Louisiana MUSIC

Also by Rick Koster
Texas Music

Louisiana MUSIC

A Journey from R&B to Zydeco, Jazz
to Country, Blues to Gospel, Cajun Music to
Swamp Pop to Carnival Music and Beyond

RICK KOSTER

DA CAPO PRESS

Designed by Trish Wilkinson
Set in 10-point Berling by Perseus Publishing Services

Cataloging-in-Publication data for this book is available from the Library of
Congress.

First Da Capo Press edition 2002
ISBN 0-306-81003-4

Published by Da Capo Press
A Member of the Perseus Books Group
http://www.dacapopress.com

Da Capo Press books are available at special discounts for bulk purchases in the
U.S. by corporations, institutions, and other organizations. For more information,
please contact the Special Markets Department at the Perseus Books Group,
11 Cambridge Center, Cambridge, MA 02142, or call (800) 255-1514 or (617)
252–5298, or e-mail j.mccrary@perseusbooks.com.

1 2 3 4 5 6 7 8 9—06 05 04 03 02

CONTENTS

PART V   LOUISIANA ROCK

PART VI   THE WONDROUS SOUNDS

FOREWORD

*L*ouisiana music, eh? Hmmmm. I can't think of a broader term than that. I mean, that single phrase can connote everything from Louis Armstrong to Britney Spears (only in *the* most technical of ways, of course). From the laconic Lee Dorsey singin' about his job in a coal mine ("Lord, I'm so tired / How long can this go on?") to the inspired intensity of Phil Anselmo of Pantera raging about the wages of personal injustice, from the creative freedom of the 1950s Louisiana Hayride offering an alternative to the bland prison of the Nashville country music establishment, to the recent success of the Cash Money rap phenomenon. . . . This can all be defined as "Louisiana Music." Amazing, isn't it?

If a single thread runs through all these stories, it's that in almost every case there was a defining moment of devil-may-care that serves not only as the inspiration for many of these glorious sounds but also as the engine of their success. Little Richard banging out X-rated songs during a break in a recording session, Better Than Ezra emerging fully-formed from an LSU frat, the entire history of Ernie (Emperor of the World) K-Doe: In each is that grand impetus of the Louisiana dream, the moment when one person turns to another and says, against all better judgment, "Why the fuck not?"

There is a casualness to the Louisiana music, musician, and spirit in general that Rick Koster captures with a flawlessness that can come only from someone who knows the shimmer of a street band echoing down the corridors of an empty Royal Street on a lazy weekday afternoon; the swampy spirit of blues in a dark Baton Rouge juke joint; the dusty celebration of indigenous folk music—Cajun and zydeco—that simmers in festivals throughout Southwest Louisiana like God's best recipe. Rick—who has logged many years as both a musician and a music writer and has written extensively about the music of Louisiana, happily sampling the region's wares and lifestyles—creates that mood with this book, riding the effortless flow that is both the state's trademark and its main asset. The man knows.

That's not to say that the success of Louisiana music in toto has been a happy accident, or that the purveyors of these slices of paradise don't know about hard work. You want to know what hard work is? Try playing in front of a New Orleans crowd. I've heard people talk about the difficulty of audiences in New York or Los Angeles. Sorry, if you ain't got the goods, and you try to play in front of a bunch of Louisianians looking for a good time, you will find out about it, and fast! You see, we *all* remember going to see the Neville Brothers (arguably the best band in the known universe) at Tipitina's on Napoleon back in 1984 for five dollars and being blown away by the harmonies from heaven and the funk from hell. It just does not get any better than that.

But what is the real glory of Louisiana? Is it a certain type of food, or an attitude, or music? Is it the laughable conduct of our most infamous politicos? Is it the tarnished majesty of the Mississippi River? Is it the inherent insanity of a state of little mind that can only be called Mardi Gras? Hell, no.

Louisiana, for all of its faults and foibles, is a place where people have always embraced their limits and their eccentricities and turned them into sources of pride and of reverence, not to be denied but rather to be celebrated—at all and any cost. *That* is the true glory of the great state of Louisiana and music—and Rick Koster has captured it, brother.

Fred LeBlanc, Cowboy Mouth
November 2001

INTRODUCTION

*T*his book is about a search for Louisiana music, and it starts not far from where jazz bubbled into existence, in the French Quarter of New Orleans.

The first thing I remember about the French Quarter is Bourbon Street, and the first thing I remember about Bourbon Street is the tawdry set of female mannequin legs swinging through the second-floor window of Big Daddy's. Every time I see them, even today—and the legs are still going, as though the hidden torso belongs to a (Playboy) Energizer Bunny—the carnival sideshow affectation still symbolizes a wealth of French Quarter possibilities that extends far beyond cheap eroticism.

I was sixteen years old, and my parents had decided that it was time my sister and I became acquainted with the myriad charms of New Orleans. Dad and Mom—R.L. and Thelm—were veterans of a romantic relationship that could hardly fit in the corny parabolas implied by Ward and June Cleaver. My folks' post–World War II years were invested together in, first, the Indianapolis bar owned by my father and uncle and where my parents met, then in Las Vegas as blackjack and craps dealers, and finally in Dallas where my sister, Michelle, and I grew up riding a bottle rocket to prosperity, fueled by my dad's visionary concept that mobile homes were the white trash housing of the future. (That he once sold a 10-wide Melody Home to a G.I. named Elvis Presley hardly elevated the long-haul per-capita financial demographics of the target customer.)

Throughout those developmental stages of their relationship, Mom and Dad spent *mucho* R&R time in New Orleans. Music, food, horse races, booze, and the endless quest for what they referred to as the Large Time had frequently lured them to the Crescent City. Later, the den in our Dallas home was furnished with a pool table, a finely crafted and lovingly stocked bamboo bar, and a primitive but powerful stereo system from which roared Ray Price and Willie Nelson, Dinah Washington and the Mills Brothers and, particularly on Sunday mornings or during hangover recovery periods, Dixieland bands, Al Hirt, and Louis Armstrong.

R.L., a trombonist of almost zero ability who spoke reverently of someone named Jack Teagarden, often regaled my little sister and me with exotic tales of the musicians and live music clubs of New Orleans. "You're not old enough, yet," he'd say when we asked when we were going to see this magical place. "But someday you will be."

And so it was that I was let loose upon the city during summer break of my sophomore year in high school. My sister had a pal along with her, and my father's mother was with us, and we all stayed in the Downtowner Inn on Bourbon Street, the site of a former opera house and now operating under the Best Western Bourbon Street banner. I had my own room, and after we checked in, R.L. ushered me down Bourbon Street on a Boys Only tour, grinning understandingly as my eyes darted uncontrollably like porn lasers into the beckoning doors of the strip joints, where naked women jerked languidly in the bored approximation of erotic fever.

R.L. knew that my hormones were skyrocketing, and wasn't about to act as though the sex on Bourbon Street didn't exist. But after we made it all the way to Canal Street and turned back, the junket took on more cultural tones. We stopped outside Arnaud's and Galatoire's, detoured half a block onto Rue Bienville to see the Acme Oyster House, and then went to Rue St. Louis so that I could see Antoine's. My parents were both excellent cooks—in post–mobile home years, R.L. would run an exceedingly fine restaurant in Dallas—and they had imbued in Michelle and me a deep appreciation for the art of cooking. (My godfather, Jimmy Vouras, owned a Dallas restaurant called the Chateaubriand, honored in the sixties on a popular television show called *Queen for a Day* as one of the top ten restaurants in the world.)

But what I remember most about that first day in New Orleans was the after-dinner outing down Bourbon with Dad. Admittedly, I harbored secret hopes that we were headed into one of the strip clubs, though the idea of visiting one with my father had distinctly creepy overtones. Instead, we went to a former jazz bastion called the Famous Door, reduced over the years to a tourist spot.

We stood outside the club in the pulsing neon of the street, which, I learned, was blocked off at night for easier Bacchanalian foot traffic. Even in the notoriously sweltering New Orleans summer, where triple-digit humidity drops out of the sky and cloaks you like wet cotton, Bourbon Street was crawling with revelers, several carrying "go cups" full of beer or a locally generated "hurricane," which I later learned tasted as though someone at a funeral home had mistakenly poured Hi-C in the embalming fluid vat. Most of the tourists were braying in such lewd or boorish fashion that I decided immediately I wanted to be a drunk when I grew up.

"Some great musicians have played here over the years," my father was saying, a trace of wistfulness in his tone as he stared at the Famous Door. He named some names and I'd be a liar if I remembered what they were, though I think Al Hirt and Pete Fountain might have been among them.

We stood a moment longer, my father presumably lost among the ghosts of evenings long past. Then, to my surprise, he stepped up to the doorman and leaned over, whispering in his ear and gesturing at me. The doorman, a muscular guy in a tuxedo, appraised me with a cocky grin: He must've been amused by my textbook geekery. I saw the flash of money change hands and Dad turned and beckoned.

"C'mon, son," he said, and led me inside. We sat down at a table about halfway back from the stage, and a melange of images swirled around me. It wasn't as though I hadn't been in a bar before—an offspring of R.L. and Thelma Koster?!—but this was different from the neighborhood joint in Dallas where all the regulars treated my sister and me like their own and a fish-fry comprised the *de rigueur* supper plans for Friday night.

For one thing, the stage was crammed with musicians, playing the brass-driven music I'd come to know from my parents' records as Dixieland. I can't say for sure—the details of that night are not as fine or plentiful as I'd like—but it seemed like the band was outfitted in straw boaters and those armbands Americans associate with Old West bartenders.

It would also be great to say that R&B legend James Booker cartwheeled in off the street, saluted my father, climbed onstage and sat down at the piano to lead the group in a raucous version of "On the Sunny Side of the Street." He didn't, though, and I think I can say with certainty that such a thing never happened.

But I suppose it could have. That evening, early on a slow weeknight in a once-famous club that had become a tourist snare, as I sat with my father, drinking a hyper-syruped bar-cola from a sticky glass while cigarette smoke as heavy as the humidity twirled in the overhead blade fans, listening the music—jaunty and loud and captivating in the way that each instrument's separate sound intertwined with the others to the greater sum of the whole—anything seemed possible.

R.L. has been dead over ten years now. I spent fifteen years as a rock bassist and visited New Orleans countless times; I even moved into a boarding house briefly in the early 1980s, on St. Ann in the Quarter, dreaming that I'd discover rock stardom in the city where Red Rockers and Zebra were starting to make national waves.

Gradually, the city and its music crept into me like sea-green absinthe dreams. I became fascinated with men whose music I'd never heard—simply because of their names. Professor Longhair. Louis Moreau Gottschalk.

Kid Ory. Mr. Google Eyes. I was overwhelmed with the idea that someone named Buddy Bolden had wandered Storyville playing his mournful cornet so loudly that it lured customers from a full-blown dance blocks away, and that photographer E. J. Bellocq once shot portraits of hookers in revealing ways that had nothing to do with nudity.

So, too, was the distinct feeling one gets, even now, that those people are still there. Maybe they're in another dimension or some wild spirit form, but the city is rich with ghosts. You taste it in the food and hear it ringing in your ears. The folks lucky enough to live there grow up with it.

There is also an uneasy tension pulsating beneath the 24/7 carnival that permeates New Orleans. It's a conflicting town of intense violence and sweet charity; of racial interaction and hidden suspicion; of secret ancestral ritual and a genuine hospitality—a city that deplores being dragged into the future even as its luxuriant past decays in the humidity.

"The image of New Orleans is that it's a progressive place," I was told by George Porter Jr. (a founding member of the Meters, the quintessential Crescent City funk band, and leader of his own band, Runnin' Pardners), "but I don't know about 'coming together.'" While many Louisiana musicians agree with Porter's assessment, most also say that the music has made things immeasurably better. Charles Neville, Grammy-winning saxophonist for the Neville Brothers, told me, "It's not so much ethnic wars going on; it's a class war, not just in inner-city New Orleans but across America. But I also think there is a spirit of hope [here in New Orleans]. . . . The blend of the cultures of the people who settled here is different than in most cities. There *are* different ethnic communities here, but they *do* mix with each other. You can walk into an Irish bar in the Irish Channel and you might find an Irish band playing—but you might find a black R&B group, too. There are second-line Klezmer bands. I think the fact that all these elements have managed to come together here is important, and not only musically."

The juxtaposition of music and culture extends far beyond the city limits of New Orleans. During my musician days, in our beaten-up band van, crisscrossing the Gulf Coast, going from gig to gig, I became as enraptured by zydeco (the music of black Creoles) and the music of the white Cajuns from the swampy vistas of Southwest Louisiana as I had been by the scene in New Orleans. I couldn't resist the musical mystery of the dusty, French-Spoken-Here communities with names such as Opelousas and New Iberia where the past had always been the present until, somehow, in the sixties and seventies, the twentieth century crept in and began making off with large chunks of heritage.

Michael Doucet, the world renowned fiddler who heads up the progressive Cajun band BeauSoleil, is a student and teacher of Louisiana music. "Where I come from are two different cultures that live in the same place," he says. "Creole culture is black and Cajun is the Acadien culture.

So there's a lot of sharing between us but there are incredible differences, too. The music is a prime way for both to preserve the heritage—and it's all related throughout Louisiana. New Orleans was the main port, and you didn't get to Southwest Louisiana unless you went through New Orleans. Whatever came through the Mississippi River stayed."

They say that once you move to Louisiana and settle in as though for a protracted, dream-clustered nap, she gets her hooks into you. And the music there is the soundtrack of those dreams. Plenty of players have moved to Louisiana in the hopes that the talent and history will seep into their own work. Jon Cleary, the British-born pianist whose reputation as a New Orleans piano professor–in-the-making has crossed the globe, came to the city almost by accident. He scored a job painting the Maple Leaf Bar—and did the work slowly so that he could study at the feet of the musicians who played there.

"I came straight to the bar from the airport," he remembers. "They took me in, bought me my first Dixie. I nearly fell off my chair when I saw Earl King climbing onstage. I saw on the schedule that James Booker played every Tuesday night. Huey 'Piano' Smith and the Clowns were at Jimmy's that night, and people I'd heard on obscure records were everywhere. . . . When I arrived it was as though all the pieces of the puzzle of my life came together."

To be sure, not every musician or band that comes from Louisiana is dusted with this magic; many are fairly generic—despite varying levels of success. It's probably true that Hank Williams Jr. or Britney Spears or Kenny Wayne Shepherd could have developed their respective styles anywhere. And it's hard to imagine anything special happening to the music of rock-kook Trent Reznor now that he lives in New Orleans.

But plenty of youngsters coming up in Louisiana *are* aware of the traditions and are affected by them. Donald Harrison, the marvelous young saxophonist whose father was the Big Chief of a Mardi Gras Indians tribe, says, "My parents taught us to listen to all types of music, and it was a wonderful experience for me because I grew up able to see the whole history of Louisiana music—and to respect it. I grew up playing in funerals and parades the same as King Oliver and Louis Armstrong. The harmony doesn't ever change; you just turn it around to reflect the times you live in and what's going on in the world today."

In Baton Rouge, drummer Sean Ardoin, leader of the millennial band ZydeKool and a member of one of zydeco's royal families, is helping a younger generation of musicians to evolve an approach to the form that's as adventurous as it is mindful of tradition. He told me: "Sometimes the traditionalists complain about what we're doing musically, but it's kinda hard to tell us about *us*. We're the Ardoins; our family *started* zydeco. Earlier generations were influenced by Wilson Pickett and R&B just like I'm influenced by eighties funk, and Chris, who's younger, is influenced by new school rap. We're just doing what every zydeco musician before us has done—with an eye on the history."

What follows is my attempt, over the course of a year, seeing and talking and listening to as many Louisiana musicians as possible—at as many festivals and concerts and clubs as I could hit without losing my day job—to integrate myself into the pieces of what Cleary called the vast puzzle of Louisiana music. My main purpose was to discover and write about all the kinds of music and musicians in the great state of Louisiana. The idea was to go for it and learn all I could—*for twelve months*. And in that finite period, I think, as my father would have said, I done good.

I have tried to cover all the important and/or popular musicians; I have also included birth and/or death dates when I could. But is this the end-all, be-all comprehensive list? Well, it's pretty thorough but it's not an encyclopedia. I'm not even sure that such a compilation is possible. Deserving artists will be left out. And of course there are some artists missing who are high on the lists of music-heads—the kinds of lists that, as an admitted but populist musical snob, I've made all my life, the sort that the guys in *High Fidelity* routinely compiled and used as weapons of superiority against innocent lay persons who wandered into their shop. Which is just one way of offering apologies to those left out, and also of confirming that I definitely ran out of time before I finished the puzzle.

But, man, it was a helluva lot of fun.

I

JAZZ

One

SPONTANEOUS COMBUSTION AND THE BIRTH OF AN ART FORM

*L*ouis Armstrong is buried in Flushing Cemetery in Flushing, Queens, New York City. That's a long way from New Orleans, where he was born and where he learned to play music. I took the train to the cemetery from New London, Connecticut. A nor'easter had blown through a few days before and the temperature was still below freezing, the ground clumped with muddy patches of stale snow and crusty ice. An odd confluence of whale-gray clouds, factory smoke, and a timid January sun gave the sky an eerie tinge.

Armstrong's headstone is black marble and impressive, a white trumpet garnishing the top. "Satchmo" is engraved in gold-leaf script and underneath, in sans-serif, "Louis Armstrong." A tattered American flag—one of those miniature jobbers seen clustering American cemeteries on Memorial Day and Veterans Day—leaned to one side. Old flowers were frozen in foil-covered holders. No one was around, which wasn't surprising; the arrows of sub-zero wind made standing outside for any reason a chore.

But I am a grave-site pilgrim, the sort constantly seeking closure or inspiration, or even a greeting-card type of maudlin rush that comes with romanticizing a hero. When I go on one of these visits—Jimi Hendrix, Wallace Stevens, Stevie Ray Vaughan, Nathaniel Hawthorne—it's the closest I can come to offering personal thanks for the gifts my favorite artists have given me. Or maybe because it's the closest I'll ever come to greatness.

I experienced no big spiritual revelations at Armstrong's tomb; no specter tapped me on the shoulder to whisper what a wonderful world it is. But it was a good thing nonetheless.

On the train ride home, listening to Armstrong with King Oliver's Jazz Band on the Walkman headphones and staring at a succession of ugly Connecticut towns, the music sounded fine, though not particularly different. But I did feel awe and a surge of respect. Two distinct images came to mind—perhaps not profound, but certainly to be considered in the light of what Armstrong accomplished, where he came from, and what his work and legend have carved into the American landscape.

The first was a quote from New Orleans banjoist Danny Barker that I read in *Louis Armstrong in His Own Words*, edited by Thomas Brothers:

> [Armstrong] be sittin' down in his underwear with a towel around his lap, one around his shoulders an' that white handkerchief on his head, and he'd put that grease around his lips. He looked like a minstrel man, ya know . . . an' laughin' you know natural the way he is. And in the room ya see, maybe two nuns. You see a street walker all up in flaming clothes. You see maybe a guy come out of a penitentiary. Ya see maybe a blind man sitting there. You see a rabbi, ya see a priest, see. Liable to see maybe two policemen or detectives, see. You see a judge. All of 'em different levels of society in the dressin' room and he's talking to all of 'em. "Sister So and So, do you know Slick Sam over there? This is Slick Sam, an ole friend of mine." Now the nun's going to meet Slick Sam. Old Notorious, been in nine penitentiaries. "Slick Sam, meet Rabbi Goldstein over there, he's a friend of mine, rabbi good man, religious man. Sister Margaret, do you know Rabbi Goldstein? Amelia, this is Rosie, good time Rosie, girl used to work in a show with me years ago. Good girl, she's a great performer. Never got the breaks." Always a word of encouragement, see. And there'd be some kids there, white and colored. All the diverse people of different social levels . . . an' everybody's lookin'. Got their eyes dead on him, jus' like they was lookin' at a diamond.

The second image, a fragment, came from Eric Taylor, the excellent singer-songwriter who lives in Texas. Taylor was standing onstage in a tiny club during a solo performance a few years ago; as he sipped a glass of red wine, he explained the muse behind the song he was about to sing from his *Resurrect* album, "Louis Armstrong's Broken Heart."

Taylor, a large, hulking man with a weathered face, stared at the floor as though transfixed by a campfire that only he could see. He talked about being at a friend's house very late one night. The friend owns a comprehensive collection of albums by Armstrong and, being an orderly sort, had filed his albums chronologically. Taylor was leafing through them, studying the metamorphosing images of Satchmo throughout his career.

"And it struck me," Taylor said softly into the microphone, scratching his blond hair and never looking up from his boots, "that, over the years,

Armstrong's smile got bigger and bigger—and his eyes just got sadder and sadder."

Although Taylor may have foisted his own melancholia onto Armstrong, one doesn't have to listen with a particular acumen to the music of Louis Armstrong (or read from his extensive writings) to discern a rainbow of human emotion. Armstrong was a musical prism through which the sum of his experiences was brilliantly extrapolated, and as such he captured the wellspring of life for us all.

On a less metaphorical level, from an early age, I always associated Satchmo with New Orleans . . . and New Orleans with jazz.

Anyone seriously interested in the history of jazz will hear many times that Buddy Bolden was the father of jazz, or that Jelly Roll Morton *claimed* he was the father of jazz (in 1902, in fact)—or even, despite the chronology of things, that its father was Louis Armstrong. In truth, it's not accurate to say that one person is responsible for such a dynamic and quintessentially American product as jazz; it is safe to argue, though, whether jazz is a dynamic and quintessentially a product of New Orleans.

The jazz musicians of New Orleans certainly think so: "New Orleans music *is* jazz," young trumpeter Irvin Mayfield told me, laughing with the ease of his conviction. "All the New York players are playing New Orleans music—and that's that."

In various ports across the country besides New Orleans—chiefly Texas, Kansas City, Chicago, and Los Angeles—various paellas of ragtime, blues, boogie-woogie, and western swing were spontaneously being cooked up. But though all those places had a role in what jazz was and is, I'm gonna go with the New Orleans guys on this one. Countless books and articles have been written about the birth of jazz, so I don't need to get specific, but here's what you need to know for our purposes: Three distinct cultural conditions swirled through New Orleans and conspired to produce a hurricane of jazz.

First, remember the name Pierre de Rigaud de Vaudreuil—and, no, he wasn't a cornet player. He was Marquis and Governor of Louisiana from 1743 to 1753 and, along with his equally Bacchanalian wife, instituted a season of never-ending parades, balls, and masquerades that sowed the seeds of the pre-Lenten blow-out now known as Mardi Gras. These activities were effectively described in *Bourbon Street Black* by authors Danny Barker and Jack V. Buerkle as "a kind of perpetual hedonistic binge with *style*." That says it all in eight words.

Second, at the turn of the twentieth century, New Orleans was not only the most European of North American cities, it was also the most Caribbean and the most African. This was because it had been marinating for over two hundred years under French and Spanish control and had soaked up the Catholicism and classical music of those cultures. These European cultures were cross-pollinated with yet more diverse rhythms, customs, foods, and ideas because New Orleans was a thriving slave port that received blacks from West Africa and the West Indies. In an effort to indoctrinate slaves into the ways of Catholicism and away from their own "heathen" faiths, the authorities in 1724 came up with the *Code Noir* (Black Code); this law banned all religions except Catholicism. Almost a century later, African religions—most of them lumped under the umbrella of "voodoo" either for simplicity or out of ignorance, or both—were still thriving. The government tried another tack and allowed slaves to gather every Sunday in Congo Square (now Louis Armstrong Park) to dance and perform religious rituals to get the so-called voodoo out of their systems (for more on this subject, see "The Music of Voodoo," Part 6, Chapter 1). The exercises became an unexpected tourist attraction as whites gathered to gape at the slaves and listen to their rhythms, undoubtedly infectious and seductive. These musical styles, dances, and customs were so alluring that they eventually spread into the community at large.

Third, as in virtually every other city in America in the late nineteenth century, brass bands were popping up in New Orleans. From New England to the Midwest, these bands gave spirited concerts from the gazebo in the town square on summer evenings as citizens sipped lemonade and wondered when the goofy handlebar moustache thing was gonna go out of style. These outfits were offshoots of military marching bands, heavy on the Sousa-esque bombosity; folks would also find them representing civic organizations and performing in medicine shows and circuses.

The New Orleans bands enjoyed their own special twist. First, they were heavily influenced by a southern piano style called ragtime. Second, they were supported by an institution particular to the city—the social or burial society. These societies had originated indirectly through the resolution of the Civil War. Before emancipation, it was incumbent on the slave owner to pay for the burial of his slaves. When the newly freed slaves were integrated into society—usually as impoverished as they had always been, and just as discriminated against—they formed burial societies to ensure their dead would have funerals in spite of the harsh economic realities of the times. In similar fashion, pleasure and social clubs were formed. For minimum dues, fish fries and neighborhood parties were organized and funded to provide cheap entertainment and build strong community spirit. Each of these societies established its own brass band—or hired the same band over and over again—to perform at virtually any function. And these bands *liked* ragtime; it had a happy, syncopated beat that added a bubbly element to the brass-band fun. When the New Orleans outfits naturally infused their city's own particular polyrhythms, something new started to boil.

It quickly became the custom for the bands not only to play at social functions but also to join in honoring the dead in a pseudo military fashion with a brass-band funeral. The rhythms and impromptu embellishments on the music began to change; for example, when mourners sang double-timing hymns in an effort to buoy their spirits as the cortege left the grave-yard, the dirges coalesced with the other sounds and pulses of the city.

Combine all these developments: the intermingling of cultures and re-ligions, a wanton and carte blanche approach to fun, food, dancing, and music—the voodoo ceremonies took place in Congo Square only a few blocks away from a magnificent opera house—and it's not hard to see how the city began to stew with the power of its own innate sound.

By 1900, a typical street-corner brass band in New Orleans was a small unit of from nine to twelve players and probably had one or two cornetists, an E-flat clarinet, a few trombone guys, a tuba player, and drummers re-spectively working a snare and a bass drum and cymbal. Whether the band was working paid dances as a professional outfit or whether it was an ama-teur group just out for beer and entertainment, you might find a baritone horn and an alto horn thrown into the mix. The most important thing is that, by the turn of the century, the brass bands were *improvising*. The rigid repertoire was slithering out the window and the new sonic salad of rag-time, popular songs, funeral dirges, gospel, blues, and standard marches was turning into something strange, exhilarating, and wonderful.

One of the first of the New Orleans brass bands to achieve true popu-larity might well have been the Pickwick Brass Band, which probably started just after the Civil War. Three of the most famous and long-lived outfits, the Excelsior, Onward, and Eureka bands, followed shortly. For the record, the Excelsior and Onward were both Creole bands, which is to say the musicians were of mixed black and white heritage and, subsequently, of lighter complexion. Theogene Baquet was the first leader of the Excel-sior Brass Band, and later musicians, such as Peter Bocage, Lorenzo Tio Sr., and Alphonse Picou, became some of the most prominent alumni of that organization. (Brass bands are discussed in greater detail in "Brass Bands," Part 1, Chapter 3).

As for **Charles "Buddy" Bolden** (1877–1931), well, we know this much: He lived much of his life in the lunatic asylum where he died. His legend, based on early and horribly exaggerated accounts of his life, chiefly from malarkey-infused interviews with Bunk Johnson and, to a lesser extent, Jelly Roll Morton, has been historically distorted. Among the many myths is the story that Bolden owned a barber shop; another named him as pub-lisher of a neighborhood newspaper.

He probably started out in music by taking lessons from one of his mother's suitors around 1895 in the well-integrated First Street neigh-borhood where he spent much of his youth. He played first in Charley Galloway's band; Galloway did own a barbershop where musicians gathered, and that's probably where the haircut stuff started. Because

Bolden mastered the cornet at alarming speed, he more or less appropriated Galloway's band, booking it under his own name. At that point, competition for gigs was fierce. Bands and orchestras played various ethnic and traditional dance music in orderly fashion—which is to say there were no soloists and the ensemble arrangements were fairly staid and predictable. Bolden changed all that.

Though what he played was probably classified as glorified ragtime, Bolden used his horn, and significant power and talent, to alter music's shape. Again, in an effort to bring attention to himself and secure higher-quality work for his band, Bolden began to infuse "blue" notes into the musical arrangements—which means that he played notes that fell between the corresponding notes on a piano, slightly flat or sharp of the rigidly written notations—and wreaked havoc on classical European structures. He began stepping out as an instrumentalist, blowing freely against or over the arrangements even as the band toyed with time signatures and rhythm, and created a newer, friskier style. The music wasn't yet known as "jazz" and wouldn't be for years, but that's essentially what he played. Along with a reputation based on his sheer strength—Bolden could reportedly be heard on a clear Saturday night from blocks, if not miles away—he did indeed garner fame as a musician.

Bolden's tightest competition came from the band led by John Robichaux, the multi-instrumentalist and bandleader whose orchestras were in demand at every level of New Orleans society. The two outfits exemplified the uptown/downtown, Creole/black, sophisticated/ragged diversities embodied by their respective leaders. Cutting contests ensued and, though Robichaux's style and elegance would always attract supporters, Bolden's wildman image made him the most popular musician in New Orleans from 1900 to 1905. It was during this time that Bolden came to be called the King, an image he strove to uphold through his art, his drinking, his affection for women, and whatever other kingly pursuits seemed appropriate.

His standout pieces included "Bucket's Got a Hole" (it's a joy to hear youngster Kermit Ruffins play this tune) and "Funky Butt, Funky Butt, Take It Away" (one of the cooler live-music clubs in New Orleans is called the Funky Butt, located at Congo Square on Rampart just across from Armstrong Park).

Unfortunately, Bolden didn't enjoy his reputation for long. In 1906, he started showing signs of delusion, and a year later he was committed to the East Louisiana State Hospital, where he lived for the remaining twenty-four years of his life. Aside from the sheer cinematic quality of his life and rumors of his godlike talent, Bolden is a primary figure in the segue between ragtime, brass bands, and jazz proper. To discover more, read Marquis's *In Search of Buddy Bolden, First Man of Jazz*. For sheer literary pleasure, read Michael Ondaatje's wonderful novel *Coming Through Slaughter*, which gloriously embraces the historical inaccuracies.

Questions of musical fatherhood aside, it goes without saying that the biggest name in all of jazz, ever, is Louis Armstrong. What in the hell am I supposed to say about **Louis Armstrong** (1901–1971) other than it's a small exaggeration, if any, to point out that books about him, written by him, and dedicated to him appear almost daily. A courageous and visionary musician, composer, singer, entertainer, ambassador, and character-at-large, Armstrong changed jazz, and, to some extent, the world.

Louis Armstrong was born to the teenage daughter of a former slave in New Orleans on August 4, 1901—not July 4, 1900, as the marketing folks and Armstrong himself would have you believe. He drove coal and rags in a wagon for the Karnofskys, a Jewish family that treated him like kinfolk, fortuitous in that it allowed him to afford his first horn, a beat-up cornet. The job took him on deliveries into Storyville, the turn-of-the-century red light district where Armstrong was first tantalized by music and, to a lesser extent, hookers.

When he was twelve he was sent to the Colored Waifs' Home for firing a pistol into the air in a celebratory New Year's Eve gesture. The experience was important for Armstrong because it taught him discipline and allowed him to practice his horn with the institution's music teacher and in the school band. To say that Armstrong was seduced by the possibilities of the instrument is an understatement. At the time, musicians were the heroes of several neighborhoods. New Orleans buzzed with stories about Bolden, and Armstrong later wrote about hearing Bolden play at the legendary Funky Butt Hall. While in the Colored Waifs' Home, Armstrong could hear the wondrous tones of Freddie Keppard when his orchestra played regularly in a white family's home about half a mile away.

When he was released at fourteen, Armstrong and his horn began to make great strides on the local scene. His chops were intuitively great, his tone assured, his instincts daring and on the money. He fell under the tutelage of Bunk Johnson and Joe (soon-to-be) "King" Oliver, magnificent artists who will be discussed presently. Both of them immediately recognized in Armstrong not just perfect pitch and an uncanny ear but something almost revolutionary in the way the young man took the horn beyond its limits.

Armstrong made a name for himself in bands and in cutting contests and eventually replaced Oliver in Kid Ory's outfit. After joining up with King Oliver's Creole Jazz Band in Chicago a few years later, he then traveled to New York to play in Fletcher Henderson's band in the mid-1920s. During this period, Armstrong had already radically changed jazz in several ways. He intuitively incorporated the New Orleans rhythms of his youth and played *around* the beat rather than *on* it, the core idea behind "swinging"; he paved the way for true improvisation by expanding the solo opportunities in the round-robin ensemble concept; he simply blew down the walls surrounding the conceived limitations of the instrument; and, too, his voice became an instrument unto itself. He created a revolutionary amalgam of the singing styles of his youth, from opera to church music to Tin Pan Alley. Though Hot Five banjoist Johnny St. Cyr's assertion that Armstrong invented scat singing during a recording of "Heebie Jeebies" has been largely discredited, Armstrong's distinctive "scatting" *was* marvelously indelible and influential.

Whether in New York or Chicago, Armstrong carved an immediate reputation with musicians and audiences, black and white, who took notice in a big way. He'd already done some recording and, in 1925, upped the bar for the world when he started sessions for the OKeh label with his Hot Five (Kid Ory on trombone, clarinetist Johnny Dodds, Johnny St. Cyr on banjo, Armstrong's second wife Lil on piano and vocals, and Armstrong on trumpet and vocals) band, a genre-changing outfit that expanded two years later to the Hot Seven (with the addition of drummer Baby Dodds and Pete Briggs on tuba, and John Thomas replacing Kid Ory). The recordings Armstrong made with these groups are arguably the most important in the history of jazz. Although people today wouldn't respond in similar fashion to such an artistic breakthrough, the work Armstrong and the Hot Five/Hot Seven laid out turned the trumpeter into a huge celebrity.

Armstrong moved to New York and by 1929 had become the first black artist to play with integrated bands, pre-dating such folk as Benny Goodman. His profile went from popular American musician to global superstar (before there *were* superstars, and certainly not African-American ones). He toured Europe, appeared in motion pictures, and, in 1947, formed His All-Stars, which at various times included Weldon Leo "Jack" Teagarden, Earl Hines, Barney Bigard, and Trummy Young. He would lead this outfit until 1968, maintaining his popularity in the wake of the Beatles, the early years of the Vietnam War, and the great sixties Celebrity Evolution.

Now, more than twenty-five years after his death, the "traditional" New Orleans jazz he mastered and transformed has come back with a clever vengeance, chiefly through the work of young artists, among them trumpeters James Andrews and Kermit Ruffins and clarinetist Dr. Michael White. But modernist Irvin Mayfield, barely twenty-one when we talked, gave perhaps the best summation of Armstrong's lingering presence: "It's impossible to be in New Orleans and pick up a trumpet and not think of Pops," he said. "There's a certain part of the city where you can go and everyone has instruments and people are dancing. Well, in Pops' time, he wasn't just doing it in the neighborhood. He was doing it to *the world*."

Despite being the first significant New Orleans jazz musician not to start out on trumpet or cornet, **Sidney Bechet** (1897–1959) made a name early on at one of his brother's birthday parties where John Robichaux's orchestra was booked. Even though clarinetist George Baquet hadn't shown up yet, the band went ahead and started—and stopped when the eerie sounds of a properly played clarinet wafted in from a deserted room away from the main party. It was the precocious Bechet, all of six years old, who wanted to play quietly along with the musicians but didn't realize they'd be able to hear what a bad-ass he was.

From there the kid was star-bound. He was quickly assimilated into the city's finest bands, where he played both clarinet and soprano sax, and usurped trumpet parts with startling ability and improvisational acuity. At eleven, he soloed with Bunk Johnson's band, and he was also an early mentor to Louis Armstrong, whom he discovered singing in a street-corner quartet.

By seventeen, Bechet had played with Freddie Keppard, Mutt Carey, Buddy Petit, and the Eagle Orchestra. After traveling through Texas for a while, he returned to New Orleans and played with King Oliver's Olympia Band before heading to Chicago and then New York to play with a variety of top outfits. Bechet first traveled to Europe during stints with Will Marion Cook's Southern Syncopated Orchestra and Louis Mitchell's Jazz Kings—and became arguably the first jazz musician to be looked upon with respect and admiration by the Continent's classical community. That first European jaunt was also where he purchased a soprano saxophone and shifted his focus away from the clarinet.

When he returned to the States, he started his recording career, backing blues artists, and then worked in Europe from 1925 to 1929. The four-year stay might have been twelve months shorter had Bechet not become involved in a gun battle in which another musician and two passers-by were wounded. Though no one was killed, Bechet went to prison for a year. As he says in his autobiography, *Treat It Gentle*, "It was something, the way it happened . . . something hard to make it clear. It's like there's somebody else inside a man, somebody that's not really that man, and when a thing happens, an anger like I had then, that other person takes over."

After his release, Bechet joined Noble Sissle's orchestra and returned to the United States. In 1938, Bechet hit the charts with "Summertime," blew in and out of Europe with Sissle for a while, then headed up his own band in Greenwich Village. He also worked with Eddie Condon and played a stint in Chicago with Vic Dickenson during the Dixieland revival. In 1951, he returned to Paris, where he was a huge star, and lived there for most of his remaining years.

Bechet left an indelible mark not just as a terrific composer and improviser but as the only person ever to use the soprano sax in a revolutionary jazz context. In fact, the *Penguin Guide to Jazz on CD, LP & Cassette* describes Bechet in luminous terms: "An exceptionally gifted and formally aware musician whose compositional skills greatly outshine those of Louis Armstrong, his rival for canonization as the first great jazz improviser. . . . His melodic sense and ability to structure a solo round the harmonic sequence of the original theme has been of immense significance in the development of modern jazz."

For most jazz enthusiasts, Louis Armstrong was an icon, but to Armstrong himself, **Joe "King" Oliver** (1885–1938) was the ultimate hero. "Joe Oliver has always been my inspiration and my idol," Pops wrote. "No trumpet player ever had the fire Oliver had. Man, he could really *punch* a number. Some might've had a better tone, but I've never seen *nothing* have the fire, and no one created like Joe."

The King was born on a plantation near Abend, Louisiana. He was blind in one eye. At the height of his popularity, he was a round, mesmerizing figure who wore a derby hat and knew how to work a crowd. He apprenticed early on in brass bands, formed his own with Sidney Bechet at thirty, and first became known as "King" in 1917, when he was playing with Kid Ory.

Oliver had the good sense to move to Chicago, and anticipated the great jazz migration. There he played with Bill Johnson and Lawrence Duhé, eventually taking over the latter's group and christening it King Oliver's Creole Jazz Band. When Armstrong came north to join the group, the one-two horn punch between Oliver and Pops was legendary.

Also in the band, still celebrated as one of the hottest traditional jazz bands ever, were vocalist Lil Hardin, trombonist Honore Dutrey, and Johnny and Baby Dodds (clarinet and drums, respectively). Armstrong's playing was without equal, but Oliver was nearly as superb, and he applied an instinctive and disciplined approach to leading a band that was top notch.

Throughout the twenties, though a variety of players came and went, Oliver's band was the best in the world. Only after the band disbanded in New York and Oliver began to tour with less-skilled groups did his reputation begin to tarnish. He demanded more money than younger and more exciting artists were asking. Suffering from severe dental problems that affected his ability to play, Oliver retired down South, where he supposedly worked as a janitor until he died destitute.

If you had a cool name like Ferdinand Le Menthe, wouldn't you keep it? Well, probably, unless you came up instead with **Jelly Roll Morton** (1890–1941). Sandwiched chronologically between the phantasm that was Buddy Bolden and the one-man explosion that would be Louis Armstrong, Morton has a secure place in history as the first significant pianist and composer in jazz. He was born in New Orleans to a Creole family, played the piano superbly at an early age, and demonstrated his skills as a stylistically adventurous teenager in the brothels of Storyville, where it's said he earned as much as $100 a night.

His affection for all forms of music, from ragtime and gospel and blues to anything ethnic, particularly Caribbean, French, and Spanish, and his ability to synthesize those disparate flavors into something unique was of particular significance. His original material still sounds terrific and retains its uniqueness: Consider "Grandpa's Spell," "Creepy Feeling," "Pep," and

"Shreveport Stomp" (just to mention a few personal favorites). Morton believed that the piano is a mirror of an orchestra's vast instrumental possibilities, and he composed parts in which specific piano keys represented trombone parts and other keys the brass or woodwinds. He also believed mightily that dynamics were the key to the music's emotion.

An intensely proud young man who used the French part of his heritage like a shield, Morton affected a diamond-studded smile and boasted a con man's aplomb at ingratiating his way into any situation. He had honed that ability as he traveled the South and the West Coast in his early years, working as a comedian, a gambler, a pimp, and a pool shark. Morton landed in Chicago during World War I and by 1923 had made history on a series of recording dates with the New Orleans Rhythm Kings for the Gennett label. Because the Rhythm Kings were a white band and the sessions took place in the KKK hotbed of Richmond, Indiana, the light-skinned Morton passed himself off as Spanish. (Later, Louis Armstrong would be the first to integrate recording sessions openly, but the NORK gig was surely one of the first to include a black musician.)

Shortly after, with fellow New Orleaneans Kid Ory, Barney Bigard, Johnny Dodds, Johnny St. Cyr, and Baby Dodds, Morton formed the band he named the Red Hot Peppers. At this point, Morton's reputation as a composer began to garner serious attention, and for the next few years he was a huge figure in the evolving jazz scene. In addition to cutting the Red Hot Peppers's recordings, he toured with W. C. Handy, the Alabamians, and Fate Marable, and also worked as a staff composer for Melrose Publishing. Despite his singular eccentricities and blooming ego, Morton paid the musicians in his band to rehearse; today, this would be one of earth's great rarities, and was almost certainly unique in Morton's time.

In 1928, Morton relocated to New York City and formed a new edition of the Red Hot Peppers (with Bubber Miley, Pops Foster, and Zutty Singleton playing at one time or another), but by 1930 the hot jazz style pioneered by Morton was losing its appeal. The maelstrom of the Great Depression didn't help matters, and it was a rough decade for Morton, who ended up playing a small bar in Washington, D.C.

Morton fell into ill health, which he ascribed to voodoo, and died just when the massive resurgence in Dixieland would presumably have brought him back into favor had he lived. Just two years before, though, he was immortalized by folklorist Alan Lomax, who had conducted a series of in-depth interviews with Morton that were fascinating not just for their documentation of the minutiae of his life but also as examples of his famous propensity for exaggeration. It's true, for example, that Morton said he "invented jazz in 1902," and equally true that critics and musicians were divided on the precise nature of his talent and contributions. Critic George Avakian said Morton was "a strange mixture of genius, musician, poet, snob, and braggart," but added that the musician could back up his musical claims.

In the end, while it's true that his personality turned a lot of people off, he still had it going on. Think of him as the Ty Cobb of early jazz.

Danny Barker (1909–1994) was a banjo player, guitarist, and composer born in New Orleans; but he was also much more than just a musician. He came to fame in New York City in the 1930s after working with Benny Carter and Cab Calloway. He hooked up with his wife, vocalist Blue Lu Barker, worked with his uncle, Paul Barbarin, ran his own orchestra at Jimmy Ryan's, and finally returned to New Orleans in 1965. There he maintained a high profile fronting the French Market Jazz Band and shepherding the Fairview Brass Band; his involvement was hugely important in resurrecting the city's eroding brass band tradition and ushering urban kids back into music and an appreciation for the traditions and cultures of their hometown.

Barker was also an author of note and was an assistant curator for years at the New Orleans Jazz Museum. He was a fine musician and a wonderful human being; but with all his accomplishments he might best be remembered as the co-author (along with Jack Buerkle) of *Bourbon Street Black*, one of the finest books on New Orleans music ever written. To learn the realities of being a black musician in the city and to read plenty of sociological and anecdotal observations about New Orleans and its music, find a copy of his autobiography, *A Life in Jazz*. An eloquent godfather, whether in print, on record, on the stage, or behind a dais as a speaker, Barker was a true municipal treasure.

Among his many fine musicial compositions is "Save the Bones for Henry Jones," which was covered by Nat King Cole. The CD of the same name is still available, and features a stripped-down Barker: just voice and instrument. It's pretty wonderful.

William Geary "Bunk" Johnson (1889?–1949), a trumpet and cornet master, confused historians for years with his creative embellishments regarding his life and the early history of New Orleans jazz; a shame because he was an estimable player and didn't need to lie. He recorded with an impressive variety of artists over the years and earned a reputation as a fine "second horn" player, a sort of rhythm trumpeter whose supportive work was often overlooked.

Nonetheless, Johnson wove quite a fantasy world when talking to scholars who'd sought him out in New Iberia, Louisiana, during his twilight years. Suffice to say that the trumpeter was born in New Orleans—not in 1879, as he told *Jazzmen* editors Charles Edward Smith and Frederic Ramsey Jr. and which for years everyone believed, but a decade later. Johnson probably played around New Orleans and the South in the early part of the twentieth century; Louis Armstrong is said to have allowed that Johnson's funeral marches "made me cry." He played regularly and with increasing ability until bandmate Evan Thomas was stabbed to death next to Johnson on the bandstand during a gig. The trauma from this experience (and, later, serious dental problems) derailed Johnson's career. He settled in New Iberia and worked at a variety of mundane trades.

In 1939, the infamous *Jazzmen* relationship started; Russell and Ramsey supplied Johnson with a new horn and new teeth (made by Sidney Bechet's brother!), then arranged for Johnson to make some recordings. Through the mid-forties, Johnson recorded a staggering wealth of material, frequently with George Lewis, Jim Robinson, and Baby Dodds, that was integral in igniting a renewed interest in traditional jazz. His own worst enemy, Johnson had antisocial tendencies and a preference for heavy drink that didn't make him the most attractive bandmate, and he ran through players with irritating frequency; it's said, though, that he could be courtly and utterly charming when he was in the mood.

Johnson briefly appeared in the movie *New Orleans* with Louis Armstrong and Billie Holiday, then formed a band of younger, swing-oriented players who worked extensively with him in perhaps the most winning of all his ensembles. In 1947, he returned to New Iberia, where he died after several strokes. Despite his own contrariness, Johnson was a gifted and important player whose ability to play behind the beat and interpret blues gave him true individuality. Recommended CDs are *King of the Blues* (American Music) and *Bunk Johnson and His Superior Band* (Good Time Jazz).

It's not belaboring the obvious to suggest that Louisiana has hundreds of early jazz musicians worthy of their own biographies, to say nothing of the jazz histories and encyclopedic volumes offering brief accounts of many others. But it's a good idea to run down the names of some of these folks. This is not a comprehensive list. It's subjective and, although plenty of good musicians were versatile on all types of instruments, I've tried to stick to the ones who are the most significant or interesting. Having said that, the trumpet-and-cornet fraternity (by the way, the cornet is more compact and has a longer tube and deeper mouthpiece than the trumpet) is overwhelmingly populated with great players.

Before World War I, New Orleans's **Freddie Keppard** (1889–1933) was one of the most important musicians in the development of jazz. A cornetist, trained also on violin, mandolin, and accordion, he ascended, some opine, to Buddy Bolden's spot after that fellow developed health problems. Keppard started out leading the Olympia Orchestra at about the age most modern teens worry about getting a driver's license, played in the Eagle Orchestra, and then headed west at the invitation of Bill Johnson. He led the group that became famous as the Original Creole Band, toured extensively, and presented authentic New Orleans music through an easily palatable, vaudeville-styled show. He ended up, like many compatriots, in Chicago. Keppard was reportedly fond of drink and, by the time he got around to recording as a leader—*The Complete Freddie Keppard 1923–1927* (King

Jazz)—his health was deteriorating; most acknowledge that the work probably doesn't represent him at his zenith.

One anecdote shows Keppard's chutzpah. In 1922, Keppard walked
into a club where Louis Armstrong was playing, marched to the bandstand, and demanded Pops's trumpet: a blatant challenge for a cutting contest. Armstrong relinquished the horn, endured while Keppard took a
flamboyant solo (his vaudevillian style made him a terrific showman). But,
as Lil Armstrong pointed out, it was best not to piss Pops off. "If you want
to hear Louis play, just hear him play when he's *angry*," she's quoted in
Laurence Bergreen's *Louis Armstrong—An Extravagant Life*. "Boy, [Arm-
strong] blew and people started standing on top of tables and chairs
screaming . . . [Keppard] eased out real slowly."

Born in either La Fourche, Donaldson, or Napoleonville, Louisiana,
the son of a poor sugar-cane cutter, **Oscar "Papa" Celestin** (1884–1954)
moved to New Orleans when he was twenty-two. A trumpeter and vocalist of significant presence in early brass bands (the Algiers Brass Band, the
Olympia Brass Band, and the Tuxedo Brass Band—the business card for
the latter reading "Music Furnished for All Occasions"), he recorded and
toured with his own band for the OKeh label before the Depression
wrought financial havoc. Celestin worked in the shipyards during World
War II and was able to return to music in the late forties. In New Orleans,
he was popular on local television, radio, and as the leader of the house
band in Bourbon Street's Paddock Lounge. He also formed and became
president of the first Negro Professional Musicians Union. A great CD is
Marie Laveau by Papa Celestin's New Orleans Band.

Emanuel Perez (1879–1946) was one of the finest teachers and leaders of the early brass bands. Born in New Orleans, Perez was a superb cornetist of whom Danny Barker said, "He played much better cornet than
Buddy [Bolden]. Perez, he was a musicianer; he was *sincere*." Barker also
claimed that Perez could hit amazingly high notes because "he had eaten
two pots of gumbo before he left [for whatever gig]."

He joined the Onward Brass Band in the 1890s before forming the
Imperial Orchestra, an outstanding and popular parade and dance outfit.
He did the Chicago thing twice, where he worked with Charles Elgar's
Creole Orchestra; he also recorded with Elgar in the late twenties. In be-
tween, back in New Orleans, he played with the Maple Leaf Orchestra in
Storyville and on the riverboats. He retired in the early 1930s to pursue
another trade—cigar making—until a series of strokes left him disabled.
(See also "Brass Bands," Part 1, Chapter 3.)

Buddy Petit (1895–1931) was born Joseph Crawford in White Castle,
Louisiana, a city that had nothing to do with the hamburger chain of the
same name. Petit moved with his widowed mother to New Orleans at
the turn of the century, so White Castle presumably didn't make much of
an impression. His mom married a trombonist named Joseph Petit, so our

Joseph called himself Buddy to avoid confusion. He took music lessons from Bunk Johnson and was soon immensely popular in the local parade bands; he also traveled the Gulf Coast, sometimes performing several gigs a night. In 1917, Petit headed with Frankie Dusen to Los Angeles to join up with Jelly Roll Morton. A pronounced stutterer with "poor boy" ways and manners, Petit was reportedly ridiculed by Morton and returned to New Orleans vowing to kill his tormentor if he ever saw him again. He seemed happiest playing in his hometown and on the old Gulf Coast circuit.

There are no known recordings of Petit, though by all surviving accounts he was a terrific player, if unusual: He preferred the second cornet role rather than the first chair. He died after over-eating and drinking at a picnic.

Louis Armstrong (a pallbearer at Petit's funeral) wrote of Petit during the times in New Orleans when the two would cross paths en route to respective gigs: "We both would meet on a corner, play our tune or a couple of tunes and we could cut out into different directions and give a big wave, playing our *cornets* with Admirations of each other's *Blowing*, which was really *Something* to hear. That alone cheered both of us up."

Mutt Carey (1891–1948) was not named for a dog. Carey was born "Thomas" in Hahnville, Louisiana, started out on drums, and then took cornet lessons from his brother before moving to trumpet. He learned much in seminal New Orleans outfits headed by Frankie Dusen, Joe Oliver, Jimmy Brown, and Bebe Ridgeley, and he eventually hooked up with Kid Ory in California in 1914. Carey was a fixture with Ory's band for over thirty years, and his darkly emotive muting techniques, learned from Oliver, earned him another nickname besides Mutt: "The Blues King of New Orleans."

Carey replaced Ory in the latter's small band, rechristened The Jeffersonians, and enlarged the unit for substantial work scoring and performing silent film music. Another victim of the Depression, Carey earned a living for a while as a railroad porter and postman before rejoining Ory during a musical redux in the forties. He remained a much-loved entertainer until his death.

Henry "Kid Rena" Rena (1900–1949) was another alumnus of the Colored Waifs' Home in New Orleans, which, in retrospect, might be thought of as the Juilliard School of Music for turn-of-the-century jazz. Rena was one of the flashiest if not the most talented of the early trumpet virtuosos. He also played in Kid Ory's band before forming his own unit in the mid-twenties. Rena essentially started the New Orleans Renaissance of the forties when he and his band recorded some dates for the Delta label in 1940.

Paul Mares (1900–1949) was born at the turn of the century and, after the usual training, moved to Chicago in 1920 and joined the Friars Society Orchestra, house band at a gangster hangout called the Friars' Inn.

The band later evolved into the New Orleans Rhythm Kings with Jelly Roll Morton. Shortly after, Mares retired and went into the family fur business, though he hopscotched between music and business until he died.

A trumpeter from Florence, Louisiana, **Tommy Ladnier** (1900–1939) moved to Chicago as a kid, worked gigs on riverboats, and possibly received his musical education—somewhat—from Bunk Johnson. He used the traditional N'Awlins style as a jumping-off point, was an excellent swing soloist, and, along with his deep appreciation of the blues he exhibited a melodic and rhythmic sympathy for them. He roomed with both Doc Cheatham and Mezz Mezzrow and co-led a band with Sidney Bechet (intriguingly called the New Orleans Footwarmers). Ladnier enjoyed a superb reputation as a session player, but he drank heavily and died of a heart attack at thirty-nine.

Last, New Orleans's **Raymond Lopez** (1889–1970) was another talent who grew up playing in the parade and brass bands. He's most remembered for copyrighting, along with Alcide "Yellow" Nunez, "Livery Stable Blues," the first jazz record ever made, recorded in 1917 by Nick LaRocca's Original Dixieland Band. LaRocca had forgotten to copyright the tune and promptly sued Lopez and Nunez; a judge later decided that neither party deserved the copyright and dismissed the case.

Some of the true Dixieland players are immortal, if occasionally considered staid by today's freewheeling standards. (I should point out that, by "Dixieland," I'm referring to the post-ragtime approach to early New Orleans jazz, infused with a bit of blues, and typically played by whites.) The foremost, of course, is **Al Hirt** (1922–1999), about whose genius the jury is always out. But he possessed superb talent and his popularity is hard to overestimate. Looking like a fusion of Sebastian Cabot and Paul Prudhomme after a beignet-and-whiskey-inhaling contest, Hirt was synonymous with New Orleans jazz for years, even while Louis Armstrong was still alive (though in the case of Pops, it was probably because he had moved out of state). And Hirt, classically trained at the Cincinnati Conservatory, was obviously skilled.

He started out playing swing, influenced mightily by Benny Goodman's band; then, after a stint in military bands, he returned to New Orleans and a variety of marginally related music gigs until 1955, when he joined forces with Pete Fountain in a sextet. They targeted traditional Dixieland as a stylistic springboard and set about conquering the record charts. The strategy worked surprisingly well, particularly after a movie star named Monique Van Vooren saw the act and turned Hirt onto her husband and manager, Gerard Purcell. Shortly after, television stardom beckoned, and by 1961 Hirt was playing the Kennedy inauguration as a solo recording star.

In 1964, Hirt, by that point a huge hometown favorite in an era when all the New Orleans jazzers had drifted away and the city's homogenous style had all but evaporated, had a massive chart hit with a song called "Java." The same year, John Coltrane released *A Love Supreme*. You can ask any jazz fan which is more important and pretty much rest assured it ain't Al, but his poppy arrangements of Dixie-swing certainly made more folks interested in "jazz." Whether many took the next step and ended up digging Thelonius Monk is another thing, but the bottom line is that Hirt was beaucoup popular.

He followed with another smash, "Cotton Candy," and surfed the crest of popularity at his own Bourbon Street club. He drifted from the spotlight after an incident in a 1970 Mardi Gras parade when his lip was shredded by a thrown brick. Though he recovered—and remained a civic treasure—Hirt was beset with rumors of drug and alcohol problems until his death.

Joseph "Sharkey" Bonano (1904–1972) was another popular Dixieland player. The trumpeter, vocalist, and bandleader was born in Milneburg, Louisiana, and enjoyed a healthy (if journeyman) career. His first taste of fame came in the twenties when he played in the New Orleans Harmony Kings with Eddie Edwards, Johnny Miller, and Jean Goldkette, and in the Prima-Sharkey group (Leon Prima, not Louis).

An active session player, he gradually scored a reputation as an "entertainer," and by 1936 Bonano was leading his own band in New York City. As with many of the Crescent City artists, the "New Orleans Revival" gave his career a boost: He was a popular and legitimately talented recording star throughout the fifties and sixties. As befitting a grown man who would call himself Sharkey, Bonano was a true character whose occasional propensity for self-aggrandizing was more charming than irritating.

Also possessed of a cool nickname was **Joseph "Wingy" Manone** (1900–1982). Despite a madcap reputation as an entertainer and sidekick to Bing Crosby, the New Orleans–born Manone was a seasoned trumpeter and an inventive vocalist and frontman. Manone scored his nickname after a streetcar accident that resulted in the amputation of one of his arms. He learned trumpet *after* the tragedy, and so effectively employed a prosthetic arm onstage that few realized he had it. After leaving New Orleans, he established a reputation as a fine swing player with Doc Ross and Jack Teagarden and the likes in Texas, New Mexico, St. Louis, Chicago, New Orleans, and New York. His tune, "Tar Paper Stomp" (aka "Wingy's Stomp"), was a big hit in 1930 for someone named Barbecue Joe and His Hot Dogs—Manone's key riff was a recurring one throughout the jazz of the period, a sort of *Brigadoon* of trumpet figures. A frenetic and idiosyncratic vocal style on an arrangement of "Isle of Capri" was a substantial hit in 1935 and turned him into a headliner. Manone then headed to Hollywood and appeared in several films (and developed his friendship with Crosby). Other big singles for Manone included "Limehouse Blues" and "Nickel in the Slot."

Nick La Rocca (1889–1961), a New Orleans cornetist, originally played with Papa Jack Laine. He founded the Original Dixieland Band, the first prominent all-white jazz band. Though he retired more than once, he kept coming back to the ODB, which recorded several popular sides for Victor including, in 1917, "Livery Stable Blues," the first jazz record ever. Unfortunately for him, his main legacy centers on his complaints, often shaded with racist overtones, that he was underappreciated for what he thought were his contributions to seminal developments in the origins of jazz.

In the annals of early Louisiana jazz there are perhaps as many memorable clarinetists as there are trumpet-and-cornet players, and again, almost all of them are from New Orleans because that's where the early opportunities were. Bechet was the biggie of course, but here are several others of note.

One of the early New Orleans guys who *didn't* migrate to Chicago, **George Lewis** (1900–1968), was a much-loved, self-taught clarinetist who performed with Buddy Petit in his Black and Tan Band. During the Depression, Lewis played funeral gigs and worked as a stevedore; then in the forties he partnered with Bunk Johnson. The two recorded for historian William Russell—who introduced them—including the Russell-produced "Burgundy Street Blues."

After a year of heading up one of the hottest bands in New York City, in 1945, Lewis and Johnson split. Lewis returned to the Crescent City and set up shop at Manny's Tavern. In 1950, when *Look* magazine ran a piece on Lewis, he was unofficially crowned monarch of the New Orleans resurgence. His career exploded. He toured the United States, Japan, and Europe as a top-paid club headliner and remained popular for the rest of his life. Critics judged him average at best, never faulting his spirit but often attacking his technique. A set worth owning is *The George Lewis Ragtime Band of New Orleans: The Oxford Series Vols 1–10* (American Music).

If he's remembered for only one thing other than being a talented tinsmith and prosperous land owner, New Orleans clarinetist **Alphonse Picou** (1878–1961) is etched in the jazz history books for a piccolo descant now accepted in arrangements of the song "High Society." He spent his early career doing the brass-band thing at celebratory and memorial gigs in the city, particularly in the Excelsior, Tuxedo, and Olympia groups, and in orchestras led by Buddy Bolden and Bunk Johnson. He worked in Chicago for a while with Emanuel Perez, but soon returned to his hometown with Wooden Joe Nichols. He also played with his band in a long-tenured gig at the Club Pig Pen. He owned his own joint, Picou's Bar & Restaurant (at 1601 Ursulines), over which he lived. One of his Mardi Gras rituals included sticking a kazoo down his E-flat clarinet, which he then manipulated as he sang. Picou was enormously popular on every level of New Orleans society, and his passing resulted in one of the most titanic jazz funerals ever.

Like many early jazzmen from New Orleans, **Albany Leon "Barney" Bigard** (1906–1980) started out on clarinet and then learned tenor sax, though it was the former on which he would become famous. He played with King Oliver and Duke Ellington, who used many of Bigard's extemporaneous riffs and chord voicings in his compositions. Bigard's's influence was so prevalent that Jelly Roll Morton said (only partly in jest): "Ellington's got Barney Bigard, a good New Orleans boy, sitting right beside him telling him what to do." From there, Bigard helped jumpstart Kid Ory's career, and later joined Louis Armstrong and His All Stars. It's true that Bigard had a fondness for drink that occasionally interrupted the flow of his career, but he stayed active professionally until the mid-sixties; after that, he worked when it pleased him until he died. His ability to use his New Orleans roots as a launching pad into the freer nuances of swing was a valuable juxtaposition of styles. One of his best, often overlooked, albums is his *Bucket's Got a Hole in It* (Delmark).

To-the-manor-born, **Edmond Hall** (1901–1967) followed in his father Edward's clarinet-tested footsteps, and by his early twenties had toured with Buddy Petit, Kid Thomas, and Eagle-Eye Shields. He landed in New York City and worked with a variety of artists during the mid-thirties, principally Claude Hopkins. He hooked up with Red Allen and then Teddy Wilson, and led his own band for five years in Gotham at the Café Society before moving on to Boston and California. He eventually replaced "Barney" Bigard in Louis Armstrong's All Stars (1955–1958) before easing off the gig circuit. Though semi-retired, Hall would play off and on with Eddie Condon and his own quartet until he died of a sudden heart attack while shoveling snow in his driveway. A gentle man who practiced yoga, Hall was one of the finest technicians of all the New Orleans clarinetists. A recording worth hearing, *In Copenhagen*, was recorded in 1966 shortly before he passed away (Storyville Records).

Jimmie Noone (1895–1944), still another New Orleans–born clarinetist from the dawn of jazz, studied with Lorenzo Tio Sr. and Sidney Bechet. Later, he worked with Kid Ory and Papa Celestin before moving to Chicago, where he started a residency at the Apex Club, and then a recording career (Fatha Hines played piano for him) that made Noone a star. Among their hits: "Sweet Lorraine," "I Know That You Know," "Sweet Sue" and "Four or Five Times." A perpetually cheerful guy with a Santa Claus gut, Noone eventually relocated to Los Angeles and worked with Kid Ory until he unexpectedly died. "He didn't drink or smoke but he couldn't leave food alone and he had very high blood pressure," his son, Jimmie Noone Jr., said. *Jimmie Noone 1930–34 & 1934–40* (Classics) is a nice collection.

Of a more recent era is much-loved New Orleans clarinetist **Pete Fountain** (1930–), who probably didn't have a shaved head when he started out at eighteen in the Junior Dixieland Band. Fountain became a founding member of the Basin Street Six, then worked with Phil Zito, Al Hirt, and Monk Hazel before starting his own band, Pete Fountain and the Three Coins. He fortuitously scored a gig on *The Lawrence Welk Show*, starring in that program's Dixieland band for two years and simply became famous. He recorded extensively (and popularly) for Coral, and opened his own soon-to-be-popular club back home, Pete's Place, on Bourbon Street.

Fountain has a terrific tone and is an undeniable talent, but like trumpeter Al Hirt, by his own choice, Fountain has become more of an "entertainer," a figurehead of New Orleans jazz rather than an innovative musician.

In recent years, Fountain has held court at the Hilton hotel in the Central Business District. Plenty of recorded material is available, but it's still worth looking in the used-record stores for the old Coral LPs.

There are more clarinetists worth speaking briefly about, from varying eras: **George Baquet** (1883–1949), a clarinetist in the John Robichaux Orchestra perhaps most noted for being late to the birthday house-party at which six-year-old Sidney Bechet filled in anonymously from another room; **Emile Barnes** (1892–1970), a traditional New Orleans clarinetist who split careers. He was a musician and mattress maker (the latter helpful in the Depression), studied with a virtual Ivy League of teachers from Lorenzo Tio Jr. and Alphonse Picou to George Baquet and Big Eye Nelson, and worked with the Camellia Band, Buddy Petit, Chris Kelly, and Kid Howard; **Albert Burbank** (1902–1976), a career clarinetist from New Orleans who played with Kid Milton, Herb Morland, Paul Barbarin, Kid Ory, and the Preservation Hall Jazz Band, also serving time with the Young Tuxedo and Eureka Brass Bands.

Irving Fazola (1912–1949), né Prestopnik, was an amazingly talented New Orleans–born player noted chiefly for stints with Louis Prima and Bob Crosby (this association ended when Fazola got into a fight with fellow Crosby sideman Ray Conniff). He did plenty of freelance recording for Sharkey Bonano and Billie Holiday. His interesting style, crossing N'Awlins roots with swing, earned him a *Down Beat* poll win in 1940–1941. Generally acknowledged to be fat, irritable, and obsessed with the Bacchanalian, Fazola nonetheless had his pals and admirers, chiefly Pete Fountain. "Faz" died of cirrhosis of the liver and high blood pressure at thirty-six. **Louis "Big Eye" Nelson** (*c*1880–1949), a New Orleans guy who worked with Buddy Bolden, became a sort of musical handyman who played any of a number of instruments as need be.

And finally there was **Albert Nicholas** (1900–1973), born in New Orleans. He literally learned on the streets and, by the end of World War I, had not only served in the navy but played with Kid Ory, Buddy Petit, and King Oliver. He worked day gigs during World War II, then led his own trio before touring and recording in Europe for several years with a variety of artists on the Continent. Nicholas was a terrific player whose fluency was pleasantly tempered by an affection for blues. He died in Switzerland.

Of his early years, Nicholas was quoted (in the excellent *Bourbon Street Black* by Danny Barker and Jack Buerkle, mentioned earlier in the chapter): "I was just like the rest of the kids—just wanted to know all about that new music called jazz. I was a second-line kid. That meant I'd follow the big bands down the streets, and man, what a thrill when [Lorenzo] Tio or George Baquet would let me carry their cases while they played. I'd walk along feeling just as important as could be."

An integral part of the early jazz and Dixieland tradition, the trombone played a significant role in the development of music in Louisiana. One of the most important practitioners was **Edward "Kid" Ory** (*c*1887–1973), a guy whose nickname, as it might reflect one's exuberance, energy, and thirst-for-life, was appropriate throughout his long career. He was born in LaPlace, Louisiana, but accounts differ about the exact year. He formed a string band quintet as a child and used the cash from those gigs to buy his first trombone.

Ory supposedly jammed with Buddy Bolden's band, then went on to become the premier "tailgate" trombonist of his generation—that player who, because of the instrumentation of the brass bands, provided rhythmic bass parts until solo time, then took off in fluid but frequently exaggerated and amusing runs. Before World War I, Ory came to New Orleans with a band that would count Louis Armstrong, Mutt Carey, and King Oliver as members.

After the war, Ory traveled to Los Angeles and Chicago and played and recorded with a succession of artists, among them Oliver, Pops, and Jelly Roll Morton. Also of that era were the Louis Armstrong Hot Five sessions; these included a recording of Ory's immortal "Muskrat Ramble." When the Depression years seemed to erase all interest in the New Orleans sounds, Ory retired until the nineteen-forties. Gigs with Barney Bigard and Bunk Johnson led to an appearance in Hollywood on one of Orson Welles's CBS broadcasts; this in turn triggered a *Time* magazine piece that headlined "The Kid Comes Back." From that point until the end of his career, Ory made occasional forays into film (he appeared in *New Orleans*, *Crossfire*, *Mahogany Magic*, and *The Benny Goodman Story*).

He continued to record, with his own Kid Ory's Jazz Band as well as with Armstrong, making such albums as *This Kid's the Greatest!* by Kid Ory's Creole Jazz Band (Good Time Jazz) and *Creole Jazz Band at Club Hangover* (Storyville). After years of touring and making records for the Good Time Jazz label, he moved to Hawaii, where he eventually died.

One of five musical brothers, New Orleans's **Georg Brunis** (1902–1974) (real name George Brunies, changed at the suggestion of a numerologist) was a Dixieland trombonist and vocalist perhaps best known for his exuberant and madcap showmanship (he played the trombone with his foot, for example). Though heavy on the tourist-pleasing schtick in home courts, the Famous Door and Nick's among them, and in bands headed up by Ted Lewis and Louis Prima, Brunis did solid recording work with Muggsy Spanier's Ragtimers and Wild Bill Davison.

Preston Jackson (1904–1983), born James Preston McDonald, was also from New Orleans, but left his hometown at fifteen. He settled in Chicago and fell in with a bunch of Crescent City musicians, including Honore Dutre in King Oliver's band. He worked with Bernie Young and Erskine Tate before catching on with Louis Armstrong in 1931–1932 (check out his solo on "You Rascal You"). He also recorded and played with Carroll Dickerson, Jimmie Noone, Frankie "Half Pint" Jackson, and Zilmer Randolph. He retired to work for the union, but in 1959 he picked his horn back up to record with Lil Harding Armstrong. Digging it, he returned to New Orleans, hooked up with the Preservation Hall Jazz Band, and was touring with them when he died.

A trombonist and bassist from Algiers, **John Lindsay** (1894–1950) was an alumnus of Freddie Keppard's Tuxedo Band who moved to New York City after serving in World War I. There, and later in Chicago, he worked with a variety of artists, among them King Oliver and Armand J. Piron, and recorded with everyone from Jelly Roll Morton and Johnny Dodds to Sidney Bechet and blues singer Victoria Spivey.

Another early master of the slide trombone, **Zue Robertson** (1891–1943) played in Kit Carson's Wild West Show and in various carnivals before joining Emanuel Perez's band. In 1917, he headed to Chicago and worked with King Oliver, Jelly Roll Morton, and W. C. Handy. He was a versatile musician, and later learned bass, piano, and organ. Robertson played extensively in New York and Los Angeles, though there are no known recordings of his work.

A variety of other entities, on a variety of other instruments (as well as vocalists) are essential to a basic appreciation of the accomplishments and history of early jazz in Louisiana.

The Boswell Sisters. Without **Martha** (1908–1958), **Connee** (1907–1976), and **Helvetia** (1909–1988) **Boswell,** it's not certain that close-harmony girl sibling acts such as the Andrews Sisters, the McGuire Sisters, or the Beverleys would have hit as big as they did. A multi-instrumental trio who learned music from the black servants in their New Orleans home, the Boswells started out in radio in Los Angeles, essentially riding on the magnificent voice of Connee (confined, incidentally, to a wheelchair by polio). When a severe cold stifled Connee's voice before a broadcast, the girls pulled up to the microphone to sing at half-volume, an untested technique that garnered rave reviews. They made records in the thirties (including *It's the Girls,* a collection of early tracks out from the ASV label) supported by the Dorsey Brothers and Benny Goodman, appeared in several films, and were bona-fide stars. They inspired other women, even Ella Fitzgerald, who once said, "Who influenced me? There was only one—Connee Boswell. She was doing things that no one else was doing at the time." When Martha and Helvetia retired to married life, Connee carried on solo. She enjoyed a terrific career as a singer in film and television and appeared in the popular television series *Pete Kelly's Blues* opposite Jack Webb.

A nationally popular entertainer, trumpeter, vocalist, and natural-born bandleader, **Louis Prima** (1911–1978)—his ex–sax man, Sam Butera, insists on "Louie"—fits in anywhere, but certainly as a singer. When still a kid, he formed his first group and worked the streets of the French Quarter, establishing connections he'd use for the rest of his life. Heavily influenced by Louis Armstrong—vocally as well as on trumpet—he headed to New York in 1935 with a band called Louis Prima and his New Orleans Gang and began a series of recordings for the Brunswick and Vocalian labels that would establish him as a star vocalist and trumpeter.

Prima, teamed with Pee Wee Russell, became a larger-than-life New York character who worked as bandleader at the Famous Door and scored a radio program called *Swing It*, after one of his favorite sayings. Rumored troubles with the mob sent Prima to California, where he opened his own Famous Door Hollywood with comedian Red Colonna. He was just as popular there, making films and recording hit songs throughout the forties with a big band ("There, I've Said It Again," "One Mint Julep"). Gradually, Prima shifted his style from pure jazz to pop music. He married the wonderful singer Keely Smith and started a high-powered nightclub act featuring Smith and hometown bro Butera and the Witnesses.

The show was astoundingly successful in Las Vegas, Los Angeles, Chicago, and New York; if it all but eclipsed memories of his superb jazz musicianship, his vocal and trumpet contributions to Walt Disney's *Jungle Book* more than made up for it. Louis Armstrong called Prima one of the "White Greats."

His legacy crosses all boundaries in works such as *Louis Prima Vol. 1* (JSP), and *Zooma Zooma—The Best of Louis Prima* (Rhino).

Lizzie Miles (1895–1963) was the *nom de gig* of a jazz vocalist born Elizabeth Mary Landreaux, reportedly on Bourbon Street. She started singing gospel in church and by her teens had musically segued from God to King Oliver, Kid Ory, and Armand J. Piron. She toured the South with the Alabama Minstrels and headed to Chicago along with everyone else. There, she worked again with Oliver, Freddie Keppard, and Elgar's Creole Orchestra. Miles went next to New York and started an extensive recording career; later she toured Europe and worked on television. She enjoyed a successful club career singing with such artists as Fats Waller, Sharkey Bonano, Clarence Williams, and Paul Barbarin. When her bluesy approach to jazz began to fade from favor, she returned to New Orleans and enjoyed a nice gig with Paul Barbarin at the Mardi Gras Lounge on Bourbon Street. Miles eventually retired and studied religion, again singing the hymns from whence she started.

The bass often seems to be the most overlooked instrument, but there have been several outstanding Louisiana bassists. Without question, **George "Pops" Foster** (1892–1969) is the monarch of the bunch. A player of almost incalculable influence, Foster was born in McCall, Louisiana, and was kicking around on his own homemade bass at the age of seven. He probably wasn't called "Pops" at that point, but he was clearly on his way to becoming the patriarch of jazz bassists. Because of the relative insignificance of the bass in early jazz, Foster turned to the bass fiddle and tuba, playing the latter in Fate Marable's riverboat band by 1918.

By the time he joined Kid Ory, Foster and his bass innovations—slapping, syncopation, bowing, and pizzicato techniques, and an intuitive sense of aggressive melodies as well as rhythmic support—had moved the instrument into the mainstream. He played with a variety of artists over the years, most notably King Oliver and Luis Russell (the latter in support of Louis Armstrong), in the Dixieland revival with Mezz Mezzrow and Sidney Bechet, and toward the end of his career with Earl Hines and Elmer Snowden.

Foster's technique was outstanding, but is perhaps more significantly captured as an extension of his exuberance for life. "Hell," he said in 1947, "I just play any old go-to-hell note, as long as it swings!"

Wellman Braud (1891–1966) was also influential. Born in St. James Parish, Braud was noted for his percussive style and recording acumen at a time when such considerations were only visionary. He worked in New York and Chicago with Duke Ellington, soloing on *Jungle Nights in Harlem* by Ellington and His Cotton Club Orchestra (RCA Bluebird), Kid Ory, and Jelly Roll Morton, among others, and later ran his own restaurant. He was a great friend of Louis Armstrong's and an occasional benefactor on the rare occasion when the trumpeter experienced hard times; he was also a major inspiration for bassist Milt Hinton.

Born in New Orleans, **Ed "Montudie" Garland** (1885–1980) is acknowledged as the Father of the Double Bass, though he started off playing tuba and bass drum in such brass bands as the Excelsior, the Imperial, the Security, and Frank Dusen's Double Eagle. He played extensively in Storyville—including gigs with Buddy Bolden—before heading to Chicago and Sugar Johnny's Creole Band (he also did stints with Freddie Keppard, Emmanuel Lewis, and King Oliver). A notoriously slick dresser, Garland was nicknamed after a New Orleans dandy of some repute during the Storyville years. He went to California with Oliver, dug the place, and stayed. He had his own One-Eleven band, worked with Kid Ory and Earl Hines, and even appeared in the film *Imitation of Life*.

Alcide "Slow Drag" Pavageau (1888–1969) was a New Orleans guy who started out on guitar and ended up on double bass. A longtime member of George Lewis's band, Pavageau apparently dressed exquisitely, spoke in a highly stylized patois, and was so popular in the annals of the city's street parades that he had an alternative nickname: the Grand Marshal of the Second Line. His forceful tone and slap-happy precision made him as much a talent as a character. He died not long after being mugged.

If the piano is overlooked, it's probably because it was hard to drag one around in a marching brass band, which, as we have seen, is where many of the early jazz masters learned. That aside, the period—as evidenced by Jelly Roll—wasn't without great players.

Tony Jackson (1876–1921) was born into poverty, but became an almost mythic figure in the annals of New Orleans piano *brujos* (sorcerers). As a musically inclined seven-year-old who had no possibility of lessons or access to a piano, he *built one!*—or at least what passed for a functional keyboard (probably harpsichord-like in design). By his early teens, Jackson was a fixture in Storyville. Though his signature style was assuredly based on ragtime (he appeared in a ragtime competition at the St. Louis Exposition of 1904), he was also blessed with a distinctive and winsome singing voice and amassed a broadly varied repertoire of over a thousand tunes. On playing club gigs with Jackson, Sidney Bechet said, "Lots of times Tony didn't need me. He could entertain three or four hundred people with just his piano." Jackson was hugely influential in early New Orleans jazz, and later worked in Chicago for several successful years until he died. Unfortunately, he was never recorded, although his most famous composition, "Pretty Baby," ensured that he would be remembered.

"Fate" wasn't a nickname, but given his status as a one-man finishing school for dozens of New Orleans musicians, Fate Marable (1890–1947), a Paducah, Kentucky, native seemed to be named with visionary accuracy. A career pianist and bandleader for the Streckfus riverboat line on the Mississippi, Marable was a disciplined fellow; he ran his band as if he were a head coach, instilling rules of behavior for his New Orleans players, many of whom had joined the riverboat organization after years of Bacchanalian excess in the Storyville district. Among his charges: the Two Pops (Armstrong and Foster), Red Allen, the Dodds brothers, Emanuel Perez, Johnny St. Cyr, Mouse Randolph, and Jimmy Blanton.

Another prominent whorehouse pianist in the Storyville glory days, Richard Myknee Jones (1889–1945), born in New Orleans, was a multi-instrumentalist who started out with the Eureka Brass Band. He moved to Chicago in the early 1920s and formed the Jazz Wizards, with whom he recorded several albums for a variety of labels. He was also a songwriter of some note, though his authorship of some material is in dispute, including "Red Wagon" and "Jazzin' Baby Blues."

New Orleans pianist **Fats Pichon** (1906–1967) relocated to the northeast at an early age. He studied at the New England Conservatory of Music, then worked in New York for several years as a composer and arranger for various artists, including Chick Webb. Later, Pichon returned to New Orleans and played solo for years in the Absinthe House bar, from which in the fifties he hosted a local television show.

Alton Purnell (1911–1987) should also be remembered. A New Orleans pianist who worked with both Bunk Johnson and George Lewis, he played with jazz musicians (Kid Ory and Ben Pollack among them) in California, and also toured Europe. Purnell's fill-the-room vocals and ever-buoyant stride piano helped establish the New Orleans piano-wizard tradition that many associate with the R&B greats.

In a town where Guitar Slim once roamed like a Peter Max–painted Tyrannosaurus, it's easy to overlook jazz guitarists–banjoists—other than Danny Barker, of course. But these musicians added diversity and richness to the sound. **Johnny St. Cyr** (1890–1966) was one of the first guitar-and-banjo champs. From New Orleans, St. Cyr was an early mentor of Sidney Bechet; he helped the fledgling clarinetist with tempo problems, and also introduced him to Emanuel Perez and "Big Eye" Nelson, who became a close friend of Louis Armstrong. A plasterer by trade, St. Cyr gradually expanded his gig schedule through work with the Tuxedo Orchestra and such artists as Kid Ory and Fate Marable. He played briefly in Chicago in the early twenties, and, after returning to sporadic jobs in New Orleans, headed to California, where he recorded with Louis Armstrong and Jelly Roll Morton. Describing the primitive recording conditions for the Hot Five sessions with Pops, St. Cyr was quoted in the September–October 1954 edition of *Second Line:* "We were only allowed two minutes and forty-five seconds per record. We could not play at ease as the musicians do now as we had no microphones then, and we had to play into a horn which was attached to a recording machine. There were several of them, one on the piano, one to the reeds, and one to the brass, and one to the banjo. I would be sitting on a small ladder, or on several packing crates stacked on top of one another."

Born in Laurel, Mississippi, and raised in New Orleans, guitarist **Mundell Lowe** (1922–), whose work in recording, television, and film demonstrates his inspired chops, started in Bourbon Street bands and worked on the *Grand Ole Opry* before the World War II. After the service, he played in swing bands with various artists, among them Red Norvo, Ellis Larkins, and Jan Savitt. He studied composition, worked on the NBC staff, recorded numerous solo albums for RCA Victor and Riverside, and even laid down a memorable version of *Porgy and Bess.* Lowe acted on occasion, scored documentary films, and for years led his own quartet. He eventually became the music director for the Monterey Jazz Festival and taught film composition. A nice introduction to his music is a reissue of *Mundell Lowe Quartet* (Riverside).

Hilton "Nappy" Lamare (1907–1988) got his nickname as a kid because he always overslept. The New Orleans–born guitarist, banjoist, and singer played around his hometown with Sharkey Bonano, Johnny Wiggs, and the Midnight Serenaders. Then, after a stint with Ben Pollack, he hooked up in Los Angeles with Bob Crosby and worked as a freelancer at San Francisco's Hangover Club. A top rhythm guitarist who recorded with Joseph "Wingy" Manone, Louis Prima, and Jack Teagarden, and gigged with Jimmy Dorsey, Lamare eventually owned his own Los Angeles nightclub and, with his band, The Straw Strutters, starred in a local television show. (He must have thought the abbreviation for Louisiana—LA—meant "Los Angeles.")

A guitarist, banjoist, violinist, and singer, **Bud Scott** (1890–1949) was born in New Orleans and started out with such artists as Buddy Bolden, John Robichaux, and Freddie Keppard. After years in Los Angeles with King Oliver, he spent time in Chicago with Erskine Tate and Jimmie Noone before returning to California for a job with Mutt Carey; later, Scott formed his own trio. Known for the catch phrase "Oh, play that thing!" which he shouted during a session with Oliver on "Dipper Mouth Blues," Scott, until he died, gigged pretty much exclusively with Kid Ory.

I would be remiss if I didn't mention some of the great drummers.

Bennie "Black Bennie" Williams was a turn-of-the-century character who played bass drum in the brass bands. Not only noted for his ability to frolic with whores, drink beer like a champ, fight for money—good naturedly—and win, Williams was a mentor to Louis Armstrong.

Minor "Ram" Hall (1897–1959) and **Alfred "Tubby" Hall** (1895–1946) were a sibling set of percussionists, both born in Sellers, Louisiana. Tubby started out in Frank Dusen's Double Eagle Band and other New Orleans outfits, worked up the ladder with Jimmie Noone, Boyd Atkins, and Carroll Dickerson before ultimately teaming up with Louis Armstrong. Ram worked with Kid Ory, King Oliver, and Noone; his work with the Kid was particularly big in the forties.

Valued beyond all else for his band-leading skills and as an evaluator of talent, **John Robichaux** (1866–1939), a Thibodeaux, Louisiana, native, started out in the Excelsior Brass Band as a drummer and shortly after formed the John Robichaux Orchestra, a long-lived and fruitful dance organization for which its leader played violin, accordion, bass, and drums. Many of the town's best musicians served time in Robichaux's outfit.

Henry Zeno was one of few men who shared the distinction of being an idol to Louis Armstrong. A snare drummer of notable talent, he came to attention as one of the original musicians to play with Buddy Bolden.

◆ ◆ ◆

Finally, before segueing into the modern age, here are some sundry folks who need to be slipped in, even if they weren't part of a specific instrumental fraternity:

Tony Parenti (1900–1972) was a terrific all-around sax-and-clarinet man from New Orleans whose abilities as a kid were so extensive that he had to turn down gigs with Paul Whiteman and the Original Dixieland Jazz Band because he was too young to go on the road. He was soon old enough to pick up riverboat jobs, though, and to play a stint with Papa Jack Laine. He led his own band at the Bienville Hotel when he was twenty-one, and six years later moved to New York; there, he subbed for Benny Goodman in Ben Pollack's band, and later worked on staff at Radio City Music Hall and at CBS. After a gig on Ted Lewis's show, he firmly embraced the New Orleans revival—whether on the road, in New York, or in Florida with Preacher Rollo's Five Saints. During the last years of his life, he led his own band of traditionalists; he was quoted as saying, "Progressive jazz is really extemporaneous tricks: it lacks feeling and expression, and gives me a cold reaction."

Though the **Dukes of Dixieland** might be thought of as the REO Speedwagon of New Orleans jazz, which is to say they enjoyed substantial record sales and popularity yet failed to score the respect of their contemporaries, they have bounced back impressively. The group was the brainchild of New Orleans brothers **Frank** (1932–1974) and **Fred** (1929–1966) **Assunto.** In high school, they formed Dixieland bands called the Basin Street Four (or Five or Six) before graduating into a four-year stint on Bourbon Street at the Famous Door with Horace Heidt in the Junior Dixieland Band. They next conceived the Dukes, managed by their father (and second trombonist) **Papa Jac Assunto** (1905–1985), and signed with the prestigious Audio Fidelity label. For years they enjoyed national success, including the recording of the first stereo jazz LP, before Fred passed away prematurely in 1966. Tragically, Papa Jac outlived both his sons. The band reformed in the mid-eighties with all new members.

James Brown Humphrey (1859–?) was an African-American music teacher from Sellers, Louisiana, who read music and played virtually every instrument. Through his happy willingness to teach both black and white musicians, he not only helped bridge the cultural gap of the times but played no small role in the birth of jazz.

Davey Jones was a multi-instrumentalist; he excelled as a mellophonist, trumpeter, drummer, saxman, and French hornist who started out playing on the riverboat S.S. *Sidney* with Fate Marable. Evidence suggests that Jones gave Louis Armstrong early instruction, and he was most certainly a good pal of Pops. (Armstrong writes most happily about Jones in a poignant incident when the two were running to catch a train in a crowded station and the trumpeter spilled a trout sandwich and some olives. Even though they were both utterly poor at that point in their lives, Jones was too embarrassed to help him pick the food up. Still, no less than Danny Barker called Jones "a phenomenal musician." Jones spent some high-quality years with King Oliver; later, he worked as a saxophonist for the Jones-Collins Astoria Hot Eight.

The first biggie of White Guy Jazz in New Orleans, **Papa Jack Laine** (1873–1966) was a drummer and altoist. He started a ragtime band when he was fifteen years old, and his Reliance Brass Band is said to be the prototype for the Original Dixieland Band. The Reliance Brass Band was so popular that Laine regularly booked several groups using that name. Laine was influential and popular as a bandleader and as a father figure to white and Creole musicians.

Armand J. Piron (1888–1943) was an accomplished violinist from New Orleans who is perhaps best remembered as being a partner with Clarence Williams in what was probably the first-ever black-owned music publishing company. A visionary concept, the business made both men wealthy, though arguably their biggest selling composition, "I Wish I Could Shimmy Like My Sister Kate," was a derivative effort borrowed structurally and conceptually from a Louis Armstrong song—and Pops received neither royalties nor songwriting credit. Musically, Piron had a vaudeville-styled act, started his own New Orleans Orchestra, and worked with Papa Celestin's Tuxedo Orchestra. He also gigged for years at the New Orleans Country Club on Lake Pontchartrain. Hear his work on *Piron's New Orleans Orchestra* (Azure).

Two

MODERN JAZZ
AND THE DISPARATE
PATHS OF YOUNG WARRIORS

*D*r. Larry Williams, my dog's veterinarian, returns from the bar with two frosty bottles of Dixie beer. It's a Thursday night before the first weekend of the New Orleans Jazz & Heritage Festival (JazzFest) 2000, and we've taxied over to Vaughan's Bar in the Bywater to catch **Kermit Ruffins** (1964–), the fine young trumpeter and trad-jazz revolutionary, play with his band, the **Barbecue Swingers.**

"Dr. Larry," I say, accepting the beer humbly, "it's interesting that, even as New Orleans's classic R&B sound is pushed to endangered-species status by the hornet-swarm evolution of hip-hop, jazz in the city has been carried on by young musicians in two encouraging ways. First, there are the retro-archivists: Ruffins, Dr. Michael White, and James 'Satchmo of the Ghetto' Andrews, who look backwards and reverently re-sod the turf of such predecessors as Louis 'Satchmo of the Satchmo' Armstrong, King Oliver, Jelly Roll Morton, and Sidney Bechet.

"And then there are bold new warriors such as the Marsalis brothers—Wynton, Jason, Branford, and Delfeayo—and Nicholas Payton, Terence Blanchard, Astral Project, Donald Hamilton, Irvin Mayfield, and Los Hombres Calientes, all of whom nod gratefully at the past even as they ride post-bop bottlerockets into the new century."

I didn't really say all that, of course. Dr. Larry is a patient and smart man; I've watched him stitch up a nasty gash in my greyhound, Moosie, as he sang along with the intricate lyrics of Robert Earl Keen's "Gringo Honeymoon." But he wouldn't put up with such bombast this early in the going.

I was *thinking* all that stuff, though.

Dr. Larry Williams is a lifelong pal who went from the fiery towhead in Little League with whom I shared a hatred of mushrooms to a distinguished veterinarian, not only to my critters but also to those of George W. Bush, at least until they became presidential. Dr. Larry is a fine and responsible companion—at least until he goes to New Orleans. Then, during the gathering storm of Jazz Fest, Dr. Larry becomes a werewolf.

But this is good. We've already feasted on the requisite roast beef po'boy at the Parasol Bar; now we have just enough room for a few cold ones and, of course, the barbecued hot sausage that Kermit Ruffins smokes during his sets and dispenses like loaves and fishes to his fans each night. That's right: It's not enough that Ruffins encloses recipes in the jewel boxes of his CDs; he travels to gigs in a red pickup truck, bed loaded with the barbecue smoker, a wondrous and much-loved cooking monstrosity that resembles a scale model of the *Merrimac*.

Vaughan's is a regular Thursday night gig for the Barbecue Swingers. Located at Lesseps and Dauphine, the bar is an amazing, nicotine-treated dive with its linoleum floors, requisite neon beer signs, television propped on a board laid across a galvanized garbage can, paintings on the walls of various Mardi Gras Indians, and, suspended from one wall, what appear to be the skeletal remains of something. "Human," Dr. Larry assures me. The place is jammed with everyone from hip college kids to older, black and white neighborhood regulars, most of whom have failed to make the *Fortune* 500 list lately. The door guy looks like an exclusively ice cream–trained Johnny Winter.

At 11:30 P.M., when the maestro arrives, the place erupts into an enthusiasm one associates with ticker-tape parades. "Hello! Happy Jazz Fest 2000!" Ruffins calls into one of those old Radio City–style microphones. The Swingers comprise Corey Henry (trombone), Kevin Morris (standup bass), Emile Vinette (piano), Jerry Anderson (drums), and Roderick Paulin (trombone). The instant the music starts, the contingency of white youth crush toward the makeshift bandstand and nod their heads knowingly in time with Ruffins's astonishingly sweet, tangy tone; and, yes, it sounds as though he's also slow-smoked his technique, over hickory and maple and perhaps the glowing embers of Louis Armstrong's casket.

When Ruffins puts his mouth to his horn, whether on an oldie such as "Ain't Misbehavin'" or his own "Hide the Reefer," the results are astonishing: fluid, somewhat jagged in arithmetic structure (often in the same two- or three-bar phrase), rolling like typhoon-lashed waves, at times blurting like a madman who'd somehow had a trumpet smuggled into the asylum. Buddy Bolden, maybe.

Indeed, Ruffins's sound, vocals, and that easy ambassadorship are all redolent with Satchmo's spirit. But alive in this unforgettable performance is something important. This is no tribute band, no cover-tunes gig. Something personal lives here, and not just in the original material. There is simply an unidentifiable quality to Ruffins's interpretation and presentation that defines his neo-traditionalistic work as art-in-progress.

Ruffins fiercely loves the Tremé neighborhood in which he grew up, just across the St. Louis Cemetery #1 from the French Quarter. A rebounding blue-collar area, the Tremé has historically been home to dozens of New Orleans musicians, and from an early age Ruffins was destined to carry the torch. In 1982, still a youngster, he helped form the ReBirth Brass Band, with whom he recorded six albums before setting sail into Solo Land. The quintet that came to be the Barbecue Swingers solidified out of regular neighborhood jam sessions, and in 1992 Ruffins signed a deal with Justice Records. He released three fine solo efforts for the label (*World on a String*, *Big Butter and Egg Man*, and *Hold on Tight*), all of which chronicled his ever-distilling love of big bands, Louis Armstrong, and his hometown's joyous funk.

Though he'd toured extensively with ReBirth, Ruffins has forged his own musical worldview; this means staying in New Orleans and playing the small neighborhood spots, hanging with family and friends, and spreading the word in his own way. To that end, he signed with the wonderful local label Basin Street Records, for whom he's put out two superb discs, *Kermit Ruffins and the Barbecue Swingers Live* and *Swing This*.

Watching the Swingers in Vaughan's during JazzFest, Dr. Larry leans over and hollers in my ear: "This is a long way from Wynton at Lincoln Center." He's referring to the cutting edge post-bop proselytized by Wynton Marsalis, reaffirming what I was thinking earlier when Dr. Larry returned from the bar. In New Orleans now there appears to be a rift between Ruffins, James Andrews, Dr. Michael White, and the other new-trad players, and the music of the Marsalis brothers, Irvin Mayfield, and the likes. But that may be an imagined perception among the press and fans more so than among the musicians, though certainly Wynton Marsalis has been pretty vocal about the direction jazz should be going.

As has Irvin Mayfield. "It's not fair to say there's a rift," Mayfield told me over the phone. "Kermit and James are playing the songs they grew up with. The difference is that Terence [Blanchard] and Wynton and Nicholas [Payton] grew up with that stuff, too, and they're using those elements, but they're going forward with them. It's kinda like having a big family and some of them work at a museum that's been around for years. And someone needs to do that; I'm not saying it's not good."

Alto saxophonist Donald Hamilton is linked to the "new school" of New Orleans jazz, yet has also released an album of old Mardi Gras Indian chants set to jazz. He told me, "We all grew up playing in the traditional sense, in funerals or parades, the same as King Oliver or Louis Armstrong. That I went on to be-bop and forward is just part of a process.

What's been done—in some cases to a greater degree of experimentation—is that each person puts [his] own spin on something. The harmony
doesn't change; you turn it around to reflect the times you live in."

So Ruffins cooks and smokes in his own happy world. Ruffins loves
good barbecue, good herb, and good jazz, which is after all a combination
that worked pretty well for Louis Armstrong.

Ruffins's brother in trad trumpetry is **James Andrews** (1970–), the
self-proclaimed—with love and admiration rather than ego—"Satchmo of
the Ghetto." There was little chance that he wouldn't become a musician
because his relatives include Walter "12" Nelson (who played guitar for
Smiley Lewis), Jesse "Ooh Papa Do" Hill, Prince Lala, Walter "Papoose"
Nelson Jr. (guitarist with Fats Domino), and Herlin Riley (drummer for
the Lincoln Center Jazz Orchestra and Wynton Marsalis), and, of course,
uncle Lionel Batiste, who gave James his first horn.

As a kid, James haunted Preservation Hall in the French Quarter, the
venerable Dixieland museum, and it wasn't long before he began a year-
long stint in Danny Barker's Roots of Jazz band; later, he formed his own
All Star Brass Band, as fine a self-perpetuated education as a young man
could hope to have. The band toured the world and prepared Andrews for
his next step: In 1995 he founded the New Birth Brass Band, one of the
most important of the new wave of youngster-led brass bands. The next
year, New Birth released a CD on NYNO Records. Called *D-Boy* in memory of Andrews's younger brother Darnell, a gunshot victim in a turf war,
the album is an amalgam of trad brass, funk, and hip-hop.

In 1998, Andrews came out as a leader on a pretty wonderful solo
disc, *Satchmo of the Ghetto*, that featured musical and professorial assis-
tance from no less than Allen Toussaint and Dr. John. Infusing dashes of
gospel and even Latin to the successful mix he'd explored on the New
Birth CD, Andrews established himself as a significant force in New Orleans jazz—and no matter that some of his contemporaries suggested that
Andrews's vision had stopped at the borders of Orleans Parish. Since the
record's release, Andrews has kept busy performing and recording, and he
helps his family in any way possible.

His younger brother Troy—Trombone Shorty—is a skilled and burgeoning young artistic force who frequently accompanies James during
live performances, one of which I witnessed at the 1999 JazzFest. With
the unbridled enthusiasm of a Chautauqua tent gathering, complete with
tunes that recalled an ebullient spirit dance by Louis Armstrong, Danny
Barker, and Buddy Bolden, the brothers Andrews led the band through a
stunning early-afternoon set that concluded with an onstage (and offstage) processional of hundreds of sweat-dotted fans jerking like happy
puppets.

The third major spoke in the wheel of new traditionalism is **Dr.
Michael White** (1954–). A wonderfully enthusiastic man and a teacher

with a doctorate in foreign languages, White's mission is to glorify the work of seminal clarinetist George Lewis. It's not surprising, then, that his debut CD, *A Song for George Lewis*, is a sweetly toned and gracefully played postcard to the clarinet jazz of an earlier age. It will be interesting to see what White and his clarinet might do as an encore, though I suppose Sidney Bechet is always out there.

On another night, I'm sitting by myself at the edge of the French Quarter across Rampart Street from Louis Armstrong Park, in the Funky Butt at Congo Square, a two-story nightclub with black walls and dozens of flickering, voodooesque votive candles. Upstairs is the principal music room; it has a tiny stage at one end, a bar, and an L-shaped listening area supplied with all manner of thrift-shop chairs, bar stools, and tables. Red overtones warm the extreme darkness, as do votives, and a few windows overlooking Rampart Street.

Like Vaughan's, the clientele consists of predominantly young white kids who, I infer, all moved here from somewhere else because of the city's reputation as a fine and Bohemian educational experience. In some ways, it is encouraging that these kids show up for Kermit Ruffins's gig or tonight's appearance by the Jason Marsalis Quintet.

If drummer Marsalis is aware of the sociological implications of his audience, I can't tell it by watching this woefully thin, tall young man who wears wire-rimmed glasses and dresses impeccably in suit and tie. Despite his William F. Buckley–esque vocabulary and quiet demeanor, something inherently mischievous always bubbles under the surface of Jason's persona, as though the whole idea that music can be channeled through his hands is nothing more than a delicious Halloween treat.

Now, seated behind his kit, he's peering out of one of the Funky Butt windows into the Mardi Gras parades and traffic, looking for one of the members of his quintet who hasn't arrived at the club yet. Marsalis elects to start the night four-piece, and does so by himself, kicking into an astonishing polyrhythmic introduction in which each foot and hand seems to operate in a separate time signature. The effect is a series of circular but distinctly disparate grooves. Marsalis's beats briefly rendezvous at a prescribed and synchronized juncture before looping back out on wild elliptical paths before returning safely and neatly to the starting point. Like passengers shakily disembarking from a roller-coaster, the patrons in the Funky Butt have woozy smiles on their faces. Although he's serious about his work, Marsalis seems to understand that carnival sense of exhilaration and translates it into his music. Indeed, his friend, the brilliant young trumpeter Irvin Mayfield, suggests that Marsalis is so musically obsessed that only lately has he been aware of other elements that might enrich existence.

But perhaps Jason's preoccupation is understandable. The musical components of his Family Royale—father Ellis, brothers Delfeayo, Wynton, and

Branford—suggest volumes about the history of jazz in New Orleans, as well as the direction of their music at the millennium. For all the legacies of the city that bubble within this family's gene pool, none could be described in the traditionalist sense of recycling the hits and runs of the masters.

Jason (1977–), born in New Orleans, is the youngest of the musical Marsalis offspring and a whirlwind talent. His production and songwriting skills are the equal of his intimidating badass-ness behind the kit. Growing up, he dug everything from Weather Report to the Peter Gabriel–era progressive rock of Genesis. Yet, unlike many kids who rebel against family traditions, Jason loved jazz from the word go and started playing violin and drums when he was six. Eventually drawn by classical percussion, he abandoned the violin and set out to master jazz and classical drumming. His skill and discipline earned him a spot in his teens with his father's trio, where he coordinated his coltish chops within the structures of balladry and the responsibilities of a drummer in a trio. Eventually, he produced records, led his own bands, and embraced Latin music. He's released two solo CDs, *The Year of the Drummer* and *Music in Motion*, both of which are pinwheels of adventurous creativity, superb performances, and ambitious songwriting. He also spent time in the groundbreaking Los Hombres Calientes, New Orleans's Latin fusion band, and produced, among other works, his father's excellent *Twelve's It* CD.

"Irrespective of individual opinions concerning the advancement or retrogression of modern music," Jason wrote in the liner notes to his *Music in Motion* CD, "something different is always happening somehow."

This night the quartet effortlessly slides through such tunes as "What Is This Thing Called Love" and "Summertime" with a blend of chops and intuitive esprit de corps that seems to evolve naturally. At one point between songs, Marsalis announces, "It looks like an evening of standards." He says this without irony or apology, which lends support to the suspicion that, no matter the source of the music—whether Cole Porter or any of the wonderfully arcane and eminently entertaining pieces from Jason's songbook—the young drummer is willing to go with the flow of jazz, whether forward or backward, knowing that the music is bigger than all of us.

Musicians Kermit Ruffins and Jason Marsalis represent the state of contemporary Louisiana jazz and the possibilities of its future, maybe more so than Harry Connick Jr. and Wynton Marsalis, who have probably reached the biggest audiences of any young Louisiana jazz musicians. But before discussing the other fine young practitioners of modern jazz, it's best to take a look at the history of the modern movement, as we did with traditional jazz in the last chapter.

Keeping in mind that most of New Orleans's early jazz musicians had scattered across the country throughout the evolution of traditional or

Dixieland, and that the bulk of those remaining in the city by the end of World War II were working in watered-down tourist traps of same, it's easy to see how something, a new form, had to evolve naturally to take up the creative slack. Starting in the late forties and progressing over the next several years, something did: bebop. A form that started with the music of Charlie Parker and Dizzy Gillespie, bebop in general isn't listener-friendly in a broad demographic context. By design, the structures of rhythm and harmony are extrapolated beyond a snappy dance beat and hummy choruses, melodies and solos interweaving around the syncopated beats in agitated fashion. Musicians found it liberating and exhilarating, but the blue-collar guy out for a Saturday night of dancing was just as likely to have a grand time trying to boogie at a calculus competition.

Although there was a solid coterie of fine New Orleans players who wanted to experiment with bebop, the city wasn't particularly warm to the idea. During the fifties, the New Orleans slithered into a stagnant holding pattern, jazz-wise, as the dynamic rhythm-and-blues empire began to rise. Survival being what it is, the New Orleans boppers quickly realized they had two possible solutions: First, they paid the bills by doing lucrative sessions in a burgeoning R&B market; second, they left the city for areas that could in some fashion support a bebop scene, chiefly Los Angeles and New York.

A third solution eventually presented itself: the New Orleans beboppers banded together and tried to form their own support system—as in 1961 when brainstormer **Harold Battiste** (1931–), in conjunction with trumpeter **Melvin Lastie** (1930–), drummer **John Boudreaux,** saxophonist **Red Tyler** (1925–1998), and bassist **Chuck Badie** formed the AFO (All For One) label.

At the center of a group of black modern jazzers, Battiste grew up across the street from the Dew Drop Inn, and though his mother didn't want him to become a musician, his father, an amateur clarinetist, showed the kid the essentials, and the boy was off. Among Battiste's neighbors were drummer Ed Blackwell and clarinetist Alvin Batiste; these musicians were surrounded by the blues and R&B scenes, but were far more interested in the burgeoning bebop movement. When Ornette Coleman moved to town and started hanging out, the musical ante was upped from bebop into even more improvisatory arenas.

Though Coleman would soon move on to the West Coast, the small group of forward-thinking musicians, which had grown to include bassist Badie and pianist Edward Frank, played where they could, often segueing from paying R&B gigs in nightclubs into after-hours, post-bebop jam sessions that would last well into the following day. Battiste, who studied music at Dillard University, became a spiritual and scholastic godfather to the movement and worked within the system to teach at various schools and to hammer on the doors of record labels trying to attract their attention.

Younger players such as Ellis Marsalis (who moved early on from saxophone to piano) and drummer James Black were introduced into the circle, and at one point Battiste, Marsalis, and Blackwell were all in Los Angeles trying to score label interest in the New Orleans scene and further experimenting with Coleman's hummingbird-wing theories.

Nothing worked, and in 1958, back in New Orleans, Battiste formed the American Jazz Quintet with Alvin Batiste, Richard Payne, William Swanson, and a merry-go-round of bassists. The group recorded one album, which intentionally or otherwise salted its bopness with elements of free jazz and the R&B sounds being dished out in sessions and clubs all over the city.

Battiste scored some success in Los Angeles: Specialty Records hired him as an A&R man with the idea of finding and signing New Orleans R&B talent, a gig Battiste hoped would bring about the integration of jazz talent into the label's mix. But although Battiste produced some nice R&B work out of the city, the jazz concept fell flat; this is when the idea of AFO was spawned. Battiste had been reading the works of Elijah Muhammed and became a Black Muslim. Because blacks essentially didn't own, well, anything, his concept was for a cooperative black-owned record label, the profits to be split equally between company members. In addition to the aforementioned founders, that crew would eventually include saxophonists Nat Perrilliat and Warren Bell, singer Tami Lynn, drummers James Black and Ed Blackwell, bassist Richard Payne, Ellis Marsalis, and clarinetist Alvin Batiste, all world-class musicians.

Ironically, the fledgling AFO's biggest success was an R&B single—"I Know"—by singer Barbara George (see the R&B section for a more detailed accounting of her work). Still, the success of the #3 hit infused the AFO coffers with cash and allowed a lot of jazz to be recorded. According to the very fine book *Up from the Cradle of Jazz—New Orleans Music Since World War II* by Jason Berry, Jonathan Foose, and Tad Jones, AFO recorded over a hundred tunes by its intermingling roster of owners and musicians, including Ellis Marsalis's *Monkey Puzzle* album. Unfortunately, very little of the label's work is available today (check out the album *New Orleans Heritage Jazz 1956–1966* on the Opus 43 label, if you can find it). A distribution deal fell through when the label's biggest seller, Barbara George, was lured away by the honchos of the distribution company. In the early sixties, with the roaring influx of British invasion rock 'n' roll, AFO went under. Following the lead of Battiste and Lastie, many of the company's founders headed for the more lucrative pastures of the West Coast.

Most of the players stayed active and moderately successful in one fashion or another; Battiste in particular did well in Los Angeles, working as music director for the Sonny & Cher show, moving cyclonically through session circles, and playing a large role in the early part of Dr. John's voodoo-rock years. His production and arrangement work in R&B was substantial, too; among other things, he arranged Sam Cooke's "You Send Me," co-produced Cooke's "A Change is Gonna Come," and produced George's "I Know," Art Neville's "Cha Dooky-Doo," and Lee Dorsey's "Ya Ya."

When he finally returned to New Orleans after twenty-five years on the West Coast, Battiste jumped headfirst back into the scene. He joined the University of New Orleans Jazz Studies Program with old pal Ellis Marsalis; he resuscitated AFO with his friend Kalamu ya Salaam, the New Orleans writer and activist; he served as executive producer on *Genesis*, the debut album by Wynton Marsalis's sideman Victor Goines; and he produced the new AFO's first CD, Edward Anderson's *Fertile Crescent*.

Battiste's vision has always shone with clarity and a concern for his community. He was honored with an exhibition at the Black Music Hall of Fame in New Orleans in 1999 and, as ya Salaam told *Offbeat* writer Roger Hahn, "Fifty years from now, Harold Battiste will be looked upon as one of the major forces in the development of New Orleans music in the last half of the twentieth century. . . . He's not the first person you think of when you think of many of the projects he's been involved in. That's because his whole energy has been to shine light upon others."

Drummer **Ed Blackwell** (1929–1992) deserves special mention, too. It's hard to sound profound when discussing someone whose premium contribution was as a member of Ornette Coleman's band. Far smarter folks than myself, and not a few excellent musicians, don't pretend to understand Coleman's arcane "harmolodics," though Blackwell presumably got it.

Blackwell's fruitful career also included dates with Ray Charles and session work with Earl King and Huey "Piano" Smith, and heavy jazz gigs in the sixties, seventies, and eighties with Eric Dolphy, John Coltrane, Don Cherry, Archie Shepp, and Dewey Redman, among others. He also led his own bands in later years.

Working bebop from a different direction was **Al Belletto** (1928–), born in New Orleans, who started playing clarinet at twelve, moved to alto saxophone at fifteen, and had an epiphany the first time he heard Charlie Parker. He raced like an ocelot into the heart of bebop, or as close as he could get because there really weren't any New Orleans bebop clubs, and the after-hours jams usually took place in the still-segregated black nightspots. Belletto, a white guy, eventually found work in strip joints. Along the way, Belletto played trad jazz around town with such artists as the Dukes of Dixieland, Wingy Manone, Sharkey Bonano, and Louis Prima. He'd also studied classical music at Loyola, visited Chicago, and in the early fifties attended LSU to earn his master's degree. After graduation, he formed The Al Belletto Sextet, who were discovered by Mel Tormé and introduced to Stan Kenton. The band relocated to New York and in 1954 released an album, *An Introduction to Al Belletto*.

The group struggled until they were incorporated into Woody Herman's big band, with whom they toured internationally through 1960 (when the national climate for jazz chilled considerably). Belletto returned to New Orleans and became musical director for the newly opened Playboy Club. Belletto's booking policies provided a biracial opportunity for modern jazzers in the otherwise barren New Orleans scene; among the musicians, white and black, who played at the Playboy Club were pianist Frank Strazzeri, trumpeter Mike Lala, saxophonist Mouse Bonati, bassist Bill Huntington (all white guys), and the black coterie from the ACO faction.

Belletto became the national booking director for Playboy and ended up playing occasionally with his own heroes: Charlie Parker, Dizzy Gillespie, and Thad Lewis. At about the time the Playboy's Club empire began to sag, New Orleans's taste for modern jazz became more voracious, and Belletto stayed busy gigging with Ellis Marsalis. He had a hand in the founding of the New Orleans Jazz and Heritage Festival in 1968, held a regular job playing with Al Hirt through 1983, and was always able to find work in the resurrected jazz environs. In 1998, Belletto's sixteen-piece big band released *Jazznocracy* on Louisiana Red Hot Records; this is a fine, seasoned, and comprehensive work that features Belletto in more of a leader's role as he provides a supportive backseat to several of the city's younger players.

This brings the modern tradition up to the present generation, of which Harry Connick Jr., Wynton Marsalis, and, to a slightly more peculiar degree, Branford Marsalis, are the most prominent. Wynton has become huge in an essence-of-the-form fashion, but Connick remains a more populist performer. Branford is a superb player, perfectly at home with his wandering muse, so if he's strayed at times into funk and even rock music, not to mention pulling a Doc Severinson–styled television gig, well, he's not the least embarrassed.

I recently had a chance to sit down with **Wynton Marsalis** (1961–), a proposition as intoxicating as it was intimidating and one I had mixed feelings about at first. Over the years, *mucho* press has tagged him as a curmudgeon who doesn't suffer fools gladly. But he *is* a genius. The more I listened to his work and read about him and digested what he said as a featured spokesman on Ken Burns's 2001 *Jazz* series for PBS, the more impressed I was. So, when I heard that he was going to give the commencement address at Connecticut College, in the seacoast town of New London where I live, I knew I had to talk to him if possible. And it was possible; I was able to arrange a brief, pre-speech sit-down in the context of coverage for the newspaper I work for.

We spoke for maybe fifteen minutes, seated at a small table in front of Sol Lewitt's mural in the foyer of the campus arts building. Though not particularly tall and perhaps a bit rounder than I'd expected, Marsalis exudes a power that suggests, indeed, he's not to be trifled with. At the same time, he projects a genuine kindness. As I observed him for a few minutes with the multitudes of folks he had to meet, I realized what he must go through every day of his life, and I was mightily impressed.

The bio goes something like this: Marsalis is the creative director of the Lincoln Center Jazz Orchestra, a musical outfit that formed in the wake of his renowned Wynton Marsalis Septet. He won the 1997 Pulitzer Prize for Music for his oratorio, *Blood On the Fields*, and is the most outspoken and arguably the most talented of his richly gifted family. When Wynton was six, he was given a trumpet by Al Hirt, in whose band papa Ellis played. By eight, Wynton was playing in Danny Barker's Fairview Marching Band; at twelve, when he heard bop trumpeter Clifford Brown, his infatuation with the horn became a mission. Always a superb athlete and student, he entered the New Orleans Center for the Creative Arts (NOCCA) and played in any situation that presented itself, including teenster gigs in both a Top 40 funk band and the New Orleans Philharmonic.

At eighteen, he moved to New York and attended Juilliard; a year later, he joined Art Blakey's Jazz Messengers and signed a solo deal with CBS Records. By twenty-two, he was a globally recognized musician known as much for his classical chops as his work in modern jazz. For a while, Wynton took a hard-line approach to modern jazz and how "real jazz" should be performed, though lately he has backed off and become a kinder, gentler spokesman. The series of albums chronicling his exploration into blues and the music of his native New Orleans—the three-disc set *Soul Gestures in Southern Blue* (which comprise *Thick in the South, Uptown Ruler,* and *Levee Low Moan); In This House; On This Morning;* and *The Majesty of the Blues*—are (to me, anyway) triumphs that offer a vision for modern jazz that incorporates the past and foretells the future.

Marsalis is also an author. He writes prolific commissions for modern dance and classical ballet, and cranks out reams of music and albums at a pace that makes me think he must be eating more Wheaties than donuts. In a way, he's become an ambassador, as his idol, Louis Armstrong, was, only within the more difficult context of the times. He's an advocate of art and, in a larger but connected fashion, of integration. He says both these issues were addressed in Ken Burns's *Jazz.* "The film had a profound effect on our culture that will resonate for the next ten to twenty years," he told me. "Kids across the country picked up horns and said, 'I'm gonna do that.' It provoked a lot of commentary, particularly in an underlying area no one touches, race." Marsalis's commencement speech a few minutes later was as eloquent as his playing.

In every way that Wynton Marsalis has advanced his conception of jazz, what it means, and the way it ought to be, **Harry Connick Jr**. (1968–), has used jazz as a trampoline from which he can spring into pop and funk. Overlooked in all this is his substantial talent. One fairly sloshed JazzFest afternoon, probably in 1991, I was wandering aimlessly and wound up in the off-limits backstage of a performance tent and, when I emerged through some straw-strewn, horsey part of the race track, I was behind Connick as he hammered away at a grand piano. I was probably ten feet from him and could clearly see the crowd staring rapturously at him. Connick, dressed in all his finery, blazed away in the humidity; a few people in the crowd looked curiously at me as though I were a Sasquatch-type of apparition: "Who is that bloodshot freak and what is he doing back there?"

The point is that I had a really nice vantage point from which I watched Young Harry play for a few minutes, and he was astounding. I don't even know what song he was performing, just that he was winging it solo for a few minutes. I'll say this, the dude can play the piano.

Born in New Orleans, Young Harry was definitely of the privileged class. Both Ma and Pa Connick were lawyers; Harry Sr. has long held the post of city district attorney, and on his own merit he's a reasonably successful hometown big-band crooner. Once Young Harry discovered the piano, when he was six, he developed a glittery form of tunnel vision. He'd joined the musicians' union by the time he was nine, and took lessons from Ellis Marsalis, James Booker (his hero), and, apocryphally, Professor Longhair. Booker genuinely liked Young Harry, and continued to teach him even though Connick, as he has reported, didn't understand what was happening when Booker got dope sick in mid-lesson and had to race out to score.

Connick, too, attended NOCCA, won numerous piano competitions, and even performed with the New Orleans Symphony while an undergraduate. He then headed to New York City to study first at Hunter College and then at the Manhattan School of Music. He was white, good looking, had significant chops, and possessed a "Jerry Lee Lewis Does Jazz" flair for showmanship, all of which was on abundant display at the club dates he scored with tenacious regularity.

Connick caught major grief from serious jazz musicians and established veterans who were put off by his "charms" and brash cockiness. Undeterred, he doggedly pursued an offhand invitation, extended years earlier in New Orleans, from Dr. George Butler, a vice-president in Columbia Records' jazz division, to come see him when Connick got to New York. Butler signed Prince Harry when he was nineteen. In the next few years, the kid released two well-received albums, *Harry Connick Jr* and *20*. One admirer was filmmaker Rob Reiner, who booked Connick to record the big-band soundtrack of the movie *When Harry Met Sally;* the soundtrack went platinum and Connick was introduced to a new audience courtesy of the film's overwhelming popularity with successful yupsters.

In rapid succession came a string of hit recordings, including *We Are in Love, Blue Light Red Light*, and, to my thinking, his best record, the funk heavy *Star Turtle* (with its amazing tune "Hear Me in the Harmony"); also, *25, 11* (another nice CD featuring traditional classics and a backing group of New Orleans jazz veterans), and a collection of original love songs called *To See You*. Along the way, Connick has starred with skill in such films as *Little Man Tate, Memphis Belle,* and *Hope Floats*. One of his latest CDs is *Come by Me*, a big band set of standards and originals, released in 2000, on which he more or less treads water, despite a nice take on "Danny Boy," an original called "A Moment with Me," and a funereal version of "Cry Me a River."

Branford Marsalis (1960–) studied music at both Southern University and Berklee School of Music, then performed the equivalent of internships with Art Blakey and Clark Terry before joining Wynton's quintet and recording with Miles Davis and Herbie Hancock. A markedly flowing player whose dexterity is often obscured by the sheer beauty of his tone and melodies, Branford caused ripples when, in 1985, he and several other bright stars of new jazz became sidemen for rock star Sting. Finally, the next year, Branford started leading his own band, a trio that ultimately expanded and would feature his good friend pianist Kenny Kirkland, who died tragically soon after. When Branford also dabbled happily in the rhythms and grooves of his hometown with his group Buckshot LeFonque, he added credence to the perception that he's like a Christmas-morning kid who views all music as bounty underneath a twinkling tree.

Cranking out superb music with a relaxed but confident pace, Branford has also appeared in films and became, for a time, musical director for *The Tonight Show Starring Jay Leno*. He's recorded a classical album and remains ever fruitful, ever curious. *Scenes in the City, Renaissance, Requiem,* and *Contemporary Jazz* are all great recordings.

It's interesting that these three highest-profile talents—the two Marsalis brothers and Connick—left New Orleans to become big. The migration indicates a central flaw in New Orleans music, no matter how rich it might be. As Ellis Marsalis told me, "The thing about New Orleans is that in some ways it's the greatest city in the world to *learn* music. But let's face it, where's Wall Street? Is that in New Orleans? Where's Broadway? Is *that* in New Orleans? The Metropolitan? Columbia Records has no office in New Orleans. When you get right down to it, people who aspire to the top level of anything have to go wherever the action is for what they do."

The Brothers Marsalis have yet another productive member—trombonist, **Delfeayo Marsalis** (1965–). He's a solid player and has toured with a variety of top jazz and R&B players (including Fats Domino, Ray Charles, and Art Blakey), but is perhaps best known as a producer (Harry Connick Jr., Kenny Kirkland, Terence Blanchard, Marcus Roberts, and most of his family). In 1992, he released a solo disc, *Pontius Pilate's Decision*.

And, oh, yeah, there's dad. Of course, **Ellis Marsalis** (1934–) is splashed across these pages like dignified graffiti. He was born in New Orleans in

1934, learned piano, ran nightclubs, taught school, played with Al Hirt, and was the house bandleader at the New Orleans Playboy Club. He was also seminal in the doomed but ambitious AFO label, worked in Los Angeles with Ornette Coleman, and was ultimately named to head the music program at NOCCA. He's been awarded so many honorary degrees and heads so many programs and committees that I can't name them all. Ellis enjoys his own productive career as a player, too, and performs frequently in New Orleans and on tour. The list of private pupils who've benefited from his insight is equally long and reads like a future induction roll at the Jazz Hall of Fame.

It's not easy to pinpoint Ellis's legacy, though he assured me it's not a family jam. "That's never happened," he laughs, "and I'm not sure I want it to. We actually were all onstage together at an award show one night, and I don't think it worked out too well."

When asked what he'd recommend to Louisiana musicians, Ellis replied, "I'd recommend two books, actually. Louis Armstrong's *Satchmo* is a great book that talks about life as a black in New Orleans at the early part of the century. And the bass player, Pops Foster, had a similar book [*The Autobiography of a New Orleans Jazz Man*] that's indispensable." As for listening to Ellis, you can't go wrong with the Jason-produced *Twelve's It*, which topped the prestigious Rick Koster's Year-End Best CDs list in the *Day* of New London, Connecticut, in 1998.

Pianos and saxophones aside, the trumpet is probably the instrument still most often associated with modern as well as traditional New Orleans jazz. Blame Louis—and Buddy Bolden and King Oliver and Bunk Johnson. And Wynton. Or, hell, maybe trumpets are cheap—but probably not. Whatever the reason, the swarm of young New Orleans Badasses of modern jazz trumpet is relentless.

Nicholas Payton (1973–) was born in New Orleans. His mom was an operatic singer and classical pianist; his father is a retired bass player and a schoolteacher. By eight he was gigging with his dad and shortly thereafter joined the All-Star Brass Band, a much-respected youth outfit. After graduating from NOCCA, he studied at the University of New Orleans with Ellis Marsalis, and before he was out of his teens had played and recorded with Joe Henderson, Clark Terry, and Elvin Jones.

In 1995, Payton signed with the Verve label and later that year released his debut CD, *From This Moment*, which was produced by Delfeayo Marsalis. A year later, he formed his already mythic Nicholas Payton Quintet (with drummer Adonis Rose, saxophonist Tim Warfield, bassist Reuben Rogers, and pianist Anthony Wonsey), and their *Gumbo Nouveau* CD made Payton, within the context of modern jazz, a star. After touring relentlessly, he hooked up with elder statesman and trumpeter Doc Cheatham for a remarkable record called *Doc Cheatham &*

Nicholas Payton, released not long before the older mentor passed away. A song from that CD, "Stardust," won a Grammy for Best Solo Jazz Performance. The album is a glorious experiment, a collection of lovingly rendered standards and pop diamonds approached as if Cheatham were looking back at yellowing pages in a scrapbook of music created during his lifetime, and Payton were taking the time to savor music he'd heard, perhaps, only in the context of impatient youth.

As Payton told *Offbeat*'s Jonathon Tabak about his friendship and teacher-student relationship with Cheatham, "It wasn't an unequal situation. I guess a lot of people would think that, because we were so far apart in age, almost seventy years, but I didn't feel that, or even think about that when we were playing. I just thought, here is a great soul and I want to try to connect with this being to create some music, it doesn't matter how old he is or where he's from or what color he is or what sex he is, and I think he shared that attitude."

Such a comment is indicative of Payton's warm, ever-curious but confident approach to life, and you can hear it in his music. The two subsequent CDs by the Nicholas Payton Quintet, *Payton's Place* (1998) and *Nick@Night* (2000), further reflect an attitude of respect for the past combined with a bold and confident insistence on going forward. He's moved from standards to composing virtually all his own material. He continues to live in New Orleans, tours heavily, and plays all sorts of extraneous gigs from global SRO shows with "The Trumpet Summit"—Payton, Wynton Marsalis, and Roy Hargrove—as well as hometown fusion experiments.

Terence Blanchard (1962–) is another blossoming musician who was born in New Orleans. He fooled around on piano early on but had an epiphany when he was eight: A jazz band came to his elementary school and he zeroed in on trumpeter Alvin Alcorn. Blanchard's father, a voice teacher, was deeply into music, and Terence had no problem shifting his focus to the trumpet, an inclination that was furthered when, in the sixth grade, he met a new friend named Wynton Marsalis. Both students attended the New Orleans Center for the Creative Arts, where Blanchard developed his molasses-smooth tone and began to expand his jazz underpinning with a fascination for other types of music.

Blanchard headed to New York City after graduating from NOCCA and hooked up with a fellow New Orleanean, saxophonist Donald Harrison Jr., in Art Blakey's Jazz Messengers. Blanchard and Harrison then teamed up to release some particularly fine CDs, including *New York Second Line* and *Black Pearl*, before Blanchard decided to form his own sextet and experiment with scoring film and television. During the several years he worked in that medium, he wrote music for several Spike Lee movies and won an Emmy award for the stunning documentary score of *Color and Light: Jazz Sketches of Sondheim*. He also worked on Dave Grusin's soundtrack for the film *Random Hearts*.

But Blanchard would be quick to tell you that he's first a jazz musician. This is why, in 2000, he returned to the fold with *Wandering Moon*, a CD of astonishing music on which Blanchard and his group exuberantly skate a fine tightrope between the calculated possibilities of classical music and the free and exuberant implications of raw jazz. Much of the record is simply gorgeous, particularly "Sidney," a tune for Blanchard's daughter (named after clarinetist Sidney Bechet), and the elegiac, elevating "Sweet's Dream."

Blanchard has now returned to New Orleans, which seems somehow fitting. He's said that *Wandering Moon* is a comment on balancing music and family. In an online chat he said, "I'm at the point in my life where I'm over the fascination of being a jazz musician. A life is complex, and involves many different equally important components. I thought this was a great time to see as much of the whole picture of my life through music—like an album of pictures set to music."

When trumpeter **Irvin Mayfield** (1979–) was nine years old, he marched up to Ellis Marsalis's house, knocked on the door, and asked Marsalis for some accompaniment. Marsalis, presumably amused and impressed, invited the kid in. What happened next? According to Mayfield, "I had been playing a little bit and I knew who Wynton was of course. So I told Ellis, 'I'm coming for [Wynton]. I'm gonna get him one day.' So he asked me in and showed me my first blues scale. And from then on he called me Hotshot." Mayfield ended up taking lessons from Ellis, attended NOCCA, played on any street corner or in any room that would have him, and in his mid-teens formed his own brass band, single-handedly booking tours of Mexico and Europe. He also turned down offers from fine music schools in order to stay in New Orleans.

"I try to describe to people how it is growing up in New Orleans—how much the music is ingrained in you—and the average person can't understand," Mayfield told me. "There are certain parts of town where everyone in the neighborhood will have instruments and people will dance; they're getting down.

"I played in those brass bands. You grow up and you get in the second line and you played in one and you danced in one. You get involved and jazz is part of all that."

Mayfield has grown up to be a marvelous player, leading his own band and playing as a member (with Bill Summers and, at one time, Jason Marsalis) of the awesome Havana-by-way-of-the-French-Quarter jazz group Los Hombres Calientes. Now in his early twenties, Mayfield is a precocious guy whose boyish enthusiasm seems almost incongruous with the articulate musical worldview that seems to come from someone very old and very wise. When Ellis Marsalis answered his door, a musical genie blew into the core of young Irvin's being.

His self-titled debut solo CD for Basin Street Records, produced by Delfeayo Marsalis, is an incendiary and wildly adventurous exercise, his horn lines and imagination bubbling like boiling oil. The quick impression is to think that the kid has great imagination, but his brain is almost moving too fast for him—and then you realize *you're* the one not keeping up. Mayfield is bursting with juicy musical ideas and pulls it off with dangerous competence, whether he's working through motorboat bop, icy ballads, standards, or Latin-tinged flights of fancy. Throughout, Mayfield builds on his hometown legacy yet adds modern touches of "burnout" to the mix. "Burnout is like where you're completely free," he explains, "but you're also very dependent on everyone else and your freedom depends on everyone else being free." And Mayfield depends on the music of others for inspiration. "You've gotta have some Louis [Armstrong], of course. Two of Wynton's: *Baroque Duet*, the classical album he made with Kathleen Battle, and *Black Codes*. And you need some Dr. John. And then Professor Longhair and James Booker—whatever compilations have the most songs."

Another area for inspiration is food: Montel's Creole Restaurant and the burgers at Snug Harbor. He also likes Kermit Ruffins's barbecue. "Wynton shows up at Kermit's gigs just to eat." Can Wynton cook? "I was staying with him in New York and he made some eggs once." And? "Well, they were okay. He dresses nice."

Though a bit older, **Joe Newman** (1922–1992) should be noted as one of the new jazz influences. His father led the Creole Serenaders, and Newman (born in New Orleans) mastered trumpet early on. When he was in college, he was discovered by Lionel Hampton. Newman worked with Hampton for a while, then moved on to Count Basie's orchestra, where he stayed for most of his career. His exuberant, versatile style led to the pioneering territory of bop, and he played on dozens of important sessions over the years. He was a frontiersman in jazz education and helped create Jazz Interaction, an outfit that promoted jazz awareness. He died in 1992. A nice sampling of his early New Orleans roots can still be found on *Salute to Satch* (RCA).

The older brother of saxophonist Illinois, Robert **Russell Jacquet** (1917–1990), born in Broussard, Louisiana, was a trumpeter and singer of considerable ability. He played in Illinois's band off and on over the years, led his own orchestra at the Cotton Club in Hollywood, and a smaller combo in Oakland, and eventually ended up in Houston, where he played with Arnett Cobb.

Also among the trumpet hotshots: **Marlon Jordan** (1970–), the son of Sir Edward "Kid" Jordan and brother of flutist Kent Jordan. He's another grad of NOCCA and pal of Wynton Marsalis, and released a solo CD called *For You Only;* **Wendell Brunious,** a remarkable young talent who heads up the renowned and venerable Preservation Hall Jazz Band; and **Stanton**

Davis Jr. (1945–), a New England Conservatory and Berklee ex who plays trumpet and was born in New Orleans. He works extensively around Boston.

The saxophonists of this era have also provided their share of showmanship. **Jean Baptiste "Illinois" Jacquet** (1922–), a Broussard, Louisiana, native who grew up in Houston, Texas, started out tap dancing as a kid, and studied soprano and alto sax. Jacquet became one of the renowned group of musicians known as the Texas Tenors (along with Herschel Evans, Budd Johnson, Marchel Ivery, Arnett Cobb, and Jimmy Giuffre), so described for their highly individual style that nonetheless segued from swing to bebop. By his late teens, Jacquet had played with Milt Larkin and Lionel Proctor and headed for California with Floyd Ray, where he hooked up with Lionel Hampton; in 1942, Jacquet recorded a solo for Hampton on the tune "Flying Home" that made jazz history. The original sixty-four-bar solo on "Flying Home" is the longest improvised solo that has been ritually incorporated to the written arrangements of a song (including the guitar solo in Bachman-Turner Overdrive's "Four Wheel Drive").

After the success of "Flying Home," Jacquet was an in-demand dude. He played with Count Basie, Lester Young, and Cab Calloway, and led his own bands, featuring his improvisatory technique, fleet noteage, and an uncanny sense of down-home blues throughout. He formed the Texas Tenors with Cobb and Buddy Tate, then settled in New York City where he led his own big band. Jacquet was also featured prominently on scores of prestige sessions. His best solo work is *The Cool Rage* on the Verve label.

Alto saxophonist **Donald Harrison Jr.** (1960–) is one of the finest of the new crop of modern jazz musicians from New Orleans. His dad was the Big Chief of the Keeper of the Flame Mardi Gras Indian tribe. Donald studied with pianists Henry Butler and Ellis Marsalis, and graduated to Art Blakey's Jazz Messengers before co-leading a superb band with buddy Terence Blanchard.

Harrison has been a guest artist on several top-flight projects and headed up his own band for such fine albums as *Nouveau Swing, Free to Be,* and *Spirits of Congo Square. Congo Square* fuses his post-bop style with the ghosts of New Orleans, similar to the remarkable (and out of print) *Indian Blues* album, which he made with his father and with Dr. John, improvising jazz next to the Mardi Gras Indian chants and rhythms. It's one of the best records made since the early eighties—if you can find it.

Other saxophonists to think about or listen to include: **Wessel "Warm Daddy" Anderson** (1964–) came to Louisiana at the recommendation of Branford Marsalis. Because Charlie Parker is his hero, Anderson focuses on alto; he studied under Alvin Batiste at Southern University in Baton Rouge for several years before joining Wynton Marsalis in 1988. His remarkable solo effort, *Warm Daddy in the Garden of Swing,* was recorded in New Orleans for the late, lamented Leaning House label, and he has recorded frequently with Wynton Marsalis. **Victor Goines** (1961–) is a New Orleans–born saxophonist and, like Anderson, has played with Wynton Marsalis in both his septet and the Lincoln Center Jazz Orchestra. Saxophonist **Doug Lawrence** (1956–), born Doug Marshall in Lake Charles, has provided fine side work for George Benson and Lionel Hampton. Tenor saxophonist **Greg Tardy** (1966–), born in New Orleans, played R&B with Allen Toussaint and the Neville Brothers and then moved to jazz to work in the Nicholas Payton Quintet; he has also played with Roy Hargrove and Ellis Marsalis. And alto saxophonist **Jesse Davis** (1965–), another NOCCA graduate, born in New Orleans, has spent time in New York with a variety of high-quality artists, from Illinois Jacquet to Nicholas Payton. He appeared in the film *Kansas City* and once again resides in his hometown.

Along with such traditional ensembles as the **Preservation Hall Jazz Band,** which has been around since the early fifties, and the ongoing **Dukes of Dixieland,** a surprisingly resilient group that has come back from the touristy dead, some truly great modern bands are playing today.

I've never understood how jazz guys can form a trio and name it after *two* of the guys in the band: the Futterman/Jordan Trio, for example. Who's the third musician and why has that artist's name been left out? As the "Jordan" in the Futterman/Jordan trio, **Sir Edward "Kidd" Jordan** leads a wide-ranging improvisational outfit (Jordan's "Sir" is official, by the way: The French government knighted him for his artistic contributions). The free-jazz saxophonist is also a wonderful educator; this New Orleans native not only teaches at Southern University in his hometown but has been integral in establishing music educational programs in Sierra Leone, Senegal, and Mali.

Jordan is one of the premier shakers in the avant-garde movement that arose in jazz in the fifties. As one bio reveals, over a forty-year period, Jordan has performed with such Grammy winners as Ray Charles, Stevie Wonder, Ellis Marsalis, Cannonball Adderley, and Cecil Taylor.

Before forming the Futterman/Jordan Trio (the third guy is drummer Alvin Fielder), Jordan was a principal in the Improvisational Arts Quartet. Also before forming the Futterman/Jordan Trio, there was the Futterman/Jordan Quintet and then the Futterman/Jordan Quartet—and I don't wanna draw any conclusions about why artists kept leaving the band. I mean, if Crosby, Stills, Nash & Young can get all *their* names in, well. . . .

In any case, when you listen to *Southern Extreme*, the 1998 CD by the Futterman/Jordan Trio, you can hear how pianist, saxophonist, and flutist Joel Futterman seems to hopscotch off Jordan's phrases, and vice versa. Much of their work evokes a stark and brooding melodicism. Jordan has said that much of his improvisation is based on the overtones from the drums and cymbals. Jordan is also quick to point out that his recorded and performance work isn't exactly the stuff of New Orleans touristry. "[New Orleans musicians] done wrote me off," Jordan said in an online interview recently. "They think I'm crazy. People been thinking I'm crazy for the last forty years. New Orleans is a museum town, and they want everything to stay like this is a museum, you understand? And art isn't like that; art has to continue to develop. But in New Orleans people will keep going around and around with the same kind of sounds, and we talk about like there ain't nothing happening nowhere else in the world but New Orleans. . . . They gonna keep me around here playing traditional music all my life? Man, I mean, I didn't wanna do that as a *kid*."

Astral Project is another modern jazz outfit. It formed in 1978 and remains one of the freshest, most creative and supremely reliable jazz bands anywhere. Comprised of drummer Johnny Vidacovich, guitarist Steve Masakowski, bassist James Singleton, pianist David Torkanowsky, and tenor-soprano saxophonist Tony Dagradi, it's named for the celestial level of Eastern spiritual enlightenment the band symbolically aspires to.

The group came together under the direction of Dagradi, a New Jersey native who landed in New Orleans after a tour with Archie Bell & the Drells. He began jamming and playing everywhere and with everyone he could, and almost immediately met and connected with the core of what would be Astral Project. In the early years, the band had a sixth member, a percussionist who left in the eighties. Since all the musicians had extensive experience in the city's funk and R&B scene—in which they still participate heavily individually—the early gigs featured a premium of funk covers and light fusion music Dagradi had already written.

But given the virtuosity of the players and the immediate and instinctual chemistry of the band, Astral Project took on a creative spirit of its own and rapidly became an improvisational group in which any given member might provide the compositional skeleton of a tune, or provide in performance the creative and directional springboard from which they collectively might blast in the heartbeat of intuition.

Almost immediately, Astral Project became civic darlings; the sheer musicality and magic of their muse and chops is indeed captivating, and their individual and in-toto work ethic is phenomenal. Over the last few years they've released three fine albums—*Astral Project New Orleans LA* (1997), *Elevado* (1998), and *Voodoo Bop* (1999), though only the last two are available (from the Compass label). *Voodoo Bop* finished third in the prestigious Critics Poll in *Down Beat*, and won the hometown *Offbeat* CD of the Year prize, the same year AP was acclaimed as Jazz Act of the Year. To listen to any of their stuff, well . . . the music roars along frenetically, literally bursts with ideas and references from pop to funk to world music, and incorporates just that proper touch of sultry New Orleans to let you know they couldn't come from anywhere else.

According to Johnny Vidacovich, "[Astral Project] got together to have fun, and the way we were havin' fun is that a lot of us were young, upcoming jazz players. At the same time, a lot of us were young, upcoming *funk* players. Tony Dagradi came around and said let's play some music that can swing and have some funk beats both, and let's make $20–$30 here and there and we'll play a few times every other week or so and have fun and make some more songs, and plus we won't stick too close to these songs, we'll freak out and change 'em all up. And things evolved and it was fun, and it was fun, and it was fun, and it became musically creative because we were having more fun bouncin' the ball around musically, not trying to stay classically jazz, or classically fusion."

And then Dagradi made a terrific statement to Jonathan Tabak in *Offbeat:* "When you come to the bandstand with Astral Project," he said, "I want everybody to give me everything. Give me everything you got. No limitations at all. And that's completely rare in this day and age, because if you go on most any gig, everybody's got an agenda, parameters that they work in. We don't. Our parameters are that we can go anywhere and whatever you do, you expect the band to support you. And they do. If, by just a couple notes sometimes, I indicate I want to go somewhere harmonically or rhythmically or melodically, there will be someone there in a nanosecond, going, 'Yeah, I'm there, too,' and you know that there's no problem with it."

Astral Project has had a longtime, semiofficial relationship with Bobby McFerrin, the Mel Blanc of vocal jazz, with whom they toured in the late seventies and early eighties and recently reunited for another road stint.

Each of the band members has been actively involved in individual projects: Among their recommended solo projects are Masakowski's *For Joe*, Vidacovich's *Mystery Street*, Dagradi's *Dreams of Love*, and, with his trio, *Live at the Columns* (referring to a stately white-columned hotel in New Orleans's Garden District).

As evidenced by their numerous members referred to throughout this chapter, **Los Hombres Calientes** is a much newer band and delights in the possibilities implied by the mixture of Havana and New Orleans. A sextet originally formed by percussionist Bill Summers, trumpeter Irvin Mayfield, and drummer Jason Marsalis (Horacio "El Negro" has since replaced Marsalis), the band won *Billboard*'s jazz CD of the year award for their debut album; they continue at this early stage to amaze even as they grow.

And speaking of Vidacovich and (by extension) Marsalis, two of the finest drummers in the world, it's impossible not to add New Orleans–born **Earl Palmer** (1924–) to the list. His timekeeping and vision are legendary even among normally jaded session players from New Orleans to Los Angeles, the two ports of recording where Palmer has ruled supreme. Though he's worked on all manner of film and television scores, rock and pop dates, and was integral to the creation of New Orleans rhythm 'n' blues, Palmer prides himself on being a jazz drummer. It's hard to listen to almost any New Orleans record released during the golden R&B era without hearing Palmer, but for an additional treat, pick up a copy of his revealing and entertaining autobiography written with Tony Scherman, *Backbeat: Earl Palmer's Story.*

Idris Muhammad (1939–) is another excellent drummer. Born Leo Morris in New Orleans, he's done a wide range of gigs from heading his own band to backing Sam Cooke, playing for the original Broadway production of *Hair,* and touring with Emerson, Lake & Palmer (!).

Brian Blade (1970–), born in Shreveport, was a brilliant tennis player before music seduced him. He moved to New Orleans and started gigs with Nicholas Payton and Johnny Vidacovich before touring with Ellis Marsalis. Blade also played with the Mardi Gras Indians before Harry Connick Jr. asked him to tour. Since then, he's been highly sought after and has played with numerous jazz stars.

Troy Davis (1965–) hails from Baton Rouge. He attended Southern University and has played with several Louisiana hotties, including Henry Butler, Wynton Marsalis, Alvin Batiste, and Terence Blanchard, as well as Betty Carter and Roy Hargrove.

Ricky Sebastian (1956–), an Opelousas native, has played with Dr. John, Ellis Marsalis, and Harry Connick Jr.

And for your further consideration:

✦ Keyboardist **John Beasley** (1958–) was born in Shreveport and started playing R&B dates in Los Angeles in the seventies. He moved to session gigs and has worked with Chick Corea, Stanley Clarke, Michael Franks, and Hubert Laws. A solo album worth listening to is 1992's *Cauldron.*

✦ **Lillian** (1949–) and **John Boutte** are New Orleans–born siblings (niece Tricia—Sister Teedy—is a popular New Orleans reggae singer), both jazz vocalists whose contributions are growing. Lillian came to fame in the lead role of the musical *One Mo' Time,* and, with her husband, saxophonist Thomas L'Etienne, formed what became known as the Boutte-L'Etienne Jazz Ensemble. She's popular on the European festival circuit and has served as the Official Jazz Ambassador for the City of New Orleans. John Boutte, a former account supervisor in the banking industry, was inspired to go into music by Stevie Wonder, who was overwhelmed by John's vocal prowess. His superb work on the exhilarating *Mardi Gras Mambo: ¡Cubanismo! In New Orleans* (2000), should break his reputation nationally.

✦ **Germaine Bazzle,** known as the city's "First Lady of Jazz," is a singer and also teaches (at Xavier University). Her recorded output is limited—a 1994 solo CD for AFO called *Standing Ovation* and some singles—but her warm personality and Ella Fitzgerald/Dinah Washington pipes are special.

✦ Bassist and composer **Roland Guerin,** a graduate of the Southern University music program, is a former member of Alvin Batiste's band; Guerin heads up his own modern-jazz unit, which has released two fine CDs, *Live at the Blue Note* and *The Winds of the Blue Land.*

✦ Another force to be reckoned with is flutist **Kent Jordan,** brother of trumpeter Marlon Jordan.

✦ New York–born Baton Rouge resident **Mark Whitfield,** a guitarist who's played with Nicholas Payton and Courtney Pine and can cover any style from George Benson to bebop, has put out numerous CDs, including *Raw* and *7ᵗʰ Avenue Stroll.*

✦ Finally, **Ron Eschete** (1948–), born in Houma, Louisiana, plays seven-string guitar. A sideman to a nice array of headliners, he's also released several solo discs, including *Soft Winds* and *Stump Jumper.*

Three

BRASS BANDS

*M*y associate for many of the sonic Louisianian excursions taken during the course of researching this manuscript was my close pal Brett Blackwell, whom I've known since we were in college together back during the Millard Filmore administration. A two-sport athlete of insane ability, Blackwell short-circuited any possibilities of a professional baseball or basketball career by fusing those skills with a sense of fun scripted, possibly, by Hunter S. Thompson.

Brett's loss was my gain, as it turns out, and we've had a large time over the years. "Louisiana Black," as he began calling himself, picked me up at the New Orleans airport for a protracted state tour in his red Firebird, dubbed the Starsky-and-Hutch-mobile for its unfortunate resemblance to a vehicle associated with an undercover narcotics officer.

Right off the bat, we decided to visit the famous Maple Leaf Bar, former sorta-home of James Booker. Every Tuesday night, the **ReBirth Brass Band** holds court. We get there early, as much to beat the guaranteed crowd as to check the place out. It's laid out rather like two side-by-side shotgun shacks with an eight-foot aperture allowing customers to pass back and forth. One room houses the main bar; the other is the live music room, anchored by a deep, almost square, stage butted up against and facing away from Oak Street. Out back and wrapping around the music room side of the building is a garden bar where customers go to talk and cool off between sets. Inside, benches ring the perimeter, the walls are rust colored, and hanging from the pressed tin ceilings are wooden-blade fans with orange lamps in the centers.

But there will be no sitting this night, at least not once ReBirth takes the stage.

Arguably the best of the nouveau brass bands in New Orleans—their immediate predecessors, the Dirty Dozen Brass Band, held that title before they shortened their name to Dirty Dozen and became more of a straight funk act—ReBirth epitomizes the regeneration of the brass band tradition in the best ways. They have the standard instrumentation of tuba, snare drum, bass drum, three trombones, and two trumpets, sax, and also a variety of supplemental percussion (cowbell, whistles) on hand. A repertoire solidly anchored in the past has rocketed the band into the future with a variety of hip-hop and funk stylings and witty, mid-song quotes from Michael Jackson or Charlie Parker songs. As they started to come into being, the new tide of brass bands was collectively against traditional brass band music, referring to it as "that old slow funeral music"; even so, there are almost always plenty of historic tunes in the new bands' club and parade playlists. So your basic "Down by the Riverside" or "When the Saints Go Marching In" is played with enthusiasm (and a bit of modernesque tweaking) alongside new and original songs that use the same compositional roux in a fresh recipe. And if the music is a mix of old and new, so, too, is the presentation. These bands exhibit plenty of enthusiasm and a clear sense of pride and history—perhaps most obvious in young black men playing tubas—which is effectively countered by a tangible, streetwise attitude that stops just shy of arrogance. For example, the brass-band tradition does not extend to the concept of uniforms; ReBirth are all clothed in standard urban–hip-hop casual; one trumpeter affects the look made city-wide famous by former band member and solo trumpet star Kermit Ruffins—which is to say he's got the handkerchief wrapped around his head underneath an angled fedora.

The crowd in the Maple Leaf is an interesting and revealing mix: apart from a few other independents besides Louisiana Black and me, probably 60 percent are white college kids who roared out of their fraternity and sorority meetings to get here in time for the first set. Though there is an element of bandwagon-hopping to their attendance, they're listening to great music that almost no other college kids in the country are being exposed to.

Most of the remainder of the crowd are friends, family, and posse of the band itself, folks who grew up in the blue-collar Tremé district from where ReBirth (and a staggering roster of other great musicians) hail.

Roger Hahn, the fine New Orleans–based freelance writer, suggests that the brass bands practice a sort of spiritual minstrelsy, a clever way of celebrating private black ritual and rhythms, yet disguised enough to make them accessible to people who aren't black. There are certainly precedents for Hahn's theory, as seen in the smoke-and-mirrors performances back in Congo Square: religious rituals modified to appease the white guys in power. But it's sweetly ironic that the brass bands, the Mardi Gras Indian tribes, and the second-line and social and pleasure clubs are possibly the most exclusive organizations in New Orleans; a black person could probably get into almost any country club more easily than a white person could join a Mardi Gras Indian tribe.

As ReBirth kicks into their first show, which consists of sixty steaming minutes of nonstop celebration, the room explodes with joy. But it's so packed that dancing isn't possible, no matter how much the music demands it. So everyone hops in place, careening off each other in a brass band equivalent of a mosh pit. Like those old-time football board games, where the electric current sent the little plastic players off on ludicrous orbits of their own that had nothing whatsoever to do with diagrammed play, Louisiana Black and I are soon separated by half the room, spinning in our respective eddies of rhythm. Occasionally, we catch one another's eye and grin happily.

Because—as we will both agree later—this is one of the most intense and amazing live performances we've ever seen. The energy created by Re-Birth is like a surge from a nuclear plant. From the initial groove—the unison chants and hand claps over bottom-end tuba snarls, the kick-in second-line beats of the snare drum, all punctuated with a shouted and casual salutation, "Welcome to ReBirth, y'all!"—the set is magical. It winds up consisting of one or two extended jams, though recognizable songs and structures are keyed off certain riffs, allowing parade stuff such as shared chants to occur at predetermined points. They roar through "Don't Start No Shit" and "Do Whatcha Wanna" fairly early on, and, wait, does a snippet from Parliament/Funkadelic's "Flashlight" cruise by like a friend waving from a passing taxi? At one point, three trombonists hit one staccato note each in a 4/4 time pattern, over and over, against the swirling collage of musical madness around them. The tension of their repetition builds wonderfully to the crescendo in the set's finale.

Watching ReBirth, I'm reminded how the young brass bands have taken something extraordinary and made it more so.

"It's music that hits you in the heart and makes you want to dance," Philip Frazier, the sousaphonist and leader of ReBirth told me. He agrees that the new generation of brass bands in New Orleans has become a cultural institution that provides a genuine alternative for young black musicians.

"In the neighborhoods we grew up in—chiefly Tremé—you hear and see the [brass band] music as part of daily life," Frazier continued. "It's a perfect time to be in a brass band in New Orleans. You practice and earn your reputation in parades and build up a name—and it's a different scene than the rap thing going on. We're performing constantly. Maybe we're not getting rich, but it's a good life."

As described in the first chapter of this section, the New Orleans brass band is for many reasons a thing of anomalous beauty. The musical segue between ragtime and jazz, born out of a national brass-band tradition and then sculpted in New Orleans by concerts, parades, and picnic gigs, as well as the requirements of the social and pleasure clubs that guaranteed funerals for its members, the brass bands probably started soon after the Civil War ended, maybe as late as 1880, and, stylistically, lacked a distinctive sound. At the sunrise of the twentieth century, as the rhythms of New Orleans began to creep into their repertoires—the beats of Congo Square, the gospel exuberance of Baptist choirs, elements of improvisation, and a gradual decline in the "reading" bands for whom recitation of written-out sheet music was rote.

According to Richard H. Knowles, author of *Fallen Heroes—A History of New Orleans Brass Bands*, the saga of New Orleans brass bands falls loosely into four periods, of which pre–twentieth century and the 1900 to World War I segments are the first two. He describes the Middle Period as postwar and lasting through the Great Depression, and the modern era as pre–World War II through the 1960s, the latter chiefly characterized by a significant decline in brass bands able to find work.

Although the brass band tradition reached endangered species status in the sixties, a wondrous resurgence has recently taken place; Knowles might call it the most-modern period. In the mid-seventies, with the formation of the Dirty Dozen Brass Band, it suddenly became hip to play in a brass band again. The form came back in exhilarating fashion, and in that most important of ways: youth. The *younger* generation fueled this resurgence with enough tradition to preserve the form, and added enough contemporary musical and cultural trends to make it attractive to their peers.

Today, in most cities across the country, kids interested in music typically want to be hip-hop or rock stars. Even in New Orleans that's true. But only in New Orleans do kids also want to play in brass bands. Only in New Orleans is it possible to walk down the street and see youngsters playing the trombone or the trumpet on the front porch. The ReBirth Brass Band and the Pinstripe Brass Band and mutations such as Coolbone lead the charge as neighborhood and city-wise heroes.

Which is particularly cool when you consider tuba ain't happening *anywhere* else. That's a fact.

Over a hundred years ago, it all began to form with the **Pickwick Brass Band,** which started sometime after the Civil War, was active for twenty years or so, and probably re-formed for a few years at the turn of the century. Little is known about the group. In its earliest incarnation, cornetist Oscar Duconge was probably a member, and its final lineup was co-led by brothers Norman Manetta (cornet) and Jules Manetta (trombone). Other pre–twentieth century brass bands probably included the Pelican Brass Band, the Columbia Brass Band, the Eureka Brass Band, and the Alliance Brass Band.

As mentioned earlier, the **Excelsior Brass Band** and **Onward Brass Band** were formed shortly after and proved far more enduring. Until that point, most of the brass band musicians were Creole and the repertoire was "read" music. Many of those players were light-skinned enough to double up and play in white orchestras. Sliding into the 1900s, though, more and more of the ranks were filled by black musicians, and the bands, which became more improvisatory, started to be associated with specific neighborhoods and social and pleasure clubs. As trained white and Creole Catholic musicians became scarcer, more homegrown black musicians and migratory players came to the city, and the intermingling of music and race made the enterprise more accessible.

Competition for gigs was fierce. Though certain loyalties existed between social and pleasure clubs and specific bands, musicians routinely joined several clubs and organizations in the hope of influencing gigs. (Jazz great Danny Barker remembers that his grandfather, Isidore Barbarin of the Onward Brass Band, drove a carriage for a mortuary. With the subsequent "insider" information from that position, he was able to secure his band's funeral bookings before death notices hit the street.)

The Excelsior Brass Band is historically referenced as far back as 1881. Headed up by cornetist Theogene Baquet, the group also included, over time, such renowned players as clarinetists Lorenzo Tio Sr., bass drummer John Robichaux, cornetists Alphonse Picou and George Moret, trumpeters Peter Bocage and Emanuel Perez, and trombonists Vic Gaspard and Honore Dutrey.

Largely based across the river in Algiers, the Excelsior had a reputation as a stylistically conservative band that upheld impeccable musical standards and employed players of consistently high quality.

Only a few years younger than the Excelsior Band was the Onward Brass Band, almost certainly organized by 1887 and in most scholarly opinions the greatest New Orleans brass band ever. A group that occasionally augmented its ranks—up to thirty musicians—to perform free concerts in city parks, the Onward earned a reputation for its extensive play list. Never a highly improvisational outfit, the band did attract musicians who were the cream-of-the-crop and who mightily influenced the next several generations of jazz players.

Over the years, the band's roster included cornetist Joe "King" Oliver, early leader and cornetist Professor J. O. Lainez, alto hornist Isidore Barbarin, cornetist and leader Emanuel Perez (Louis Armstrong's mentor and resident wild man), Black Benny on bass drum, trumpeter Peter Bocage, clarinetists Alphonse Picou, George Baquet, and Lorenzo Tio Jr., and cornetist Papa Celestin. Even Armstrong reportedly subbed for the band on occasion.

The organization would be reprised in 1960 by drummer Paul Barbarin (Isidore's son). The new version was more streamlined—eight players instead of twelve—and included, at various times, banjoist Danny Barker, clarinetist Louis Cottrell, and drummer Placide Adams. The later edition of the band, which broke up in 1978, can be heard on *10th Anniversary Jazz and Heritage Festival*.

Of the other early brass bands, the most famous are the **Pacific Brass Band,** the **Henry Allen Brass Band** (for whom it is said Buddy Bolden occasionally played), the **Indiana Brass Band,** the **Marching Band,** the **Melrose Brass Band, Amos Riley & the Tulane Brass Band** and, of course, the **Colored Waifs' Home Brass Band.**

There were also the so-called "country brass bands" based in rural areas outside the city, occasionally coming into Orleans parish to perform: the **St. Joseph Brass Band,** the **Cypress City Brass Band,** and the **Holmes Brass Band.**

Of the early "non-reading" bands that were starting to proliferate at the turn of the century, the two major ones were both connected to Buddy Bolden: his own short-lived brass band and the **Eagle Brass Band.** The latter *was* the Bolden band; after the leader defected with mental problems in 1906 (the next year he was committed to a sanitarium; see Chapter 1), Frankie Dusen took over. While the group existed through the twenties, it was a "who's available to play today" organization. A third such group that helped spread the influence of non-reading improvisation was the **Kid Ory Brass Band.**

Three important "Professors"—those black musician-teachers whose work of musically schooling young black musicians far surpassed their own accomplishments as players—should be noted: **James Brown Humphrey, Paul Chaligny,** and **Dave Perkins.**

Between 1920 and the end of the Depression, a new era in brass-band music gradually took shape and built on the new tradition of the improvisational bands. The most important group of that time was the **Tuxedo Brass Band,** apocryphally organized in 1910, though it emerged probably eight or ten years after that, by trombonist William "Bebé" Ridgley and Papa Celestin. Moving rapidly in the direction of jazz, the band's repertoire shifted away from the dirges of the period and adopted a more popular and contemporary songlist; at the same time, Celestin come up with such innovations as commissioning material and arrangements.

The band also prospered from its membership. Starting in 1921 with the inclusion of Louis Armstrong, other players were added over the course of the band's existence: cornetist Peter Bocage, trombonist Sunny Henry, South Carolinian trumpeter Amos White, and brass band vets Isidore Barbarin, Lorenzo Tio Jr., tuba wizard Eddie Jackson, and trumpeter Louis Dumaine.

In the improvisatory context of the new wave, a coterie of trumpet greats each headed up his own brass band for secondary gigs and dance-band work—and the groups were almost always pick-up in nature. At funeral gigs, they relied on standard hymns that everyone knew, but for everything else they cut loose, freely blasting through repertoire. The best of these admittedly patchwork but excellent organizations were the **Henry Rena Brass Band,** the **Chris Kelly Brass Band, Punch Miller & the Zulu Band,** the liquid membership of the **Buddy Petit Brass Band,** the **Tonic Triad Band,** and groups led respectively by **Sam Morgan, Alcide Landry,** and **Kid Howard.**

As the brass bands maneuvered into the next phase, roughly World War II through the sixties, a significant stylistic innovation came in the form of the saxophone, which until then hadn't had a place in the rigid instrumental makeup of the brass bands.

The heavyweight of this era was the **Eureka Brass Band,** a group with roots going back to 1920. When the house orchestra of the Hobgoblins, a secret society noted for its Halloween night parades, was splintered by clarinetist and bass drummer Willie Parker into a smaller unit for purposes of a Labor Day parade, Parker came up with the Eureka tag because he was not permitted to use the Hobgoblins name.

For two decades the band worked extensively in a fairly traditional "reading" context, and opinions about their abilities range from fairly awful to competent. They persevered, and as the bigger bands such as Onward, Excelsior, and Tuxedo trickled to a halt in the mid-thirties, the Eureka, by virtue more of their "last man standing" status than true ability, suddenly found itself the premier brass band in New Orleans—even as the Depression slowed gigs and forced the departure of musicians for brighter economic pastures.

In 1937, trumpeter Dominique "T-Boy" Remy assumed leadership, but the players were getting old, dying, retiring, or were just no longer interested. When Remy retired and trumpeter Percy Humphrey took over, the chemistry of the membership and musicianship suddenly began to take a new form. By 1951, with the influx of alto saxophonist Ruben Roddy, snare drum bad-ass Arthur Ogle, trumpeter Willie Pajeaud, clarinetist George Lewis, and bass horn man Red Clark, the Eurekans cross-pollinated just the right elements of traditional brass band history with a forward thinking and modern instrumentation. They recorded for the first time with *New Orleans Funeral & Parade.*

By 1954 the band had expanded to fifteen pieces. They played at Papa Celestin's funeral and began recording practice sessions (the newly released *In Rehearsal 1956* is now available). Throughout the fifties and into the sixties, the band's momentum and reputation were strong; it was only—once again—when age began to take its toll and the membership rolls starting rotating that things began to fall apart. Though the group recorded live at Preservation Hall for Atlantic Records in 1962, much of the magic had dwindled, and their once unique sound was more or less indistinguishable from that of the lesser brass bands that had cropped up to take advantage of burgeoning tourist interest.

Another great band carrying on that era's tradition is **Harold Dejan's Olympia Brass Band**, continuing the sound into the modern era. Saxophonist Dejan (1908–), founded the Olympia squadron in 1958 as a neotraditional group committed to the classic recitation of funeral hymns, parade marches, and Dixieland standards. Typically, a twelve-piece unit with standard instrumentation—three trumpets (usually one lead, the others alternating on melody), two trombones, two saxophones, clarinets, tuba, snare, and bass drum. Renowned trumpeter Milton Batiste played with the band, as did George "Kid Sheik" Colar, and the Olympia has enjoyed quite a bit of hometown notoriety as well as success on national and international junkets. They've also released several CDs, foremost among them *New Orleans Jazz Preservation*, which includes guest performances from modern jazz heavyweights Donald Harrison Jr. and Terence Blanchard.

Older by almost two decades, the **Young Tuxedo Brass Band** was started by clarinetist John Casimir. A kind of traditional modernist, Casimir insisted on the old-time alto and baritone horns as well as the new-fangled saxophone. Despite problems keeping a steady lineup, the Young Tuxedos were one of the best and most popular brass bands in the city by the end of World War II, a status they enjoyed for some time. In the early fifties, they appeared in the film *Cinerama Holiday*, and by the end of the decade they had recorded for Atlantic Records. In 1961, they joined fellow stylists the Eureka Brass Band in playing for Alphonse Picou's funeral.

After Casimir died, trumpeter Wilbert Tillman assumed leadership responsibilities until his death six years later. The band maintained popularity through the sixties with a varied lineup, and they held the torch aloft until the great wave of younger bands churned into action.

Among the other bands of the 1960s are the **George Williams Brass Band,** the **E. Gibson Brass Band,** the **Young Excelsior Brass Band,** the **Anderson Minor Brass Band,** and the revived **Onward Brass Band.** Despite their existence, though, it wasn't a healthy time for the brass bands. When jazz banjoist Danny Barker, who'd played in brass bands until he left New Orleans to become a star in New York, returned to the city in 1965, he was alarmed to find that brass bands were hurtling toward extinction. Plucking young musicians from their high school marching bands, Barker formed the **Fairview Baptist Church Christian Band**. Barker told writer Michael Tisserand that at least 120 kids passed through the band. They made money and sparked energy. Gradually, a few groups of kids formed their own brass bands, the most successful and influential being one that was started in 1975 by trumpeter Gregory Davis—the **Dirty Dozen Brass Band.**

Using the old style reverentially but as a trampoline, and shifting the emphasis of the tuba from its "oompah" role to the sort of melodic figures that could be played by an upright or even electric bassist, the Dirty Dozen would march down the streets blowing typical hymns and then suddenly launch into bebop-toasted R&B. Formed as a sort of rehearsal exercise for a group of friends whose instrumental virtuosity conveniently fit the brass band format—two trumpets, one trombone, a pair of saxes, sousaphone, a snare, and a bass drum—the Dirty Dozen Brass Band started playing a neighborhood bar called the Glass House. Soon, they were filling the joint with curious and grateful patrons. A regional hit song followed, "Feet Can't Fail Me Now," and suddenly the band had inspired several imitators amongst the young black musicians in the city.

"We weren't actually trying to start a brass-band resurgence," Davis says. "The whole idea was just to play some music and throw some new ideas into the old stuff, just because it was fun and it was cool to experiment in that fashion. But then certain people started to put it down because we *were* taking it to another level."

If the conservatives grouched, far more folks woke up to a style of music that held the key to a large chunk of the city's past. The Dirty Dozen Brass Band shot to popularity on a global scale so fast, Davis says, that fifteen years passed before he realized what an impact the band had made.

Seminal records from the formative years include *Voodoo* and *The New Orleans Album*, and the band has recorded for such labels as Rounder and Columbia. In the mid-nineties, though, the band lost both drummers at a pivotal time. Davis said that it was easier to replace them with a standard traps drummer; shortly after, they added a keyboardist and began to supplement the bottom-end sousaphone with electric and acoustic bass. Almost without being aware of what they'd done, the group had become more of a funk band than a formatted brass band. When the name was abbreviated to the **Dirty Dozen**, the stylistic shift was official—and the *Ears to the Wall* and *Dirty Dozen* CDs commemorated the move.

"We all grew up with New Orleans funk, too," Davis told me. "As much as we love the brass band stuff, the Meters and the Neville Brothers are part of the heritage, too. And that's worth exploring." Davis himself loves the traditional sounds of "any and all Louis Armstrong, some Sidney Bechet, Danny Barker, Fats Domino, Professor Longhair, and James Booker."

Having toured in the new incarnation with such rock bands as the Black Crowes, the Dirty Dozen is expanding its fan base as surely as they have broadened their musical horizons.

The **ReBirth Brass Band** has, since the stylistic left turn of the Dirty Dozen, become the kingpin of the nouveau brass band scene in New Orleans. They started in 1983 at Joseph Clark High School (their first gig was at a teachers' convention) in the Sixth Ward. Although trad-jazz trumpeter Kermit Ruffins is probably the most famous of the ReBirthers, founders and coleading siblings Philip and Keith Frazier (sousaphone and bass drum, respectively) are the mainstays and master cylinders of the band.

"After the Dirty Dozen, we started carrying on in the early eighties," Philip Frazier told me, "and we were pretty much the only young band writing music that incorporated hip hop and hits from the radio. The old connection was still there—still is—and we play the old stuff in the old, traditional lineup, but we worked in all these new ideas and styles. And before you know it, it just took off."

Within a year, they'd appeared in Clint Eastwood's *Tightrope* and shortly after they signed with Rounder Records. Their debut, *Feel Like Funkin' It Up* scored two hits, including "Do Whatcha Wanna," which landed in heavy rotation on the city's commercial radio stations.

The band began to tour Europe and Africa, and even though membership rotated a bit, they consistently maintained excellent standards. Other records include *Kickin' It Live* and, the two most recent, on the Shanachie label, *We Come to Party* and *Main Event Live at the Maple Leaf Bar*. Benefiting from their status, they've also guested on records by such diverse artists as Maceo Parker, Robbie Robertson, Aaron Neville, and G. Love and Special Sauce.

Two of ReBirth's albums were recorded live, which fits into my theory that brass bands sound better live than when they are recorded in the studio. This could be argued of most bands, and I'm not saying the brass band CDs aren't good—some of them are honkin' great—but the integral energy and ritual of the live brass band heightens the experience quite a bit.

As the Dirty Dozen migrated from brass-band musings to straight funk, **Coolbone** logically embraced hip-hop. The first nouveau brass band to sign with a major label—Hollywood Records/Polygram—Coolbone grew up on the West Bank in Algiers. Band members happily acknowledge influences ranging from opera and Frank Sinatra to Nat King Cole and Bill Withers, all helping to further season the hip hop–brass band recipe.

Leader and trombonist Steve Johnson has always maintained that Coolbone is just doing what comes naturally. He told Timothy White of *Billboard*, "When I was in grade school or junior high, everybody I knew wanted to blow a trumpet, valve trombone, or a sax in a marching band, but friends of mine in places like Washington, D.C., or New York would never think of doing something like that as a kid, telling me their friends would have laughed at them and said they should be into sports instead! . . . And since New Orleans was the cradle of jazz, why shouldn't this city be the place 'brass-hop' gets created?"

Their debut CD, *Brass-Hop*, and the first single, a moody but infectious hit called "Nothin' but Strife," is only one of several insightful tunes the band has that addresses life in inner-urban New Orleans: "[The song] explains what it's like growing up in New Orleans, which has the crime, turbulence, and negative peer pressure of a lot of urban areas, but also a web of culture that helps us keep it together," Johnson told White.

With that cross-section of influences and the band's innate stability, Coolbone is a true force. Though the band lost its deal in a honcho-shift at Hollywood Records, they rebounded with a neotraditional (for them, anyway) CD called *Bone Swing*, which featured chillingly great versions of "Bye Bye Blackbird" and "Do You Know What It Means to Miss New Orleans."

The **Soul Rebels** brass band comes off sizzling in any context, rather like a marching band competition at Chuck D High School, but with a reggae beat. Such are the components of this exciting eight-piece unit. *Let Your Mind Be Free* and *No More Parades* are the band's CDs to date, and both are well worth owning.

Another interesting group is the **New Birth Brass Band,** its members hailing from the Young Olympians Brass Band. Featuring trumpeter James Andrews, New Birth fuses the traditional sounds with blues, funk, and even ragtime to generally excellent results. Their 1997 CD, *D-Boy*, named for Andrews's little brother, a victim of violence in the projects, is, despite the somber implications of the title, a rollicking record that has great tunes, particularly "Shake That Ass" to "Mardi Gras in New Orleans."

There are dozens of other nouveau brass banders, and the **Tremé Brass Band,** led by snare drummer Benny Jones Sr., is one superb outfit. They're much in demand not only for parades but in clubs, including Donna's, *the* brass-band hangout located on Rampart Street at the edge of the Quarter.

Tremé is also an experimental brass band, fusing contempo-funk and hip-hop with Dixieland roots. On their half-studio and half-live *I Got a Big, Fat Woman* CD, they brought in vocalist Henry Youngblood to sing some material that is a decided twist for the genre. They repeated the experiment on *Gimme My Money Back*, sweetening the mix with a great version of "The Old Rugged Cross" and a clever adaptation of George Gershwin's "Oh Lady Be Good." Kermit Ruffins teams with his trad-jazz trumpeter pal, James Andrews, on this scorching disc.

In 1990, Danny Barker called the **Algiers Brass Band** the "best damned brass band in New Orleans." High praise indeed. Headed up by trumpeter Ruddley Thibodeaux, the Algiers Brass Band is more traditional than the other young bands, though they don't mind throwing some funk or high-energy gospel into the recipe. Their *Lord, Lord, Lord* is an outstanding CD.

As with early Dixieland springing forth from traditional jazz, white musicians are appropriating the brass-band tradition. **The New Orleans Nightcrawlers,** whose *Funknicity* CD probably best represents their blend of old, new, and original, is an outstanding unit whose members have played with the Neville Brothers, Dr. John, Harry Connick Jr., Clarence "Gatemouth" Brown, Danny Barker, and even Rosemary Clooney.

It is encouraging to see that more and more brass bands are cropping up all the time in New Orleans. Not only are the parades and clubs open for new acts but the street corners of the city are stages unto themselves.

As such, the **Pinstripe Brass Band** *(Your Last Chance to Dance)*, **Tuba Fats** and the **Chosen Few Brass Band** *(Tuba Fats)*, **Li'l Rascals Brass Band** (featuring the much-in-demand leader and trombonist Corey Henry, *We Shall Walk Through the Streets of the City)*, the **Magnificent Seventh's Brass Band** *(Authentic New Orleans Jazz Funeral)*, the **Mahogany Brass Band** *(Mahogany Brass Band)*, and the **High Steppers Brass Band** *(New Orleans Jazz Greatest Hits)* all offer tremendous new music.

"It's a great scene right now," Philip Frazier assured me. "All the bands get along"—he laughs—"except at parade time, when we're all hustling gigs. But we get along. It's a different thing than the scene with rap, though we take some of their ideas—Soulja Slim was on our newest CD—and the Cash Money folks or Master P will refer to the second line. The brass bands are moving forward."

II

RHYTHM & BLUES

One

THE FOUNDATIONS
AND PIANO GIANTS

*I*t's Mardi Gras morning in New Orleans and I have been unable to obtain a hallowed silver or gold foil-wrapped coconut from the Krewe of Zulu as their parade makes its protracted way down St. Charles Street toward the Quarter. Zulu, though now integrated, was the first African-American Mardi Gras krewe. (A "krewe," I should point out, is nothing more than a carnivalesque spelling of "crew," and refers to a private club or organization that parades during Mardi Gras: the Krewe of Zulu, the Krewe of Bacchus, the Krewe of Proteus, the soon-to-be-commissioned Krewe of Koster, and so on. . . . More on such minutiae in "Mardi Gras Indians and Carnival Tunes," Part 6, Chapter 3.) Apocryphally, when Louis Armstrong served as the King of Zulu, back in the days when the krewe tossed the coconuts to the crowd as opposed to the current practice of handing them out—decidedly safer, though less accessible for those not on the front lines—it's said that when Satchmo wound up and let fly one of the treasures, it smashed the windshield of a parked Cadillac.

Though I have spent the weekend with my close friend and old college roommate, the perpetually cherubic and hysterical Steve "Dixieland Steve" Pace, watching Mardi Gras parades and/or kooks, he has now returned to his duties as a school principal in East Texas, a career that, in the context of our history together, is somewhat like finding out that the dope-addled sorority trollop you once knew is now Mother Superior of a convent. My host today is a new pal, Ian McNulty, a Rhode Island transplant with whom I share mutual Connecticut friends and who is happily ensconced in his first year of New Orleans residency. He's been kind enough to offer lodging even though we've never met, and I'm staying at his apartment in the lower Garden District. Ian is costumed appropriately today as Pan, and has headed out with friends to explore the morning. I appreciate and briefly consider their kind offer to join them in full-scale merriment, but I have work to do.

The exuberant parade ebbs and flows to the edge of St. Charles—families barbecuing, folks in Halloween splendor, kids playing: a day-glo quilt of citizenry focused on the revelry at hand. I pass a family standing on the sidewalk and looking down the street happily as a beaming little girl races towards them from the other end of the block, calling out, "Look mama! Look what I got!" She's wearing a dress of Easter finery, and in her outstretched hand is one of the silver Zulu coconuts.

It's a great moment, but it's in sharp contrast to what I see when I walk on a bit. At an intersection, I glance toward St. Charles and see a grandiose float of Zulu, besieged by a biracial crowd, passing in front of the enormous statue of Confederate general Robert E. Lee. It's hard not to make pompous judgments, or at least observations, particularly when the issue of the Confederate flag's flying over the South Carolina capitol building has been subject to national scrutiny, but in truth the parade route does throw a brief chill of irony into the day's celebration.

I realize, though, that if it's Fat Tuesday and you're in New Orleans, there's only one thing you can do. You head into the lower Quarter to Matassa's Grocery at the corner of Dauphine and St. Philip to introduce yourself to family patriarch Cosimo Matassa. For roughly twenty-five years as the *brujo* at his three recording studios, Matassa produced and essentially served as a primary sculptor of New Orleans rhythm & blues.

This fine morning, Matassa is standing on the corner in front of the small grocery, whose narrow and Byzantine aisles I've just navigated to buy a turkey po'boy from the food counter in back. Now in his seventies, Matassa is smiling, wearing a baseball cap, talking with a small coterie of friends and neighbors, and taking in the mellow sunshine. I lean against the wall, not wanting to interrupt, and inhale the very fine Matassa po'boy.

After a few minutes, when everyone's attention seems glued on a twenty-ish female masker who is clad in blue and green paint and little else, I approach Matassa and introduce myself. He fields my bumbling salutations with the grace of Jackie Robinson. It is not my intention to interrupt Matassa's Mardi Gras, but it seems symbolic to make his acquaintance on such a day; this, after all, is the man who made records for a hall-of-fame legion of New Orleans musicians—the George Martin of the French Quarter, one might say. He is a white man who for much of the last century worked primarily with black artists and couldn't care less about such distinctions, and that is important indeed.

So we chat a moment and he smiles indulgently as I reel off a litany of musicians he's worked with. It isn't as if he's somehow forgotten that part of his life, but I want Matassa to know that I know. His legacy is an amazing thing to ponder; it has changed modern music.

Later, he tells me that his participation in the great tsunami of fifties New Orleans R&B was "a happy accident. I'm the luckiest man in the world. I got to sit and watch this all happen." Indeed he did, though "watch" isn't exactly the correct verb. True, as he would be the first to tell you, he's not a musician. "I can play a radio," he laughs. What he and his best friend, **Dave Bartholomew** (1920–), the black saxophonist and bandleader at Matassa's studios, did along with producer and songwriter Allen Toussaint and his business partner, Marshall Sehorn, was bring the city's R&B scene into the open (also discussed in "The Indigenous Sound," Part 5, Chapter 1).

Rhythm 'n' blues, along with their slightly less frenetic sister, Soul, and their nephew, Funk, are not exclusive to New Orleans. Memphis and Detroit are also cities whose respective Stax/Volt and Motown labels are just the representative tips of the sonic icebergs. But, as always, the New Orleans twist on things creates another sound. The evolution of R&B was a natural for the same reasons that jazz was born in the city: the confluence of intermingling ethnic communities and their respective musical styles; the town's geographical status as the northernmost port in what might be called the Caribbean Rim; the strange and bewitching charm of the Mississippi River and its sway over the rhythms of industry; the neo-Pagan dancin'-in-the-streets delight in a 24/7/365 Celebration of Life regardless of circumstances; the inherent musicality of family and the passing of music from generation to generation; the tropical air and its siren song to outdoor activity; and, indeed, the town's poverty in general.

The R&B split from jazz is understandable. The basic second-line parade rhythms that function as New Orleans's funky heartbeat had been pushed out of jazz as new time signatures were taking root in its modern forms—the traditional Dixieland musicians had in many ways more things in common with the emerging R&B than with bop—and those rhythms simply had to surface somewhere. The difference between R&B and pure blues is a question of degree rather than species. Both rely on a basic I-IV-V chord progression. While R&B *does* get out of this structural pattern, the divergence is negligible.

One significant question is whether classic New Orleans R&B is a dinosaur genre. Young jazz musicians are carrying their music into the new century in a variety of ways. There are a variety of educational options, from the neighborhood brass bands that have returned from the dead in the past twenty years—the Dirty Dozen, ReBirth, Coolbone, and dozens more—to the New Orleans Center for Creative Arts (NOCCA) and splendid undergraduate and postgraduate music programs at Tulane and Xavier Universities in New Orleans and Southern University and Louisiana State University in Baton Rouge. Wither goest R&B, though? You don't see a lot of young artists singing soul and R&B in the nightclubs, whether they are interpreting the classic repertoire or writing new contemporary material. To be sure, on a national level, there *is* a small contemporary rhythm & blues scene, and such folks as Erykah Badu, Jill Scott, and Macy Gray are a few who are expanding the form—as opposed to the dozens of truly crappy recording "artists" who wouldn't recognize Stevie Wonder if he landed in their front yard with a space ship. But in the meantime, Louisiana R&B is languishing.

There is one hot contemporary Louisiana rhythm & blues act. **Profyle,** a vocal quartet from Shreveport (of all places) has hit the *Billboard* charts in a big way. Made up of brothers Face and Hershey and cousins Baby Boy and L'Jai, Profyle was initially motivated by Boyz II Men, Take 6, and Jodeci and Stevie Wonder. They impressed a series of increasingly important folks, and in 1997 they scored a contract with Motown Records. Their debut, *Whispers in the Dark*, came out in 1999, followed a year later by *Nothin' But Drama*. All four members are strong singers, and they work the hip-hop beat–lush harmonies sound so prevalent in contemporary urban music. The ballad-heavy sound of the first album is timid, but the newer record is more profane and musically aggressive. In November 2000, their new single, "Liar," overtook MTV fave Sisqo at the tops of the R&B charts and hung there impressively.

But Profyle seems to be the exception. The bulk of young artists who might have been interested in going in that stylistic direction appear to be pursuing hip-hop instead. Some would suggest that R&B as Fats Domino would know it is going under in the rising tide of hip-hop. Others would say that hip-hop *is* R&B, or at least the next evolutionary step in the genre's path. The truth probably falls somewhere in between.

"As far as New Orleans R&B, it's not going anywhere," Cyril Neville assured me. "It's evolving. In my estimation, the true hip-hop musician—true to the art—is constantly making the same kind of gumbo we work with. The Meters, for example, are one of the most sampled groups by hip-hop artists. People like Erykah Badu are taking the R&B feeling and adding hip-hop and saying, 'This is our roots and this is how we can take it forward.' And Bounce [a poppy, dance-happy variety of hip-hop; see Chapter 6 for more] is *exclusive* to New Orleans."

Producer Cosimo Matassa agrees, but only to a point. "Hip-hop has a lot of its roots right here in New Orleans," he told me. "And it was kind of a square format until our artists gave it a little *oomph*—a little soul, if you will. So in that sense New Orleans is still contributing. But it's still so—to me, anyway—restrictive. Aside from the way you dress and conduct your life, it doesn't give an artist real expression in the way the stuff we did, did. It's the difference to me between the tenor in the opera and the chorus."

Whether hip-hop is the logical extension of soul and R&B is probably moot; regardless, it's happening in a big way. But the Old Guard is also making efforts to preserve the past and educate the new generation—similar to the efforts of the jazz community. Chicago's Loyola University has instituted a music business program to help aspiring players pay attention to the fiscal side of their careers. The New Orleans Music and Culture Preservatory was formed recently as an extension of an early eighties group called NOMO (New Orleans Musicians Organized), both spearheaded in part by Cyril Neville to coordinate opportunities and education for local musicians with the caveat that local musicians are integral in the workings of the preservatory.

"Hopefully," Neville told me, "there will be an ethnomusicology course, an archive where younger musicians can go and learn about the older session cats, the Mardi Gras Indian tribes and the brass bands and social and pleasure clubs [see also "The Mardi Gras Indians and Carnival Tunes," Part 6, Chapter 3]. To continue the tradition, you've got to get the younger musicians interested in the old R&B. With so much emphasis put on jazz, R&B is getting swept under the rug, so to speak."

Neville also faults the city in general. Though he acknowledges that jazz educators and musicians have done a more efficient job, perhaps, than the R&B folks at perpetuating their tradition, Neville thinks the city has been negligent in meeting its obligation.

"Consider Nashville," he says. "An entire city that supports and educates the community of country musicians. It's a resource and it's not just the music but the culture. Musicians there don't *have* to go to New York or L.A. because the industry is *there*. New Orleans has so much it *could* be doing, but the city cuts off its nose to spite its face."

Indeed, given the glorious birth of New Orleans R&B in the forties and fifties, and its hall of fame gallery of artists and individuals who were around to create the scene, it is a shame that they're frequently overlooked in the big scheme of American music.

In many ways, New Orleans R&B started by accident, with Matassa, who never planned to get into the record business in the first place. After World War II, he became a partner in an appliance store where, as a sideline, he began selling the used records extricated from a bunch of jukeboxes his father owned. In time, because record stores were scarce, so many folks ended up coming into the store looking for records that Matassa eventually phased out the appliance part of the business and opened the J&M Music Shop.

Matassa eventually bought out his father's interest in the jukebox business (as well as his dad's partner's), and along the way it occurred to him that, given the significant demand for records and the high-quality musicians in New Orleans, there were few in-town recording options. He bought a disc cutter, put it in a back room, and started J&M Recording Services—a set-up so primitive that a screw-up in a recording take meant the actual acetate had to be thrown away. Since the house band included leader and trumpeter Dave Bartholomew, saxophonists Red Tyler, Joe Harris, and Clarence Hall, pianist Salvador Doucette, drummer Earl Palmer, and guitarist Ernest McLean, it's not surprising that virtually any-one who walked in the door could be made to sound hot.

Indeed, Bartholomew was a huge factor. Born in Edgard, Louisiana, the trumpeter's father was a noted tuba player named Louis Bartholomew. Dave is an imposing, no-nonsense sorta guy who learned the horn as a kid and had played professionally with Papa Celestin's big band and Fats Pichon by the time he was eighteen. Bartholomew went into the army at twenty-two, played music throughout his service stint, and, when he got out, formed a popular dance band parts of which would become the house band at Matassa's and include at various times saxophonist Herbert Hard-esty, guitarist Justin Adams, bassist Frank Fields, guitarist/pianist Dr. John, and keyboardist James Booker.

Bartholomew also recorded briefly for the DeLuxe label, and in 1949 he scored a regional R&B hit with "Country Boy." He then met Imperial Records honcho Lew Chudd who, wanting an "in" to the lucrative New Orleans rhythm & blues scene, hired Bartholomew as an A&R man and producer. One of the first artists Bartholomew and Chudd discovered was Fats Domino, whom they recorded at J&M.

"I'm pained Dave never got the recognition he should have, especially early on," Matassa told me. "He ran sessions the way sessions are supposed to be run: We can enjoy ourselves, but we're here to do our best. I remem-ber one time Dave thought the drummer wasn't playing hard enough, and he took the stick to demonstrate and hit the drum and the stick went through the batter head and the other head, too!"

There isn't enough room in this book to list the Bartholomew-produced hits Domino had; but it's easy enough to say that the work of Matassa and Bartholomew put them on the studio map and set the stage for a floodtide of rich and seminal New Orleans R&B to roar forth for the next several years. Besides Domino, Bartholomew signed and produced Frankie Ford, Shirley and Lee, Lloyd Price, Smiley Lewis, the Spiders, and Tommy Ridgley, to name a few. The sessions he played on and artists he wrote tunes for are even more extensive and range from Allen Toussaint and T-Bone Walker to Hank Williams Jr. and the Dirty Dozen Brass Band.

He also released several records, efforts ranging from wide-open jazz to Dixieland to classic R&B. In recent years, since his induction into the Rock 'n' Roll Hall of Fame, he has been most active in the pursuit of his own record-ings. In 1991, Bartholomew released an eclectic effort called *In the Alley* that called on the services of many of his old studio mates, and in 1998 he came out with *New Orleans Big Beat*, a further extrapolation of his musical experi-ments that segues winningly from big-band jazz to funky R&B and rock.

A similar partnership in the annals of the New Orleans sound was that of **Allen Toussaint** (1938–) and Marshall Sehorn. Toussaint is a shy mogul who has always been more comfortable in the background, or at least in the recording studio, than onstage. He did wear a luminous green jacket during his set at JazzFest 2000, one of his relatively rare performances, which was going along wonderfully until first Bonnie Raitt and then Jean-Claude Van Damme insisted on coming out to jam.

Toussaint was born in New Orleans. In elementary school he attempted to play piano like Professor Longhair. He worked in his teens with a group called the Flamingos and quickly became good enough to do sessions for Dave Bartholomew, laying down tracks for no less than Shirley and Lee and even Fats Domino. Toussaint was also starting to experiment as a songwriter. By 1958, he'd released an instrumental solo album, *The Wild Sound of New Orleans,* for RCA under the name "Tousan." One of the tunes from that record, "Java," would later become a huge success in the hammy hands of trumpeter Al Hirt (see Part 1, Chapter 1).

Minit Records formed in 1960, and Toussaint, though he also produced material for the Fury and AFO, became the label's house writer, arranger, and producer. He was a one-man gold mine for that label, as well as for the Minit sister company, Instant Records. Toussaint's writing was magical in effortlessly capturing the feel and spirit of New Orleans and, at the same time, placed a premium on melody and high-quality lyrics. In rapid succession, Toussaint worked his magic on Jessie Hill's "Ooh Poo Pah Doo," Ernie K-Doe's "Mother in Law," Chris Kenner's "I Like It Like That," Bennie Spellman's "Lipstick Traces," Barbara George's "I Know," and Lee Dorsey's "Ya Ya." He also sculpted sessions for Aaron Neville and became in essence, at least for a while, Irma Thomas's personal songwriter.

"Allen wrote some customized songs for me," she remembered in a phone conversation, "and it was so obvious he'd put a great deal of thought into who I am and how I sing. He's a gentleman; a very talented, very shy gentleman."

After a three-year stint in the military, Toussaint returned home and formed Sansu Productions with Marshall Sehorn; this was another black guy–white guy partnership, like that of Bartholomew-Matassa, that clearly bucked the segregationist trends of the era. Their work made Lee Dorsey a hit-single machine and the Meters a remarkable backing band.

In 1970, Toussaint released his second solo effort, the magical *From a Whisper to a Scream*, an album that fostered the gradual national segue from roadhouse R&B to a velvety soul style. A few years later, he and Sehorn opened Sea-Saint Studios, a world-class recording facility that would lure all manner of prominent global musicians from Johnny Winter and John Mayall to Paul McCartney and Paul Simon. Along the way, Toussaint's reputation as a producer and arranger exceeded his fame as a songwriter. In spite of that, two years after the studio opened, Toussaint issued perhaps his signature record: *Southern Nights*, the title song of which is a masterpiece (and was a monster hit for Glen Campbell). Some of the other artists who have covered Toussaint's material over the years include such varied folks as Boz Scaggs, Bonnie Raitt, the Oak Ridge Boys, Herb Alpert and the Tijuana Brass, Little Feat, Devo, and Lawrence Welk.

Since those high-watermark years, Toussaint has been content to sit out the tides of popular music—be it punk, heavy metal, country, or hip-hop—and remains easily settled in his New Orleans studio, writing or producing or arranging at his leisure. Occasionally, as on the JazzFest afternoon in his sparkly green coat, he takes the stage. And even Jean-Claude Van Damme can't screw it up.

Sehorn stayed strictly on the fiscal side of the partnership. As he told writer Jeff Hannusch in the book *I Hear You Knockin'*, "It don't matter how good ya sound, it don't mean a thang if ye ain't got no money behind ya!" Sehorn and Toussaint's teamwork was divided along creative and financial lines, while Matassa and Bartholomew had slightly more crossover; but both partnerships worked, and they resulted in many awesome records.

With the production mechanisms in place, a vast tapestry of artists, and a gradual network of regional and national label and distribution possibilities kicking in over the years, the Golden Age of New Orleans R&B was set to explode. But it wouldn't get there without the piano.

From the days of the Storyville whorehouses through small nightclub and street-party gigs to the royal tradition of entertainment in the city's many luxury hotels, pianists from "Champion Jack" Dupree, Kid Stormy Weather, and Kid Sullivan Rock through Tuts Washington and Professor Longhair to fresh torchbearers Jon Cleary and Tom McDermott held the title of "Piano Professor"—an apt description of an artist who could play what people wanted. The Professors were paramount in the development of rhythm & blues because the piano was the structural bridge from Dixieland, swing, and even ragtime—and it *kept people dancing.*

It's essential to start with **Professor Longhair** (1918–1980). Wild high notes, trills, and figures that are musical exclamation points to the seductive amalgamation of barrelhouse blues, boogie-woogie, and calypso all buzzing together like a cluster of bees trying to get out of a jar—*that's* what Professor Longhair's piano playing sounds like, and it's impossible to be anything other than happy when you listen to his records.

His voice is something else, too: a joyful, yowling thing that can ache with raw emotion or cackle with mischief as it speaks and sings in a lexicon purely of his own design and comfort. Just listening to his lyrics allows you to grasp the idea of Longhairian vernacular. According to Dr. John, to whom Professor Longhair served as a father figure after the Doctah's own dad passed away, Longhair referred to such things as the "key of E-minus," and often ordered the boys to "frolic presto," a verb command that indicated the band was well-toked and ready to blister.

I never saw Fess, as he's known to most citizens of New Orleans. When he died, I was still convinced that Humble Pie and such people were musical visionaries. Still, I was at least aware of him, and by now the facts of his life are pretty familiar. By all accounts, he was a singular fellow: warm, loving of children and animals and the medicinal properties of the good herb; a wonderful family man who enjoyed to the fullest the rich New Orleans concept of "neighborhood" sovereignty, though he spent far too many years in impoverished obscurity.

But those who knew him well rejoice in his singular wonder. The Professor was born Henry Roeland Byrd in Bogalusa, Louisiana, and he grew up in New Orleans (where he was called Roy by friends and family), zeroing in on an innate rhythm at an early age by dancing with pals for coins at the corner of Bourbon and Rampart Streets. His early efforts to learn guitar didn't pan out, but during his teen years he began hanging around nightclubs; there, piano players such as Sullivan Rock, Archibald, Kid Stormy Weather, and Tuts Washington caught his attention, and, early on, the playing of Chicago boogie-woogie wizard Jimmy Clancey also created an impression. Byrd was able to seduce Rock and Washington into giving him foundational lessons of a sort.

Byrd practiced on an abandoned piano he and some friends found in an alley behind his house, and his musically adept mother helped out with scales and chording. That the instrument was missing several keys and many more were inoperable was of huge import; young Byrd was forced to adapt his fingering only to the workable portions of the keyboard. The result was that the songs he'd learned from Washington or Rock quickly began to bear Byrd's own characteristic and instinctual stylistic flourishes to make up for the missing keys. "He progressed not in the general way of the world, he progressed in Professor Longhair's world," said Allen Toussaint in Don Snowden's liner notes to 'Fess: The Professor Longhair Anthology, from Rhino.

Before long, Byrd scored his first pro gig playing with Champion Jack Dupree, whom he showed piano licks in exchange for vocal lessons. Stints in the Civilian Conservation Corps and the army in World War II followed. (He was never shipped overseas and spent the duration of the conflict stationed in Louisiana, entertaining troops on the rec-room piano or relieving them of their cash in card games—a skill at which Byrd displayed the same intuitive genius as he did playing piano.)

When he was discharged, Byrd learned to cook and became a partner in a soul food restaurant, but he continued to hammer away at the house piano. By 1948, when New Orleans had become a southern recording mecca, Byrd had been playing around sporadically with such groups as the Mid Drifs. A spontaneous solo performance at the Caldonia Club, during a break by Dave Bartholomew's band, caused the crowd to go so berserk that Bartholomew was fired—and Byrd was booked on the spot. The burgeoning strain of post-barrelhouse music that would become rhythm & blues, and Longhair's affinity for the tropical nuances of Caribbean rhumba and calypso, as well as ragtime and pure New Orleans jazz, were growing in the musician's pesky left hand. This unique style was further augmented with a fevered onstage dynamic, a metamorphosing blend that torched the Caldonia audience.

Where did the Spanish flavorings come from? Byrd professed to be a big fan of Perez Prado, and it's probable that he heard a lot of Latin music while hanging around the military base during the war. In his marvelous autobiography *Under a Hoodoo Moon*, Dr. John suggests, "The closest thing I could ever find to his style among the earlier cats was a guy named Joseph Spence, who was a guitar player from the Bahamas who played rhythms like Fess."

"A lot of bass players had problems with [Fess's] left hand," George Porter Jr. told me. "What I figured out early on was just play half the notes that he'd play and it would make sense. A lot of bassists tried to compete and it was a train wreck. I tried that a few times and he'd just look at me and say, 'Get off my left hand.' Half-time was the way to go."

"I threw myself in the deep end when I tried to learn the song 'Tipitina,'" says pianist and British expatriate Jon Cleary, one of the latest of New Orleans's R&B pianists. "For years I tried to get *one lick* down from that song, and it finally worked out for me. What's important to remember about Fess is his originality and what that says about style. People start off learning by imitation and too many people stop there. You have to take that vocabulary, respect that tradition, and move forward. And that's what I hope I'm doing. Because I had to get on a plane and come half way around the world to get here where it all happened."

In any event, for support at his new job, Byrd hired a backup group. According to legend, the club's owner, Mike Tessitore, taking note of the musicians' slipshod approach to barbering, came up with the moniker Professor Longhair. The band worked the Caldonia for a year before Fess was approached by Star Records in 1949 with an opportunity to record, though the proposed record never materialized because of a union snafu.

It wasn't long, though, before Mercury Records came sniffing around. Fess and band found themselves back in a studio and, less than a year later, the Professor hit the newly titled R&B charts with "Bald Head," which went to #5. There was a flurry of gigs and bands (the Four Hairs Combo, the Cha-Paka-Shaweez, Professor Longhair and His Blues Scholars, Roy Byrd and His Blues Jumpers, Professor Longhair and His Shuffling Hungarians), and soon Longhair was signed to Atlantic Records after label honchos Ahmet Ertegun and Herb Abramson "discovered" the pianist on a talent-hunt in Algiers, across the river from downtown New Orleans. Sessions for Atlantic, and later for smaller labels such as Edd, Ric and Ron, and Ripp, produced the now-recognized classics "Tipitina," "Stack-O'Lee," "Hadacol Bounce," "Hey Now Baby," "Big Chief" and, naturally, "Go to the Mardi Gras." But Fess never duplicated the early success of "Bald Head."

As a result, while he continued to gig and record sporadically, the Professor spent most of two decades living with his wife, Alice, and their family in a small house on South Rampart Street and working creepy jobs or playing cards to supplement a meager cash flow. Depending on which story you believe, he was either busted on a marijuana charge or blacklisted by shady union honchos in the early fifties and was subsequently kept from gigging in Orleans and Jefferson Parishes. Issues such as royalties on the original material he'd recorded were moot; either Byrd had received a straight session fee for the record or, as was typical for the times, he just got screwed.

By 1970, people questioned whether Longhair even existed. A few journalists tried to track him down, and rumors ranged from "He's crippled" to "He's dead." But a booking at the relatively obscure second Jazz and Heritage Festival in 1971, held in Congo Square, resurrected Fess. The Professor's set was so incendiary that it brought all activity to a stunned standstill: Musicians and fans alike were transfixed.

George Porter Jr. shares a great anecdote: "I got a call from Zig [drummer Zigaboo Modeliste] the first year JazzFest was [moved to] the fairgrounds, asking if I wanted to play the date backing Professor Longhair [who was by that time a regular featured performer]. I was so anxious and excited. Well, I lived three blocks from Fess when he was on Rampart Street, and we were supposed to rehearse Wednesday before the festival. I couldn't wait and I knocked on the door thirty minutes early, and he answers the door and I say, 'Hi, Mr. Professor Longhair. My name is George Porter and I'm here to rehearse for JazzFest.

"He looks at me and says, 'You're early,' and closed the door. So I sat on the steps in front of his house for forty-five minutes, knocked again, and he said, 'C'mon in!' And that was that. The gig was great!"

Things started to turn around; festival founders Quint Davis and Alison Miner began to manage his career with near-parental concern, and Atlantic re-released all the early Ertegun sessions on a well-received LP called *New Orleans Piano*. A European tour with the Meters not only proved that there *was* a Professor Longhair but brought global recognition for his inspiring talent. Hot recording sessions in New York and Memphis—supposedly some of the best stuff Byrd ever did—were tied up by the estate of Bearsville Records label founder Albert Grossman. Longhair was dealt another crushing blow when his house burned to the ground and everything the family owned was destroyed.

It seemed, though, that his spirit had been revitalized by the resuscitation of his career, and Fess hung in. Three days after the fire, in 1974, he recorded the *Rock 'n' Roll Gumbo* album with Clarence "Gatemouth" Brown (for more on Gatemouth, see "The Baton Rouge Scene and Statewide Guardians," Part 3, Chapter 1). Released in France for the Blue Star label, it's now available in the United States, and it's great work that includes definitive versions of "Mardi Gras in New Orleans," "Meet Me Tomorrow Night," "Junco Partner," "Stag-o-Lee," and the wonderfully titled "(They Call Me) Dr. Professor Longhair," the musical and grammatical structures of which are everything one needs to know about the universe of The Professor.

In 1975, Paul McCartney brought Byrd to England to play a private party, a recording of which, *Live on the Queen Mary*, came out three years later. Back home, a nightclub called Tipitina's opened at Napoleon and Tchoupitoulas, providing Fess with a regular performance venue. Another live album was recorded, the double-set *The Last Mardi Gras*, though it, along with *House Party New Orleans Style* (later reissued as *Mardi Gras in Baton Rouge*), would become a posthumous release.

A documentary of live, interactive piano and conversation between Professor Longhair, Allen Toussaint, and Tuts Washington—three generations of the New Orleans piano tradition—was also in the works for record and video at the time of Byrd's death. Called *Piano Players Rarely Ever Play Together*, it's an overwhelming experience. "What comes out of that session is what a sensitive player Professor Longhair was," says Henry Butler, an extraordinary New Orleans contemporary pianist who studied with Byrd on a few "marathon" lessons. "With Tuts and Allen, Fess was the mediator; the go-between or groove that kept that session going. I can recognize that after studying with him. He was a very humble guy who just had a way of letting you know what he thought should happen—and he was right."

Also underway were plans for Fess to tour in support of the British rock band The Clash, a group of musicians intuitively aware of rock's past and committed to making their audiences aware of the genre's roots.

In 1979, Fess bought a house and even filed a tax return. He then inked a deal with Alligator and recorded *Crawfish Fiesta*—with such empathetic musicians as Dr. John and all-world drummer Johnny Vidacovich—still acknowledged by most as his finest effort. Fess died in his sleep just as the album was scheduled for release. Given the frequent obscurity of his life and career, perhaps his family, friends, and supporters took some comfort in the fact that his funeral procession was so well attended that it extended over a mile long.

There's not much else to say about Professor Longhair other than listen to the music. He was so unutterably unique, so otherworldly wonderful that wizard pianists today still discuss his technique and style with reverence. That he recorded so little solo piano work is a tragedy. His voice was great and he played with some terrific side musicians, but just to listen to him as he sits at the piano and goes nuts is something to remember.

A genius is seated at the piano in the Maple Leaf Bar on Oak Street. Wearing an eye patch with a star on it, he rips off an astonishing and unique take on a Bach fugue, then stops halfway through and mumbles distractedly. After a moment, he rises from the piano bench as though miming the actions of a malt-liquored marionette, makes his way behind the bar oblivious to the creatures gathered in the room to see him play, and with an athlete's precision, vomits into the open bin of crushed ice.

It's hard to sustain the romantic notion of **James Booker** (1939–1983) as a beautiful madcap genius after you talk to several people who describe a litany of scenes like this one. To be sure, Booker *was* a beautiful madcap genius. A postcard of a Michael P. Smith photograph of Booker, taken at the 1978 Jazz & Heritage Festival, is titled "Music Magnifico." A medium shot snapped with a wide-angle lens from onstage, with the crowd in the background and a Schlitz tall boy propped on the piano in the foreground, the image of Booker is transcendent as it captures the buoyancy of the artist in one of his "up" periods. Booker, wearing a ludicrous Afro wig, his star-crusted eye-patch, and a form-fitting vest, is smirking with easy confidence, his supple wrists and serpentine fingers poised in mid-attack. But after a certain point, his tortured but charming persona went from bizarre to worse, assimilating the worst qualities of a thief and a junkie.

Having said all that, in the robust and day-glo canon of New Orleans musical characters, nobody could intrigue like James Carroll Booker III. "Most of Booker's torture was self-torture," says George Porter Jr. "As loving as he was, he never found peace within himself or put himself in a winning situation. There was never enough 'I like *me*' in him. But I'll tell you this: On the road, I *always* have a Booker CD in the disc changer."

As has been pointed out by every chronicler of the pianist's life—because he was so fond of pointing it out himself—James Booker was born the same year Jelly Roll Morton died. The implication has always been that some sort of spiritual transference took place, which was hardly the strangest of Booker's observations. He was born into a musical family at Charity Hospital in New Orleans (where he would die forty-three years later). He was raised in his early years by an aunt in Bay St. Louis, Mississippi, and was considered a child prodigy on the piano. With his older sister, Betty Jean, he studied classical music, but James was innately absorbed by blues and assimilated any style from classical to barrelhouse with ridiculous ease. After their aunt died, the siblings rejoined their mother in New Orleans where, when he was ten, Booker was struck by a speeding ambulance, his leg severely fractured.

The prescribed morphine had more than just a temporary effect, at least according to Booker, who blamed the accident for introducing him to what would be a lifelong affection for narcotics. A sinister reliance, though, was yet down the road. He was enrolled in Xavier Preparatory School, where he excelled scholastically. He was introduced by his sister, then singing gospel on a local radio program, to the station's managers; shortly after, Booker was playing his own blues and gospel show on Saturday afternoons. He formed a band with Art Neville—Booker Boy & the Rhythmaires—which scored radio time, and at fourteen Booker auditioned for Dave Palmer, releasing a single for Imperial called "Thinking About My Baby" (b/w "Doing the Hambone").

Though the record did nothing and it would be a while before he released more of his own stuff, Booker's name was circulating in the New Orleans music scene. He began working sessions at Matassa's J&M Studio with another young wizard named Mac "Dr. John" Rebennack, and eventually the two were accepted as regulars within the J&M house band's incredibly tight family.

Booker also worked gigs with the Rhythmaires and as a support pianist for many hot regional R&B acts, including Shirley & Lee, Smiley Lewis, and Earl King. In 1956, Booker was signed by Chicago's Chess label as a quick-fix effort to enter the burgeoning rock 'n' roll market, but a single did little and Booker was dropped. Not long after, Booker recorded a few sides for Johnny Vincent's Ace label ("Little Booker" and "Teenage Rock") but the pianist was angry when he discovered Vincent overdubbing Joe Tex's vocals on one of the tunes.

By that time, Booker was also perhaps the hottest organist in New Orleans. He entered Southern University, probably in an effort to overcome his narcotic tendencies, although he left school to tour with Dee Clark. Clark's band broke up in Houston, and Booker worked for a while at Don Robey's studio, siding for Duke/Peacock artists Junior Parker and Bobby Bland. In 1960, he released his own single on Peacock, "Gonzo," which charted with surprising strength on the national R&B charts though, sadly, it would be his only hit.

He returned to New Orleans, became more heavily involved with dope, worked plenty of gigs, collected advance payment for stuff he didn't then make, and spent the cash on getting high. He was busted for heroin possession at the Dew Drop Inn and sentenced to a two-year stint at Angola. Though he served only six months, the situation did little to help Booker's increasingly fragile mental state. Later, it was revealed that Booker was gay and, while being gay and black is probably not the most easily assimilated societal lifestyle at any time, to come to terms with it in the South in the sixties in prison couldn't have been much fun.

On the streets, Booker did session work for Fats Domino to cover for the Fat Man while he was touring, and played clubs on Bourbon Street until more police trouble convinced Booker to vacate New Orleans for a while. For years he wandered about, a sort of musical hobo, doing primo session work in New York, Nashville, and Los Angeles with Aretha Franklin, Maria Muldair, the Grateful Dead, the Doobie Brothers, and Ringo Starr. Also in the seventies, he toured with Dr. John, who by that time had hit big with rock 'n' roll audiences.

"There's no other way to say it," Cosimo Matassa told me. "He was a genius. Until you saw him play a variety of styles in different circumstances—until you *got it*—you didn't know how phenomenal he really was. And he was *phenomenal*—fantastic! That guy could play *anything.*"

Booker returned to New Orleans in 1975, and by most accounts that's the point when his distinctive eye patch surfaced; in some sordid fashion, he'd been blinded in his left eye. Still, the patch and the propensity for appearing onstage in a cape leant a certain sorcerer's look to his persona and, in addition to his session work and tours with Dr. John, Booker's name became, if not household, at least legendary amongst a certain cognoscenti. He also made his most valiant effort to get off heroin and was moderately successful. That he seemed to substitute increased quantities of liquor and cocaine didn't particularly add to his sobriety, but it wasn't heroin.

An appearance later that year at the New Orleans Jazz and Heritage Festival was so stunning that German musicologist Norbert Hess booked him overseas at festivals where his idiosyncratic and brilliant sets—combining pop fluffery, R&B seduction, and deft classical touches—astounded audiences. Some months later, in 1977, he recorded the *Junco Partner* album for Island and toured Europe to fine acclaim. Two in-concert records were issued from those dates: *James Booker—The Piano Prince of New Orleans* and *James Booker Live.* The latter won the Grand Prix de Disque de Jazz for best live album, which Booker accepted at the Montreux Jazz Festival in 1978. (Rounder released the album in the states as *New Orleans Piano Wizard: Live!*)

The hopeful surge of all this activity ushered in the final chapter of Booker's life. Unfortunately, it was a creepy but compelling period of often inspired performance and recording and an equally bizarre and tragic descent into near-lunatic behavior.

Cyril Neville giggles when he relates this anecdote:

> I don't remember what Jazz & Heritage Festival it was, but I had the privilege of hanging out with James—one of the greatest piano players that ever lived, by the way—the night before and during the day of his set. James rented a white Bentley and drove *through the crowd* at Jazz Fest—I don't know how we got actually on the grounds—and he was passing reefers out the window! The crowd parted like the Red Sea when they realized who it was, and when we got to the stage he held court, wearing a long, flowing cape. And I don't know if it was his grandmother or his aunt who came home from church and

had taken off her wig, [but] James put it on and wore it to the gig. I knew I was riding with royalty that day—and to watch one person sitting behind the piano and it sounded like three or four people playing—well, he was just one of the best players *ever*.

As he got older, the darker aspects of his persona seemed to surface with greater regularity. Sometimes no one knew where he stayed or where he was. He drank more heavily and, despite his efforts to stay off dope, he was certainly in and out of that arena. He speculated about conspiracies: UFOs and government maneuverings. Gigs at the Maple Leaf were hit or miss.

At other times Booker seemed perfectly normal. He worked at City Hall as a clerk—he liked the physical therapy of typing—and walked to work wearing a three-piece suit. He taught piano—and Harry Connick Jr. was surely the most famous of his pupils.

Henry Butler also spoke about Booker's final years: "We did double bills together from '77 to '80. He was a real character but in the end he started encouraging me and saying I was getting into the energy—which to me was a real compliment. Playing in nightclubs and living the way he did, a lot of his best stuff just evaporated. If you were there you could appreciate it, but it was hard to know it was even played after a bit of time passed."

Perhaps the period is best typified by the sessions for his final album. Based on the success they had with the live album, Rounder Records signed Booker in 1981 and shortly after sent their ace producer-wizard, Scott Billington, down from the company offices in Cambridge, Massachusetts, to oversee recording sessions. Billington lined up three days at Ultrasonic Studios in New Orleans, but Booker was in bad shape and the dates had to be rescheduled several times while the pianist recovered from first one malady and then another. When he was well enough to try to work, Billington brought in Booker's regular Maple Leaf band for the gig: drummer Johnny Vidacovich, bassist Jim Singleton, and saxophonist Alvin "Red" Tyler.

The first two days were a disaster. Booker refused to cooperate and generally behaved erratically.

"By the third day I was distraught," Scott Billington told me, "but I went in early—and there was Booker, ready to play. He had me come out of the booth and into the room and I sat next to him at the piano while he played all the material. It was astounding. He did the darkest version of 'Angel Eyes' maybe anyone has ever recorded. And basically that album came from that one day. I learned how delicate some people can be. No matter how talented [they are] you can't always just put 'em in front of a mic and tell them to do a great job. The spirituality or psychology is very much a big point.

"People talk about Professor Longhair, and he was great, but Booker had all of the music of the world in his ears and hands."

After that, Booker wandered off back into his private universe. Appropriately, his last live appearance was on Halloween night at the Maple Leaf. A week later he died in the corridor of Charity Hospital, after an apparently fatal dose of cocaine.

Louisiana Black and I made the pilgrimage to his grave. From the reporter's notebook:

I've seen uglier cemeteries in uglier places, but certainly not in New Orleans, which among other things has the most beautiful graveyards in America. We're trapped in [the suburb of] Metairie between a mobile home park and a railroad yard. Behind us is Airline Highway, junked up with used-car dealerships and dark under the threat of rain.

High up on a mausoleum wall in the back right corner of the graveyard is the morgue-style shelf that holds Booker's remains. The lettering is straight out of a hardware store, the sort you'd find stuck on the back of a pickup truck window that said, "CARPENTRY WORK DONE" or "ED TATE, PLUMBER." It reads JAMES CARROLL BOOKER, III. It's supposed to mean "the third," of course, but it looks as if he was the hundred-and-eleventh.

Standing around in the muddy grass, trying to figure out a way to get high enough in the air to take a usable picture, we realize that one of us has disturbed an ant pile and that swarms of the red demons have crawled into our shoes and up our ankles.

What a holy experience.

Probably most readers have never made roux before—and those not from the South probably don't even know what roux is. Roux (pronounced *roo*, by the way, as in what comes after "kanga") is a thickening agent made from slow-cooking lard and flour. Roux is a staple of southern cooking and perhaps the most vital ingredient in gumbo. Making proper roux isn't the easiest or quickest thing in the world to do, and this takes on added significance when you realize that **Antoine "Fats" Domino** (1928–) never toured without his own gumbo-making kit in the trunk or on the front seat of his Cadillac. Even when he was the biggest R&B star in the world—he's sold over 65 million records—and was on the road extensively, Domino always took the time to make his own gumbo—and a glance at his Santa Claus–like frame shows that he always took the time to eat his own gumbo, too.

Now ensconced in his gaudily regal enclave off St. Claude in New Orleans, Fats lives out of the spotlight. As Irma Thomas said when I asked her about him, "You mean the hermit?" She laughed. "Fats *used* to get out, he'd come to [my club] The Lion's Den and visit with my husband and me, but he's decided his career's done and he's happy with the decision. God bless him."

True, along the way, he made a fortune (he gambled some of it away over the years, living large as he did for a while during visits to Las Vegas), but has settled into being a sweet, home-happy guy; apparently he's content to relax with his wife, children, and grandkids, presumably padding around what I imagine is a large, state-of-the-art kitchen, eyeing his roux skillet with the scalpel-sharp eyes of a kestrel, slicing okra and andouille with heavenly glee.

From the reporter's notebook:

Louisiana Black and I are out in the Starsky-and-Hutch-mobile, driving toward St. Claude in search of Fats Domino's house, listening to WWOZ and sipping warm beers on a hot afternoon . . . WOW. I'm sure the Domino family is happy that we've pulled up out front, the better for me to jot this down rather than trying to write as Black negotiates the pothole-clustered streets.

The house is a sprawling ranch with bricks the color of those vanilla-creme wafer sandwiches. Surrounding is a white wrought-iron picket fence interwoven with vines and alternating yellow and pink roses. The drapes look like gold lamé, and adjoining is some sort of family business: FD Publishing reads the big yellow-and-black sign. There is no evidence of life; I don't know what I expected—Fats to jog out with some fresh-baked crawfish bread? Castle Fats doesn't seem particularly unapproachable, though it's not a great neighborhood and the property is surrounded mostly by boarded-up shotgun shacks. There is a nursery school across the street. Driving away towards the Saturn Bar, Black wonders if the nursery school kids know "Blueberry Hill."

Domino, of course, has earned his private and low-key kingdom; it's that easy-going approach to life, at once evident in any song he ever cut, that makes him such a special artist.

Born in New Orleans and active on the piano by the age of nine, Domino quit school at fourteen and worked in a mattress factory to facilitate playing nightclub gigs. His first work was with Billy Diamond's band in the Hideaway Lounge in his native Ninth Ward neighborhood. Influenced by the boogie-woogie style of such artists as Fats Waller and Albert Ammons, Domino was further schooled playing alongside Professor Longhair and Amos Milford.

As one story goes, producer Dave Bartholomew and visiting Imperial Records honcho Lew Chudd caught Domino at the Hideaway one night in 1949 and shrewdly realized that, while Domino's style was somewhat primitive, it was primitive in an utterly compelling way. They hustled Domino into Cosimo Matassa's studio and out of the first eight-song session came a single called "The Fat Man" (some argue this was the first rock 'n' roll song ever recorded). The tune, a structural takeoff of "Junker's Blues" and "Tipitina," was the first of many hits co-written by Domino and Bartholomew and, precisely because it sold over a million copies, became the record that established The New Orleans Sound.

I shall reiterate here that the difference between early rhythm & blues and early rock 'n' roll is that the latter was recorded by white guys after black guys had recorded the former (more about this in Part 5, Chapter 1). This means that the floodtide of Domino hits—"Goin' Home," "Every Night About This Time," "Goin' to the River," "My Blue Heaven," "I'm in Love Again," "Walkin' to New Orleans," "Blue Monday," "I'm Walkin'," "Ain't That a Shame," "Blueberry Hill," and "Valley of Tears" being just a sampling of instantly recognizable songs—that followed "The Fat Man" were frequently called R&B tunes despite their innate "rockness." And Domino *did* rock.

A perpetually rollicking player whose hammering right-handed triplets were anchored solidly by the boogying tempos of his left, Domino, who spoke French before he did English, sang with a Louisiana drawl that was simultaneously gleeful and lazy, and his music captured the early spirit of fun-blasted youth and the mild rebellion of the times.

"What was magic about Fats," Matassa told me, "was that, we'd be at a session and Dave [Bartholomew] would come in with a song he'd written or that he and Fats had done together, and you could just watch Fats listen to it and play with it—literally sitting at the piano and playing with it. Then he'd walk away, talk about it, and go *back* to the piano . . . and somewhere along the way—BAM!—it was *Fats!* It was *his* now, and it just sounded like Fats, note to note. And he did it over and over again; I must have seen it a thousand times."

It is also important to remember the sound of the records: They featured Bartholomew's warm and blasting sax-giddy arrangements and the terrific contributions of his house band. (Indeed, Domino was frequently so busy at the height of his fame that he didn't have time to do anything other than record his vocals; piano players such as James Booker often stepped in uncredited.)

When Imperial Records was sold in the early sixties, Domino switched labels to ABC–Paramount at about the same time the Beatles came along. (Not many people know that, in 1964, before the Beatles's New Orleans concert, Domino was ushered into their trailer, at which point they serenaded him with a version of "I'm in Love.") These two occurrences somewhat derailed the Fats Wagon, though he continued to sell with moderate power. By 1968, though, when psychedelics had tinted rock 'n' roll the color of a marmalade sky, Domino released a nicely received album called *Fats Is Back* (which included an imaginative arrangement of the Beatles's "Lady Madonna"), although he suspected the ride was over.

When a car accident during a 1970 tour killed one of his band members and injured two others, Domino seemed to take it as a sign, and he gracefully stepped back. Though he continued to play sporadically, and even record, he did it at his leisure and for his own purposes rather than at the crack of a record label's whip.

Domino still surfaces occasionally; for example, at the 1993 Montreux Jazz Festival in France. He performed a wildly successful hometown gig at the House of Blues in 1995, and encored for his own fiftieth anniversary show at the 1997 JazzFest. He also occasionally shows up at award ceremonies.

A comprehensive eight–CD boxed set, *Out of New Orleans*, contains Fats Domino's best work and is available from Germany's excellent Bear Family label.

In many ways, more than any other living artist, Malcolm "Mac" Rebennack—a.k.a. **Dr. John** (see also "The Music of Voodoo," Part 6, Chapter 1)—is the glue that holds Louisiana music together. A genius with a healthy musical curiosity and distinct persona, the Doctah has that ambassador's quality sported so iridescently by Louis Armstrong; this is to say he knows everyone and draws them together musically and otherwise for the greater good of the whole.

Mac Rebennack (1940–), as a sixteen-year-old hustler, was a musician who sought narcotics as passionately as he looked for session and club work. Born in New Orleans, he grew up in the Third Ward in a comfortable and close family and learned piano at a very early age. His dad owned an appliance store that was stocked with all styles of music—and young Mac expressed a keen interest in virtually all of it, from hillbilly to blues. As he got older, Mac started learning guitar. A family friend happened to be Cosimo Matassa, and he made it possible for Rebennack to hang out at the J&M Studios, watching sessions and running errands.

His teachers at Jesuit High School probably wished he was as fervent a student of scholastics as of the city's R&B scene. When rock 'n' roll landed with an audible thump on American shores, Rebennack blew school off permanently, settled for a correspondence-course diploma, and began scrounging gigs anywhere he could find them.

By his late teens, Mac was a sought-after session guitarist, a songwriter, an A&R man for Ace Records, and an all-around studio whiz. He was also busy playing the Gulf Coast club circuit when gunplay in a nightclub fight hit Mac in the finger and forced him to reconsider his guitar career. He returned to the piano and, with the help of compatriot James Booker and father-figure Professor Longhair, added substantive keyboard work to his repertoire.

After legal troubles over his narcotic appetites, Mac decided to leave New Orleans for a while; he followed friends out to Los Angeles, hoping for some session work. His buddy Harold Battiste, who hung out with a gang of expatriate New Orleans musicians, helped Mac with all sorts of nice session gigs and eventually arranged for the free studio time that evolved unexpectedly into what would become the Dr. John sound. The music was a refreshing, hauntingly drugged-out combination of Mardi Gras Indian music, spiritual church rhythms, and funky rock. And when in 1967 Atlantic agreed to release the album—*Gris-Gris*—it became necessary to create a stage vehicle for the Dr. John character. He designed the stage show as a cross between old minstrel shows, voodoo shtick, and what looked like a fire sale at a Mardi Gras Indian bar; the Dr. John character was based on a nineteenth-century Louisiana root doctor–voodoo traiteur.

With smoke and incense and snakes and dancing girls—and a bad-ass New Orleans rock 'n' rhythm band—Dr. John took off in a bigger way than he'd probably ever expected. Over a series of ensuing albums for Atlantic, Dr. John enjoyed rapt critical adulation from such rock royalty as Mick Jagger and Eric Clapton, and began gradually to expand the boundaries of his confining concept.

On such albums as *Babylon; The Sun, Moon and Herbs;* and *Gumbo,* he did a fine job incorporating his N'Awlins foundations into the confines of radio-friendly rock. Out of this period came the hits "Right Place, Wrong Time" and "Such a Night." Still, bored with the limited implications of rock proper and longing for a more distilled exploration of his hometown's music, Mac seized the opportunities afforded by fame. For the next two decades he recorded an all-over-the-landscape collection of records, the results admittedly varied. He's worked with orchestras, played solo piano, and explored everything from pop standards *(In a Sentimental Mood)* to hometown grooves *(Goin' Back to New Orleans)* to jazz *(Bluesiana Triangle* with Art Blakey and Fathead Newman, and *Duke Elegant)* and even alt-rock *(Anutha Zone).*

Some despaired the Doctor's often uneven and sometimes uninspired forays into the wilds of music, but when he hit, as on *Goin' Back to New Orleans* and *Anutha Zone,* he was brilliant. After sobering up at long last, Mac has entered into late middle age with an air of true dignity and wisdom. He speaks profoundly in an unmistakably original dialect all his own, and plays with sweet respect and profound ability.

From the reporter's notebook:

To watch him perform [in this case at a small nightclub called the Wolf Den in the Mohegan Sun Casino, Uncasville, Connecticut] *is to watch a man play piano for the love of the instrument and to pay homage not just to his hometown's unparalleled musical past, but to great music in general. A friend with me says this isn't what she expected; she thought he'd be some wild apparition out of a Mardi Gras hangover.*

I had to explain that he probably was—thirty years ago. And if his repertoire is predictable—I can't remember a time I've seen him when he didn't open with "Iko Iko"—well, I, too, wish he'd just cut loose and do some Booker and Fess and go nuts. But maybe that's stuff he does at home, in the privacy of his own study. I certainly like to think of him like that: capering with ghosts of heroes he actually knew and played with. Maybe it's all too private, too personal . . .

Another enormously talented piano player whose skills influenced a host of fine players, **Huey "Piano" Smith** (1934–), wrote whimsical songs—for example, "Rockin' Pneumonia and the Boogie Woogie Blues"—that were as infectious as they were zany. Born in New Orleans, Smith studied at the Grunewald School of Music, was influenced heavily by Professor Longhair, and by the time he was fifteen was gigging with Guitar Slim. Soon after, Smith began playing lucrative sessions and writing hit songs for other artists. His own voice left something to be desired but, on a package tour playing piano for Shirley & Lee, Smith decided to hook up with vocalist Bobby Marchan—and the Clowns were formed.

Their onstage show was wittily comic, the music tight and entertaining, and with hits such as "Pneumonia" and "Don't You Just Know It," Huey "Piano" Smith & the Clowns proved to be a popular live draw in the late fifties. *Having a Good Time* (Edsel Records) is a fine and representative sampling of Smith and the Clowns's best years.

Smith wrote and planned to record a tune with the Clowns called "Sea Cruise." But, though accounts of what happened differ, it seems safe to say that Smith and Marchand had argued and Ace Records's honcho Johnny Vincent, to whom Smith was signed, decided to have a young white vocalist named Frankie Ford sing the tune. The song was a hit. Smith was bitter; Ford remains confused about the situation and suggests, probably correctly, that he was just doing what he was told. Later, after Smith had left the label, Ace released another Smith tune with overdubbed vocals, "Do the Popeye"; this was a minor success and Smith *was* given credit.

But his best days were behind him. Smith stayed in the business for a while—he even started his own label—but eventually got heavily into drink and, later, religion.

Too often overlooked, probably because he recorded only one album in his long, rich life, is **Isadore "Tuts" Washington** (1907–1984). Born in New Orleans, he started playing piano at the age of ten and, with no lessons or instruction from anyone, always believed his talent was a gift from God.

By his teens, he was playing in top-flight Dixieland bands; he also worked solo, absorbing the blues magic of the barrelhouse pianists of the day. Soon, many players (younger *and* older) were looking up to Tuts, and among the younger artists he taught in his early years were Professor Longhair, James Booker, Fats Domino, and Smiley Lewis. Tuts claims he wrote a lot of Lewis's early material without getting credit, and scholars believe he's probably telling the truth.

Washington never sought out the recording studio himself; he preferred music in the live environment. For years he was the embodiment of the working-class New Orleans piano player who held down a lucrative gig at the Bayou Room in the Pontchartrain Hotel. In 1983, when he was seventy-six, he recorded the delightful *New Orleans Piano Professor* album for Rounder. It's a tantalizing record and makes one wonder what sort of legacy Washington might have left had he not been averse to the studio. When Washington died, he was appropriately playing onstage at the New Orleans World's Fair.

Jeff Hannusch, author of *I Hear You Knockin'*, told me: "Tuts was a rascal and a gentleman; just a great musician. He was the kind of guy who, even if he didn't have a gig, sat down and played the piano—and he was the last guy who needed to practice."

Of all the times I've seen **Eddie Bo** (1930–)—including the time when he headlined the annual Professor Longhair Tribute/WWOZ Benefit at Tipitina's Uptown in 2000, a pretty goddamned incinerating environment— my favorite performance happened by accident. Dr. Larry and I were escorting some New Orleans novices around the French Quarter on a mellow spring Friday afternoon during JazzFest 1999, and the sliding, garage-style doors at the Downtown Tipitina's were open to entice happy-hour drinkers. Onstage was Bo with his band, and though the crowd was sparse indeed, the music was scorching. Now in his early seventies, Bo, who resembles a cross between Ed Bradley and Redd Fox, has navigated the curious waters of a career in music with skill and self-control, and has come out a wise and philosophical man whose presence exudes a spiritual serenity.

That doesn't mean he can't rock the hell out of a piano, though, and indeed he did that afternoon. It was a virtuosic performance of classic New Orleans rhythm & blues piano and extemporaneous boogie woogie performed with such gusto and love that the few of us in the meager crowd were collectively overwhelmed with Bo and his band's enthusiasm.

"Eddie is the most infectiously rhythmic guy I've heard in person, ever," says musician Marcia Ball, "and he's such a nice guy. There's a thing about New Orleans: It's about education and sharing, and that's why New Orleans draws the players. Eddio Bo just exemplifies that to me."

He was born Edward Joseph Bocage, grew up in Algiers and the Ninth Ward, and after the service enrolled in the Grunewald School of Music. He started out as a jazz musician influenced by Oscar Peterson and Art Tatum. He also dug his mother's R&B stylings on the piano, as well as Professor Longhair, and like many of the city's jazz artists, he switched to R&B because of its lucrative session possibilities.

After polishing his chops on the club circuit, Bo signed with Ace Records, then Apollo, for whom he recorded the hit "I'm Wise." He also worked for the Chess and Ace record companies before hooking up with the Ric label, for whom he released numerous singles and served as a producer, arranger, session wizard, and songwriter. Among his popular tunes from that era are "Hey There Baby," "Tell It Like It Is," "It Must Be Love," "Every Dog Got His Day," and "Dinky Doo"—and eventually "Ask Mr. Popeye," his biggest hit, which was released in 1962 and spawned a national dance craze.

But when he realized that he could never move up to the truly successful level, Bo soured on the music business. He continued to record for a variety of small labels, but eventually his ire for the industry and its white honchos led him to form his own label, Bo-Sounds. He'd also become interested in the Muslim faith, and, curiously, spent years as a carpenter. He lived in Florida for many years, has remained deeply religious, and somewhere along the way achieved a peace that seems to embrace everyone and everything. He returned to New Orleans and jumped back into music as a revered elder statesman—and it's a joy to behold his work and energy. *Nine Yards of Funk* was released a few years ago on Bo's own label; containing fiery and full-band material, it includes the second-linish "Jukin'," the creeping "Black Cat Bone," and the easy-flowing "Driftin' in the Breeze."

If there's ever been a society closed to females, it's probably been R&B piano, whether by design or otherwise. To be sure, blueswoman Katie Webster could hammer the keys, but of the modernists, **Marcia Ball** (1950–), who was born in Orange, Texas, and grew up in Vinton, Louisiana, is certainly the finest.

A bipartite musician who lives in Austin and has claimed New Orleans as home, Ball grew up learning piano in a family atmosphere with a supportive grandmother who could play her ass off. A literature major at Louisiana State University, Ball became seduced by nightclub and honky-tonk music, started singing with a roommate, and began to channel her piano skills into country and blues gigs. Before long, Ball, whose wonderful voice and spongelike ability to distill the influences of the 6/8 Gulf Coastisms and Professor Longhair, coalesced her favorite sounds into a unique style. She signed a short-lived contract with Capitol, which tried to pigeonhole her into country with the *Circuit Queen* album; but shortly after she signed with the estimable Rounder label and has since released a decade-and-a-half's worth of extraordinary records. These include *Hot Tamale Baby, Let Me Play with Your Poodle, Soulful Dress, Gatorhythms,* and *Blue House.*

Whether reworking an obscure bit of classic R&B or writing her own clever material, Ball uses her evocative voice and ten nimble fingers. Totally at home in any honky tonk with a piano, she is one of the supreme babes in contemporary rhythm & blues.

Ball and that other R&B lady, Irma Thomas, with pal Tracy Nelson, released *Sing It!* in 1998, a delectable hash of soul, neogospel balladry, and second-line funk; conceptually it mirrored an earlier Ball collaboration with Texas blues singers Lou Ann Barton and Anglea Strehli called *Dreams Come True*. Goes to show that Ball is not just talented; she makes friends easily.

On the social and cultural interaction and tolerance in the musical community, Ball told me, "My cousin, who is not a musician and who fights the race battle daily with rednecks, points out to me that we musicians do not live in the real world. She's right; we live in a wonderful world. . . . I just think for the most part musicians can't be racist. It doesn't make any sense in *any* area, but musicians seem instinctively to know it. Once you get into the music, the other stuff just doesn't make any difference."

You can probably count on one hand the New Orleanians who, despite summer days where the sun bleeds heat, enjoy an afternoon cup of hot tea. But **Jon Cleary** (1964–) is probably one of them. Now in his midthirties, Cleary came to the city several years ago from England to experience the music of New Orleans he'd grown up loving through the record collection and anecdotes of an uncle who'd lived in the Big Easy. At the airport, he ordered the taxi driver to take him straight to the Maple Leaf Bar, where he had his first Dixie beer and was quickly hired to paint the joint. The job stretched out for months, allowing him to absorb the sounds of the city.

Cleary never set out to be a professional in a town full of them. "I never took [playing piano] seriously," he told me. "I was doing it for a laugh until I actually got hired to play it. New Orleans kinda blew my mind, really, and introduced me to a lot of stuff I'd only heard on record before. So I ended up doing all kinds of jobs to get by just so I could go home and play the piano."

His worshipful and diligent approach paid off. A pianist who plays with the fire of the converted and the intelligence of a free-spirited artist, he learned everything from Booker and Professor Longhair to Dr. John to Little Feat and Robert Palmer. His backing band, the Absolute Monster Gentlemen, is comprised of guitarist Derwin "Big D" Perkins, bassist Cornell Williams, and drummer Jeffrey "Jellybean" Alexander.

Cleary received further education during a two-year stint in Walter "Wolfman" Washington's band, has toured extensively in Bonnie Raitt's band, recorded with Junior Wells and Bobby Charles, worked with Taj Mahal, and in 1998 released with the Gentlemen his major label debut CD, the terrifically infectious *Moonburn*. An earlier indie effort, *Alligator Lips and Dirty Rice* (picked up for distribution in 1990) is a great disc if you can find it.

Davell Crawford (1975–) has superb bloodlines; his grandpa, "Sugar Boy" Crawford, wrote the oft-covered "Jockomo." It's not surprising, then, that Davell turned into a musical giant himself. Young Crawford inhaled the intricacies of the piano like a thirsty man going through a Barq's, and by the age of twenty had released his first gospel-teased funk album, *Let Them Talk*, on the prestigious Rounder label no less. His playing is instinctually assured, and his appetites seem to bound with equal abandon between blues, jazz, R&B, and gospel. Subsequent CDs—*B–3 and Me, Born with the Funk*, and the most recent, *Love Like Yours & Mine*—are as dazzling as they are multifaceted. *Love Like Yours & Mine* almost moves into Harry Connick Jr. territory, covering everything from "Fly Me to the Moon" to the Beatles's "Let It Be." It helps that Crawford has an emotionally charged voice that he puts to good use, particularly on ballads. It all comes together live, too. I saw him in a sultry afternoon set at the 2000 JazzFest, backed by his brothers-in-arms band, and he was stunningly good. My wife thought he was hot, too, and had movie-star good looks.

Plenty of other young, aspiring piano masters are lurking, many of whom I saw at the 2000 WWOZ Piano Night/Professor Longhair Tribute at Tipitina's. There were some big names, of course, including Bo, Ball, Crawford, and Cleary, but chief among the youngsters was **Tom McDermott,** a St. Louis–born magician who moved to New Orleans years ago and, by way of improving his piano skills, set about more or less to learn the complete James Booker canon. But he's developed into far more than a one-artist jukebox. Though the Bookerisms abound, McDermott is very much his own man. His solo CD, *All the Keys and Then Some*, and his work with such diverse acts as the New Orleans Nightcrawlers and the Dukes of Dixieland show incredible range.

Joe Krown is another notable transplant to New Orleans. As fluent on organ as he is piano, Krown has a regular gig with Clarence "Gatemouth" Brown, works with his own Joe Krown Organ Combo, and is the honored guy who works the Traditional Piano Night every week at the Maple Leaf Bar. Check out any of his CD work: *Buckle Up, Down & Dirty*, and the superb *Just the Piano . . . Just the Blues*.

Joshua Paxton and **Nelson Lunding** are also staggering talents. Lunding frequently plays with his band, Blues in the Pocket, with whom he's released the CD *Whiskey & a Beer to Go*. Paxton does plenty of solo gigs and has contributed to the perpetration of the form with incisive magazine articles on James Booker, a transcription in book form of Professor Longhair songs *(The Professor Longhair Collection)*, and session work for the Afghan Whigs.

Two

SINGERS
AND HITMAKERS

*F*or years the Neville Brothers have been the traditional second week-end, Sunday afternoon show-closers at JazzFest, and of the dozens of times I've seen them, they played the best set ever as the finale to the 1991 soiree. By the end of their performance, which, as I recall, was their take on Bob Marley's "One Love," the massed thousands in front of the Ray-Ban stage were in a patchouli-scented snake dance of joy—and Satan himself couldn't have found a bad vibe anywhere in the fairgrounds. They rocked—and at that moment all the hype they've enjoyed over the years about being the best live band on the planet was justified. (This was not the only time I made that judgment, either; it's just the particular experience imprinted itself on me as one of life's singularly great events.)

I mention this as a precursor to this section because the Nevilles are a uniquely famous example of a Louisiana vocal tradition that highlights the great soul and R&B singers, another wonderfully rich area of the state's musical past.

In retrospect, it seems as if it took the Neville Brothers a long time to figure out that, given their respective talents, it would be a sensible idea to play together. After all, they are the poster guys for contemporary New Orleans soul-funk, a sort of Olympian four-man relay team sprinting with a baton they've inherited from the generation that included Professor Longhair, Fats Domino, and Huey "Piano" Smith.

But the Brothers Neville had some other stuff to get out of the way first. They came from a musically curious family—five of the six children play instruments or sing—though neither parent was a musician. Amelia, their mother, had been part of a dance team with her brother, the boys' Uncle George "Big Chief Jolly" Landry. Their father, Arthur Neville Sr., a hard-laboring blue-collar guy who worked on the waterfront and for the post office, occasionally went on fishing trips with Smiley Lewis, so perhaps a bit of musical magic was infused to the kiddos in that fashion.

Art (1937–) is the oldest of the brothers, and he grew up enamored of street corner doo-wop and early R&B. The family lived on Valence Street in the Uptown Thirteenth Ward and moved during the 1940s to the Calliope projects. Regardless of their surroundings, they enjoyed a collective affection for music and education, and the brothers tried to replicate the sounds of popular singing groups of the time as they entertained at house parties or sang on street corners.

By 1954, Art led a band called the Hawketts (with drummer John Boudreaux and George Davis on sax), who spun out a little ditty called "Mardi Gras Mambo," now certainly one of the two or three perennial carnival anthems. Art, who was blessed with a smoky baritone even as a teen, was tapped by Specialty Records as a solo artist; he released a few regional faves, including "Cha Dooky-Doo" and "Ooh Wee Baby," before jumping to Instant for 1962's "All These Things."

Charles (1938–) was the second, and he gravitated towards blues and jazz and wanderlust. He became proficient at saxophone early on and pinballed back and forth to Memphis where he worked with artists from Big Joe Turner and Johnny Ace to Bobby "Blue" Bland and Willie Mae Thornton. In New Orleans, he played with such as folks like Ernie K-Doe and James Booker and basically scored an incomparable musical education.

The third brother, **Aaron** (1935–), learned that he possessed a special voice when he sang ballads and soul tunes to combat the drudgery of various blue-collar jobs. He's often joked that he knew at birth he had a gift when the doctor spanked him and that magical falsetto spun forth—and it's true that Aaron was still a teenager when he released a single called "Over You" in 1959. He continued to dabble in song until 1966, when he temporarily hit big with the timeless ballad "Tell It Like It Is," though corporate shenanigans not only deprived him of any profits but also the momentum to generate a career.

The youngest Neville, **Cyril** (1948–), is quick to point out that he's essentially of a different generation than his siblings, and he's right. By the time he was in his teens, his temperament and social ideas were solidifying in a more militant direction, though he was just as intrinsically musical as his older brothers. He learned drums and percussion and was starting to gig in bands at the time Art, Charles, and Aaron worked together briefly in Art Neville and the Neville Sounds.

Just after that, Art and the rhythm section of the Neville Sounds split off and became the Meters, with Leo Nocentelli on guitar, George Porter Jr. on bass, and Zigaboo Modeliste on drums. Out of the Meters loop, Charles headed on to New York City, where he played jazz and experimented with such creative outlets as playwriting; he ended up teaching college in Vermont. Aaron, who was exploring various musical styles from gospel to hillbilly and trying to build on the success of "Tell It Like It Is," hooked up with Cyril in an outfit called the Soul Machine, a group that worked clubs doing contemporary R&B covers. But after the Soul Machine failed to make it in Memphis and New York City, Cyril went over to the Meters. They'd been booked to open the Rolling Stones's 1974 American tour, and Cyril, with his highly visual persona and distinctive percussive seasonings, brought a lot to the table.

Despite their vast experimentation with song, the Neville brothers weren't noted for their community spirit at that point. Drugs and crime came into play throughout the early years, and there was a bit of jail time doled out while they were respectively building their careers. Everyone but Art had problems with drug addiction, and Aaron scored his notorious "dagger" tattoo—the one etched in sinister fashion on his cheek—from a bit of lock-up cosmetic surgery during a stretch for auto theft. Charles received five years in Louisiana's Angola State Prison for possessing two joints—a goofily strict sentence that was unfortunately indicative of the time. He eventually served three-and-a-half years and, not surprisingly, jail had a profound effect on his worldview.

Crime aside, though, in 1976, with both their parents now dead, the Nevilles began to share a collective focus. The brothers cleaned up (Cyril credits the music of Bob Marley for his own spiritual and wake-up call) and convened at the request of their uncle, Mardi Gras Indian Chief George Landry, a.k.a. Big Chief Jolly, to record the **Wild Tchoupitoulas** project (more about this in "The Mardi Gras Indians and Carnival Tunes," Part 6, Chapter 3), an early attempt to fuse the Fat Tuesday chants of the Mardi Gras Indian tribes with second-line Crescent City R&B.

Comprised of the four Neville brothers—Aaron, Cyril, Art, and Charles—along with the rest of the Meters and various vocal members of Jolly's Wild Tchoupitoulas, the sessions were produced by Allen Toussaint and his partner, Marshall Sehorn, in their Sea-Saint studios (discussed earlier in this chapter). The tunes were wildly infectious, mostly Indian chants written for carnival by Big Chief Jolly and arranged by Art and Charles with a Caribo–second line complement of R&B groove. Tossed in to the album for empathetic flavoring were Cyril's "Brother John" and the Meters's staple, "Hey Pocky A-Way." *The Wild Tchoupitoulas* was released by the Island label in 1976 and remains a cure-all for glum moods or bad luck. To be sure, many of the words are the nonsensical-but-compelling phraseology of the Mardi Gras Indians (discussed in more detail in "The Mardi Gras Indians and Carnival Tunes," Part 6, Chapter 3). But that's part of the fun. Even the jewel-box liner notes are unforgettable, showing the Tchoups dressed in their day-glo, feather-and-bead Fat Tuesday finery.

Big Chief Jolly realized that each of his nephews brought a different ingredient to the musical gumbo. Imagine Big Chief Jolly as Emeril. He takes Charles for the cerebral aspects, Aaron for That Voice, Art for the soul, and Cyril for the conscience. Bam! A melange of flavors the world has never tasted before—and the Big Chief knew it. The unique vocal harmonies provided hot sauce for the dish.

That energy and spirit must've blown like a sweet wind through the Neville brothers, too, for gradually the four officially convened as **The Neville Brothers**. Capitol Records signed them and in 1978 released their self-titled first album. *The Neville Brothers* didn't sound like them—it was too slick and neo-disco—and it didn't sell well, either. Three years later, Nevilles devotee Bette Midler implored her producer, Joel Zorn, to record the group. They signed with A&M and in 1981 came out with *Fiyo on the Bayou*, a wonderful amalgam of their varied influences, all simmered together. From honeyed doo-wop ("The Ten Commandments of Love") to slick soul ("Sweet Honeydripper") to Aaron's taking on Nat King Cole ("Mona Lisa") to the pure, humid voodoo of their after-midnight funk (fresh versions of "Hey Pocky Way" and "Brother John," the latter segueing into perhaps the definitive version of the carnival anthem "Iko Iko" (discussed later in this chapter; also, see "The Mardi Gras Indians and Carnival Tunes," Part 6, Chapter 3), the Nevilles for the first time displayed their true potential.

Unfortunately, *Fiyo* sold poorly, and the Neville Brothers lost their record deal. Gigs with the Rolling Stones fueled all sorts of recording rumors, but instead they released two live albums for the hometown Black Top and Spindletop labels (1984's *Live Nevillization* and 1987's *Nevillization 2*, respectively, now represented on Rhino's 1982 *Live at Tipitina's*). They are most notable for Aaron's rendition of the ballad "Wildflower," and both albums are well worth owning.

The Neville Brothers's live reputation was starting to spread when they still dazzled crowds with mid-show sets dressed as the Wild Tchoupitoulas. Thousands of white college kids came onboard during those years, captivated as much by costumes as by the addictive groove, which hinted of a mysterious New Orleans culture having nothing to do with puking hurricanes in Pat O'Brien's.

In 1987, the band got another major label deal (EMI) and released *Uptown*, an album widely vilified for its ultra-crisp production and sterile disco flavorings. Two years later, when they'd hopped labels again, this time to A&M, they hooked up with atmospheric producer Daniel Lanois to create one of the greatest records ever, by anyone at any time. *Yellow Moon* is almost perfect.

Much of the credit goes to Lanois; his eerie, predawn swamp feel and the sinister voodoo rhythms create a seductive aural incense. But just as important were the brothers. Whether on Neville-generated material or shrewdly chosen cover tunes, they created a cohesive document that addressed a myriad of social concerns, as well as such time-honored musical anxieties as female trouble, and indigenous experiences such as Mardi Gras.

Throughout, the Nevilles and their awesome road band—drummer "Mean" Willie Green, bassist Tony Hall, and guitarist Brian Stoltz—were superb. The record ultimately went platinum and made year-end "Best Of" lists across the United States. The Neville Brothers, always respected, were suddenly successful, too. True, Aaron would skyrocket his way to million-seller status later the same year on the strength of four duet numbers with chanteuse Linda Ronstadt for her *Cry Like a Rainstorm, Howl Like the Wind* album. The radio and video airplay for the single "Don't Know Much" broke-out Aaron—and helped break his brothers—in a huge way.

Though that was a decade ago, the Brothers haven't reunited with Lanois. In an interview a few years back, Charles told me that it was simply a matter of conflicting schedules. In any case, despite what appears to be a concrete following, the Brothers haven't enjoyed the same critical or commercial success since, regardless of a fine succession of albums. The immediate follow up, *Brother's Keeper* (1990, A&M) was coproduced by the band with Malcolm Burn, who had essentially trained under Lanois and carried to the table a similar sense of evocative space. Highlights include Art's weary and sad spoken-word recitation of street violence on "Falling Rain," the infectious anthems of "River of Life" and "Brother Jake," and the prayerful "Jah Love" and "Steer Me Right."

Three studio CDs have followed since, spaced around various compilations and a superb in-concert document called *Live on Planet Earth* (1994, A&M). In order they are: *Family Groove* (1992, A&M), *Mitakuye Oyasin Oyasin—All My Relations* (1996, A&M), and *Valence Street* (1999, Columbia). They have also produced an autobiography together, called *The Brothers* (co-written with David Ritz and published by Little, Brown in 2000).

The Nevilles's place as a low-key national force appears secure, and their place as New Orleans royalty seems an inalienable right. In December of 1999, the Nevilles were awarded the Mayor's Medal of Honor in their hometown, which is assuredly a long way from grand theft auto or drug possession. They'll play the honored farewell set at JazzFest as long as they're physically able, and there's a certain sense of security in knowing the Neville Brothers are, at any time, in one configuration or another, somewhere on Mother Earth, bringing us all that wondrous Creole Funk.

Art, Cyril, Charles, and Aaron, of course, continue their various solo projects when not heeding the umbrella call of the Neville Brothers proper. Aaron and That Voice are probably the most high-profile. Since the Ronstadt duets brought him to national fame, he's released numerous big-label solo CDs. 1991's *Warm Your Heart* is one of my favorites, though all his collections are redolent with his musical curiosity; his fascination with country and gospel-spiritual tunes take equal billing with his pop tendencies. Other recommended efforts include *The Tattooed Heart, Grand Tour* (featuring a superb reading of the George Jones–associated title track), and *Soulful Christmas.*

Charles has always been a jazz enthusiast, and his solo efforts seem firmly rooted in the jazz experimentation first realized in his New York City days. Back in New Orleans, he first formed Charles Neville & Diversity, a post-bop outfit that released a seductive, self-titled (and reasonably hard to find) album in 1990. The band included two saxes, a guitar, and a string section and they swung through a history of standards and pop. Diversity metamorphosed into various units—the Charles Neville Quartet and the Charles Neville Jazz Ensemble, in particular—and work came steadily in New Orleans's premier jazz clubs. Charles's most recent release, *Safe in Buddha's Palm*, features a premium of original material played with passion and a swinging style.

Cyril Neville is perhaps the most active civically. In addition to producing and recording a variety of family, friends, and side-band albums, including his reggae-toasted Uptown All-Stars and solo CDs (*The Fire This Time, Soulo*, and the tribute to community, *New Orleans Cookin'*), he runs his own record label, Endangered Species, and is in partnership with Tipitina's in a variety of beneficial ways, including the New Orleans Music and Culture Preservatory. A man of the city and its music, he recommends this list of Louisiana music:

> You'd definitely have some Louis; some Pops. Danny Barker's gotta be in there. And Papa Celestin and King Oliver. AFO Records if you could find all of the stuff in the catalog. A mixture of the jazz of the time: Ellis Marsalis's Quartet, Barbara George and Dr. John, James Black . . .
>
> And then you'd have to have Professor Longhair—but to really understand Fess properly you'd have to have Tuts [Washington] and Huey Smith and Fats [Domino]. Louis Prima and Keely Smith.
>
> And then I'd say try to get as much stuff from the fifties and sixties—boxed sets from Specialty Records and Minit Records and the anthologies of the singles called *Creole Kings* going from one era to another: Allen Toussaint, Robert Parker, the Meters . . .
>
> [He laughs.] . . . Well, another would be the Wild Magnolias's *The Call Is Wild*. You need *The Wild Tchoupitoulas*. You gotta get your Dr. John in there. And, to cleanse the palate, you need Jesse Hill.

And speaking of food, "You gotta go to Nora's Creole Kitchen. It's got anything you could possibly name; Nora is the kind of person who will come up with something special. It's not far from Jazzland. I'll tell you what I've had from there: she does lamb chops and several shrimp dishes and she has something called Ricky Chicken after [New Orleans Saints running back Ricky] Williams."

Art's primary extra-Neville activities center around the perpetation of the **Meters,** the band that laid the foundation of modern New Orleans funk—

and also the group that broke the music outside the boundaries of Orleans Parish. Formed in 1967, the original Meters might be thought of as a wonderfully successful chemistry experiment.

"I think New Orleans in its finer parts is a bunch of small communities—we call 'em wards—and in each one a small musical mecca is going on," a jovial George Porter explained to me one January afternoon in a protracted phone conversation. "The Meters brought four of them together and created a gumbo."

Porter grew up in a household where his father dug jazz players Sonny Stitt, Dexter Gordon, and Stanley Turrentine. George studied guitar; but when he walked by the home of bassist Benjamin Francis, who played on the porch, spinning great, thick grooves into the air, he was bewitched by the bass. Porter mastered it and the concept of "the pocket"—the groove—and in his late teens, when he was working for Earl King, he met Art Neville, who was then playing with the Hawkettes.

George struck up a friendship with Zigaboo Modeliste, a neighbor and second cousin who had scored a three-piece drum kit from his grandmother. His hero—in a ward stuffed with great drummers—was Joe "Smokey" Johnson, a one-time member of the Hawkettes and a session guy at Cosimo Matassa's studio. Modeliste had a unique acumen for the drums, so much so that, when he was in the seventh grade, Art Neville asked him to join the Hawkettes. The kid wasn't quite good enough at that point, but, after practice, he began to back Irma Thomas, Tommy Ridgley, and Deacon John.

Leo Nocentelli grew up in the Irish Channel. His father, who played banjo in the Louisiana Black Devil Band, gave young Leo a cheap ukelele and, when the kid was twelve, a guitar. Within a year he was playing with Honey Boy Otis and Melvin Lastie and, by fourteen, was backing Otis Redding and Clyde McPhatter. Then he joined the Hawketts. By that point, the Hawk thing had pretty much played out, so when Neville came across Porter, he decided to start a new group, Art Neville and the Neville Sounds, bringing Nocentelli and Modeliste along. Also in the band were vocalist Cyril Neville and saxophonist Gary Brown, but within two years the lineup had been pared down to just Art, Porter, Nocentelli, and Modeliste.

The band's funkiness took hold at once during a six-night-a-week residency at the Ivanhoe club on Bourbon Street. Unlike traditional soul or R&B bands, the Meters preferred to let each of the four musicians go anywhere at any time instead of forcing the bass and drums to hold down the fort. They played screwed-tight, riff-happy instrumentals that bubbled with a sense of impending explosion. While such a free-form approach might have been disastrous in any other format, the guys in the Meters had an innate sense of groove, instinctively keeping the pocket solid even as the players pinwheeled off into intoxicating orbits.

They worked prestige studio gigs (Lee Dorsey, Earl King, Chris Kenner) for Allen Toussaint and Marshall Sehorn at their Sansu Enterprises. When the band cut some of their own instrumentals, Sehorn took the tapes to New York where he scored a contract with Josie Records. Despite a perceived lack of enthusiasm from the music community at large, the Meters's first four singles clocked in the Top 100—"Sophisticated Cissy" (#34, 1969), "Cissy Strut" (#23, 1969), "Look-Ka Py Py" (#11, 1969), and "Chicken Strut" (#11, 1970). The group also cut three superb albums in two years: *The Meters, Look-Ka Py Py,* and *Struttin'.*

In 1972, the Meters signed with Reprise Records, thanks in part to their burgeoning, underground reputation amongst famous and rich musicians as *the* bad-ass backing band on the planet. Paul McCartney & Wings, Dr. John, King Biscuit Boy, and Robert Palmer are among the artists who sought out the Meters for session work. The Rolling Stones, who have always championed relatively obscure artists, handpicked the Meters to open their 1975 American and 1976 European tours.

Of the Meters's Reprise years, *Cabbage Alley* and *Fire on the Bayou* are favorites; the latter, released in 1976, heralded a new era for the band in that Cyril Neville again joined up as a vocalist and percussionist. But the Meters, plagued by business difficulties, a few internal riffs, and drug and alcohol problems, soon went on hiatus.

Their legacy over twelve years and ten albums is still being calculated. Every time a new funk band starts, particularly in the Crescent City, or a hip-hop act samples a Meters groove—the Meters are probably the most sampled band in the history of rap and hip-hop—their influence and importance clicks up a notch.

"Growing up in New Orleans, I was certainly unaware of anything special going on," Porter said. "I thought Mardi Gras happened everywhere—not just us. I think we *did* realize the Meters were special. There were some stressful moments toward the end because Art and Zig were getting along less and less. But when we were on, there was always that pocket and at the same time things were always on the [musical] edge. We'd be going off but there was always the basic groove; we'd hit these little turnarounds I call ditties. We'd hit one out of nowhere and I'd smile and say, 'Yeeaaaah!' It gives me chills thinking about it."

In 1989, after a relaxed jam at JazzFest, the core unit of the band regrouped as the **Funky Meters;** only Modeliste was missing. Young honcho Russell Batiste Jr.—a member of the royal New Orleans musical family and an atypically hot drummer who'd played with Harry Connick Jr., Allen Toussaint, and Robbie Robertson—took the chair. In 1994, Nocentelli amicably split, and former Neville Brothers guitarist Brian Stoltz segued into the lineup with ease.

Though the band hasn't released any material yet, Porter assures us it's inevitable. "The Funky Meters have product," he said. "We've got a number of songs we've recorded that we're sending out to test the waters. We've got management and they're sending out about fourteen songs to prospective buyers. The chances of there being a new Funky Meters album is definitely better than it was a year ago."

In the meantime, Porter has, for years, been the guiding force behind one of New Orleans's finest funk outfits, George Porter Jr. and Runnin' Pardners, whose debut CD, *Funk'n'Gonuts*, came out at JazzFest 2000. Comprised of Porter, Batiste, guitarist Brint Anderson, and keyboardists John Gros and Michael Lemmler, Runnin' Pardners mines, as one would expect, Metersesque territory, but with a distinctive twist. More attention is paid to vocals, with Anderson and Porter taking turns, and the songs have a sense of lyrical fun and adventure often absent from the Meters, where singing frequently takes a back seat to the music.

Modeliste played with Ron Wood and Keith Richards in the New Barbarians, and later relocated to Berkeley, California, where he remains musically active conducting clinics, doing sessions, and playing with his Zigaboo Modeliste New Aahkesstra. In the spring of 2000, he released his first solo CD, *Zigaboo.com*. Modeliste is one of the most influential of today's New Orleans drummers. His innate sense of syncopation, borne of the second-line parade rhythms at a time when the subgenre "funk" was evolving from R&B, is as regular as clockwork.

In the fall of 2000, the original Meters reunited for one gig in San Francisco. Historical? Sure, but none of them made it out to be such a big deal. It was a good opportunity, and life goes on for Modeliste and for the guys in the Funky Meters. As for history, they'll always have history.

"If you come from New Orleans and you haven't been influenced by the Meters, then I don't know what to tell you," Cyril said. "You walk in that city and you hear [the Meters]. You're breathing it. It's in the air and water, it's from the soul and heart. But it wasn't the Meters that put it there. They just *harnessed* it—the way a lot of musicians have. And not just the musicians; if you *live* there, you got it."

If the Nevilles and the Meters are the greatest of the modern New Orleans R&B groups, it shouldn't be forgotten that the city's scene has always boasted wonderful vocalists. A lot of them are gone now—Johnny Adams and Tommy Ridgley in the last few years—but it's still possible to see legends perform.

In Mid-City, at 2655 Gravier, around the corner from a bail bonds joint, is the Lion's Den, a friendly neighborhood bar and home turf of New Orleans soul queen **Irma Thomas** (1941–). Thomas, who owns the place with her husband, Emile Jackson, runs it more like a Cub Scout den mother than a bar owner. One can envision setting up pup tents, staying up all night, and eating enormous amounts of the red beans and rice and smoked sausage that Thomas herself prepares and sets out in generously apportioned, sterno-driven bins for free sampling by patrons.

The lounge is dimly lit in a comfortably lambent way—not pitch black like the French Quarter wino bars, where no one wants to see the denizens (and where certainly the drinkers themselves don't want to be visible). The Lion's Den bar, shaped like a backwards *J*, fronts a small entry area where the well-stocked juke box sits alongside a table piled with Irma Thomas merchandise. Follow the *J* around and you're in the "backroom" area where the red-carpeted stage angles across the far corner. Kitchen chairs are set up, revival tent–style, in anticipation of a crowd.

The employees are the friendliest people in the solar system. The beer is cheap and cold, and I'm greeted with "There's some free beans and rice and sausage over there—you're welcome to as much of it as you'd like. We think it's pretty good."

It's Sunday night, the first weekend of JazzFest, and Thomas and her band, The Professionals, can bank on sold-out crowds of regulars and visitors for both of the two shows they'll play each weekend night for the duration of the festival. I am indeed seated at the bar with a plate of red beans and rice, and a happy drunk guy, sixtyish, wanders over to assure me, jabbing his finger wildly at the sounds emanating powerfully from the jukebox, "Thass Aaron Neville! Thass . . . Aaron . . . *Neville!*"

A short while later, fresh beer in hand and a new heap of red beans on my lap (but only because the waitress gently chided me: "You only had *one* plate? I'm gonna tell Irma you didn't like it"), I watch as The Professionals file in with their instruments and begin those rituals indigenous to working musicians. They're wearing black jeans or slacks and black Irma Thomas T-shirts, except the keyboardist, who wears a white one. The seats have filled up quickly, and soon enough the band launches into a bit of instrumental fanfare before the announcement is made that it's time for the Soul Queen of New Orleans—and Irma walks around the bar from the entry area and smoothly glides onto the stage.

Though she is indeed a regal presence, there's a comforting dichotomy to her shimmering persona: for every bit of starry electricity she generates, and it's a lot, she emanates a homey kindness as well. This is a queen, all right, but one who doesn't mind telling you that her feet hurt after a long day. As she takes the mike with a tired but full-blast smile, she is superbly genuine. When a grade school kid approaches her with a song request his dad has scrawled on a cocktail napkin, she looks at the youngster happily and explains how she might have to fake that particular choice—that it's been a while since she or the Professionals have even thought of the song. So she performs another song perfectly, all the while flipping through the phonebook-thick song catalog on the music stand to one side as she tries to find the requested tune. She doesn't, but that's okay; the attempt is so effortlessly . . . *Irma* that everyone is charmed and the kid walks away with a crush on a fifty-something nightclub singer who bears little resemblance to the Christina Aguilera pinups he's got on his wall.

Thomas was pinup material in her teens, which is when she got started not only in the music business but also in the having-kids business. Born about an hour north of New Orleans in Ponchatoula, Thomas grew up in the Crescent City, singing in church and school talent shows. She made her first recording when she and Henry Carbo (brother of Spiders Chuck and Chick Carbo) sang their class song at Cosimo Matassa's studio.

She became pregnant when she was fourteen, got married, left school, and went to work in a restaurant washing dishes—where her singing bothered customers so much that she was fired. Her first marriage ended soon after, as did a second job as a waitress in the Pimlico Club, when she sat in with singer Tommy Ridgley's band. Ridgley asked her to join his band, then introduced her to Joe Ruffino at Ron Records, for whom she cut two tunes. One was a clever Dorothy LaBostrie number "(You Can Have My Husband but Please) Don't Mess with My Man," which Thomas tattooed as her personal property in a sizzling performance that became a hit. In many ways it is still her signature song—something she trots out every night with a gracious good humor.

Thomas moved over to the Minit label, had another hit with Jesse Hill's "Ooh Papa Doo," and, perhaps more fortuitously, met Allen Toussaint, a kindred spirit who set out to write original material for Thomas that reflected the pain and joys of her experiences: "Ruler of My Heart" (later a huge hit for Otis Redding), "Wish Someone Would Care," and "It's Raining" among them. When Toussaint joined the service, Thomas signed with Imperial and scored hugely with "Time Is on My Side"—yeah, later recorded by the Rolling Stones.

With the British Invasion came a changing of the guard in radio and record sales; combined with the devastation of Hurricane Camille, the Gulf Coast music biz was in disarray by 1970. Thomas relocated for a time to Oakland, where she worked at a Montgomery Ward and recorded ineffectual sides for a variety of small labels. In the mid-seventies, she returned to Louisiana, signed with Rounder and, along with other New Orleans artists, seems to have grown comfortable with the way things are. She has her club, her family, her church, her charities, her bowling night, her red-beans-and-rice recipe; she's secure in the knowledge that she's a true goddess in her hometown and makes wonderful records (among them *The New Rules, Simply the Best Live, True Believer, Story of My Life*, the gospel collection *Walk Around Heaven*, the collaborative *Sing It!* with Marcia Ball and Tracy Nelson, and the pretty terrific *My Heart's in Memphis—the Songs of Dan Penn*).

"I'm not comparing, but before they gave Aretha Franklin the title 'Queen of Soul,' Irma was the Queen of Soul," Cyril Neville told me. "Some of my favorite New Orleans songs are hers—'Ruler of My Heart,' and 'Breakaway.' Some of my vocal antics I got from Irma, but you know what I like about her? She's one of the nicest people you'd ever want to meet."

Among Thomas's contemporaries were Johnny Adams and Tommy Ridgley, both of whom died recently and both of whom—like Thomas—were around so long that they could fit comfortably in either the pioneer R&B chapter or the moderns chapter. Because their careers carried on until today, they are included here.

Johnny Adams (1930–1998) was called the Tan Canary. And no less than Cosimo Matassa said, "Johnny sang like an angel. He was the best. Aaron [Neville] has a marvelous, really great voice. But he doesn't have the range of expression Johnny had. [Johnny] could do jazz, he could do blues, he could do country. . . . The times conspired against him, I guess. About the time he showed up and started singing, we weren't doing much in the record world."

Adams was a remarkable talent—a dignified, slender, sharply dressed guy who vocally tap danced between musical genres with liquid and heartfelt ease. He was born in New Orleans and began his career singing gospel with the Soul Revivers and then Bessie Griffin and the Consolators, shifting to secular music when he was about twenty-five. As the story goes, New Orleans songwriter Dorothy Labostrie—the writer who penned Irma Thomas's "You Can Have My Husband" and who came up with G-rated lyrics for Little Richard's "Tutti Frutti"—lived in the apartment above Adams and heard him in his bathtub singing "Precious Lord." She persuaded him to try one of her tunes, "Oh Why," and was instrumental in getting him signed to the local Ric label.

In the studio, the song was changed to "I Won't Cry" and produced by a precocious eighteen-year-old named Mac Rebennack—soon to be known globally as Dr. John. "I Won't Cry" was a local hit. A few years later, "A Losing Battle," a tune Adams co-wrote with Rebennack, echoed the regional success, and he bounced through a succession of small labels, among them Watch, Pacemaker, and Smash. But it wasn't until 1968, when he signed with the national SSS International label, that he experienced a small run of attention through such country-tinged songs as "Reconsider Me," "Release Me," "It Can't Be All Bad," and the truly great album *Heart and Soul*. In the early seventies, Adams had disappointing stints with both Atlantic and Ariola Records, though in 1978 he charted with a classic R&B song called "All the Good Love Is Gone."

Finally, in 1983, Adams was shrewdly signed by the visionary Massachusetts Rounder label and recorded nine must-own albums—all produced by Scott Billington—including *Room with a View of the Blues*, *The Verdict*, and *Man of My Word*.

During his years with Rounder, Adams's reputation as a vocalist and entertainer grew substantially. He would become at home on the stages of

Europe in particular, and in his later years he won a W.C. Handy Award and several hometown (Big Easy and *Offbeat*) trophies. Of all the folks who could have sung gospel at Professor Longhair's funeral, Adams was chosen.

Adams, who was a heavy smoker, was ultimately diagnosed with lung cancer. The disease cut his life and career short, but it's comforting to recall this statement, which Adams made to *Offbeat* magazine in 1993: "I keep telling myself that when the time comes when I can't enjoy what I'm doing, I'll stop. Because I don't want to be out there, seventy-five or eighty years old, you know, still trying to get somebody to feel something that you don't feel anymore. Lots of guys just go until they can't go anymore, but I would rather have people remember me from when I sang with a lot of inner soul and feeling and spirit. I say give me my flowers now, because I don't want to go on with this after it stops happening for me."

It never stopped happening for Adams—and he earned his flowers.

When it comes to entertainment versus sheer talent, there was **Ernie K-Doe** (1936–2001). Born Ernest Kador Jr. in New Orleans and raised by an aunt, he was singing by the age of fifteen with the Golden Chain Jubilee Singers and the Zion Travellers. As he was exposed to secular tunes, he gradually turned his attention to soul and rhythm & blues and, after stints in Chicago singing with the Moonglows and the Flamingos, the K-Man returned to New Orleans and joined the Blue Diamonds.

K-Doe, as he would come to be called in an obvious condensation of his surname, eventually decided, in a gesture of typical modesty, to anoint himself "Emperor of the World." He was instantly noticeable in any configuration because of an outrageous stage persona that might be described as a unique martini comprising equal parts Little Richard, Muhammad Ali, and Jimi Hendrix. Not bad, particularly when you think that perhaps any of those folks could just have easily been influenced by K-Doe as the other way around.

After a few marginally successful singles, K-Doe hit it big in 1961 with an infectiously goofy Allen Toussaint–produced number called "Mother-in-Law." (Interestingly, the bullfrog-voice calling out "Mother-in-law!" at the end of the verses in the song isn't K-Doe, but Benny Spellman.) For the next several years, K-Doe remained a hard-working entertainer who would occasionally chart a single, in particular "Te-Ta Te-Ta-Ta," "I Cried My Last Tear," and "Later for Tomorrow." That's pretty much the bulk of the national noise K-Doe has made, though his presence in New Orleans continued to prevail. He was an outlandish character—The Emperor—in stage tuxedos who held court on Sunday nights in his Mother-in-Law Lounge at 1540 N. Claiborne Avenue. His yearly appearances at Jazz Fest always commanded a large audience.

Unfortunately, the persona took on grotesque overtones during Jazz Fest 2000 when *New York Times* writer Neil Strauss came to the Lounge to interview K-Doe before his regular Sunday night set. After they'd talked in a van outside the club, Strauss went inside to watch the show, innocently holding his interview tape recorder on his lap. K-Doe saw the recorder from the stage, thought Strauss was trying to bootleg the performance, and freaked big time. K-Doe's wife, Antoinette, got into the act, and the police were called; all this suggests that perhaps K-Doe was taking his legacy a bit too seriously. Strauss wrote a witty and understanding piece about the incident, and K-Doe settled back into his routine. He died at 65 in July 2001.

New Orleans's **Lloyd Price** (1933–), worked from a blueprint similar to K-Doe's. He kicked off his career as a second-line rocker on the strength of a radio station commercial tag-line, "Lawdy Miss Clawdy," that became a massive success when he transformed it into a single. With soulful and expressionistic voice, and a penchant for mixing the comic aspects of life with the world's bluesier moments, Price has a unique sound—and he plays the trumpet, too.

Price was seventeen when he auditioned for Art Rupe of Specialty Records, and the wringing emotion with which he delivered "Lawdy Miss Clawdy" was sufficient for Rupe to gather Dave Bartholomew and Fats Domino for sessions at Cosimo Matassa's J&M Studio.

By some accounts, "Lawdy Miss Clawdy" was the first "black" single that became a "white" hit. The song went gold, was the *Billboard* #1 R&B record of 1952, and copped Price the *Cash Box* R&B Singer of the Year honors. Price, a handsome young guy who resembled Mike Tyson, suddenly found himself a star. Though "Clawdy" was the standard bearer, Price followed with "Restless Heart" and "Ain't That a Shame" before having his career interrupted by service in the Korean War.

By the time he got out, Little Richard had hit with Specialty. Price moved to ABC Paramount, spent a short time with his own cofounded and ill-fated KRC label, then returned to ABC Paramount in 1958 for a #1 version of the classic "Stagger Lee." The tune was a fresh-to-the-moment rendition of the violent old N'Awlins blues classic, notable not just for Price's typically emotive vocals but also because Dick Clark booked Price to sing the song on *American Bandstand*. Clark insisted on re-doing the tune with an upbeat ending more suitable for *Happy Days* than a New Orleans barroom; the record sales probably made up for any indignities suffered by the artistic process.

Oddly, it was with that success that Price stylistically abandoned New Orleans and moved into the mainstream. Over the next few years, he enjoyed fame with such velvety singles as "Personality," "I'm Gonna Get Married," "Where Were You (On Our Wedding Day)," "Come Into My Heart," "Lady Luck," "Misty," "Question," "No If's—No And's" and, in 1969, his final chart effort, "Bad Conditions," this one released on another of Price's co-owned labels, Turntable Records. Price also owned a New York nightclub called the Turntable, and he smoothly segued from performance to artist management and record production.

When Price's frequent business partner, Harold Logan, died in 1969, Price moved to Africa for a while and concentrated on nonmusical pursuits. Since the eighties, though, he's periodically done package tours with Jerry Lee Lewis and Little Richard, and has even guested with such (relatively) younger folks as Huey Lewis & the News. In 1998, Price was inducted into the Rock 'n' Roll Hall of Fame.

Many have claimed to be the Father of Rock 'n' Roll and at least one has claimed to be the Godfather of Soul. New Orleans's **Roy Brown** (1925–1981) would certainly be entitled to toss his hat into both rings if he were still living. Born in 1925, Brown made plenty of records in the forties and early fifties that tight-roped the burgeoning and swirling gray area between shoutin' blues, gospel-flavored jump blues, and R&B that would eventually explode as rock 'n' roll and soul.

Brown spent his seminal musical years in first Shreveport and then Galveston, Texas (at that time a cesspool of whoring, gambling, and drink; in other words, a fun place to be), singing smooth tunes that might be described as supper club music. Indeed, Bing Crosby was one of Brown's favorite artists. But Brown began touring the clubs and developing his own wild style that incorporated the emotion of gospel and the raucous celebration of jump blues.

Though he recorded briefly for Gold Star in Texas, he returned to New Orleans and, in a high school gym in 1947, recorded a tune called "Good Rockin' Tonight," which, depending on who you believe, was either penned by Brown or a school teacher–keyboardist in one of his Galveston bands named Joel Harris. What is certain is that the song, released on the local De Luxe label, was an immediate sensation in New Orleans and soon started to make waves nationally. From its sensational opening line—*Have you heard the news, there's good rockin' tonight?*—the piece is an irresistible chunk of churning, good-time sensuality.

The tune was eventually covered by everyone from early competitor Wynonie Harris to seminal rockers such as Elvis Presley, Ricky Nelson, and Jerry Lee Lewis. As with any hot new artist, Brown was ushered into the studio to crank out follow-ups, and over the next few years scored big-selling singles with "Hard Luck Blues," "Rockin' at Midnight," and "Party at Midnight." Between 1948 and 1951, Brown tacked fifteen hits on the charts. Though his popularity unaccountably slid after that—despite a world-class stage show and a string of tunes for the King Label including "Hurry Hurry Baby" and "Black Diamond"—Brown kept plugging away, suffering more of the business indignities than was typical even for black artists of the time.

Still, he carried on. Dave Bartholomew signed Brown to a deal with Imperial and they had a million-selling success with "Let the Four Winds Blow" and minor triumphs with "Party Doll" and "Saturday Night." Those appeared to be the final highlights of his career, particularly when Brown got into legal troubles (including a bout with the IRS). Subsequently, though, Brown enjoyed a revival in Europe, where he toured to a hero's welcome, and, as though he'd scripted the final scenes himself, he eventually returned to New Orleans for a triumphant Jazz Fest appearance; shortly afterwards, he died of a heart attack.

Lee Dorsey (1924–1986) stumbled on immortality while drinking beer in an uptown bar with Marshall Sehorn; the record company talent scout had heard "Lottie-Mo," a regional single by the New Orleans–born Dorsey, and searched the singer out in his Ninth Ward home. Though Dorsey didn't have any material to record at the time, some neighborhood kids were singing a homemade nursery rhyme—about a mother's bowel movement, oddly enough—that was irresistible; so the two men retired to a tavern to quaff a few cold ones and re-work the lyrics into a more acceptable song.

The result was "Ya Ya," a goofily infectious novelty tune, and in 1961 Dorsey, signed to Fury by Sehorn, sold over a million copies of the single. It was a surprise for Dorsey, an ex-Marine and former boxer who stood barely five feet tall, but the powerfully baritoned singer followed up with Earl King's "Do Re Mi," a similarly constructed song that sold almost a half million copies.

Dorsey had grown up in a musical home; his mother sang around the house incessantly, and at an early age he developed a passion for country music. The family lived in Portland, Oregon, for a while, and after the service Dorsey fought as a featherweight and a lightweight. When he tired of that, he returned to New Orleans and happily became a mechanic. A perpetually cheery, positive, and hard working guy, Dorsey would sing while working on cars. One day, independent record producer Reynauld Richard came to pick up his repaired car, heard Dorsey's velvet voice, and took him into the studio to make a record.

When Fury went bankrupt, Dorsey landed with Sehorn's future partner, Allen Toussaint. They released a Toussaint piece called "Ride Your Pony," which went on to become a radio and nightclub favorite. "Get Out of My Life Woman" was another early cut, out about the time Toussaint and Sehorn cemented their partnership: Sea-Saint Productions, a giant of a New Orleans–based music-biz success story.

Dorsey, a big part of the early days, earned various nicknames: "Mr. TNT," "Kid Chocolate," and "Cadillac Shorty." He rode his good natured persona and foghorn voice through a slew of successful singles: "Holy Cow," "Yes We Can," "My Old Car," "Go Go Girl" and, of course, "Workin' in a Coal Mine." Having Toussaint as a writer, arranger, and producer didn't hurt, but Dorsey's style was such that "Coal Mine" was a perfect fit. One can't imagine, for example, that Aaron Neville would bring the same drama to the song (though Art Neville could probably pull it off with dramatic flair). In any case, through the sixties and into the seventies, Dorsey did well without leaving New Orleans. When things slowed up in the seventies, he went back to his garage, and in 1977 he released an album, *Night People*, that never gained momentum.

A hit-and-run accident broke both of Dorsey's legs in 1979 and he was wheelchair-bound for a few years. Eventually he got back on his feet and continued working with his accustomed enthusiasm and energy—both Dorsey and Texas songwriter Joe Ely were tabbed by the Clash as opening acts in the eighties. Dorsey died after a long bout with emphysema.

Percy Mayfield (1920–1984) was born in Linden, Louisiana, and survived a car accident (that disfigured his movie-star looks) to become a terrific songwriter and, to a lesser extent, a performer. He grew up in Texas, worked clubs as a singer in Houston, and got his start in the jump blues movement in Los Angeles in the forties. He sold "Two Years of Torture" to Specialty Records, then recorded his own version of the tune.

He followed with a hit recording of "Please Send Me Someone to Love" and seemed star-bound until the car wreck. Still, with dignity, courage, and a distinctly spiritual perseverance, Mayfield carried on. He maintained his own (if low-key) recording career, scored seven hits for Specialty, and carved a reputation as a writer that soon had other artists begging for his material.

He signed a contract to write songs for Ray Charles and kicked out a series of terrifically unique and expertly crafted tunes such as "Hit the Road, Jack," "Danger Zone," and "Tell Me How Do You Feel." In return, Charles signed Mayfied to his own Tangerine label, for which he recorded and did relatively well until the rock 'n' roll charge of the early sixties slowed R&B sales.

Though Mayfield gathered many nicknames during his career, the touching and accurate "Poet of the Blues" is the best.

The "Sweethearts" angle was always hyped, as in sweethearts of the blues, sweethearts of R&B, or even sweethearts of rock 'n' roll. Shirley Goodman (1936–) (whose maiden name was Pixley) and Leonard Lee (1936–) weren't girlfriend and boyfriend and were never married to each other. But the high-school, let's-go-steady innocence perpetrated by the records of **Shirley and Lee** certainly lent musical credence to the "I'm wearing his letter sweater" angle. After all, the time was 1952, a postwar, pre–*American Graffiti* era of well-being; Goodman and Lee were high school classmates at Joseph Clark High School in New Orleans's Seventh Ward when they recorded a song called "I'm Gone"—which bottle-rocketed up the charts to #2.

Written by the thirteen-year-old Goodman along with several of her pals during one of their daily after-school song-fests, "I'm Gone" was originally recorded by Cosimo Matassa for $2 in a gesture he made simply to persuade the kids to stop bugging him. When Aladdin's Eddie Mesner accidentally heard the master—and Goodman's angel-quaking soprano complementing Lee's blues-toasted baritone—he went nuts. Mesner used band leader Dave Bartholomew and the J&M house musicians to chronicle in song the evolving "relationship" between Shirley and Lee. Each single was the next saga in their high-school romance—a sort of soap-opera opera. The duo would release a song, go on the road, sell a slew of records, and come back to New Orleans; there, the youngsters would write another tune further describing the antics of their "love," and the cycle would start again. The three biggest hits were "Feel So Good," "I Feel Good" and, of course, "Let the Good Times Roll," the latter becoming their signature song.

After the dissolution of Shirley and Lee, Goodman worked briefly with Jesse Hill (Shirley and Jesse), then headed to California and became a session singer backing such New Orleans artists as Harold Batiste and Dr. John. In 1975, recording with a backing group as Shirley and Company, Goodman scored a huge disco hit with "Shame, Shame, Shame" before easing into semiretirement. For his part, Lee recorded a few solo discs for Broadside and Imperial in the mid-sixties, but didn't chart.

Often overlooked, **Tommy Ridgley** (1925–1999) was another great soul singer. That he died tragically around the same time as Johnny Adams was a one-two gut punch to the fertile tradition of New Orleans R&B vocalists. Ridgley was a friendly and kind man, born one of seventeen kids into a religious family in Shrewsbury, a suburb of New Orleans. His first performances were singing spirituals on street corners and in a church choir.

A fan of primal shouters Roy Brown and Big Joe Turner, Ridgley could rock, too, and developed his own torrid style. In short order a popular pianist and singer at the Dew Drop Inn, he caught the eyes and ears of Dave Bartholomew, who in 1949 produced and provided the backing band for Ridgley's first single, "Shrewsbury Blues" b/w "Early Dawn Boogie" (Imperial Records).

Sales were less than inspiring, but Ridgley kept plugging and a few years later scored a contract with Decca Records; shortly after, he landed another with Atlantic. Both deals resulted in nice work, most notably the instrumental "Jam Up"—a strange story since it had more to do with the honkin' saxophone of Lee Allen than with Ridgley.

Though unsuccessful at cracking national charts in a big way, Ridgley stayed consistently popular in New Orleans and the southeast. He put on blistering live shows, but over time his abilities as a smooth balladeer began to compete with his frenetic, uptempo image.

In 1957, he signed with Herald Records and made his three biggest hits: "When I Meet My Girl," "Baby Doo Liddle," and "I've Heard That Story Before." He formed his own band, the Untouchables, and for years was a mainstay as the house bandleader for the Municipal Auditorium in New Orleans.

In the sixties, Ridgley's career was at a standstill; he worked driving a cab and in department stores, but he never stopped gigging. The seventies were kinder to New Orleans R&B artists, and during the eighties Rounder reissued several of Ridgley's records. He continued to record new material—the marvelous "Let's Try and Talk It Over" and "Should I Ever Love Again" chief among them—for a variety of small but high-quality labels.

In 1995, Ridgley released *Since the Blues Began* on the BlackTop label, but shortly afterwards he suffered kidney failure. He received a successful transplant and was able to resume working on a limited basis.

Clustered amongst all these singers are two exceptional guitar forces, Earl King and Walter "Wolfman" Washington, whose contributions certainly extend beyond mere ax mastery.

As the Meters are to the world, so is **Earl King** to New Orleans, which is one way of saying he has been a substantive force in the evolution of funk. A spectacular guitarist and songwriter, he was born Earl Johnson in the city in 1934. He was influenced by Isadore "Tuts" Washington and Clarence "Gatemouth" Brown (among others) as a kid; but when the man who would be King met Guitar Slim, he found a guiding force and a close friend.

After a few local recording efforts, the musician signed with Specialty, and changed his name to Earl King after that name was mistyped on the label of a 45. When label honcho Johnny Vincent started a new subsidiary, Ace Records, King became one of the imprint's main artists. After the raving funk of "Those Lonely, Lonely Nights," King, working out of Cosimo Matassa's J&M studio, began to forge a guitar funk style on a series of regionally popular singles.

In 1960, he signed with Dave Bartholomew at Imperial, then recorded a tune that he had written called "Come On." It would have been a hit if Vincent hadn't released an earlier demo version of the song as "Darling Honey Angel Child" at the same time. A bigger hit, "Trick Bag," quickly followed, and King's work became sought after by other artists, including Professor Longhair, Fats Domino, and Jimi Hendrix.

These days, content to trot out his considerable flash with discretion and leisure, King is a subtle presence on the New Orleans funk scene. But his contributions are enormous.

Before the searing guitar work carves its way into your brain, the first thing you notice about **Walter "Wolfman" Washington** (1943–) is his smile—at once predatory and seductive. Looking lean and much younger than his fifty-seven years, Washington is one of the finest of the contemporary R&B artists in New Orleans: a monster guitarist, a spookily great singer, and a solid writer and interpreter whose hash of blues, R&B, and funk is joyfully concocted. He's also a riveting entertainer who grew up watching his cousin Ernie K-Doe mesmerize audiences.

Starting in his teens as guitarist for Lee Dorsey, he also played with Irma Thomas in the Toronados before starting his own outfit, The All Fools

Band, in the mid-sixties. After a tour of Europe, his reputation now extending into international territory, Washington formed a new band of loyal and merry musicians in the early seventies. The group, known at first as the Mighty Men, and then the Solar System, before settling in as the Roadmasters (keyboardist Jon Cleary was a member for two years), spent several good years at Dorothy's Medallion Lounge; there they backed vocalist Johnny Adams and opened each show with their own set before kicking out the hits for the veteran singer.

Washington released a solo album in 1981 called *Rainin' in My Heart* on the local Hep' Me label, but it wasn't until a few years later that Washington signed with Rounder, for whom he released three solid records, *Wolf Tracks*, *Out of the Dark*, and *Wolf at the Door*. After some confusion and an ebb in momentum, Washington and the Roadmasters released the excellent *Sada* for Virgin/Point Blank in 1992, then three years later recorded *Blue Moon Rising* (re-released on the European Go Jazz label) before re-upping with Rounder imprint Bullseye Blues for *Funk Is in the House*.

In early 2000, *On the Prowl* was released; from the agitated "You Got Me Worried" and the carefree "It Was Fun While It Lasted" to the heart wrenching soul balladry of "Without You," it's a stunning work.

Several other artists had big moments in the development of New Orleans rhythm 'n' blues.

An Uptown New Orleans kid who grew up loving to sing church music, **James "Sugarboy" Crawford** (1934–) first played piano with a locally popular group called The Cha-Pake Shaweez. In 1952, under the name The Sha-Weez, they recorded a single with Dave Bartholomew for Aladdin Records—"One Sunday Morning." The 45 went nowhere, but a year later, Leonard Chess of Checker Records heard the band rehearsing and gave them $5—promptly spent on red beans and rice—to record a couple of original numbers for him at a local radio station. A month later, one of the tunes, "I Don't Know What I'll Do," was played on the radio.

The disc was released under the name Sugarboy Crawford and the Cane Cutters—"Sugarboy" having been Crawford's nickname since childhood. The record did reasonably well, enough to justify sending the band, which now included Snooks Eaglin on guitar and Frankie Fields on bass, back into the studio. One of the tunes they cut, "Jock-A-Mo," is quite simply one of the most important songs in the history of New Orleans R&B, to say nothing of the town's Mardi Gras celebrations. Later recorded as "Iko Iko" by the Dixie Cups, Dr. John, the Neville Brothers, Irma Thomas, and on and on, the carnival anthem, penned by Crawford, was based around the songs of the Mardi Gras Indians, who once fought their battlefield skirmishes not far from where Crawford grew up.

Crawford toured extensively for years for various labels until 1963 when, in the wake of the freedom marches and the resultant southern redneck reactionary violence, Crawford was pulled over one morning on tour, accused of speeding and driving drunk, and clubbed in the head with a pistol. He suffered brain damage and was paralyzed for a year. He couldn't see, hear, or speak, and, in a painfully laborious and protracted process, he had to be re-taught how to function. Although he recovered substantially—and is reportedly not bitter about the incident—Crawford has never performed again. The bloodline goes on in his grandson, Davell Crawford, the astonishingly talented young keyboardist and singer whose work is discussed in greater detail earlier in this book.

When he wrote "Land of 1000 Dances" in 1963 New Orleans's **Chris Kenner** (1929–1976) had no idea that he should have probably called it "Land of 1000 Royalty Checks." Structurally inspired by an old hymn, it charted in 1965 with Cannibal & the Headhunters and again with Wilson Pickett a year later. The tune was also covered by a variety of folks, including Kenner himself, with substantial success. In addition, he wrote songs for such artists as Fats Domino and Tom Jones.

Kenner had scored his first major success as a singer a few years earlier with a Grammy-nominated tune that he and Bartholomew wrote together called "I Like It Like That" (later covered by British Invasion rockers the Dave Clark Five). Kenner went through some label difficulties and developed an affection for liquor, but he managed to stay reasonably productive. Over time, though he continued to record some nice tunes, Kenner's creative fountain began to dry up. His drinking turned into alcoholism, and in 1968 he was convicted of statutory rape and served time in Angola. After he got out, he continued to perform sporadically, and seemed to be turning his life around when he died of cardiac arrest.

A Youngstown, Ohio, native with a wonderfully emotive voice, **Bobby Marchan** (1930–1999) fell in love with New Orleans when his troupe of female impersonators, The Powder Box Revue, played a two-week gig at the Dew Drop Inn. Marchan moved to the city and was discovered by Ace Records's Johnny Vincent at the Club Tijuana. Marchan's first sessions at J&M Studios produced a modest hit, "Chicken Wah-Wah," written for him by Huey "Piano" Smith. Together they formed the Clowns, for whom Marchan sang such late-fifties hits as "Rockin' Pneumonia and the Boogie Woogie Flu" and "Just Know It." (Marchan ran the Clowns on the road because Smith didn't like traveling. It was Marchan who hired James Booker to tour with the band in Smith's place).

Eventually, Marchan went solo, alternating a female impersonator gig with sporadic recording efforts. He went to #1 in 1960 with "There Is Something on Your Mind," and was instrumental in the creation of Cash Money Records, the New Orleans hip-hop empire (more about this in "Rap and Hip-Hop," Part 6, Chapter 6).

One of the early singers on the Minit label, **Benny Spellman** is maybe best known as the bass voice on Ernie K-Doe's hit "Mother-in-Law." Spellman had some success on his own, too, with the single "Lipstick Traces (on a Cigarette)," and he also sang for a while with Huey Smith's Clowns. A collection, *Fortune Teller* is available; the Rolling Stones later covered the title track.

The Spiders were originally a late forties–early fifties gospel group known as Zion City Harmonizers or the Delta Southernaires (depending on whether they were live or on the radio). The group segued into a secular, rock-flavored R&B vocal outfit. Comprised of brothers Chuck and Chick Carbo, Joe Maxson, Matthew West, and Oliver Howard, The Spiders charted several Dave Bartholomew–produced hits in the mid-fifties, including "I Didn't Want to Do It," "You're the One," and "For a Thrill." The Carbo siblings split after a few years for solo careers.

It's true that the career of **Jean Knight** (1943–) is predicated around one song, the infectiously bossy 1971 hit "Mr. Big Stuff." She also enjoyed a modest hit some years back with a remake of Rockin' Sidney's "My Toot Toot," and in recent years has released a couple of CDs, *Shaki de Boo-Tee*, and 1999's *Queen* (off which the sinewy "Slide" should have grabbed some attention). A New Orleanian, Knight is a vital woman, more than capable of blasting through in a big way yet again.

King Floyd (1945–) would probably still be working at the post office if a New Orleans disc jockey hadn't accidentally played the "B" side of King Floyd's first single, a grabbing, accent-on-the-backbeat slice of wicked soul called "Groove Me." A New Orleans kid who grew up digging Tommy Ridgley and Irma Thomas, Floyd's circuitous route to Crescent City soul stardom included stints in the army and a stay in Los Angeles, where he gravitated to songwriting and hung out with Dr. John, Sonny & Cher, and Jimi Hendrix. When Floyd returned to his hometown, he couldn't find gigs, and settled in at the post office. But he kept hustling and in 1970, with producer Wardell Quezergue, recorded a mellow, Otis Redding–esque piece called "What Our Love Needs." He flip-sided it with a one-take effort that happened to be "Groove Me"—which, because of the DJ snafu, rocketed to #1 on the R&B charts and #6 on the pop charts and pulled Floyd and the tiny Malaco/Chimneyville label along with it. Atlantic Records took note of the smash, inked a distribution deal for Malaco, and set out to turn King Floyd into a star.

Floyd followed with three more hits, "Baby Let Me Kiss You," "Got to Have Your Love," and "Woman Don't Go Astray." He continued to record (all told, he sold over 5 million records in five years), and world tours made Floyd even more prominent.

When several New Orleans jazz musicians—Melvin Lastie, Harold Battiste, John Boudreaux, Red Tyler, Roy Montrell, and Chuck Badie—got tired of being ripped off and decided to start their own label, AFO, in 1961, a singer named **Barbara George** (1942–) provided them with their best shot at success. George (see also "Modern Jazz," Part 1, Chapter 2), an unknown and essentially unschooled singer born in New Orleans, was signed to the label on the strength of an audition, an untamed but teasing blues voice, and a song she had based around an arrangement that copped the melody of the hymn "Just a Closer Walk with Thee." Called "I Know," the tune became AFO's biggest hit when it went to #3 in the pop charts in the late fall of 1961. "You Talk About Love" followed "I Know" with some chart presence but, unfortunately, the naïve singer was lured away from the nurturing but crumbling arms of AFO. Subsequent efforts for the Sue label went nowhere. Collectibles Records has a collection of George's material, *I Know (You Don't Love Me Anymore)*, that features her hits and a nice taste of her brief catalog that includes several self-penned tunes.

Clarence "Frogman" Henry (1937–), born in New Orleans, has an expressive voice with a monstrous range—and the bottom end gave birth to his sobriquet. Influenced by Fats Domino, in 1956 Henry wrote and recorded a huge smash, "Ain't Got No Home," which remains his biggest hit. Other nice tunes include "It Won't Be Long," "(I Don't Know Why) But I Do" and "I'm in Love." He worked for years playing clubs on Bourbon Street before 1964 when, as mentioned in the last chapter, he opened a string of dates for the Beatles.

In a town full of colorful nicknames, **Mr. Google Eyes** (1931–) is one of the most memorable. That would be Joe August, born in New Orleans, whose singular nickname came along while he was working at Dookie Chase's restaurant. Given to ogling babes, he was described by coworkers as "the googlest-eyed motherfucker" ever, and it was under that nickname that he began sitting in as a singer anywhere anyone would let him clamber onstage. He quickly became known for his energetic showmanship and powerful vocals, so much so that Dr. John, in his early days as a bandleader, would take his singers to clubs to study the way Mr. G worked a crowd. At the age of fifteen, Mr. G recorded his first single for Coleman Records, "Poppa Stoppa's Be-Bop Blues." It was a hit, followed with similar success by "No Wine, No Women," and then "Rock My Soul."

Columbia Records bought out Coleman, and Mr. G's next several releases were for that label. Over the next few years, he blasted through on a variety of labels before the momentum trickled to a halt. Mr. G worked in music-related jobs in Newark and Los Angeles before returning to New Orleans, where he remained active on a local level in his own clubs for years. He was integral in Blacks That Give A Damn, a political outfit offering aid to youth in trouble.

For a "one-hit" guy—that would be "Ooh Poo Pah Doo"—**Jesse Hill** (1932–) led a life rich in New Orleans music. Included in his bloodline were Lawrence "Prince La La" Nelson and Walter "Papoose" Nelson, younger heroes such as trumpeter James Andrews and his brother, trombonist Troy "Trombone Shorty" Andrews—and then the Lastie clan which, if not as globally familiar as, say, the Nevilles, is sonically substantial nonetheless.

They grew up in extreme poverty in a Ninth Ward ghetto. Hill gravitated to drums, worked bars in the early fifties in the Houserockers (playing

Hank Williams tunes), and eventually gigged with Professor Longhair and Huey "Piano" Smith and the Clowns. When the Houserockers performed, though, it was with Hill out front, singing and pounding a tambourine.

Desperate for cash in 1960, he tried to sell "Ooh Poo Pah Doo," a tune he'd written in two parts, nonetheless, to Minit Records. Execs Larry McKinley and Joe Banashak liked the demo so much that they released an Allen Toussaint arrangement of the song, Hill singing and the Houserockers backing. A manic, greatly infectious tune of screeched gibberish, "Ooh Poo Pah Doo" went to #28 on *Billboard*. It would be Hill's only hit, though similarly structured songs such as "Can't Get Enough," "Whip It on Me," "I Need Your Love" and "Sweet Jelly Roll"—all of which can be heard on the *Golden Classics* collection, demonstrate that Hill was underappreciated as a performer.

If classic soul and R&B has dried up, a preponderance of younger funk bands is making a mark on the Crescent City. A few worth listening to include:

Galactic, originally known as Galactic Prophylactic, crosses the jam-band tendencies of Phish or the Dead with serious funk nuances and jazz chops. The resulting ambrosia is decidedly New Orleans–esque, which means they could probably be pigeonholed in a variety of areas. CDs include *Late for the Future, Crazyhorse Mongoose,* and *Coolin' Off.*

Iris May Tango is an intriguing and popular local band whose experiments in funk, jazz, and hip-hop are typically more successful than not. Their recordings include several authorized live bootlegs and a studio disc called *Let 'Em Have It.*

All That band has a great CD out, *The Whop Boom Bam,* from Rounder Records. Its sound conjures Spike Jones and The Olympia Brass Band and the Meters.

Smilin' Myron infuses Latin and reggae into their raw funk. A terrific band with a lot of momentum, the group was tragically stopped in their tracks by the death from cancer of guitarist Tim Guarisco a few years back. Whether they regain their form or not is up in the air. In the meantime, recordings such as *Live from the Hoochy Kooch Highway* and *What About the People* are recommended.

The New World Funk Ensemble crosses guitar hard rock with sublime funk and improvisation.

Michael Ray & the Cosmic Krewe suggests what it might be like if, on a full moon, Sun Ra turned into Ornette Coleman and crashed a Mardi Gras second-line parade. *Funk If I Know* and *Michael Ray & the Cosmic Krewe* are tasty samples.

Finally, take note of producer and arranger **Wardell Quezergue, "The Creole Beethoven."** For over forty years, he's done masterful work for everyone from Jean Knight to the Wild Magnolias, and his solo CDs, *Funky Funky New Orleans* and *Masterpiece,* are prime demonstrations of his skills.

III

THE BLUES

One

THE BATON ROUGE SCENE AND STATEWIDE GUARDIANS

*I*n the Baton Rouge phone book it's listed as Neal's Restaurant & Lounge, but amongst the blues cognoscenti around town it's known simply as Raful Neal's—Raful Neal being the veteran blues singer and harmonica player who serves as patriarch of the largest and most important blues family in the state. Son Kenny, a mid-level blues hero known internationally, and daughter Jackie, who is performing this very evening, are just two in the Neal bloodline who make their living strutting the blues.

In Louisiana, only the Guy brothers—Buddy and Phil—can claim a larger following, and that's like the homerun statistic that says Hank and Tommie Aaron have hit more homers than any other big league brothers in history. (Hank, of course, hit 755 of their aggregate 768.) In that fashion, Buddy Guy is without question the biggest of living Louisiana blues monsters and, although brother Phil had a modestly successful career, there's only one Buddy.

Well, in any case, there are plenty of Neals, and plenty of blues to be had in Raful Neal's enticing little lounge.

On a September Friday afternoon, nearing the end of the fifth annual Baton Rouge Blues Week, festival honcho Johnny Palazzotto has taken me and my pal Brett "Louisiana Black" Blackwell down to Neal's for a late lunch. While New Orleans is the dominant musical force in jazz, R&B, and hip-hop, and southern Louisiana is the fortress of Cajun and zydeco music, Baton Rouge is pretty much the central clubhouse for Louisiana blues.

Palazzotto is regarded as kinfolk here, as the greetings from employees and afternoon beer enthusiasts attest. He takes Louisiana Black and me on a brief tour of the place, shepherding us into the kitchen to meet various Neal relatives whose job is to make God's food.

Neal's is a classic joint, the sort of roadhouse that has long peppered certain corners of the American musical landscape, but it was a secret to much of the Wal-Mart nation until Dan Ackroyd and John Belushi brought such places to the forefront in the movie *The Blues Brothers*. Located in a part of Baton Rouge far removed from all the Scarletts living in their Tara-styled sorority houses at Louisiana State University, Neal's is an aesthetic thirst quencher: haunted-house dark as one comes in out of the white afternoon sun, blood-red industrial carpeting, mirrored brick walls. Record albums and musical instruments are positioned around the perimeter of the small stage at one end of the club, and gold cardboard G-clefs, swaying gently in the breezy force of the air conditioning, hang on string from the acoustic tile ceiling. Along the back wall runs the long and friendly bar.

Louisiana Black and I had spent part of the afternoon with Palazzotto in his recording studio watching a fine interview with Clarence "Gatemouth" Brown, a man with a tendency for self-promotion. I've interviewed Brown three times and found him pleasant on each occasion, though he is fond of his own work; indeed, one of the journalists I spoke with during the writing of this book quoted him as once saying, "Enough about me. Let's talk about my record."

Palazzotto, a Baton Rouge native who worked for years with various moderate musical heavyweights in Los Angeles before returning to his hometown some time ago, is a gregarious mover-and-shaker-about-town whose affection for Louisiana blues is a driving force in his music business career.

"I haven't scored a major label deal for anyone in a long time, not since I left California," he cheerfully admits. "But it's very gratifying to be a part of a scene like this. Highway 61 cuts right through here, and this is a close-knit and spiritual scene of musicians and fans. Maybe it's not the biggest scene in the musical world, but it's heart and soul to the people here. It's genuine."

It's every bit as genuine as the home cooking that is brought out: heaping Styrofoam plates of fried pork chops, boiled cabbage, dirty rice, potatoes smothered with shrimp and sausage, cornbread, and, perched precariously atop the whole thing like a star on Charlie Brown's Christmas tree, a prewrapped Hostess chocolate cupcake.

From the reporter's notebook:

Let me just say right now, as an aspiring fat man: If I've EVER eaten anything as good as the smothered potatoes with shrimp and sausage, I don't remember it. Cross my rapidly congealing heart and hope to die— with my mouth full.

While we inhale food, Palazzotto talks about the Baton Rouge blues scene and the Blues Week it has spawned. Originally, there was just a weekend Baton Rouge Blues Festival, started in 1980, but the "Week" evolved to add attraction and scope to the original concept. Now, there's music each evening at a downtown stage on a blocked-off street. The early evening concerts serve as a springboard to a related web of nightly activity in the city's blues clubs—chief among them Neal's, Tabby Thomas's Blues Box, and the Thirsty Tiger. Earlier this week, "Gatemouth" Brown, Deacon John, Barbara Lynn, Cosimo Matassa, and Allen Touissaint showed up, some performing, at the festival.

Baton Rouge Blues Week also includes photo and art exhibits, a video festival, television specials, and a *Blues in the Schools* program that educates and introduces young students to the meaning of the blues and the cultural and provincial associations of the music.

Though it's nowhere near the attraction of New Orleans's Jazz & Heritage Festival, as a microcosm of Louisiana blues, Baton Rouge Blues Week is a healthy and growing infant. The farsighted and multifaceted approach being taken by Palazzotto and other folks emphasizes that blues, rather than remaining just an ingredient in jazz, R&B, and zydeco, and despite its low profile, makes an important contribution to the history of Louisiana music.

Blues here doesn't have the star-spangled roster of practitioners one would expect, or that could compare with the rosters of Mississippi and Texas. Thanks to the innate rhythms of New Orleans, which by their tropical definition preclude standard blues structure, it wasn't a particularly good breeding ground. The vast stretches of southwest Louisiana that might have been expected to turn out blues artists were instead culturally occupied by the Cajun and Creole cultures; Cajun and zydeco music evolved rather than blues, though there are certainly bluesy aspects to those forms (particularly in zydeco). Baton Rouge, though, located conveniently between New Orleans and the gateway to southwest Louisiana, also happened to be a blue-collar refinery town surrounded by rice fields. As such, plenty of oil workers and farmers, almost all beset by the poverty and life conditions necessary for proper blues nourishment, settled in the area, which became a hotbed for what came to be known in Louisiana as swamp blues. Meanwhile, Shreveport became home to an electric blues-rock mentality typified by Buddy Guy, Kenny Wayne Shepherd, Mighty Joe Young, and the late John Campbell, and even New Orleans produced a few soulful, R&B–tinted blues heroes.

Blues guitarist Tab Benoit, who grew up outside New Orleans and has played the Baton Rouge clubs hundreds of times, says that even these distinctions shouldn't be taken seriously: "Everyone in Louisiana plays music, and there's a lot of stuff going on—stuff that isn't recorded—that the public doesn't know about. So you have guys in Shreveport doing the Baton

Rouge thing, and guys in Baton Rouge playing New Orleans style." And swamp-and-voodoo blues guitarist Coco Robicheaux points out that all Louisiana blues share the triplet pattern on the high-hat cymbals. "Plus," he told me, "it's not always something you can technically describe, but if you listen to Slim Harpo or Clifton Chenier, that's Louisiana blues—and you *know* it."

Not surprisingly, Baton Rouge's swamp blues fuses all things Louisiana: piano, a rural underpinning most obvious in vocal inflections and percussion, twangy and exuberant electric guitar—perhaps best typified on a familiar level by New Orleans's Guitar Slim—and a spiritual evocation of Bayou proper.

"Blues is just what everybody—black and white—did. It's what we listened to," said Robicheaux, who grew up in Ascension Parish and moved to Slidell outside New Orleans when he was thirteen. "Country musicians had a hard time in New Orleans, but Baton Rouge had Standard Oil and you could get a job. And outside town, everyone's farms were butting up against one another. The culture just sorta bled."

The blues history of Shreveport can't be ignored, either: In addition to the guitar greats that originated there, the town became a post–World War II blues recording center. A visionary entrepreneur named Stan Lewis opened a small record shop on Texas Street that would eventually become the Paula-Jewel-Ron conglomerate, sister record labels that would put out blues, R&B, country, and pop artists ranging from Dale Hawkins and Big Joe Turner to Lowell Fulson and John Lee Hooker.

Sitting in Raful Neal's this afternoon, though, Baton Rouge seems to be the sun in the solar system of Louisiana blues. After we eat, Louisiana Black is so impressed that he buys a round for the bar and insists on heading back to the kitchen to tip the staff and wait-folks.

A confluence of events similar to those that gave Stan Lewis his Shreveport empire helped usher in Baton Rouge's blues resurgence in the early seventies. A white businessman named Jay Miller from Crowley, Louisiana, unveiled a talent for discovering and harvesting Louisiana musical talent (which some would say was matched by his ability to pay them less than acceptably). His Feature label was distributed nationally after Miller hit with a recording of Lightnin' Slim's "Bad Luck Blues."

Most of the state's blues giants aren't part of the Baton Rouge scene, and in most cases they had to leave Louisiana to make it. But because the cohesiveness of the Baton Rouge scene is organic, as though its practitioners and advocates (like Palazzotto) would rather eschew the limelight to keep intact the purity of what they have in Baton Rouge, I'll start my blues survey with them.

Henry Gray (1925–) is the grand old man of Baton Rouge blues. A superb pianist, a gentleman, and a former member of one of Howlin' Wolf's finest bands, Gray was born in Kenner, Louisiana. He taught himself piano as a child and refined his burgeoning technique throughout his teens by playing in various area churches. After serving in the army during World War II, Gray moved to Chicago and started working with Little Hudson's Red Devil Trio; he moved on to a variety of club gigs with Little Walter and Junior Wells before joining up with the Wolf from the mid-fifties through the late sixties. He was also a sought-after session player who backed Bo Diddley, Jimmy Reed, and Jimmy Rogers, among others.

Gray returned to Louisiana in 1968 and began recording his own projects for the Arhoolie/Excello label. A master of Chicago blues and barrelhouse touches, with more than a hint of New Orleans–style R&B and swamp blues, Gray finally settled in Baton Rouge with his own band, the Gray Cats. He's worked steadily—including performances at the New Orleans Jazz & Heritage Festival—and returned to Chicago in 1988 long enough to record a solo record, *Lucky Man*, for the Blind Pig label. He remains a Grand Old Ass-Kickin' Gentleman in the thriving Baton Rouge blues hive.

From the reporter's notebook:

Apparently, [Henry] Gray has played every night of the [Baton Rouge Blues Week] until tonight. Naturally. Still, cruising through downtown, looking for Tabby Thomas's club, we saw Mr. Gray—in a suit and tie— strolling happily down the street by himself, as though headed somewhere fun where it didn't make any difference how late it was. My immediate idea was to offer him a ride. But there was a pretzel twist of one-way streets conspiring against us, and by the time Brett got us pointed in the right direction, the piano player was gone.

Tabby Thomas is another of the Jay Miller pool of Baton Rouge talent. Thomas was born in the city, got into blues through his mom's Peetie Wheatstraw and Arthur Crudup records, but didn't gain musical fame of his own until he won a talent contest in San Francisco after having served there in the army. A fine singer with capable skills on piano and guitar, he was signed to Hollywood Records and released an immediately forgotten disc of California-styled blues called *Midnight Is Calling*.

The label dropped him and he returned home, formed a band called the Mellow, Mellow Men, and in 1962 broke through with a tune called "Voodoo Party"; soon afterwards, he returned to obscurity. He quit the business for a while, but in 1970 he started his own label, Blue Beat Records.

In 1979, Thomas played a killer set at the New Orleans Jazz & Heritage Festival. Producer Miller immediately signed him to his Unlimited label and released the now out-of-print *25 Years With the Blues* and *Live at Tabby's Blues Box*—the latter featuring his talented son, Chris Thomas King. Perhaps Tabby's biggest accomplishment was in opening Tabby's Blues Box and Heritage Hall, the club at which the live CD was recorded. Along with Neal's, it's the pre-eminent blues club in Baton Rouge.

As musical host, Thomas displays his unique style, which might be thought of as swamp blues after a bout in the electric chair, and serves as a generous and supportive grandfather to young bluesmen across the South. From the reporter's notebook:

The night we were in town for the Baton Rouge Blues Week, Louisiana Black and I cruised the empty downtown streets searching for Tabby's Blues Box. A kindly guy on a street corner, pausing to light a cigarette, gave us precise directions—and we followed them with ease to Tabby's, only to find it PADLOCKED. The next day, a bemused local musician told us we'd gone to the old location, and that the new Tabby's was only a few blocks away.

One of the living maestros of Baton Rouge blues had dropped out of the business for many years. Cornelius Green, a.k.a. **Lonesome Sundown** (1928–1995), from Donaldsonville, Louisiana, loved music as a kid, and at twenty he moved to New Orleans to turn pro as a pianist, taking along an uncle's guitar for fun. Little worked out for him in the piano business, though, and he found time to practice guitar; eventually he gigged and recorded in the fifties as one of two badass guitarists in Clifton Chenier's Red Hot Louisiana Band (the other was wizard Phillip Walker).

Eventually, Sundown went solo. He recorded several sides for Jay Miller's Excello label, and it was Miller who gave him the moniker Lonesome Sundown. Probably his best-known song for Miller was the maudlin "Lost Without Love," though several of his tunes—among them "My Home Is a Prison," "Hoodoo Woman Blues," "I'm a Mojo Man," "Leave My Money Alone," and "I'm a Samplin' Man"—typified his unique sound: a guttural, somber blues guitar accompanied by an evocative and deep voice, as though he were sinking slowly in some bayou quicksand and had just enough time to ruminate on the implications of a bad situation.

A member of an apostolic church since the mid-sixties, Lonesome Sundown spent long periods away from secular music. In 1977, though, he recorded arguably his best record, *Been Gone Too Long*, for Hightone. You should also hear *I'm a Mojo Man—The Best of the Excello Singles*.

Another kingpin in the Baton Rouge–swamp blues family, **Lazy Lester** (1933–), was born Leslie Johnson in Torras, Louisiana. His nickname was yet another inspired PR effort by the same man who came up with Lonesome Sundown. Lester started out as a self-taught harmonica wizard who formed his first band, the Rhythm Rockers, in his late teens. He soon found himself working house parties and dances in Crowley with Lightnin' Slim after Slim literally ran into him while searching for his missing harpist.

Johnson became Lazy Lester in the mid-fifties when he began recording for Excello; the relationship lasted about a decade and resulted in some fine material, including "If You Think I've Lost You" and "Sugar Coated

Love." He also worked as a valued session player for Miller, throwing in much creative input as virtuosic harp. After working briefly with Buddy Guy in Chicago in the early seventies, Lester broke from the music business for several years to settle in Michigan for a while. He mounted a comeback in 1988 with an album for Alligator, *Harp & Soul*.

Silas Hogan (1911–1994) was a guitarist and harmonica player who learned to play from his uncles. He grew up in Irene, Louisiana, and perfected his craft playing house parties through the thirties. Trained in the rural tradition, Hogan went electric several years before Dylan at Newport and, finally recording in his fifties, was soon a mainstay for Jay Miller's Excello stable.

Unfortunately, Excello went bust shortly thereafter, and Hogan went to work in oil. By the seventies, though, his archetypal blues were in demand on the festival circuit—including the New Orleans Jazz & Heritage Festival—and he recorded for the Arhoolie and Blue Horizon labels. A sampling of his work is *Trouble: The Best of the Excello Masters*.

And of course there's the Godfather, **Raful Neal** (1936–), a most prodigious and talented Blues Daddy. Neal is not only a world-class harmonica player but also a songwriter and singer.

Neal was born in the Baton Rouge suburb of Chamberlin, where he picked cotton as a kid and, at ten, learned the harmonica. Influenced by Little Walter, and slow-smoked in the blues of his childhood environs, Neal started playing along with the radio. At seventeen, he and the soon-to-be-called Lazy Lester formed a band called the Clouds; when Lester headed to Chicago, he was replaced by Buddy Guy.

Though other top players migrated out of town, Neal stayed put because he had started a family that would eventually include ten kids; without regret he set out to become the giant of the Baton Rouge blues scene. Since 1958, Neal has compiled a fine series of mostly small-label singles. His first album was the renowned *Louisiana Legend*, available from Alligator. In 1991, he released the compatibly great *I Been Mistreated*, which features sons Kenny and Noel and is largely self-penned.

Though he continues to watch over the family bar, Neal has retired from day gigs and most recently came out with a warm tribute album to his clan, his pals, and the Baton Rouge blues community at large, *Old Friends*.

From the reporter's notebook:

Louisiana Black and I had watched an entire set of Jackie Neal's funky soul review, drinking beer and just taking it easy, and I kept studying the doorman—a big guy with a pleasant smile and a Panama hat, gnawing on pieces of fried chicken secured from the wondrous kitchen in back of the club—because he looked familiar. Finally, when Jackie Neal started the second set by asking her father to come up and sing, the door guy sets his chicken atop a bar stool, hands the door money to another guy, dusts

*off his hands, and makes his way through the happy throng to the stage.
The doorman was Raful Neal!*

*Oh, yeah. He sang his ass off with the warmth and discretion of
someone who didn't wanna take any momentum from his kid's gig—a
true gentleman. Then he went back to his post and picked up his chicken.*

If the Baton Rouge scene is in fact a form unto itself, it does not account
for all the blues artists in Louisiana. Indeed, as I mentioned, there are far
more successful, old-guard Louisiana blues artists than those mentioned
above, at least in terms of global renown. **Buddy Guy** (1936–), who spent
plenty of high-quality years in the Baton Rouge coterie, is probably
thought of, with justification, as the most famous and influential. He was
born in Lettsworth, Louisiana, not far from Shreveport, and played extensively in Baton Rouge before heading north to Chicago, where he's the
heart of Chicago's millennial electric blues scene. He's also a hero to Eric
Clapton, a good pal of the late Stevie Vaughan's, and a self-proclaimed inspiration to Jimi Hendrix.

Guy began to garner a reputation in Baton Rouge in the early fifties,
playing first with John "Big Poppa" Tilley and then with Raful Neal. His slashing fretwork, coupled with a stage persona fueled by Guitar Slim, served him
well when he relocated to Chicago in 1957, where he was soon rubbing musical elbows with Otis Rush, Muddy Waters, Freddy King, and Magic Sam.

Guy released a few fiery but interpretive, Willie Dixon–produced
sides for Cobra, then went to Chess. During the sixties he recorded solo
material for the label; along the way, he became their session guitarist, no
small achievement. Guy backed Muddy Waters, Big Walter Horton, and
Sonny Boy Williamson. His own best work from that period can be found
on *Buddy Guy Complete Chess Studio Recordings, Vol I* and *Vol II*.

He then hooked up with Vanguard Records and with harmonica-
meister Junior Wells, an incendiary live partnership that lasted throughout
the seventies and produced several great international tours (including prestigious dates with the Rolling Stones) and albums such as the in-concert
Drinkin' TNT and Smokin' Dynamite. Though his solo recording efforts remained sporadic and his reputation with American fans low-key, Guy
opened his own Chicago music club and, through his friendships with Clapton and Vaughan, began to seep into a substantial fan-base consciousness.

His 1991 Silvertone, *Damn Right I've Got the Blues*, not only won a
Grammy, it caught on in a big way and made Guy a star. His club is a
must-see attraction in Chicago, and he headlines his own tours or travels
with biggie packages featuring B. B. King and the likes (or, as on the one
that found Guy, in Wisconsin in August, 1990, playing with Robert Cray,
Clapton, Jimmie Vaughan, and Stevie Ray Vaughan—after which Stevie
Ray perished in a helicopter crash).

Guy's recorded work since his ascension to superstardom has been erratic, but high points include *Heavy Love* and *Slippin' In*. For all his efforts to be all things to all people, Guy sometimes misses the mark. But he's still one of the best blues guitarists in the world.

Kenny Wayne Shepherd, who at the age of fourteen spent a day eating barbecue with Guy, marvels over him. "Buddy's just so good. I mean, he's *good*. That's the only way to say it."

Tab Benoit says he thinks of one word when he hears Guy: "Fire. That's what I got out of Buddy Guy, that fire. How to turn the heat up."

The list of legendary Louisiana blues artists automatically includes **Clarence "Gatemouth" Brown** (1924–). Brown, still going strong in his late seventies, is a remarkable and innovative musician. He bristles at being pigeonholed as a "blues" musician, or as any stylist, and prefers to call himself a purveyor of American music. Fair enough: versatile at fiddle, accordion, drums, and guitar, and having performed jazz, blues, zydeco, and even country with aplomb, skill, and wit, Brown's own assessment of his work is astonishingly accurate, if not particularly modest.

As for my pegging him a blues artist, well, it's mostly for convenience and because he came up with a signature blues riff on the song "Okie Dokie Stomp," which most aspiring blues players must now practice with the fervor of a yeshiva student roaring through Torah.

Brown was born in Vinton, Louisiana, in 1924, and grew up in Orange, Texas, where he watched zydeco-blues songsters entertain at fish fries and house parties. "Gatemouth" is the nickname given him by a music teacher in an attempt to describe his voice. He was a quick study on first the fiddle and then the drums, and he developed into a versatile singer. Brown played in professional bands on the southern and eastern seaboard from his teens until he was drafted into World War II. When the war ended, he became entranced by T-Bone Walker and shifted his musical stylings in the direction of electric blues. One night at Don Robey's Bronze Peacock Club in Houston, where Brown was in attendance, the headlining Walker became ill. Brown seized the moment to get onstage and, using T-Bone's guitar, ripped up the joint. Walker raced back onstage, so the story goes, suddenly healed.

"No, he wasn't happy about it, I can tell you that," Brown told me during one of three interviews I conducted with him over the years.

Robey immediately signed Brown to a management deal, and not long after started his own Peacock Records label as an outlet for Gate's music. Brown started releasing records in 1949, and at first they were admittedly derivative of Walker. But by the time "Okie Dokie Stomp" came out a few years later, Brown had established his personal imprint on whatever he played—and that encompassed everything from sizzling swing and heart-ripping blues to lively zydeco and rich R&B.

His live shows were legendary and led him to host the television variety show *The Beat*. He drew huge crowds on the European festival circuit in the sixties, and later he experimented with mainstream country music, recording at one point with guitar virtuoso Roy Clark. By the end of the decade, Brown had signed with Rounder and began to release a stunning series of blues-based records, among them *One More Mile, Real Life*, and *Alright Again!* (which won a Grammy in 1981). He then started to experiment more with jazz on *Texas Swing* and *Pressure Cooker*, a tendency that only intensified toward the millennium on CDs such as *The Man, Gate Swings, Long Way Home*, and *American Music, Texas Style*.

Clearly, the old man is going strong and touring heavily. "I'm working on my autobiography," he keeps telling me. "I guess I work too hard. I don't have time for anything but the music."

Brown now lives in Slidell, just outside New Orleans. When he's not on the road, he heads into the French Quarter and hangs at the House of Blues, where he has his own booth, his own parking place, and his own signature dish: Gate's Catfish Bites.

As for his recommendations on Louisiana music, Gate suggests several of his own records and strongly suggests avoiding anything by young whippersnappers such as Kenny Wayne Shepherd. "It's not just him, though, it's all those younger players," he said. "Stevie Vaughan was a wonderful person but all he wanted to do was be Jimi Hendrix. Until people get their own IDs and stop being copiers, there's not really anyone up and coming I'm interested in playing with. If they want to pay me to play on their records, I'll help 'em out. But that's about it."

Presumably, had the chronology worked out, Brown would have helped **Huddie Ledbetter** (1888–1949), had he been asked. But apparently Ledbetter didn't need help. While serving two prison sentences, he improvised songs for two governors and won parole thanks to his tunes each time.

A complex man with a Jekyll-and-Hyde personality, Ledbetter, also known as **Leadbelly**, was born on the Louisiana side of Caddo Lake on the Texas state line. He mastered guitar, accordion, and piano, but his one stroke of instrumental vision came when he put down the six-string guitar in exchange for the twelve-string variety, which many of us in the older generation associate with the chiming sound of the Byrds or even the Plimsouls. In the hands of Leadbelly, though, the ax took on a haunting but aggressive quality, the shimmering strings anchored by a heartbeat bass pattern.

Starting out, he honed his burgeoning skills at house parties in his native Mooringsport and in nearby Shreveport, influenced by the sounds rising out of the post–Civil War Reconstruction era. He was also writing his own material by the time he moved to Dallas, and somewhere in the early years of the new century he adapted the song he's best remembered for,

"Goodnight Irene." He gigged regularly (in houses of ill repute) with Blind Lemon Jefferson from around 1912 to 1917. That arrangement was interrupted when Leadbelly was convicted of murdering a man and served six years of hard time in Shaw State Prison Farm. In a legal maneuver that probably wouldn't work today (unless Johnnie Cochran's been taking guitar lessons), Leadbelly improvised a song in front of visiting Governor Pat Neff, who then pardoned the inmate!

Leadbelly returned to Louisiana and continued to play the blues, evolving over time into a fine songwriter. In 1930 he was imprisoned again, this time for assaulting a woman. Leadbelly performed for visiting folklorist John Lomax, who was taping authentic chain-gang songs, field hollers, and rural blues at Angola Penitentiary. One of the tunes Leadbelly performed was a plea for clemency aimed at Governor O. K. Alan, who, not wanting to be outdone by a Texan, one supposes, pardoned Leadbelly yet again.

Lomax became Leadbelly's manager and Leadbelly became Lomax's chauffeur. They relocated to New York, where Leadbelly's public image grew substantially. He performed with Burl Ives and Woody Guthrie, and recorded a vast repertoire of original material and clever arrangements. Part of Lomax's strategy was to publicize Leadbelly in a striped prison uniform; another part was to sign his name on the song copyrights as a collaborator.

Leadbelly recorded sides for the Library of Congress and the American Recording Company, but met with only modest success. By the forties, though, he'd split with Lomax and continued to evolve artistically. His later material developed a conscience, and he gained popularity as an entertainer of children, whom he loved.

Leadbelly was never the star he'd hoped or deserved to be. But as a strikingly original artist and one who laid ground for the next generations of folk and blues artists, he's become a justifiably renowned figure.

There's a wealth of material to choose from, but anyone wanting an introductory taste of Leadbelly would do well to pick up Rounder's *Midnight Special* or *Gwine Dig a Hole to Put the Devil In*, or Columbia/Legacy's *King of the 12-String Guitar.*

He might have been the second most famous alumnus of New Orleans's Colored Waif's Home, but it's probably true that William Thomas **"Champion Jack" Dupree** (1909–1992) could have beaten up the most famous—who was, of course, Louis Armstrong—because in addition to being a marvelous and influential blues pianist, Dupree was the veteran of over a hundred professional prizefights.

When you think about it, boxing isn't the most physically sympathetic occupation for a would-be pianist, but Dupree, whose parents died either in an accidental fire or one started by members of the Ku Klux Klan (he was often ambiguous about that), hustled coins in the streets of the French Quarter until he learned enough barrelhouse piano from local legends Don Bowers and Willie "Drive 'Em Down" Hall to begin earning cash indoors.

At twenty, hoping to escape suffocating racism, he headed for the Midwest, playing piano and bootlegging whiskey between Chicago, Detroit, and Indianapolis for years. For a while, though, boxing was his passion; he spent some time as the lightweight champion of Indiana. Gradually, his reputation as a pianist began to spread and he started a recording career, only to have it interrupted when he was drafted in World War II and served two years as a prisoner of war in Japan. Upon returning, taking on as much work as he could get, he recorded for a variety of labels under several names, though his 1955 duet with Mr. Teddy Bear, which was called "Walking the Blues" and went to #6 on the R&B charts, was under his real name. His best work happened for the King label, at least until 1958, when he released what most regard as his masterpiece, *Blues from the Gutter* (Atlantic). Featuring quintessential takes of such N'Awlins fare as "Stack O'Lee," "Junker's Blues," and "Frankie and Johnnie," the album is not only a superb relic of a quickly fading piano style but also influenced younger players, Professor Longhair and Fats Domino among them.

In the late fifties, Dupree moved to Europe, where he enjoyed solid popularity, recorded for several labels, and in general had it pretty good. It wasn't until 1990 that Dupree returned to the United States to play his hometown Jazz & Heritage Festival. He encored the performance a year later, and also released three albums for the prestigious Bullseye Blues label: *Back Home in New Orleans*, *One Last Time*, and *Forever and Ever* (featuring an awesome version of "Yellow Pocahontas"). The collection, *New Orleans Barrelhouse Boogie (The Complete Champion Jack Dupree)*, available from Columbia/Legacy, offers the best sampling of Dupree's work.

There are two "Slims" in the annals of Louisiana blues. In terms of sheer influence, Slim Harpo had massive effect, particularly with the British rock invasion of the early sixties. On the other hand, Guitar Slim without question had an impact on Jimi Hendrix and several others with his onstage aura and attitude.

If you're a rock fan, you know a lot more about **Slim Harpo** (1924–1970) than you think you do—if for no other reason than his work was covered in reverent fashion by no less than the Kinks and the Rolling Stones (who had a hit with Harpo's "I'm a King Bee"). Born James Moore, Harpo grew up in Port Allen, Louisiana, played youthful gigs—under the nickname Harmonica Slim—as a matter of survival after his folks died, and became an integral part of the Baton Rouge blues scene.

Characterized by clever material, raw arrangements, and stripped-down instrumentation, Harpo's music was most identifiable by his adenoidal vocal delivery, sleepy but effective guitar style, and punctuation-mark harmonica riffs. His songs were special. He co-wrote with his wife, Lovelle, and felt no guilt about borrowing from rock beats and country structures—all of which paid off when he charted such hits as "Rainin' in My Heart" and "Baby Scratch My Back"—before the Brits picked up on his peculiar genius.

He became Slim Harpo just before releasing the "I'm a King Bee" single, and fame ensued. He called his old pal Lightnin' Slim for some national tours. They went extremely well, particularly with young white audiences, and plans for a European tour were in the works when Harpo died suddenly of a heart attack. *Hip Shakin'—the Excello Collection* is probably his most definitive work.

The other Louisiana "Slim"—**Guitar Slim** (1926–1959)—was from Mississippi. Born Eddie Jones, the ax hero started singing in church as a kid. He says he grew interested in guitar after a choir tour, but little is known about the details of his guitar education. What is known is that he showed up in New Orleans in 1949 and was soon playing lead in Huey "Piano" Smith's trio.

Influenced by Clarence "Gatemouth" Brown, Slim graduated to session work over the next few years. But it was his explosive approach to live performance that led to Slim's own recording dates. After a few mediocre efforts, he cranked out a serving of chicken-fried gospel called "The Things You Used to Do" in 1954. It was a smash. It nestled atop the R&B charts for several weeks and brought plenty of bookings that enabled Slim to perpetuate his own image, which, in turn, sold more records.

Guitar Slim must've been amazing to watch. He had a guitar cable longer than a football field; he trod with it across table tops, the bar, and out into the streets. He wore Easter-egg colored suits, dyed his hair to match, and sang bluesy R&B with undercurrents of gospel with pre-Hendrixism guitar inventiveness.

An account from Jerry Wexler's autobiography, *Rhythm & the Blues— A Life in American Music,* describes a recording session with Slim, which took place on an abusively hot day in Cosimo Matassa's studio. Slim was dressed up in full stage regalia—he insisted on recording in such finery— and they were trying to get a take on a soulful tune called "There's Plenty Good Room in My House." The problem was that Slim, very much a free spirit, kept forgetting lyrics in his exuberant flights of fancy. Here's Wexler:

> We try to explain: "You have to go from here to here," I point out. But Slim is adamant. "When I get there, my natural soul brings me to here."
>
> We get an idea. Leaning against the wall, there's a big cardboard placard announcing a R&B show at the San Jacinto Ballroom. . . . We turn it over, rip it into sections, and separately print the lyrics for the verses, bridge, chorus, and coda. We appoint someone to hold the appropriate section—and that section only—as Slim makes his way through the song. Slim, though, is unhappy with the holder. We try a

second holder, and a third, and a fourth. We finally get to the tag—
and Slim skips it.

"Slim, you missed the coda."

"Motherfuck the motherfuckin' coda," he says. "I'm here to sing
'There's Plenty Good Room in My House.'"

His reputation was as an R&B artist, and because he insisted on playing bluesier material in performance, he would often end up losing his
deals. But in 1956, after some extremely frustrating years, he got new management and a fresh contract with Atco. Producers commercialized his
sound on such songs as "If I Had My Life to Live Over Again" and "Hello,
How Ya Been, Goodbye." But over the next two years, the alcohol began to
catch up with him; eventually, it was obvious on and off stage. He refused
to heed doctors' warnings and died at the age of thirty-two while on tour
in New York City.

As with Hendrix, with whom he'll always be associated, Guitar Slim
remains a character about whom you can't help but wonder: What the hell
could he have done had he lived even twenty more years?

"Outrageous," says Tab Benoit. "That guy was just outrageous. Not
only was he the first guy with the long guitar cables, but he used to wear
these insanely colored suits and wanted his hair to match. So he'd have to
paint his hair because there were no hair dyes that wild."

Pick up either the *Suffering Mind* or *Things That I Used to Do* collection, though probably nothing recorded compares with the live legend.

Of equal stature, both as a musician and all-around character, was harmonica wizard **Little Walter** (1930–1957). Few would dispute that the
two harping Walters—Little Walter (born Marion Walter Jacobs in
Marksville, Louisiana) and Big Walter Horton—were probably the best
blues harmonica players ever, and certainly better at it than Dan Aykroyd
and John Popper. Little Walter's flighty and instinctively great runs and
jazz-flavored shuffles were mainstays not only of Muddy Waters's sound
but also of his own fine solo work.

He hauled ass from the Louisiana countryside to New Orleans when
he was twelve, formed his own band, then traveled through Memphis,
Arkansas, Texas, Montana, and St. Louis before landing in Chicago in the
mid-forties. Instinctively brilliant on the chromatic harmonica, the movie
star–handsome young man started hanging out with Tampa Red, Big Bill
Broonzy, and Memphis Slim. He was doing sessions and extensive club
work within a year, and before long had hooked up with Waters. The two
of them called themselves The Headhunters and swaggered into clubs
looking for musical gunfights—and taking no prisoners along the way.

The Muddy Waters Band, formed in the late forties, toured and
recorded to great acclaim. In addition to his work with Waters, Little Walter was the house harpist for the legendary Chess label, for whom he

recorded the hit single "Juke" in 1952. The single made him a star in his own right, and for the next several years he laid down fourteen chart-topping hit songs for quasi-sibling label Checker, including "You're So Fine," "Mean Old World," and "You Better Watch Yourself." Little Walter never really ran out of gas; rather, it was the decline in popularity of Chicago blues that hastened his descent into chronic alcohol abuse. Though efforts to help were made by everyone from Waters to Bo Diddley, Walter couldn't pull out of his own tailspin. He died reportedly from a bloodclot that formed after a disastrous streetfight.

If you own only one Little Walter project, get *The Chess Years, 1952–1963*, which is a one-of-a-kind musical textbook on blues harmonica.

My pal Rocky Lawrence, the terrific Connecticut blues guitarist who plays with Hubert Sumlin, relates a story Sumlin told him about some Little Walter justice from the Chicago days:

> Hubert and Wolf were upstairs at the Chess Building doing some recording and heard an explosion outside. Hubert went to the window and looked out and said, "It's not an explosion." There was a new Caddie *smashed* through the front wall of the building, and the car was stopped inches in front of the Chess brothers' desks and they were standing there in horror.
>
> It was Walter's car, and it was so caved in that he had to crawl out the back window and into the office, where he held out an empty suitcase and said, "Fill it up." And they did—with overdue money. Little Walter came upstairs and paid all the musicians—every one. Hubert told me, "Son, that's when we started getting the money we earned." And an hour later there was a new Caddie out front for Little Walter.

Just as Little Walter and Champion Jack prove that not all blues stars are guitarists, all blues stars aren't necessarily killer players, either. **Lizzie "Memphis Minnie" Douglas** (1897–1973) was born in Algiers, just across the river from New Orleans.

Minnie was arguably the greatest female country blues singer of all time. She started playing banjo shortly after her family moved to Walls, Mississippi, when she was seven, then ran away from home when she was eleven to perform in the streets as Kid Douglas.

Shortly after, she landed in Memphis, hooked up with the Ringling Bros. Circus, and worked tent shows until she was in her early twenties. By the time she quit that gig and returned to Memphis, she'd learned guitar and started to sing in Beale Street bars, gigging frequently with Jed Davenport's Beale Street Jug Band. By the end of the decade, Minnie had cut sides with the Memphis Jug Band (for the Victor label), and then moved to Chicago and formed her own group. She began to record for the OKeh label, and in the early thirties won at least one guitar-cutting contest that included such competition as Tampa Red and Big Bill Broonzy.

With her southern roots, neo-vaudeville experience, and immersion in the Chicago scene, Minnie developed a unique style that was as virtuosic as it was appealing to musicians and fans alike. In performance, she'd use comical songs and tell jokes to blend with spirituals and moaning country blues. She frequently worked duets, and over the years she married three of her male onstage partners.

For the rest of the thirties, Minnie released sides for a variety of labels including Vocalion, Decca, and Bluebird, teaming up at one point with Bumble Bee Slim, whom I mention out of numerous collaborators just because his name is so cool. Minnie spent the next several years making records for just about every recording company in America, working extensively in clubs throughout the Midwest, including her own bar in Indianapolis with someone named St. Louis Jimmy.

She also formed and worked with a vaudeville-styled troupe for several years until the mid-fifties, when she more or less retired. Not long after, Minnie began to suffer from declining health. She lived in rest homes for several years before suffering a fatal stroke.

Among her most memorable tunes are "I Want to Do Something For You," "Meningitis Blues," "Bumble Bee," and "Nothing in Rambling." Her best albums are *Hoodoo Lady (1933–1937)*, available on Columbia, and *Kansas Joe* (Blues Classics).

Johnny "Clyde" Copeland (1937–1997), born in Haynesville, Louisiana, inherited a guitar after the premature death of his father. By the time the family moved to Houston while Clyde was still young, he was doing paid gigs in the tonks.

Working with Albert Collins, Big Mama Thornton, and Freddy King, Copeland's style developed quickly. His synthesis of New Orleans–styled funk and the sort of jazzy swing you'd hear from the Kansas City players made him unique amongst his fellow bluesmen.

After playing the swamp circuit, Copeland headed to New York City in 1974 and signed with Rounder Records in 1981. He released several fine albums for the label, including *Texas Twister*, the Grammy-nominated live album *Ain't Nothin' But a Party*, and *When the Rains Starts a Fallin'*.

With his fluid guitar style, shouting, exuberant, gospel-drenched voice, and crafty way with a song structure and lyric, Copeland was a refreshing presence on the blues scene. In later years, he suffered heart problems. A few months after a heart transplant, complications set in and Copeland died in surgery.

Simply one of the best electric bluesmen going, **Lonnie Brooks** (1933–) was born Lee Baker Jr. in Dubuisson, Louisiana. His first gig was lead guitarist for Clifton Chenier, the musical equivalent of an all-around Ivy League education (Chenier is discussed in detail in "Early Cajun and Creole Music," Part 4, Chapter 1).

He was slow coming around, though; it wasn't until he was in his twenties and living in Port Arthur, Texas, that he took the instrument seriously. Calling himself Guitar Junior, he recorded his own successful swamp-pop song—"Family Rules"—for the regional Goldband label, and followed with a successful dance floor rave, "The Crawl."

At the invitation of Sam Cooke, he headed to Chicago, only to find there was already a Guitar Junior. He worked a variety of sessions, eventually releasing some poorly received soul singles by the early seventies. Along the way, however, his own slicing style began to emerge, coupled with an engaging stage presence and powerful singing voice. When four of his cuts were high points on one of the *Living Chicago Blues* compilations released by Alligator Records, a contract was quickly in the offing. In 1979, he released *Bayou Lightning,* the first of a remarkable series of albums that includes *Hot Shot, Deluxe Edition,* and the very fine *Roadhouse Rules.*

In 1999, Brooks was featured along with Long John Hunter and Phillip Walker on a consistently sizzling CD called *Lone Star Shootout.*

As Brooks adapted his swamp pop–influenced sound into the context of Chicago, **Snooks Eaglin** (1936–) is a guitarist from New Orleans who's stayed true to the sounds of his hometown. Eaglin (born Fird Eaglin Jr.), who lost his sight while an infant, learned guitar by replicating sounds from the radio and jamming with his harmonica-playing father. He has spent most of his career as a session wizard and his work with Professor Longhair alone is legendary. He also played in the renowned Flamingos, headed up by thirteen-year-old Allen Toussaint, then worked solo, billing himself "Little Ray Charles."

He was discovered in the French Quarter by folklorist Harry Oster, who released three albums of Eaglin's rural and acoustic blues material on the Folkways label. In 1960, Eaglin was signed by Dave Bartholomew, who subsequently produced several sessions for the guitarist. Though none of the singles hit big, Eaglin was able to sustain himself with extensive club and session work throughout Orleans Parish. His local status went through the roof after an inspired pairing with Professor Longhair at the inaugural Jazz & Heritage Festival in 1971.

Since the eighties, when Eaglin signed with local blues label Black Top, he has released several sturdy albums of note: *Baby, You Can Get Your Gun* (which featured contributions by Bartholomew, blind piano great Henry Butler, and R&B vocalist Tommy Ridgley), *Teasin' You,* and *Live in Japan.* As a writer, interpreter, and acoustic and electric maestro, Eaglin is the real deal.

Excerpt from an e-mail diary entry sent to the author by Cowboy Mouth drummer Fred LeBlanc:

> *The other night I was at Mid-City Lanes Rock 'n' Bowl. Cool place,*
> *great vibe. There was a guy playing there, a local blues guitarist named*
> *Snooks Eaglin, great player and singer. . . . Anyway, his drummer for the*

evening was a guy I know called Jellybean (who is a GREAT drummer)
and he and I have known each other around the circuit for years. During
a break [the drummer] asked me if I wished to play a song [with] Snooks
& the band. Now Snooks is kind of a local legend, so I was honored to be
asked. . . . So what song does local blues legend Snooks Eaglin choose to
play with me? "Back That Ass Up," of course. . . . You see, only in New
Orleans can a white guy in a punk/country/rock band get on stage
[with] a local black, blind blues guitar legend in order to play a rap song
and make it feel like the most natural thing in the world.

There are plenty of notable Louisiana blues players who have stayed local
but aren't part of the Baton Rouge scene. Of the guitar players, **Clarence
"Bon Ton" Garlow** (1911–1986), a Welsh, Louisiana, native, grew up in
East Texas. His guitar playing and songwriting were largely overlooked outside that region despite heavily influencing Clifton Chenier and Johnny
Winter. Early on, Garlow was taken with zydeco—his father was heavily
into it—and studied fiddle and accordion in addition to guitar.

When he heard T-Bone Walker for the first time, though, he shifted all
focus to blues guitar. He recorded for a variety of small labels in the region,
and developed a scalpel-sharp style to be envied, but Garlow's only true
taste of success came in 1941, at the relative dawn of his recording career,
when a single called "Bon Ton Roula"—"let the good times roll"—made the
national charts.

Long John Hunter (1931–) was born in southeast Louisiana and grew
up near Beaumont, Texas, but his legacy will rest on his having played the
blues for years in Juarez, Mexico—being one of few, to be sure, who
worked that hotspot. He was in self-exile down there because he felt
duped in an early deal with Don Robey of Duke Records; in any case,
Hunter used his time on the border honing his considerable guitar skills. In
1995, he headed back into mainland Texas, signed with Alligator, and released the very strong *Border Town Legend* CD.

A Mississippi native called **Louisiana Red** (1936–) was born Iverson
Minter. His mother died the week he was born and his father was lynched by
the Ku Klux Klan five years later. Red was raised by grandparents in New
Orleans and learned enough guitar to record some primitive sides for Chess
before joining the army when he was sixteen. After the service, he began
performing blues guitar as Rocky Fuller, Guitar Red, and Playboy Fuller, releasing singles for small labels. He played with John Lee Hooker in Detroit
for a while, and his ability to assimilate the hot styles of the best lead players
of the genre ultimately resulted in Red's own fiery brand of musicianship.

His solo writings are haunting and poetically bizarre, like "Red's
Dream," surely inspired by the tragedies of his childhood as well as the
active imagination one associates with writer Ray Bradbury. In the song,

the singer imparts a unique twist to blues subject matter by solving the Cuban missile crisis during a visit to the United Nations. Evidence Records has released a nice compilation, *The Best of Louisiana Red.*

Another guitar monster is **Mighty Joe Young** (1927–?), who was born in Shreveport in 1927 but grew up in that most bluesy of towns, Milwaukee. After migrating to the fruitful Chicago scene, he has devoted his life to solid, steady blues. He returned to Louisiana briefly in 1955, hoping to catch on with a label there, but returned to Chicago. By the early sixties, he'd hit with "Why, Baby," "I Want a Love," and "Voo Doo Dust." For years he released high-quality, soul-flecked records, but in recent years the infirmities of age have restricted his ability to play. His 1974 album *Chicken Heads* is a fine sampler.

Born in New Orleans, **Frankie Lee Sims** (1917–1970) ran away from home as a kid, learned guitar, taught elementary school, served in World War II, and finally settled in North Texas, where he set about playing the country blues. He was a witty lyricist, if a hackneyed structuralist, and sang in a breathy, faintly sinister tone. He recorded extensively during his career, most notably for the Specialty and Ace labels. It's hard to find his stuff, but look for a CD called *Lucy Mae Blues.*

A few other Louisiana blues guitarists worth mentioning:

✦   **Sam Collins** (1887–1949). Originally known as "Crying Sam Collins and His Git-Fiddle," he was one of the earliest Mississippi bluesmen, born in Louisiana. He played a clumsy but prototypical slide guitar, and may have been the first one to record a song about being in the pokie: "The Jail House Blues," in 1927.

✦   **Boogie Jake** (1929–?). A fine guitarist and pianist from Marksville, Louisiana, he worked early on with Little Walter and ended up in Baton Rouge as a vital ingredient in the Excello blues package, mostly as a sideman.

✦   **Arthur "Guitar" Kelley** (1924–?), a Clinton, Louisiana, native, Kelley who played guitar with Silas Hogan for years and recorded a few sides for the Excello label.

✦   **Lemoine "Lemon" Nash** (1898–1969), a multi-instrumentalist stringster (guitar, mandolin, banjo, ukelele), was from Lakeland, Louisiana. He worked for tips virtually all his life in every conceivable musical situation from railroad yards to house parties to nightclubs to the streets of the French Quarter.

✦   **Robert Pete Williams** (1914–1980), an unorthodox artist, from Zachary, Louisiana, was a born guitarist and was discovered while in prison. An acoustic player with no interest in playing in any expected patterns or style, and who frequently made up his own tunings, Williams either mesmerized or irritated the listener.

✦ **Phillip Walker** (1937–) was born in Welsh, Louisiana, and grew up copping licks from Clarence "Gatemouth" Brown and Long John Hunter on the Gulf Coast. His biggest hit was an early effort called "Hello My Darling."

Louisiana blues pianists outside Baton Rouge who made significant contributions include **Roosevelt Sykes** (1906–1983), a guy who embodied the cheerful concept of Santa Claus going as a blues pianist on Halloween. Sykes used a swaggering, post-barrelhouse style and a comic's sense of punning and sexual humor. He grew up in Arkansas and worked extensively in Chicago, though he recorded for Dave Bartholomew in New Orleans and later settled in the city for the final years of his life. Known as The Honeydripper, Sykes was a vitamin blast to the blues genre, and his primordial take of "Sweet Home Chicago" is a treasure.

Eurreal "Little Brother" Montgomery (1906–1985), born in Kentwood, Louisiana, was a truly big musical deal. A pianist and vocalist who segued from seminal American blues to Chicago electric blues, Montgomery taught himself to play when he was five, singing in church along the way. He quit school at eleven to work in juke joints and never looked back.

After extensive training in a variety of New Orleans clubs, Montgomery landed in Chicago in his twenties, and within four years was writing and recording for the Paramount label. He returned to the South for a few years, recorded in New Orleans for Bluebird Records, then settled permanently in Chicago. He later formed his own label and recorded some nice boogie woogie and barrelhouse material, but the *Complete Recorded Works (1930–1954)* is probably the best-bet look at his career.

Boogie Woogie Red (1925–1992) was a Rayville, Louisiana, native born Vernon Harrison. Red's family relocated to Michigan while he was still an infant. He learned piano as a kid, studying with local legends Big Maceo and Dr. Clayton, and by the time he was a teenager he was a versatile player with a unique style. He became a favored sideman for Sonny Boy Williamson and John Lee Hooker in Chicago and alternated the bulk of his career between Chicago and Detroit.

Dave Alexander (1938–) is a Shreveport-born pianist-drummer-singer who grew up in East Texas and, after settling in the Bay Area and working with Big Mama Thornton, became a fine practitioner of West Coast blues. He's released some nice records for the Arhoolie label, and his original material has a distinctly urban tint. He also goes by the name Omar Hakim Khayyam, under which he writes blues and African American music.

Born just outside of Shreveport, **Willie Egan** was a solid piano player who scored a series of hits in the fifties—"Wow Wow," "What a Shame," "Wear Your Black Dress" among them—for the Mambo and Vita labels.

A keyboard inspiration to Dr. John, James Booker, and Fats Domino, **Leon "Archibald" Gross** (1912–1973), a New Orleans pianist, worked clubs as an entertainer in the French Quarter and recorded briefly for Imperial and Colony.

Blues singers you should know about include:

Blue Lu Barker (1913–1999), born in New Orleans, was a reclusive vocalist with a wonderful personality who was perhaps known too much as the spouse of jazz guitarist and writer Danny Barker. Still, when she could be coaxed to sing, she did so with a distinct (if limited) voice. The biggest of her numerous hits in the thirties was "Don't You Make Me High," though, late in life, she released *Live at New Orleans Jazz Festival.*

Carol Fran & Clarence Hollimon met in New Orleans in 1957. She was a young singer with a powerful voice from Lafayette who'd worked with Guitar Slim and who'd enjoyed a big solo hit called "Emmit Lee." He backed Clarence "Gatemouth" Brown, Big Mama Thornton, and Bobby "Blue" Bland. But it wasn't until about twenty-five years later that the two got together permanently and became the blues equivalent of *Love American Style.* In the early nineties they signed with Black Top and released such fine (if hard to find) albums as *See There!, Soul Sensation,* and *Gulf Coast Blues.*

Al King (1926–) was born Alvin Smith in Monroe, Louisiana, and relocated in his early twenties to Los Angeles where he enjoyed a steady club career; he formed his own label, Flag Records, in the mid-sixties.

Lizzie Miles (1896–1963) was a classic New Orleans–born blues belter who started singing with jazz musicians Kid Ory, Joe Oliver, and Bunk Johnson. She worked in Chicago through the Depression and was out with a serious illness for years, but rebounded to continue a sterling career as an old-time, all-purpose blues singer and nightclub entertainer.

Richard "Rabbit" Brown was a New Orleans–born songster who frequently worked the street corners of his hometown and Baton Rouge, led a good life, and is resting comfortably in whatever passes for heaven. Still, his ability to extemporize rhymes and work as a singing boatman on Lake Ponchartrain made him a minor legend.

William Carradine of Garden City, Louisiana, was another street singer whose bluesy gospel resulted in at least one Folkways recording in the fifties.

Ann Cook (1903–1962) was a New Orleans–based barrelhouse blues singer who started out singing in Storyville and graduated to clubs and bars when Storyville was closed. She recorded jazz sides with Louis Dumaine, but her own improvisatory work was blues.

Two

YOUNG PUPS

*S*till wandering around Baton Rouge Blues Week, Louisiana Black and I check into a hotel and head on downtown to the Rhythm & Views Stage on Third Street, where two young and future turks of Louisiana blues are appearing. **T. J. Black**, now twenty-one, and eighteen-year-old **Joe Starks**, both past winners of a local contest for amateur guitarists, are splitting the bill in suitably impressive fashion.

It's late afternoon and a skein of clouds provides some relief from the sun. Behind the flatbed stage, traffic lights change, pointlessly, since the tree-punctuated street has been blocked off. Fine red-brick buildings housing hardware stores and insurance companies, their entryways covered by blue-and-white striped awnings, line the block. The crowd is substantial and a nice mix: Louisiana State University kids, post-work happy-hour folk, young civic types, and teensters dancing to Black's version of Hendrix's "Machine Gun"—a tune that predates their own parents' high school graduations.

Both players possess talent beyond their years—they're some of the best of the post–Stevie Ray movement that spawned Kenny Wayne Shepherd. For that matter, I'd pit T. J. Black against Shepherd right now.

As Louisiana Black and I only have a few hours here, it would be nice if we could see one true fave of the young guard—someone like **Corey Harris** (1969–), a dreadlocked acoustic guitarist who fairly drips the delta as well as Mother Africa and is arguably the most exciting young bluesman in Louisiana today. His fingerpicking style is astonishingly adept and punctuated with moaning slide work. His stage work uses poignant and clever original material within parenthetical doses of neatly arranged archival material. Harris is a burgeoning Louisiana treasure.

Born in Colorado, Harris grew up in a household filled with the sounds of gospel and Stevie Wonder. He was an award-winning trumpeter in his high school's marching band until he quit school in his sophomore year to pursue a new romantic interest: the guitar. Sponging up material from such diverse sources as Bob Dylan, Odetta, and Lightnin' Hopkins, Harris began to play in the streets for the experience as much as any coinage. Armed with a National Steel Standard guitar, he attended Bates College in Maine and played in the groups backing campus theatrical productions. Although he obtained a degree in anthropology, part of his education was travel; particularly enlightening was an eye-opening and ancestrally connective visit to Cameroon in West Africa.

Harris was staggered by the polyrhythmic seductions of the country's juju music, which he absorbed and thematically incorporated into his own work when he returned home. He settled in the Louisiana countryside and taught French and English in local schools, but on weekends and at night, he'd head into New Orleans and refine his musical skills on the streets of the Quarter—and soon he was playing in clubs and coffee houses.

Signed to the prestigious Alligator label in 1995, Harris released the *Between Midnight and Day* CD, which the *New York Times* described as "invoking the ghosts of Robert Johnson, Lightnin' Hopkins and Howlin' Wolf." All true—but the record also carved a big slice of Corey, for there is much original styling going on. Songstress Natalie Merchant was so taken with the album that she invited Harris to open on her West Coast tour later that year. The publicity generated by the album's reviews and his tour with a high-profile artist led to solo and international work for Harris.

In 1997 he came out with *Fish Ain't Bitin'*, an ambitious and logical thematic expansion that adds touches of brass and a new culturally aware lyrical edge to his tunes. Again, critical response was overwhelmingly positive and Harris became a favorite not just among blues fans but among musicians as well. He was invited by Billy Bragg to work with Wilco on the *Mermaid Avenue* project—the critics' favorite collaboration on which modern musicians took lyrics from the Woody Guthrie notebooks and wrote fresh and sympathetic music.

Harris's last solo album, *Greens from the Garden*, was another masterpiece, infusing dollops of reggae, ragtime, ska, and even hip-hop into his marvelously twisted take on rural Louisiana and Delta blues. It also boasted, on two songs, New Orleans jazz-and-blues piano wonder Henry Butler, a collaboration that led, in 2000, to the jointly released *Vu-Du Menz* CD.

"I met Corey in New Orleans a few years ago," Butler told me. "It's exciting to work with the very intricate rhythmic thing we've got going. Hopefully, the full-blown collaboration [*Vu-Du Menz*] demonstrates some of the magic we had together."

It does, and here's hoping they try it again. Corey Harris has a sparkling future.

Better Than Ezra with my wife and me, backstage after an out-door show at the submarine base in Groton, CT. I had left New Orleans at six that morning; a voodoo ceremony I was to attend the night before had been cancelled, so of course I was forced to stay out drinking with Louisiana Black most of the night be-fore a mad dash to the airport. My wife Eileen picked me up in Providence and we drove straight to the Ezra show. When we were introduced, they said, "Oh, you're the guy always emailing our request list to play 'WWOZ.'" Did they play it? No.

Jason Christley

Guitarist Tab Benoit

Jason Christley

Al Pjura

I can't count the times I've seen pianist Marcia Ball. This particular set was at the Rhythm & Roots Festival in Charlestown, Rhode Island; Steve Riley and Geno Delafose also played that day.

Blind guitar wonder
Snooks Eaglin

Ian McNulty

Photographer Ian McNulty and I caught retro-trumpeter Kermit Ruffins in a variety of spots around New Orleans, from Vaughan's in the Bywater to his regular Wednesday night gig at Les Bon Temps. This shot was taken at Les Bon Temps about ten minutes before a break and some of Kermit's free barbecue.

Dr. Larry's lovely wife, Deanna, took this picture of voodoo bluesman Coco Robicheaux at JazzFest. The week before, Coco spent a few hours graciously teaching me about the nuances of voodoo, of which he is a serious practitioner.

Deanna Williams

Jacquie Glassenberg

Say what you will about casinos, but the two in Connecticut bring in some amazing acts—in this case a free show by the Funky Meters. Art Neville saw my friend Jacquie Glassenberg shooting pictures and ushered her up onstage, where she got this image of Papa Funk and George Porter, Jr.

Fred LeBlanc of Cowboy Mouth

Jacquie Glassenberg

Bust of Professor Longhair, one of the many Fess images that dot Orleans Parish. This was located in an "Idol's Field of Honor" at JazzFest.

Steve Riley and the Mamou Playboys followed Marcia Ball at the Rhythm & Roots Festival in Rhode Island. That's never an easy job, but the Playboys were smoking.

Al Pjura

Buckwheat Zydeco playing a Fat Tuesday show

Dana Jensen

Beausoleil's Michael Doucet onstage at the Mardi Gras Ball in Cranston, Rhode Island

Eddie Bo at his regular Happy Hour set at Tipitina's in the Quarter

Eileen Koster

Brett Blackwell

Speaking of **Henry Butler**: Like a lot of Louisiana players, he could easily fit a variety of categories, whether it's blues, jazz, R&B, rock, or gospel. I decided to include him in the blues section when he said, "I believe in the evolving essence of music, which in my opinion has very little to do with physical style or genre. The essence of music can be expressed in any style, and I think most of us are very infantile in our understanding of it. So, as far as what kind of music I play, I chose a long time ago to move towards the essence—or spirit—of the emotional part of what we call music." I think that's a pretty blues-worthy statement.

Blind since his birth in New Orleans (as for his age, Butler said he was "as old as God and as young as eternity"), his mystical and philosophical approach to song and life are wonderfully refreshing, and the results are like a huge musical popcorn ball lovingly glued together by Jelly Roll Morton, Isadore "Tuts" Washington, and Professor Longhair. An innately gifted kid, Butler was performing at the Louisiana School for the Blind in Baton Rouge by seven. It was the first educational stop along a road that included studies at Southern University and Michigan State University, and landed him at such varied record labels as Alligator, Windham Hill, and MCA/Impulse.

He's traveled a bit, settling in New Orleans not only because it's home but because of the constant ebb and flow of musical styles. Butler has released some adventuresome and typically great records: *Blues and More, Vol. 1, Orleans Inspiration, Henry Butler—For All Seasons, Blues After Sunset,* and, of course, the collaboration with Corey Harris, *Vu-Du Menz.*

Butler is also an enthusiastic and quasi-professional photographer; he loves the food in his hometown and recommends Brigtsen's, Bayona, and Mandina's.

Representing another side of Louisiana blues entirely, and a significantly larger public recognition quotient, is **Kenny Wayne Shepherd** (1977–), a genuine, fill-the-arena star. A disciple of Stevie Ray Vaughan's to the extent that his first album is transparently derivative, it's important to remember the kid had a recording contract two years before the state of Louisiana would let him buy a daiquiri.

Born in Shreveport, Shepherd, whose father was a veteran radio programmer, was only seven when he saw Vaughan in concert for the first time. At an age when most youngsters are learning to chew bubble gum, Shepherd experienced the "musician's epiphany."

By the time he was thirteen, the kid was good enough to clamber onstage during a family vacation trip to New Orleans, jamming for several hours with Bourbon Street bluesman Bryan Lee. Soon after, he formed his first band. With the connections of his father (also his manager), Shepherd began working clubs, parties, and music conventions, drawing a substantial amount of word-of-mouth attention in the industry.

Not long after, he signed with Irving Azoff's Giant Records label and released his first CD, *Ledbetter Heights*, in 1995. Keeping in mind that the average seventy-year-old career bluesman probably won't have sold 50,000 records in his lifetime, note that Shepherd scorched out of the gate and moved a half-million units of his debut CD—which spent about twenty-four weeks in the #1 slot on *Billboard*'s Blues Chart.

True, he did sound like Stevie Ray. And yes, his blonde hair and cheek-bone-happy, "Why isn't he in *Party of Five?*" good looks probably didn't hurt. Cynics might suggest that white America was still clamoring for a white, blues-based guitar hero to take the late Vaughan's place—and they'd be right.

"Sure, Stevie Ray influenced me," Shepherd told me during a phone interview. "And I'm sure it's obvious. But I'd say with each album we've grown musically and you can hear it. Anytime you play two-hundred dates a year, you're gonna get better and develop your own style. But the passion has always been there. I was born with it; the guitar was an extension of my childhood, and when other kids were playing Little League, I was talking about Muddy Waters."

Shepherd does have some mighty fine chops, and he's clearly listened and learned from Albert and B. B. King, Muddy Waters, Duane Allman, Robert Johnson, and Billy Gibbons in addition to SRV.

Shepherd doesn't sing lead—yet. He's had two lead vocalists in his young recording career: Corey Sterling sang on the first CD before Noah Hunt assumed the role. Both have that *basso-blueso* tone that reminds one of James Dewar from the old Robin Trower days. Shepherd had said, just as *Ledbetter Heights* was coming out, that he was a little uncomfortable singing as he wasn't sure his voice had finished changing—but that it was something he'd be working on.

In 1997, Shepherd came out with *Trouble Is . . .* and it was already possible to discern a shift in his guitar style—not earthquake-like in significance, but a shift nonetheless. This time around, the Kenny Wayne Shepherd Band was an official unit (though permanent personnel has been a shuffled concept). Again, the blues-simmered rock sounds topped the *Billboard* Blues Chart—this time for two years—received a Grammy nomination, and three singles ("Blue on Black," "Slow Ride" and "Somehow, Somewhere, Someway") were radio hits.

By early October, 1999, Shepherd had released his third CD, *Live On*. This time, in addition to the KWS Band, numerous luminaries from the world of rock and blues participated in the sessions, including Dr. John, Double Trouble (Vaughan's magical rhythm section: drummer Chris "Whipper" Layton and bassist Tommy Shannon), Les Claypool of Primus, and Third Eye Blind bassist Arion Salazar.

For all the guesting musicians, the CD sounds a lot like its predecessors. Shepherd's songwriting continues to become more refined, which in this case is leading him in a rock direction, and his playing blends influences with personal discovery.

As for influences, KWS lists four necessary CDs by Louisiana blues artists: "*Brown Blues Daddy* and *Memphis Bound* by (New Orleans) guitarist Bryan Lee. He's one of the most underrated players I've ever heard. Buy a couple by Buddy Guy—for sure you should have *Damn Right I've Got the Blues*. And, what the heck, get *Live On* by the Kenny Wayne Shepherd Band."

A Shreveport precursor to Shepherd was **John Campbell** (1952–1993). He was playing guitar by the age of eight and was opening for big name acts such as Clarence "Gatemouth" Brown and Albert Collins in his early teens.

Campbell didn't get serious about music until he had a drag racing accident when he was sixteen. Left bedridden for months, blind in one eye, and with permanent facial scars, Campbell turned inward and sought release in his guitar. Not surprisingly, he flew like a kestrel straight into the arms of the blues.

Campbell was heavily into spiritual church and sundry voodooisms—"folk magic and the power of the earth" was how one friend described it; that imagery peppered not only his material but also his stage show, adding a Robert Johnson–esque sense of menace to his already vibrant and haunted conviction (see also "The Music of Voodoo," Part 6, Chapter 1). His guitar tone was searingly great, his chops fueled by a fury, and his voice and songs came straight out of hell.

After moving to New York in the late eighties, Campbell was nominated for a W. C. Handy award for his first CD, *A Man and His Blues*, released in 1989 on a German label. That led to two albums with Elektra, *One Believer* (1991), an urgently impressive effort, and 1993's *Howlin' Mercy*, one of the best modern blues albums ever made. Infused with tortured, voodoo-cloaked images of loss, sorrow, and decay, *Howlin' Mercy* lives up to its title.

For all the darkness, Campbell was a generous person. He went to war with his record label because he wanted unsigned artists of his choice to open tours for him, and he frequently performed charity shows benefiting the homeless.

Campbell passed away shortly after *Howlin' Mercy* of causes that are still a mystery. He'd experienced drug and alcohol problems in the past, but had reportedly been clean at the time of his death. Campbell's friend Dr. John delivered a eulogy at the funeral—he had, years earlier, performed the wedding ceremony for the guitarist and his wife.

One of the coolest of the younger Louisiana bluesmen is **Tab Benoit** (1967–), who was born in Los Angeles but grew up and still lives in southern Louisiana in the petroleum-happy town of Houma, about an hour outside New Orleans. A singer, guitarist, and songwriter of fluid and instinctual ability, Benoit has the work ethic of an NFL football coach and a down-to-earth grasp on the business of blues.

Influenced at an early age by the music of Ray Charles, Benoit was nonetheless forbidden by his parents to play in bands, a concept that backfired. On stage, he'd slip in Muddy Waters tunes and eventually played straight blues gigs at Tabby's Blues Box and Heritage Hall. It was a true education.

"You can play as much as you want in New Orleans," Benoit says, "but Baton Rouge was really the main focus of the blues. That's where I can play the blues; where they like me for it."

Benoit eventually attracted the attention of Justice Records, primarily a country label at the time, for whom he released several solid CDs of swamp blues, including *Nice & Warm*, *What I Live For*, *Standing on the Bank*, and *Live: Swampland Jam*. Benoit jumped to the Vanguard label for *Homesick for the Road* and *These Blues Are All Mine*.

In a giddy sort of way, Benoit's work has progressed steadily. His style exudes Louisiana and the bayou, lyrically and in the humid, warm sound of his guitar. He's a great player with a gunslinger's style, and he writes vitally honest material. Although he doesn't have the movie-star looks or hyped appeal of Shepherd, he's another of the "young white guys playing blues" fraternity. Some blues purists dismiss his work because it has been used heavily in television on such shows as *Northern Exposure*, *Baywatch Nights*, *Melrose Place*, and *Party of Five*. But as far as I'm concerned Benoit's absolutely authentic.

Kenny Neal (1957–) is the heir apparent to the Raful Neal Baton Rouge blues monarchy. Although he was born in California, he's as Louisiana as it's possible to get. Slim Harpo gave him his first harmonica when the kid was three, "Uncle" Buddy Guy was always hanging around, and, by thirteen, Kenny was playing in the Old Man's band. Four years later, he was playing bass for Guy.

With that background, it's not surprising that young Neal wanted to test the waters for himself, and soon he gathered younger brothers Noel, Larry, and Ray to form the Neal Brothers Blues Band, which featured Ken on guitar, harp, and vocals.

In 1986, Kenny recorded *Bio on the Bayou*, a remarkably assured first CD that was picked up for release a year later by Alligator. Neal is a gifted player with a guitar style like boiling oil, and his voice lands somewhere on the warmer side of John Campbell and Johnny Winter. Since his debut, Neal has consistently delivered high-quality CDs almost annually, each a churning synthesis of swamp blues with R&B overtones. All his albums feature superb original material and Kenny's high-voltage instrumentation, but *Bayou Blood*, *Walking on Fire*, and *Hoodoo Moon* stand out as truly special.

A few years back, Neal and his band motored several hours to make a 2:00 A.M. gig in Baton Rouge as part of an all-night blues festival, only to arrive and find the place deserted because the city was preparing for an ap-proaching hurricane. Only a soundman was there to greet the arriving mu-sicians and apprise them of the situation. Neal shrugged and cried that he wanted to play some blues—and the band went on to the appreciation of the sound guy and several derelicts clustered in the area.

(Oh yeah, the storm turned away and spared Baton Rouge.)

Sonny Landreth (1951–) is the pre-eminent slide guitarist in Louisiana blues; a bespectacled and quasi-reclusive player who combines traditional slide technique with fingerpicking and fret-board hammering adaptations, three-finger right-hand chordal work, spider-bite sustain, and eerie harmon-ics to create something spectacular. Born in Canton, Mississippi, Landreth is a true swamp rat whose family settled in southwest Louisiana; he's lived in Lafayette all his adult life.

He played trumpet early on but dabbled in guitar from his early teens. To say he was a quick study is putting it mildly. He absorbed the tech-niques of Scotty Moore, Chet Atkins, Ry Cooder, Gregg Allman, and Leo Kottke, even as he basked in the rural waltzes of Cajun music and the swel-tering, soul-infused zydeco. He formed a band called Br'er Rabbit, went briefly to Colorado and gleaned from Robben Ford, then moved back to Lafayette; there, a jam with Clifton Chenier led to Landreth's joining the zydeco king's Red Hot Louisiana Band as its first white guy.

Chenier died in 1987, but Landreth's years on the circuit had bol-stered his reputation. He did scores of prestigious sessions (Kenny Loggins, Junior Wells, Zachary Richard, Mark Knopfler) and joined first John Hiatt's critically acclaimed band and then John Mayall's Bluesbreakers. Finally, in 1992, signed to the Zoo/Praxis label, Landreth released his first major label solo record, the luminously good *Outward Bound*. It was followed three years later by *South of I–10*, a more introspective but equally compelling effort, and 2000's *Levee Town*, which confounded critics in its stylistic wanderlust; I liked it. Some early tracks have been released, revealing ma-terial Landreth recorded in the seventies. *Prodigal Son—The Collection* is probably the best of these efforts.

I saw Landreth play a particularly interesting gig at the 2000 Festivals Acadiens, where he performed as part of a Cajun supergroup called Trai-teurs; the group included Michael Doucet from BeauSoleil and was formed by the musicians to honor the late Cajun musician Tommy Comeaux.

It was a sizzling performance by all parties; the September sun was not intrusively hot, and, although dancing is the rule of the day at the festi-val, the one-time assemblage of talent—comprising two fiddles, standup bass, triangle, acoustic guitar, fiddle, and a drummer working with just a snare and brushes—brought fans to the lip of the stage to watch in rever-ence. Landreth, looking pale and rock-like, tuned his Les Paul and sipped from a long-neck Miller Lite. While the music they played was comprised

of material exceptionally familiar to most of the musicians—all of whom
are veterans of the Cajun circuit—Landreth, as a blues-rock guy, was probably less versed in the songs. He brightened noticeably when it was time
for him to solo.

From the reporter's notebook:

> *When it comes time to rip, SL kicks ass; at one point, the interplay be-*
> *tween him and [Doucet], on opposite sides of the stage, though not a cut-*
> *ting contest, is invigoratingly impressive and you can tell they're pushing*
> *each other on in a sense of respect and fun—and because, frankly, they're*
> *good enough to do it.*

If **Anders Osborne** (1966–) lacks Shepherd-like success, he more than
makes up for it in emotion. It's hard to say that his music is more authentic
than Shepherd's; Kenny Wayne can't help it if he grew up a suburban kid
with talent and dedication. It's just that Shepherd hasn't seen the world—
literally or figuratively—the way Osborne has.

Born in Sweden, Osborne ended up in New Orleans after traveling
the globe and hanging in Greece, Egypt, Yugoslavia, and Israel. On the
road, Osborne, who started playing drums in kid bands in Sweden, picked
up the guitar and spare cash playing in pubs and on street corners. He visited New Orleans to catch up with a good friend he'd met on his travels
and, after moving to California for a year, settled in the Crescent City permanently in 1987. "New Orleans had excitement in a way that New York
or LA didn't," Osborne told me. "There was a sense of acceptance; it's a
very relaxed town and multicultural area."

Osborne worked at a sound company and on a horse farm while he
honed his music. Growing up, he'd always been aware of such rural blues
artists as Robert Johnson through "late night radio," and, later, he learned
about Little Feat, Ry Cooder, and other such folks. As his style solidified,
Osborne began hustling gigs and ended up working at Checkpoint Charlie's on Esplanade before the joint was even a music club, gradually earning
a reputation that brought him more lucrative shows at Carrollton Station
and Mid-City Lanes Rock 'n' Bowl.

"[Musician friends and I] talk sometimes about how much music
plays a vital part in the structure of the city—historically and now," he says.
"The respect that the listener and the white musicians have for black
artists has crossed over into the city at large.

"I'm so impressed [whenever I see] the little kids with their musical instruments coming home from school. They're not in the cases—the kids are
playing them. It's a poor town and people live close together and music is
one of the big ways we figure out how to communicate with one another."

Osborne's music is a melodic assertion of the validity of that statement. Though dipped in a piquant batter of blues, Osborne has nonetheless

absorbed various folk and rural influences and wrapped them in the veneer of rock. Musically, for every acoustic Robert Johnson–ism, there's a slashing bit of Rory Gallagher slide; a funky nod to Little Feat is countered by the yearning melodic acumen of Gregg Allman, all of which underpins the lyrical textures of Osborne's own bittersweet tunes.

He's released several CDs during the last ten years or so, and while some are out of print, *Which Way to Here* and *Live at Tipitina's* aptly chronicle his musical and personal journeys—especially his drug and alcohol tribulations. Fortunately, all of that seems to be behind him.

Osborne, a world traveler, has an eclectic taste in food. "In New Orleans, you should go to Maximo's on Decatur. It's food from the Tuscany region with a Louisiana twist. Also: Pearl's on Baronne." But his musical tastes are pretty straightforward, and he recommends the greatest hits collections of Clifton Chenier, Louis Armstrong, the Meters, Allen Toussaint, and "the last solo thing Danny Barker did."

Another guitarist blending disparate styles and geographies is **Coco Robicheaux** (1947–). Over the phone from Colorado, he told me, "You know how the Blues Nazis are: Unless you're ninety years old and black and from Mississippi, you don't qualify. So be it, but I put blues in everything I do. And if there's a bluesman on every corner, well, I can only do what I do."

Like Campbell, Robicheaux is mystically inclined. But where Campbell's friends duck the voodoo question, Robicheaux readily admits he's a practitioner. His family is from Ascension Parish, where he lived until he was thirteen (Robicheaux was born "on the side of the road in California" during a road trip). He spent his teens in Slidell, and started playing music after sonic love affairs with Elvis Presley, Professor Longhair, and selected country artists.

"I was taking trombone in school and I hated it; I just used it to make fart noises. At the same time, I worshipped Louis Armstrong. It broke my heart when he went in the hospital near the end. I saw a photograph of him lying in the bed with his trumpet, with that facial expression that said, 'If I die this trumpet's going with me.' I started to play the trombone very seriously after that."

By the time Robicheaux was seventeen he had his own television and radio programs, broadcast out of a car dealership in Mississippi, and shortly after began recording at Cosimo Matassa's New Orleans studio and for the J&M label. When the British rock thing took over America, Robicheaux couldn't get a gig; he holed up with his National Steel Standard guitar and carved his own unique style: a sinewy, dangerously low-key, oozing-with-swamp-funk sound topped off by his peculiar and great mouthful-of-porcupine-quills approach to singing.

Voodoo had a profound effect on his music, adding a particular and discernible worldview that exudes power and comfort. These distillations are best represented on the three CDs he's put out in the last decade: *Spiritland, Louisiana Medicine Man,* and *Hoodoo Party.*

Kipori "Baby Wolf" Woods is so nicknamed because he's a sort of musical godchild to Walter "Wolfman" Washington. A New Orleans guitarist whose education started with his grandfather, Lloyd Lambert (bassist for Ray Charles), and has continued through Washington's tutelage, Woods is willing to jam with or back any artist who comes through town. In 2000, Woods released his solo debut, *Big Black Cadillac.*

A special mention should be made of two other artists. **Marva Wright** is an ultra-cheery, gospel-belter-turned-bluestress who was born and raised in New Orleans. Along with jazz trumpeter Kermit Ruffins, she more or less has the city eating out of her hands, and the nourishment is in the form of her canyon-sized voice. A popular and much-anticipated JazzFest veteran, Wright has released several CDs, among them *Marvalous* and *Heartbreakin' Woman.*

Finally there's **Keb' Mo',** a huge star and Grammy fiend. A fine guitarist, singer, and songwriter, Mo' is an acoustic blues archivist whose visionary concepts about the future of blues have breathed oxygen into the form. He's lived in New Orleans for a few years; not long, but certainly enough, he told me, to add color to his musical palette.

IV

MUSIC OF
SOUTHWEST
LOUISIANA

One

EARLY CAJUN
AND CREOLE MUSIC

*L*ouisiana Black and I, on a lovely September Saturday morning, have roared in the Starsky-and-Hutch-mobile down the causeway over Henderson Swamp from Baton Rouge to Lafayette for the Festivals Acadiens and Bayou Food Festival.

Festivals Acadiens (also see "Young Pups," Part 3, Chapter 2) is a three-day soiree of Big Fun held in celebration of Cajun culture and victuals; it takes place annually in oak-clustered Girard Park hard by the campus of the University of Louisiana at Lafayette, home of the Ragin' Cajuns. The single-stage event is a triumphant, throwback-to-the-old-days kind of event: Norman Rockwell on roux.

It's still a manageable festival; you can park your car nearby, wander up to the park—it's free—and, well, enjoy. It can be brutally hot when you're bunched up at the front of the stage or dancing during the waltzes, and it's sufficiently populated to make its people-watching possibilities intriguing; but there's never the sense of suffocation or sheer claustrophobic misery that plagues JazzFest and Mardi Gras.

Having parked on the other side of campus, we amble through a casual mixture of students playing frisbee, two guys washing a car and talking about the Ragin' Cajuns's football chances against Texas Tech tonight, and suddenly find ourselves amid the proceedings—no barricades or fences or large signs block or point the way. Louisiana Black and I buy some official Festivals coinage from the monetary exchange booth and avail ourselves of cheap cans of Coors Light.

"Why is this just a Cajun festival and not a Cajun and Creole festival?" Louisiana Black asks—and it's a fair question to anyone not familiar with the thing.

"Well, in terms of music, there really *isn't* Creole music anymore," I explain. "Creole music has become zydeco music. And the new zydeco music is called *nouveau* zydeco."

Louisiana Black pulls at his beer as we instinctively aim for the U-shaped cornucopia of food tents at the bottom end of the park, pleased at the prospect of fanging-down all manner of cheap and good things: po'boys, shrimp on a stick, seafood gumbo, crawfish étoufée—none of it emblazoned with nationally recognized logos or served by people in McFranchise outfits.

"If Creole music has become zydeco music—"

"Sort of," I interject, stepping to the front of the line to buy a crawfish pie with seafood sauce. "There is a separate Creole music, but there really aren't too many Creole musicians playing it anymore. Most have moved on to zydeco, which is a modern form using contemporary instrumentation and a helluva lot of funk."

"Okay. Sort of," Black says. "Then what's Cajun music?"

"Cajun music is still Cajun music. It's just evolved somewhat, though not as much, in my opinion."

Black points over his shoulder, back up to the music stage, where a large preteen ensemble is singing a traditional French two-step. "So those kids are playing Cajun music—even though they're, like, eight years old?"

"That's Cajun, bro."

Walking awkwardly, spooning food and balancing beers, we make our way back to check out the tunes, halting a few yards behind the canopy-shaded mixing board set up in the middle of a large clearing, about thirty yards from the music. Steve Riley, the fine accordionist who heads up the great modern Cajun band called the Mamou Playboys (see also "Swamp Pop," Part 6, Chapter 2), is relaxing under the sound tent, drinking a beer and watching the children jam, a big smile on his face. The little kid on fiddle is pretty amazing—I don't know who he is and guess I won't unless they take pity on me. Everything seems to be conducted in French, which is also more or less the reason for the entire gathering.

Traditional Cajun music is typically rendered in French, of course; that's part of the long story of the Cajuns in Louisiana, and includes a foul post–World War II period in which American culture threatened to stamp out virtually all traces of its French heritage. That's no longer the case; the Cajun heritage is alive and well, merci beaucoup, and it's easy to document that Cajun music—and its Creole cousin, zydeco—is more popular than ever before.

The music is intoxicating. Cajun music sounds like an aural snack mix: The Cheez Doodles are hillbilly music, the Rice Chex are French lullabies, the pretzels old-time Anglo-Saxon folksongs and, playing the triangle and calling everyone to the table is French crooner Maurice Chevalier. It's seductive and sad and exuberant all at the same time.

Directly in front of Louisiana Black and me, two little six-year-old girls practice waltzing not five feet from a senior-citizen couple dancing with wild abandon. Louisiana Black nudges me and points at a group of college girls who are also watching the dancing senior citizens. He asks me, "Ess there a Hooters in zis town, mon ami?"

"Just keep talking like that and ask one of them to dance," I respond, nodding at the area directly in front of the stage, which is packed with two-steppers hoofing up great mushroom clouds of dust.

Louisiana Black shrugs and drinks. "They're too young. Do they zydeco?"

"This is *Cajun*, bro. Stick with me and one day you'll understand the difference."

When the kids finish the song, an emcee leads the applause and intones in French and then, for morons like us, in English, that the children in the band are handpicked from music programs in neighboring parishes.

"They speak French fluently," he says proudly, and it's an exclamation point to emphasize that the Cajun culture is rebounding. These are people retaking their culture.

I wander around behind the stage, where there's an expansive shadow land of oaks curtained with Spanish moss. A small village of extravagant portable tents is set up, each emblazoned with names like KREWE DE CANAILLE. Inside, the gentrified sit on portable chairs or couches and cluster about tables heaped with impressive arrays of food. Folks converse amiably with one another, holding tankard-sized beverage glasses or long-neck bottles of beer and waving cardboard fans.

Onstage, the Traiteurs, a one-off supergroup of Cajun musicians, are assembling to perform in support of the Dr. Tommy Comeaux Endowed Fund for Traditional Music at the University of Louisiana at Lafayette. (Comeaux, a medical doctor and musician who played with BeauSoleil and Coteau, among others, was killed in a cycling accident a few years back.) The Traiteurs include Sonny Landreth (discussed in the last chapter), the bluesy slide guitar wizard transplanted to the bayou from his native Mississippi, and BeauSoleil fiddle-maestro Michael Doucet (see "Modern Cajun," Part 4, Chapter 2).

When they start, I see that it's a large but fairly traditional Cajun lineup (except for Landreth's electric guitar): two fiddles, acoustic guitar, standup bass, triangle, accordion, and a drummer working out on a snare with just brushes. The tunes have a paradoxical quality: a heaving, mournful sound that's contradicted by the innate cheerfulness of the music. Most Cajun music—be it two-step dance stuff or the slower waltzes—holds an undercurrent of melancholy despite the exuberance of the tunes, as though musically proclaiming that, no matter how much we've been screwed over, tonight we're gonna rock.

In that sense, the Traiteurs do kick ass. There are plenty of dancers but, probably because of the presence of the reclusive and legendary Landreth in the band, there is a mob of folks pressing the stage, watching his every move as though he were a sort of crawfishy Rory Gallagher. It's irresistible music and I can't help but bounce around despite my criminal lack of rhythm.

Looking around to see how the distant crowd is reacting to the band, I can see they love it, even far back by the food tents, and I start laughing as I notice two Mormon missionaries working the crowd.

Cajun and Creole music have come a long way since the nineteenth century, when the two similar styles of music started to evolve in a tiny section of southwest Louisiana. Things were set in motion as far back as 1764, when the area was settled by Acadians (later shortened to "Cajuns"), a French-speaking group booted out of Canada in the Grand Dérangement for refusing en masse to take an oath of loyalty to the English king. Over time, Creoles—French-speaking ex-slaves and free persons of color who had, over the years, mixed with immigrant Haitians, American Indians, Spanish, and French—also began to occupy the region as they left post–Civil War New Orleans to head west. Both the Creole and Cajun cultures, though different, have intermingled in a variety of ways, and archivist John Lomax characterized the early music from both groups as being a collision of French European, Afro-Caribbean, and Mississippi Indian influences. Working in the same fields in the same impoverished, family-oriented environments, Cajuns and Creoles have withstood extreme prejudice—frequently from one another. Still, the similarities between them caused no small amount of empathy among the more enlightened of their respective citizenry. As time passed, much of the food and music cross-pollinated and the results have been spectacular.

In early Cajun families, singing was a tradition that passed from one generation to another through house songs and dance music. The former consisted of solo narrative ballads typically sung by mothers to their children, and the latter generally by men to one another in working or post-work relaxation environs. Both often served as musical history lessons depicting the origins and hardships of the culture. They were always French language and French ancestral songs, rendered solo or with fiddle and accordion accompaniment. Some of the early practitioners included the Stafford brothers, the Hoffpauir family, Wayne Perry, and the Segura brothers.

On the Creole conversion chart, the ancestrally based sonic equivalents would be found in the *juré* singing—rhythmic call and response patterns—and hollers that had their origins with slaves and Haitian fieldworkers and were fueled by the Afro-Caribbean polyrhythms and songs of the Native Americans. These call-and-response creations, punctuated often with gull-like cries from the musicians, were focused on the emotions of jubilant hope and spiritual sorrow—the same feelings that simmer in the blues. The tunes were often accented with dance steps and intricate percussion figures on makeshift instruments. Jimmy Peters and Wilford Charles were two traditional Creole artists recorded by Alan and John Lomax for the Smithsonian Institution.

Because of the proximity of the two groups, the European-born folk songs and waltzes intermingled with the blues-based field hollers, early gospel music, and Caribbean and African rhythms. Eventually, the songs and lullabies that developed were given instrumental accompaniment. After long and brutal weeks in the fields, people of both cultures celebrated with Saturday night dances and house parties, observed along segregated lines. For years, the primary instruments at these entertainments were the guitar and fiddle; later the accordion was added.

"Basically, you had two different cultures living in the same place," Beau-Soleil fiddler and leader Michael Doucet told me. "There was a lot of sharing but there were incredible differences, too. If you had a 180-degree graph, put Creole culture on the left and Cajun culture on the right. Go up 30 degrees from the left and you'd have blues and field hollers and a very rhythmic sensibility. On the Cajun side you'd have ballads and fiddle tunes. And then there'd be 120 degrees of gray area with varying degrees of overlap."

Over the years, certain things have happened that affected these musics: The concept of two fiddles—one to carry the melody, the other to weave in and around for support—came into play and further thickened the musical texture. Improvements in the construction of accordions also expanded their base keys beyond A and F to include other possibilities, thereby opening the music to a new element. In many ways, because the accordion isn't capable of the scalular intricacies of the fiddle, it limited the Cajun–Creole repertoire, but the confluence of accordion and fiddle was nonetheless a beautiful one.

In 1916, the government in Louisiana outlawed French as an official language, and the French-speaking culture began to decline. French continued to be spoken, of course, and, for years, advancement in the music of both Cajun and Creole artists was substantial. But legislation had compromised the culture and the effects would eventually be felt.

In time, of course, *Creole* music would become *zydeco* music (discussed in detail in "Zydeco," Part 4, Chapter 3). If, in the meantime, it sounds as though Creole and Cajun music became indistinguishable, well, that would be an exaggeration. When I listened to old recordings of Creole and Cajun artists, I sensed differences between the two despite marked similarities, but I couldn't describe what, precisely, I felt the differences were. So, doing what any confused author would do in a similar situation, I picked up the telephone and called Michael Tisserand, author of the wonderful book *The Kingdom of Zydeco*. Despite being blindsided, Tisserand could not have been more gracious or helpful.

This is what he told me:

Creole music in general tends to be of a historical period. It's not something you would describe as a vibrant scene right now. The old-style Creole music, as played by Canray Fontenot, is typified by the early fiddlers and accordions, and it *is* very similar to Cajun.

There are, though, certain African influences that make it different, too. [Creole artists] Bois Sec Ardoin and Canray Fontenot couldn't play blues at dances but they still found a way to slip that element in. . . .

People setting out to play Creole music now—as opposed to zydeco—are doing so as revivalists, and are doing so in a stripped-down, elemental style. It's pretty rare that anyone actually does it, though Goldman Thibodeaux and Calvin Carriere have just come out with a contemporary but old-style Creole CD from louisianaradio.com.

According to Tisserand, Cajun music grew through three distinct periods: the early accordion era, the string-band era, and the modern era (the latter including a segue between the old-time accordionists and the new generation of nouveau revivalists). Creole music paralleled many of these stylistic changes. But as the Cajuns moved into the modern era, Creole music, through the infusion of blues and R&B, was becoming "la la" music, a synonym for the old Creole style, which, in turn, became zydeco.

The cultures ebb and flow between their similarities and differences. But the respect, camaraderie, and, most important, musical cooperation, is an encouraging sign for many reasons.

Maybe it doesn't rank up there with the Yalta conference, but one of the huge and concrete examples of these elements all coming together occurred back in the early part of the twentieth century when Creole accordionist **Amédé Ardoin** (1898–unknown) and Cajun fiddler **Dennis McGee** (1893–1989) began to collaborate.

Unfortunately, Ardoin met a premature end. As one story goes, Ardoin, kicking it out at a house party for some white people, made the egregious mistake of asking the homeowner for a rag so that he could mop the sweat from his brow. When Ardoin accepted a handkerchief from one of the homeowner's daughters, he apparently crossed some line in the minds of a few of the white revelers; he was followed home and en route beaten so senseless that he never recovered. Another version holds that he was intentionally run over by an automobile after being pummeled and left lying in a ditch. And partner McGee suspected that Ardoin was poisoned by a jealous fiddler.

The details aren't known, but the consensus is that Ardoin courted disaster. The magic of his music gave him an innate power and sensuality that probably placed him in quantifiable danger every time he played, whether for white audiences (two-steps and waltzes) or black (a bluesier bout of field hollers and *juré* tunes), and he frequently did both in the same night.

Ardoin's grandmother was a slave; his father was also born into slavery but eventually became a landowner with over a hundred acres on Bayou

Nezpiqué. There are plenty of gray areas in Ardoin's biography, though *The Kingdom of Zydeco* probably gives us the best portrait we're likely to find.

Starting a life that would be chiseled with tragedy, Ardoin's father died a few months after Ardoin was born. The kid grew up with his mother, learning and playing single-row accordion after being given one by his older brother. A diminutive man who probably didn't stand over five feet tall, Ardoin was as instinctively gifted at music as he was spiritually allergic to working in the fields.

As such, he probably wasn't much help at home. He would, though, get up every morning and head off with his accordion and a lemon (to maintain his singing voice) and usually return from wherever with a little cash. After his mother died, Ardoin frequently gigged for room and board. So great was his virtuosity and so powerful his high keening voice that his original material was immediately accepted and clamored for. His strength was legendary; he could play five- or six-hour dances without a break or the benefit of a support musician.

He became an anomaly because he was soon in demand at house parties and fais do dos in white and black neighborhoods alike. When Ardoin and McGee met and hit it off, they began to play together regularly, soon taking their places at the top of early twentieth-century Cajun–Creole music. Throughout the twenties and thirties, Ardoin and McGee were a musical and sociological force.

It's said that in 1929 Ardoin and McGee went to New Orleans to cut half a dozen tunes for Columbia Records. Among the future standards laid down that day were "Two Step de Eunice" and "Two Step de Prairie Soileau." Over the next several years, the duo recorded additional sides for Brunswick and Bluebird/Victor Records. The evolution of the material and dynamics suggests two things: 1) that McGee's participation gradually became less equal and more supportive, and 2) that, on songs such as "Crowley Blues," Ardoin was anticipating the spawning of zydeco.

Ardoin had one more session: laying down a dozen solo tunes in New York City with Cajun musicians Joe and Cleoma Falcon. Back home, Ardoin became a drawing card: Folks would come from all over when the word was out that he was going to play somewhere, either by himself, with McGee, or with a backing band that might comprise guitar, fiddle, triangle, and even rubboard (or *frottoir*, discussed in "Zydeco," Part 4, Chapter 3). The hypnotic energy of his playing drew huge crowds.

After Ardoin was beaten, his mind began to deteriorate; similar, one supposes, in a strange way to jazz cornetist Buddy Bolden's gradual descent into lunacy. Ardoin ended up and probably died in a mental asylum in Pineville, Louisiana; but because no records exist, he could've died anywhere from 1941 to the early 1950s.

As for his legacy, accordionist Chris Ardoin (for more, see "Zydeco," Part 4, Chapter 3), the masterly young lion of nouveau zydeco and

Amédé's great-nephew, told me, "I don't even try to learn his stuff. There's no way I could follow that. He had this great, high voice and, as for his playing, he was simply the best."

Pretty much all of Amédé Ardoin's recordings are available. Arhoolie's *I'm Never Coming Back* is a complete package.

Dennis McGee hailed from Bayou Marron, where his widower father, himself a fiddler, worked in the fields while Dennis shuttled from cousin to cousin. At fourteen, he got his first fiddle and was reportedly functional on the instrument within forty-eight hours, at once beginning to pick up technique and influences from other sources. He worked a variety of trades—sharecropping and cutting hair among them—but his music was a constant spiritual boost.

Early on, he played extensively with "rhythm" fiddler Sady Courville, with whom he traveled in 1928 to New Orleans. There they recorded several songs, many of them McGee's original material. A master of several different (and often eccentric) tunings, and as much a fan of the older fiddle music as he was an innovator, McGee might be thought of as a sort of cornbread Paganini.

"He was actually a friend of my family, so I grew up hearing him play," young Cajun accordionist Steve Riley told me. "In fact, I actually got to play *with* him. David Greely [who plays fiddle in Riley's Mamou Playboys] likes to say Dennis was the first Cajun-punk fiddle player."

For all the obvious reasons, McGee's early recorded work with Amédé Ardoin frequently stands out. McGee also recorded with fiddler Ernest Fruge, but his gigs with Ardoin in both black and white venues were the stuff of legend. After Ardoin died, McGee played sporadically until the 1970s, when a resurgence of Cajun music took place. He reunited with Courville and performed nationally and internationally, touring and playing festivals. He taught BeauSoleil's Michael Doucet and even reentered the studio; indeed, he was an icon until his death.

"It's hard to put into words how totally amazing Dennis McGee was," Doucet told me. "I met him in 1972 and I had to completely relearn everything because he was doing the old French style from the 1800s. I used to tape Dennis playing; I would just go over to his house and take coffee and let him be a mentor."

Among McGee's available releases are *The Complete Early Recordings*, on which he blasts through all manner of early traditional music, incorporating reels, waltzes, and polkas; and *La Vieille Musique Acadienne*, which he recorded with Courville when he was eighty-four years old.

He was a major influence until the day he died, perhaps fearing unnecessarily that, after he was gone, his work might disappear. As he told musician and writer Ann Savoy in her terrific book *Cajun Music—A Reflection of a People*, "In a little bit, I'm gonna' go on my long trip and if I don't play my songs, nobody's gonna' know them."

If McGee and Ardoin are the patriarchs of fiddling and accordion, respectively, certainly plenty of great artists followed. In this chapter I'll stick with the Cajuns.

Of the squeeze-box coterie, probably the second great Cajun musician was accordionist and balladeer **Amédé Breaux** (1900–1973), born in Rayne, Louisiana. He was probably the first artist to record what is arguably the best-loved song in the Cajun repertoire, "Jolie Blonde" (a.k.a."Ma Blonde Est Partie").

The Breaux family was musically active: father Auguste was a fine accordionist and a big influence, and brothers Ophy and Clifford (fiddle and guitar, respectively) often accompanied Amédé on stage and in the studio. (Sister Cleoma Breaux Falcon was an even bigger deal: Evidence suggests that she wrote "Jolie Blonde," and in any case went on to have a successful career independently of her brother.) Typical of early Cajun singers, Amédé had a high, caterwauling voice, and his stage persona included a propensity for drinking heavily, tearing his accordions apart barehanded, and often brawling with anyone nearby—including family and band members.

Equally fiery was his playing, which was interestingly counterbalanced by his skill at composing and singing haunting ballads. In the 1930s, with his brothers in his band, Breaux Frères, Amédé recorded for several small regional labels, but it wasn't until later work for J. D. Miller and the Fais Do Do and Feature labels that his best material was put on tape. Though Breaux's religious feelings interrupted his career—he promised God after surviving an illness that he wouldn't play secular music ever again—he eventually returned to the fold, recording (for labels such as Arhoolie) and performing until his death.

Some of his greatest music can be heard on *Home Sweet Home* (Breaux Frères) and *Cajun Dance Party: Fais Do Do*.

In the early 1900s, vocalist and accordionist **Joseph Falcon** (1900–1965) was the highest profile Cajun musician, though his wife **Cleoma Breaux Falcon** (1905–1941) didn't hurt the recipe for success any. Joseph was born in Robert's Cove, Louisiana; Cleoma, born in Crowley, started out on a guitar backing her brother, Amédé. Suitor Joseph used to hang around the house playing triangle behind the siblings.

After Joseph and Cleoma married, Joseph returned to his accordion duties and the two began performing together. The duo gelled immediately. Each had a terrific singing voice that blended well with the other; their frequently alternating lines were piercing in intensity. In 1928, in a hotel in New Orleans, Joseph and Cleoma made the first Cajun recording, "Allons à Lafayette." It was immediately popular and the pair recorded several other pieces, not only as a duo but with their band, a hugely popular dancehall unit that played traditional Cajun tunes and French-language arrangements. Joseph and Cleoma also sculpted the Cajun repertoire by writing material and coming up with lyrics and vocal melodies for pre-existing instrumental pieces.

After Cleoma died under mysterious circumstances, Joseph's enthusiasm for music dwindled. He stopped playing for years, but in the 1960s, with his second wife, Theresa, on drums, he formed Joe's Silver String Band.

It's not easy to find recordings of Joseph and Cleoma Falcon, though Arhoolie released a live recording made in 1965 called *Cajun Music Pioneer.*

The accordion has fallen in and out of favor in Cajun music, and two artists who pioneered its resurrection, at different times, were **Nathan Abshire** (1915–1981) and **Iry Lejeune** (1928–1955).

Abshire was one of the most fluent Cajun musicians; it's probably not a coincidence that he was heavily influenced by blues and Creole as well as by honky tonk. Born in Gueydan, Louisiana, to a family of accordionists, he taught himself to play at six, and by eight he was playing dances. He was immensely influenced by Amédé Ardoin—and eventually filled in for Ardoin in clubs while the older musician was on break.

Abshire had just started a recording career in the early thirties with Happy Fats and the Rainbow Ramblers when western swing roared onto the scene. Bowing to the stylistic demands of the times, he turned to the fiddle, another instrument over which he demonstrated mastery. After World War II, Cajun music experienced a resurgence and Abshire went back to the accordion.

A plaintive, powerful singer whose exposure to country music and honky tonk mingled enticingly with his bluesy Amédéisms, he scored a hit with 1949's "Pine Grove Blues," which would become his signature tune. The song helped reintroduce the accordion into Cajun music, and Abshire became a household name in the region.

A decade later, when Cajun music had again fallen on hard times and out of favor with its own people, Abshire helped generate an international curiosity about the music when he toured with the Balfa Brothers. He continued to perform and record with the Pine Grove Boys—the Balfa Brothers did stints in that outfit too—and to solo. Abshire recorded for a variety of labels, including Swallow, cranking out a remarkable string of high-quality disc hits, among them "Tramp sur la Rue" and "Lemonade Song."

In the seventies, Abshire continued to do sessions, though he was battling the alcoholism that would eventually kill him and it's only fair to say that the quality of his work had diminished. Nonetheless, he toured colleges and the festival circuit to favorable response, appeared in the documentary film *Good Times Are Killing Me,* and kept working the job he had held for most of his life: caretaker of the Basile, Louisiana, town dump. Of the available albums, *A Cajun Legend: The Best of Nathan Abshire* and *French Blues* are his best.

The accordion resurgence that Abshire had kicked off was made even bigger by LeJeune, born nearly blind in Pointe Noire, Louisiana. He grew up unable to attend school or to work; he occupied his pivotal childhood time practicing on his uncle's accordion. Influenced by Amédé Ardoin to the point of musical obsession, he imbued his original songs with the pain that had characterized Cajun music since the move to Louisiana, and his rhythmic style was evocative. After World War II, Cajun soldiers returned to discover that hillbilly music had wrought a powerful effect on the music of their youth; fortunately, the nostalgic veterans had LeJeune to fall back on. His single, "Love Bridge Waltz" b/w "Evangeline Special," rocked dance halls across Acadiana.

After the label's funds petered out, LeJeune garnered some radio attention and subsequently signed with Gold Band Records, with whom he began an ascent up the ladder of regional record and dancehall success. He was frequently recorded in his own tiny shack; the raw emotion of those recordings is telling and transcendent. Unfortunately, returning from a gig when he was only twenty-seven, LeJeune and fiddler J. B. Fuselier stopped to fix a flat tire when a passing motorist hit them. LeJeune died instantly; Fuselier was critically hurt.

As such, LeJeune's legacy is criminally short. Few collections are available, but *Cajun's Greatest* is a fine one.

Lawrence Walker (1908–1968) was also a superb and important accordion player. Walker was born near Scott, Louisiana, and learned accordion and fiddle from his French-speaking musical family. When the Walkers moved to Orange, Texas, as the Walker Brothers, Lawrence, his father Allen, and his brother Elton (both fiddlers) recorded Cajun and hillbilly songs ("La Breakdown la Louisiane" and "La Vie Malheureuse") for the Bluebird label. Seven years later, with an all-star group of Cajun musicians, Walker helped take home the first-place trophy at the National Folk Festival in Dallas, Texas.

After World War II, Lawrence, a rice farmer, relocated to Louisiana and formed a new band called the Wandering Aces, which performed only original material and established itself on the nightclub circuit.

Though embracing a conservative musical style, Walker was as powerful a singer as he was a player, and it's a shame he wasn't recorded more extensively before he died. As it is, the recently released *Tribute to the Late, Great L. W.* serves as an effective introduction to his work.

A similar giant in Acadiana dancehalls, **Aldus Roger** (1916–1999), leader of the Lafayette Playboys, was born in Carencro, Louisiana. He reportedly learned accordion by sneaking off during work time with his father's instrument. Influenced by his old man, Walker, and Amédé Breaux, Roger became a proficient and inspired player.

He married as a teenager, became a carpenter, and spent much of his early adulthood providing for his family. In the mid-forties, he formed the

Lafayette Playboys and developed a reputation for hiring the best available musicians (including future swamp popper Johnnie Allan and fiddler Doc Guidry). Not surprisingly, the band was immensely popular. They started recording for the TNT label in the early fifties.

Roger and the Playboys also maintained a high profile thanks to their popular local television show, aired on Lafayette's KLFY from 1955–1970. Among their hit songs are "Mardi Gras Gig," "Channel 10 Two-Step," "Louisiana Waltz," and "Johnnie Can't Dance." Although there was nothing innovatively flashy about Roger, who also didn't sing, he was a solid player who should be slotted one of the top five Cajun accordionists ever. A fine sampling of his music can be heard on *Plays the French Music of South Louisiana*.

Serving as a living stepping stone between traditional Creole accordion styles and the young zydeco players who are interpreting them is **Alphonse "Bois Sec" Ardoin** (1914 or 1916–), born in Duralde, Louisiana—and Amédé Ardoin's cousin. That he's a lifelong farmer is kind of amusing since his nickname—Bois Sec, French for "dry wood"—refers to his childhood reputation as being the first in the fields to seek shelter during rainstorms.

He taught himself accordion when he was twelve, and became an excellent player almost immediately after performing on triangle at several of Amédé's gigs (where he studied his brilliant older cousin's technique close-up). Because Bois Sec's mother was adamant about keeping him away from the musician's lifestyle, it wasn't until he was in his thirties and hooked up with fiddler Canray Fontenot that Bois Sec made a musical imprint. They called themselves the Duralde Ramblers and became so popular at house parties and dances that they were invited to appear at the Newport Folk Festival in 1966, the same year they released *Le Blues du Bayou*, an album dusted with sad French ballads and hellfire-quick two steps and considered essential listening for anyone seriously interested in the form (and still available as *La Musique Creole*).

He later fronted the Ardoin Brothers Band (known also as the Ardoin Family Orchestra and the Ardoin Family Band), which included Fontenot and Bois Sec's sons Morris, Gustave, and Lawrence. But when Gustave was killed in a car accident in 1974, Bois Sec's spirit for the music seemed to vanish.

Through an intriguing association with the youthful Cajun band Balfa Toujours, Ardoin has again become a force in the recording studio and on the festival circuit. In 1998, their collaborative CD, *Bois Sec Ardoin with Balfa Toujours*, was released. Another great recording is *Allons Danser*.

From the reporter's notebook (JazzFest 1999):

I am standing at the rickety fence separating the crowd from the security space in front of the stage, watching an early afternoon performance by

Balfa Toujours with Bois Sec Ardoin. It's impossible *not to watch the old man, who is grace and dignity personified.*

As the unit exuberantly roars through a tight set of classic French archival two-steps, Bois Sec is seated primly on a folding chair, stage right, in a lacquered straw riverboat gambler hat and a checked western shirt with pearl buttons. Despite the adoration of a considerable and antic crowd dancing in steamy celebration, Bois Sec takes it all in pacifically. His playing is beautifully assured, but for all its complexity, he could be sitting in the lazy afternoon torpor of a post–Easter brunch on a screened-in gallery, grinning indulgently at his grandchildren. This feels *like history.*

Even as Bois Sec Ardoin represents a living, breathing connection between the past and future, **The Carriere Brothers** were perhaps more of a literal one with the link they forged between their traditional early Creole tunes and the soon-to-come zydeco.

Eraste "Dolon" Carriere (1900–1983) began playing accordion when he was fifteen; sibling Joseph "Bebe" Carriere (1908–2001) started playing guitar shortly after. Both quickly established themselves on the house party circuit, plying a modern version of "la la" music. The evolution in the form was a result of gradual changes in music across the board from swing to country, elements that crept in small ways back to the bayou. As a teenager, Bebe did some gigs with Amédé Ardoin; in fact, both brothers played apart from one another, at white and black house parties and dances, but when they played together they made the biggest impression.

The duo became the Lawtell Playboys with the addition of Eraste's daughter Beatrice on rhythm guitar and son Calvin on violin. Fiddler Canray Fontenot also played with the group frequently, and by the sixties they had gradually segued their sound to a strict zydeco.

Two great records are available: *La La: Louisiana Black French Music* and *Cajun Fiddle Styles, Vol. 1—The Creole Tradition.*

Other accordionists who played significant roles in the development of Cajun and Creole music are **Sidney Brown, Joe Bonsall, Austin Pitre** (1918–1981)—who, in instrumental anticipation of Jimi Hendrix and Guitar Slim, played the accordion behind his back, under his legs, and behind his head—and in particular **Sidney Babineaux,** a contemporary of Amédé Ardoin who never recorded but whose reputation as a supreme musician was passed down by fiddler Canray Fontenot.

Of the fiddlers, a wonderful player and hugely important figure was **Dewey Balfa** (1927–1992), born in Bayou Grand Louis, Louisiana. Again, bloodlines tell: Balfa came from a virtual harvest of fiddlers. His father, grandfather, great-grandfather, and older brother Will were all fiddlers. Dewey quickly learned the instrument as a kid and began performing with his brothers—Will and guitarists Harry and Rodney—as the **Balfa Brothers.** They not only performed material from the canon but wrote their own songs, many of which would, in time, be incorporated into that very body of classic work.

Balfa was exposed to western swing music when he shipped off with the Merchant Marines, and later he would use some of those stylistic twists in his own exuberant playing. Back with family, Dewey orchestrated the brothers' blend of the old twin fiddle sound, delicious but hangdog vocals, and accordion. At various times, Nathan Abshire, Hadley Fontenot, and Marc Savoy played with the Balfa Brothers. The group became a staple on the Acadian circuit until it faded with the waning French culture.

But because he went to the Newport Folk Festival in 1964 and rocked the house with indigenous music that was being laughed at back home, he's known as a true savior of not just Cajun music but, in many ways, the culture. Performing with Gladius Thibodeaux and Louis "Vinesse" LeJeune, Dewey nearly blew the walls down. Few of the 17,000 in attendance had ever heard Cajun music and were overwhelmed; the subsequent standing ovation buoyed the trio and renewed Balfa's conviction in Cajun pride.

As the world opened its ears to the sounds and lifestyle behind them, Balfa returned to Louisiana committed to championing the cause of his people. He founded CODOFIL (Council for the Development of French in Louisiana) to teach French in public schools, started a Cajun music festival, and became an adjunct professor at the University of Southwest Louisiana's Center for Acadian and Creole Folklore.

Musically, the Balfa Brothers enjoyed hero status—and maintained a rigorous touring and recording schedule until 1979, when Rodney and Will died in an auto accident, an unfortunate recurring motif in the area. Even then, Dewey persevered. Several musicians comprised the Balfa Brothers over the years (including his daughter Christine on guitar and Rodney's son, Tony, on drums), and Dewey collaborated on various musical and Cajun culture projects with the younger musicians he'd inspired, among them Steve Riley, Michael Doucet, and Marc Savoy.

In 1982, Dewey won a fellowship from the National Endowment for the Arts, and after ten more years of activity slowed by cancer, he passed away. *Cajun Fiddle Old and New* and *Fait à la Main* are recommended samplers of his astonishing legacy.

Creole fiddler **Canray Fontenot** (1922–1995), born in L'Anse aux Vaches, Louisiana, made an indelible mark in his state's music. He frequently partnered with Bois Sec Ardoin, much as Dennis McGee and Amédé Ardoin played together.

In addition to his generous nature, quick smile, and quicksilver style, Fontenot was a hard-line musical conservative who emphatically stated that he did not play zydeco music (though it could be argued that some of the work he did with the Carriere Brothers was moving in that direction). He started out with a fiddle he constructed out of a cigar box and strings he fashioned from screen-door wire. He played with his father, renowned accordionist Ada Fontenot, his mother, his maternal grandfather, and neighbor Douglas Bellard—the first Creole fiddler to record. Amédé Ardoin invited Canray to accompany him to New York for what would be the former's final recording sessions, but Fontenot's mother thought he was too young for such a mission.

After his parents died when he was fourteen, Fontenot went to work in the sugar-cane fields and supplemented his pay by performing at house parties and dances. Fontenot worked "day gigs" all his life—as a farmer and at a feedstore—and always maintained that he played music because it was fun.

Live, he was a pyrotechnic performer, spinning off primitively structured but lively runs and often stamping his bare feet in time. Like most of the Creole artists, Fontenot had a bluesy twist to his style, and he was a master of slipping blues elements into the traditional music even though blues weren't allowed at many of the dances. As he told author Michael Tisserand, "They didn't want no blues, because they would dance too close to one another, they didn't want that at all. You was out of business if you played blues. So we started to slip up on them with something like the 'Prison Bars,' where you could blues it or you could waltz it."

In the thirties, Fontenot formed his own string band, soaking up a variety of fairly typical influences—jazz and western swing—and later hooked up with Bois Sec Ardoin. They formed the Duralde Ramblers in 1948.

The duo appeared at the Newport Folk Festival, recorded a massively influential album *(La Musique Creole)*, and generally waved the banner for Creole music proudly in the face of zydeco. Along with Cajun fiddler Dewey Balfa, Fontenot won a fellowship from the National Endowment for the Arts and was appointed an adjunct professor at the University of Southwestern Louisiana.

Fontenot was in his seventies when he toured with the popular Cajun group Filé. Plans were underway for him to make albums with both that group and young trad-zydeco accordion *brujo* Geno Delafose when Canray passed away in 1995.

He left us one solo record, the remarkable *Louisiana Hot Sauce, Creole Style*, a pastiche of older and newer material, which featured backing by BeauSoleil.

During the "down period" of accordion, Cajun string bands rose to prominence. In the early 1930s, an influx of workers roared into southwest Louisiana to pursue jobs in the oil biz explosion, bringing with them an interest in hillbilly and western swing music. The accordion and triangle, which had been integral to Cajun music, were phased out. The fiddle, which had shared the spotlight with the accordion, came to the fore, and the recently introduced guitar took on a new, if rhythmic, prominence.

When drums were added to the mix, the string band suddenly created a different Cajun music. The traditional songs in the oeuvre stayed the same but were arranged for the new style, which served as a trampoline to original material that naturally emphasized a new set of possibilities.

Maybe the first biggie of the new form was the Ville Platte, Louisiana, fiddler and vocalist **Leo Soileau** (1904–1980), a Dennis McGee devotee who was the second Cajun musician to record—and the first on his instrument.

After mastering the fiddle in his youth, Soileau and accordionist and vocalist Mayuse LaFleur struck gold in 1928 with a recording of "Mama, Where You At," a biographical lament in which the orphaned LaFleur musically wonders about the identity and whereabouts of his mother. The song was great, but the pair never encored their initial session; LaFleur was killed in a barroom brawl nine days after taping "Mama." Another gem from their brief partnership is the tune "Grand Basile."

With accordionist Moise Robin, Soileau recorded several successful singles, including "La Valse Pènitentiaire," for several labels. But Soileau's style, a deft blend of traditional music and lightning-strike fiddle runs, seemed to leave the accordion behind in virtuosic compatibility. With his cousin, the fiddler Alius Soileau, Leo recorded some experimental material, including the scorching "Lake Arthur Stomp" and, in 1934, he started Leo Soileau's Three Aces, with two guitarists and a drummer. Twisting the familiar French language repertoire with the drummer's backbeat, adding healthy doses of western swing, and in turn applying that recipe to American standards, Soileau's group essentially defined the Cajun string band sound. Between 1935 and 1937, Soileau and the Three Aces, later the Four Aces and then the Rhythm Boys, recorded over a hundred singles for such labels as Bluebird and Decca.

At the height of their popularity, Soileau and the Rhythm Boys peppered lucrative house-band stints in Lake Charles, Louisiana, and Orange, Texas, with tour dates in Chicago, Memphis, Richmond, Atlanta, and San Antonio. They were also in demand as a live-radio outfit.

Soileau's run stopped in the early fifties when the accordion returned to prominence. He retired from music and worked as a janitor and, like his brothers, a general contractor, for the remaining twenty-five years of his life. It's said Leo Soileau didn't own even one copy of any of his recordings.

Early Recordings of Leo Soileau is a recommended album.

Soileau was the innovative kingpin of the string-band movement, but several other artists were also prominent, especially the **Hackberry Ramblers**.

Where Soileau was the first Cajun fiddler to record, the Ramblers were the first band to add amplification to the mix—and anyone who's heard Ted Nugent from the first five rows can surely appreciate the idea of volume. Though Cajun in principle, the group would ultimately represent a sort of musical buffet—All-You-Can-Hear helpings of western swing, rock 'n' roll, swamp pop, and blues—and some traditionalists look upon them less than favorably. But over seventy musicians have worn the uniform of the Ramblers, and their popularity is still undisputed.

Ramblers bandleader **Luderin Darbone** (1913–), born in Evangeline, Louisiana, spent much of his youth with a fiddle in East Texas and was appropriately influenced by western swing. Also a fan and student of Cajun music, he formed the Ramblers after a stint at business college. By 1935, they were the hottest band in the region. The early lineup included Darbone; vocalist Lennis Sonnier; guitarists Glen Croker, Lonnie Rainwater, Floyd Shreve, and Joe Werner; bassist Johnnie Parket; and accordionist and future guitarist Edwin Duhon.

The band began using amplification—powered by the battery of Darbone's Model-A Ford; the increased volume made it possible not just for the musicians to use greater dynamics but also for the crowd to hear the subtleties. Although their early Bluebird recordings were sung in French, a Hackberry Ramblers radio program sponsored by Montgomery Ward caused the band to change their name to the Riverside Ramblers (after a brand of the store's automobile tires), and sing tunes in English. Hits from that period include "Wondering, Wondering" and their version of "Jolie Blonde."

That segment of the band's career ended with World War II, when the Ramblers temporarily broke up. But after the war they kicked back up, established a popular club residency in Lake Charles, and scored a deal with the Deluxe label. When rock 'n' roll was born in the fifties, the Ramblers's momentum dulled. Only noted musicologist and Arhoolie Records honcho Chris Strachwitz kept the unit buoyed up, offering them a new contract and reissuing earlier material.

Renewed interest, sparked in part by Dewey Balfa at the Newport Folk Festival in 1964, helped the Ramblers become a sort of Harlem Globetrotters of Cajun music. In 1992, they recorded *Cajun Boogie*, their first album of new material since the Strachwitz record three decades before, and followed up four years later with *Deep Water*, a millennial tour de force that features guests Jimmie Dale Gilmore and Marcia Ball.

Much of the new energy for the band seems to come from young drummer, writer, producer, and fireball Ben Sandmel. Of late, they've been nominated for a Grammy and are said to be the subjects of a documentary-film-in-the-works. Between Sandmel and Darbone, the band possesses youth and wisdom, and however they've flaunted tradition by going outside the form, the Ramblers have certainly introduced Cajun music to a massive new audience.

Leaning heavily in the country direction was fiddler **Chuck Guillory** (1919–), who once beat both Harry Choates and Leo Soileau in a fiddling contest. Born in Mamou, Guillory recorded with accordionist Milton Molitor; later, Guillory founded and headed up a popular seven-piece Cajun country band, the Rhythm Boys, which included at various points Jimmy Newman and George Jones. A much-loved tune from that period is "Grand Texas."

Though he retired in the late fifties, Guillory would pull out the fiddle on special occasions. In the eighties, the Rhythm Boys united for an album released by Arhoolie. A collection of the Arhoolie sessions, including versions of songs spanning his career, is available under the title *Grand Texas*.

Another force in the string-band era was the fluently talented fiddler and mandolinist **Oran "Doc" Guidry** (1915–1992). Born in Lafayette, Guidry recorded early on for Bluebird with guitarist Happy Fats as well as the Rain-bo Ramblers, then formed (with family members) Sons of the Acadians and recorded for Decca, for whom he translated hillbilly tunes into French.

After a break for World War II, Guidry reconnected with Fats in Happy, Doc & the Boys, a group that was the first successful recording stars for J. D. Miller's Fais Do Do label ("Colinda"). After the short-lived band broke up, Guidry and Fats continued to record and play together, and Guidry subsequently worked with various Cajun and hillbilly artists over the years, including Vin Bruce. Guidry recorded one solo album, *King of the Cajun Fiddlers*, and in the early eighties actually toured Asia with D. L. Menard.

Harry Choates (1922–1951) of Rayne, Louisiana, gets a great deal of attention for three reasons: He was a great fiddler, his "Jolie Blonde" is accepted by many folks as the ultimate version, and he was a wild man and liquor enthusiast who died in an Austin, Texas, jail under mysterious circumstances.

Choates grew up in the Depression, taught himself fiddle and guitar, and gleaned much about life, it's been said, by sneaking into bars as a teen, hiding under tables, and listening to jukeboxes.

His over-the-edge style (his stage presence was supposedly riveting) and stunning musical ability were undeniable, and he worked with such big time acts as Leo Soileau and the Rain-bo Ramblers. But while cutting sides for labels such as Bluebird, Choates developed a fondness for alcohol that cost him work in bands. As such, he played solo or headed up his own recording projects for labels that included DeLuxe, D.O.T., and Cajun Classics, and managed to stay busy with live shows in Texas and southeast Louisiana despite having been banned by the musicians union in Texas for missing gigs. In 1946, his French-language western-swing version of "Jolie Blonde," released by the Gold Star label, was the biggest Cajun record outside Louisiana *ever*. Unfortunately, the cruel grip of alcoholism began to tighten around Choates; he started pawning instruments for drink and supposedly sold the rights for "Jolie Blonde" for fifty bucks and a fifth of liquor.

Three days after he was jailed for contempt in a nonpayment-of-child-support case, Choates was found dead in his jail cell. Some said the cause was police brutality; others said that Choates went into convulsions or banged his head against the bars in a fit of delirium. In either case, the official cause of death went down as cirrhosis of the liver and complications due to alcoholism.

Despite his brief life and erratic career, Choates's onstage persona and superb melding of jazz, western swing, and pure Cajun influenced beaucoup performers that followed in his adventurous footsteps. Most of his recorded work is available; probably *Cajun Fiddle King* and *Five-Time Loser 1940–51* are the best collections.

Other Cajun fiddlers of note are **Wade Frugé, Adam Hebert, Lee Miller**, and **Allen Fontenot.**

The fiddle and the accordion aren't the only instruments required to make this music happen, at least not all the time. Certainly the guitar never blasted to the instrumental fore to create an Alvin Lee or an Andy Timmons of Cajun–Creole music. However, the guitar gained some prominence in early Cajun and Creole music in a generally rhythmic capacity.

Guitarist, songwriter, and vocalist **D. L. Menard** (1932–), born Doris Leon in Erath, Louisiana, brings a true country twinge to Cajun music. By all accounts a generous and sweet person, Menard has always said the D. L. stands for "darned lucky." Perhaps, but he worked his ass off, too.

Because he listened to country and western music on the radio as a kid, and plays guitar rather than the more high-profile fiddle or accordion, his music adds a unique sense of country song craft to the French- and occasionally English-language repertoire. For that reason Menard is known throughout southwest Louisiana as "The Cajun Hank Williams." It's interesting that a young Menard once met Williams in a New Iberia bar called Club Teche, where the country genius was extraordinarily kind to the kid and encouraged him to study the music of his heritage.

Before that, though, Menard was a teenager working in the cane fields. When he first heard his uncle's Cajun band, he was so inspired that he went out and bought a guitar. Within a year, he was playing in the band. Two years later, he joined a popular outfit called the Louisiana Aces; eventually Menard took over the band and ran it for eighteen years. Meshing his Hank-esque C&W with the sounds of Cajun heroes Lawrence Walker and Aldus Roger, Menard's Aces carved a delicious niche in the genre.

The group signed with Swallow and started to record some hits. First was "Valse de Jolly Rogers," then, in 1962, Menard cemented his burgeoning reputation as a songwriter with "La Porte dans Arriere" ("The Back Door"), the whimsical story of a carousing Cajun who is reduced to whipped-dog status when he arrives home at dawn and tries to creep through the back door. It's the rollicking counterpart to the mournful classic "Jolie Blonde," and, in the decidedly hard-working Cajun tradition, Menard wrote the song during his day gig pumping gas.

The original Louisiana Aces broke up in the sixties, but Menard continued to perform and record; he even expanded his influence during national and international tours. He formed a new Louisiana Aces, has been nominated for a Grammy, and eventually won a Folk Heritage Fellowship from the National Endowment for the Arts. His best records include *Cajun Memories, The Swallow Recordings,* and the English-language *Cajun Saturday Night.*

Guitarist and vocalist **Vin Bruce** (1932–), born in Cut Off, Louisiana, took a country-spiced version of Cajun music to the world by the way of Nashville—a true rarity.

A veteran of regionally popular country bands by nineteen, Bruce, who has a moss-draped baritone voice, began to focus on his own songwriting, and ended up in Nashville with a contract with Columbia Records. His purely Cajun repertoire, including the hit "Dans la Louisianne," was made doubly compelling by the backing of Nashville session wizards Owen Bradley and Chet Atkins.

Bruce was catapulted into brief if intense stardom and was one of the first Cajun musicians to appear on *Louisiana Hayride* and on the stage of the Grand Ole Opry. Unfortunately, the looming apocalypse of rock 'n' roll crashed into the recording business in the mid-fifties and Bruce lost his deal. He moved to smaller labels sympathetic to his unique style—Swallow and La Louisianne among them—and has maintained a substantial touring popularity with his band the Acadiens.

In recent years, Bruce had another hit with his version of "Jolie Blonde," and in 2000 saw two CDs released, *Essential Collection* and *Carousel for Two.*

Guitarist, songwriter, and vocalist **Shirley Ray Bergeron** (a man, by the way) played box and steel guitar for the Veteran Playboys. A consummate composer, Bergeron was perhaps best noted for his pure and perfectly-suited-to-Cajun singing voice.

Beyond guitar, at least one drummer deserves note: **Fernest "Man" Abshire,** who played with Lawrence Walker and Aldus Roger, and, more important, was the composer of such tunes as "One Scotch, One Bourbon, One Beer," "Family Waltz," "Tout les Deux Pour la Même" and "Lafayette Two-Step."

Two

MODERN CAJUN

I just remember being in the middle of it all. I remember old people speaking French and everybody gathering at someone or another's house to eat big suppers and play cards—and of course there were always people playing music.

It was part of my life and I grew up being involved in it—wanting to be involved in it. There are probably a lot of different pockets in this country with unique cultures who have a different way of doing things. I travel a lot but not enough to suss it out. But, hell, [Cajuns] have been down here in Louisiana since the 1700s keeping our culture and our language going, even though a lot of people my age didn't grow up speaking French and were ashamed of the music. It's not that way anymore.

—Steve Riley, accordionist
Interview with author, August 2000

*A*t a Rhythm 'n' Roots Festival in 1998 in a small Connecticut community about twenty miles in from the coastal city we live in, my wife, Eileen (a.k.a. The Vegetarian Who Walks Among Us), and I, our friends Jacquie Glassenberg (whose photographs help illustrate this book), and Young Dan Pearson (who accompanied me to JazzFest a year later largely because of the inspiration he received on this day), all braved a ludicrously chilly June day to catch Steve Riley & the Mamou Playboys, Geno Delafose & French Rockin' Boogie, and young female zydeco temptress Rosie Ledet fill out a Sunday afternoon bill.

It was bad enough that it felt like mid-February in the Yukon, but after we got inside the RV park where the festival was being held, we found out that it was a BYOB event, too. As Connecticut doesn't sell beer on Sundays, we were reduced to sending Young Dan—a cub reporter with the features of Opie Taylor—around from campsite to campsite, begging the good people for handouts. God love him, he came back with a sturdy paper grocery sack filled with a fine sampling of cheap beer—just in time for the music to start.

When Rosie Ledet and her band kicked off and were smokin', I noted with interest just how traditional her set was. I've since seen Delafose several times, and he's pretty traditional, too; on the big zydeco curve, both are conservative for their generation. The radical that day was the Cajun, Riley, and his monstrously good band, the Mamou Playboys. They'd just released their *Bayou Ruler* CD, a stylistic leap away from Cajun music tradition, singing in English on some cuts and infusing all the songs with great doses of infectious swamp pop and rock 'n' roll rhythms. On the Connecticut tundra, they rocked the house.

As I had told Louisiana Black at that (much warmer) September Festivals Acadiens (see "Young Pups," Part 3, Chapter 2 and "Early Cajun and Creole Music," Part 4, Chapter 1), Creole music evolved into zydeco around mid-century. Cajun music has traveled less far from its roots, which were characterized back when McGee played with Ardoin. But that afternoon I learned that the young Cajun musicians were reinventing the form. The Cajuns have added bass and drums. They've gone electric and pumped up the volume and energy, and where the zydeco folks sneak in R&B and blues (described in more detail in the next chapter), the Cajun kids add healthy doses of Louisiana swamp pop, honky-tonk country, and boogie-laced southern rock. Within the next year, I'd learn about Chris Ardoin and Keith Frank, and I'd see just how radical zydeco has been getting, too.

BeauSoleil avec Michael Doucet is without question the best-known proponent of Cajun music in this solar system, chiefly through their ability, highlighted in almost two-dozen albums and world tours, to embrace tradition even as they explore futuristic visions of the music.

BeauSoleil means "Beautiful Sunshine." Not coincidentally, it was also the nickname of eighteenth-century Acadian resistance fighter Joseph Broussard. The band has been around for a long time. When founder Michael Doucet (1951–) was asked to explain how they've survived, he answered, "Well, we've gotten a lot better. In the old days, we worked out the songs on the bandstand during the shows. Practice? Hah! We just put an ice chest on the stage and played until the beer ran out. It sounds hedonistic but it was fun and we learned—we *needed* to learn where the music came from.

"And then, we started to put in a lot of things people hadn't heard. It wasn't a plan; it was *never* a plan. We were never trying to do anything but play what we felt and feel."

With twenty-five years now on the bandstand, it could be said Beau-Soleil has done all right with that concept.

Fiddler Doucet, born in Scott, Louisiana, started the band as an original folk trio with Bessyl Duhon on accordion and Kenneth Richard on mandolin. He'd grown up speaking French but became interested in music at the height of the Americanization period. Like his friend, musician and songwriter Zachary Richard, Doucet reinvigorated his passion for the Cajun heritage through exposure to its early music. When BeauSoleil began to triumph at folk festivals, the lineup gradually expanded. In 1977, they recorded their American debut for Louisiana's Swallow label and, when they played at President Jimmy Carter's inauguration, the word began to spread.

In the eighties, as they grew to appreciate the true Cajun roots and got comfortable with their mastery of them, BeauSoleil began to incorporate new components—jazz, rock, Caribbean, and even Hawaiian flavors—and decided to move from acoustic to electric. With albums such as *Zydeco Gris-Gris* and *Belizare the Cajun* (a soundtrack work), the Grammy nominations started to roll in.

The group also expanded their touring circuits, often rolling into communities that had never heard of Cajun or zydeco music and then blowing out of town leaving a wake of zealous converts. They still perform over a hundred dates a year—and count numerous fans on several continents. The definitive BeauSoleil lineup is Doucet on fiddle, vocals, and songwriting, his brother **David Doucet** on guitar, **Jimmy Breaux** on accordion, multi-instrumentalist **Al Tharp**, drummer **Tommy Alesi**, and percussionist **Billy Ware.**

"It's pretty amazing what Michael has done," Cajun accordionist Steve Riley told me. "He's made the best-known Cajun band in the world and they've stuck to their guns. Whether they play old stuff or write their stuff, it's just great song after great song; an endless well of great material. And what a fiddle player."

Fueled by the renaissance of the French-speaking culture, Michael has felt comfortable enough to write original material and incorporate it into the vast body of Cajun music. On more recent CDs—*Cajunization* and *L'Amour ou la Folie*—the mixture of indigenous songs (traditionally played or adapted in a modern context) and new originals is breathtaking. And the same goes for an older record, *Hot Chili Mama*, as well as the in-concert disc, *Live from the Left Coast*. In performance or on CD, BeauSoleil provides the magical opportunity to sample Cajun past, present, and future. It's as good as it gets.

And don't forget the performer's solo works. People up here [in Connecticut] still ask, "What *is* it?" about David Doucet's *1957—Solo Cajun Guitar,* which I named Best Album of the Year in 1999. I tell them, as the title says, it's a CD full of solo Cajun guitar by Michael's younger brother, David Doucet, the lead guitarist in BeauSoleil. From the moment I first listened to it, I felt its magic: It's like Leo Kottke and Michael Hedges sitting around drinking shooters of Tabasco. Michael's catalog—in particular *Beau Solo*—is just as illuminating. When asked to name his favorite Louisiana recommendations, he replied, "Get a Fats Domino collection, a Bobby Charles album, and a Dr. John album. As far as the French-language stuff is concerned, get some Amédé Ardoin and Dennis McGee. And you need to own the soundtrack and the video of the movie *Went to the Dance Last Night.*" As for food in southwest Louisiana, he recommends Shuck's in Abbeville: "It's just a great oyster and gumbo place."

Arguably the most elastic and unique modern Cajun artist would be **Zachary Richard** (1950–), whose militant French-Restoration stance persuaded him to leave Louisiana and live in Montreal from 1976–1981. Born to the mayor of Scott, Louisiana, Richard is a spectacular songwriter and multi-instrumentalist whose creative muse has led him to attack hardcore Cajun party music, inventive rock 'n' roll, and near-ambient swampy-styled material. Influenced as much by New Orleans rhythm 'n' blues as he is by old-line Cajun, Richard is the only sailor in his particular musical sea.

He grew up at the height of the Americanization storm and spoke French only around older relatives and on special occasions. Early in his musical career, he was enamored of the Rolling Stones. He played in rock bands throughout his matriculation at Tulane University—Richard is also a respected and published poet—and headed afterwards to the pulsing music scene of New York City.

Richard was signed to Elektra Records after sending them a demo tape. After a protracted series of imbroglios with the label, he bought an accordion and taught himself to play by listening to Aldus Roger records. When a duet performance at a festival in France with old pal Doucet further awakened in Richard a fascination with the music of his ancestors, he and Doucet returned to Louisiana to experiment with the idea of a Cajun rock band.

It didn't work out, though, and when Doucet decided to form Beau-Soleil, Richard headed north to Canada and became a star with his adventurous, French-language mix of musical styles. Several albums resulted, among them *Mardi Gras* and *Bayou des Mystéres*, before he returned to Louisiana. Two English-language albums followed for Rounder, *Zack's Bon Ton* and *Mardi Gras Mambo.* When a gig at an Acadian festival in Nova Scotia sealed his commitment to Cajun activism, Richard started commuting between Canada and Louisiana in an attempt to restore the Cajun culture to his home state.

Using his American and Cajun backgrounds to work for the cause, Richard began to step into his own. He signed with A&M Records, for whom he released the superb *Women in the Room* and *Snake Bite Love*, and has since recorded for French and independent labels. Some of his best work is filled with haunting melodies contrasted with funky Mardi Gras songs; listen to it on the two-disc *Cap Enragé*.

Active in a variety of rights movements (animal, environmental, and Cajun), Richard remains a visible force in Cajun music.

Special mention should be made of the band **Coteau,** which was the first experiment at Cajun rock. Employing a base of traditional instrumentation, then throwing some Wishbone Ash–style twin guitar into the musical étouffée, Coteau came together in the seventies for two short years when younger Cajun musicians, who'd grown up Americanized and into rock 'n' roll, rediscovered their French musical roots.

Although the original band never recorded, the success of the similarly adventurous BeauSoleil—plus Michael Doucet's being *in* Coteau— inspired a slightly altered lineup to make a Coteau album in 1998. The new incarnation consisted of bassist Gary Newman, drummer Kenneth Blevins, accordionist and fiddler Bessyl Duhon, Doucet, Danny Kimball on rubboard, and guitarists Bruce MacDonald and Dr. Tommy Comeaux, the latter stepping in for original guitarist Dana Breaux, who committed suicide not long after Coteau had played a reunion set at the 1981 JazzFest. Bizarrely, Comeaux, as mentioned in the last chapter, died shortly after the recording in a cycling accident; another of the band's original guitarists, Sterling Richard, passed away in an oilfield crash.

Inspired by the memory of their lost members, the new Coteau took the old-time Cajun music and rearranged it so the fiddle-accordion lines were played by guitars. The resultant CD, *Highly Seasoned Cajun*, is an exercise in exploratory, free-form Cajun–rock–jazz.

If BeauSoleil represents a visionary traditional band, and Richard a wild card in Cajun music, then **Balfa Toujours** is a high point of purely traditional bands. An acoustic group out of Basile, Louisiana, formed as a tribute to the late Balfa Brothers Band, Balfa Toujours, "Balfa forever," was conceived upon Dewey Balfa's death in 1992 by his daughters, **Christine Balfa** and **Nelda Balfa.** Both women played guitar with their dad and various relatives as kids but never pursued music as a career until their father passed.

After Dewey died, Nelda and Christine both started writing traditionally flavored French tunes unbeknownst to each other. When they realized what was happening, they put the material on tape and sent it to Louisiana's Swallow Records for constructive criticism—and ended up with a record deal.

Accordionist **Dirk Powell** (now Christine's husband) and fiddler **Kevin Wimmer,** who'd become friends of the family over the years, came on board. The reception for that first release, *Pop, Tu Me Parles Toujours,* "*Dad, You Speak to Me Still,*" set the Balfa Toujours legacy in motion in a way that would become bigger than all of them. Subsequent CDs included *Vielle Terre Haute* and the recently released *Live at Whiskey River Landing.*

The Cajun music they perform is pristine, but it's also more than rote recitation of Balfa Brothers material. They continue to write their own songs and, fueled by the spirit of sharing inherited from Dewey Balfa, Balfa Toujours have always generously given their time in supportive and instructional contexts. Nelda has since retired, but Christine continues along with mainstays Powell on the accordion, fiddler Wimmer, and bassist Craig Guillory.

In April, 2001, the first Dewey Balfa Cajun & Creole Heritage Week was held in St. Martinville, an event spurred on by Balfa Toujours and the Louisiana Folk Roots Foundation in commitment to one of Dewey's fondest dreams: to perpetuate the two cultures in all fashions, as well as foster unity between Creoles and Cajuns.

It's the sort of thing that one sees regularly at Balfa Toujours shows, when their guest performers might be Creole accordionist Alphonse "Bois Sec " Ardoin (with whom they did the splendid *Allons Danser*) or young zydeco hero Geno Delafose (described in the next chapter) who told me, "Balfa Toujours is simply a great Cajun band."

Another similarly devoted (and connected) band is an acoustic trio, the **Savoy-Doucet Cajun Band;** it includes accordionist and accordion-maker **Marc Savoy** (1940–), born in Eunice, Louisiana; his wife, guitarist **Ann Savoy** (1952–), born in St. Louis, Missouri, author of the highly recommended *Cajun Music: A Reflection of a People*; and BeauSoleil's Michael Doucet. The group exists to perpetrate traditional Cajun music; not only are they spectacularly good at it but they also serve as a hub outfit for various related projects (even as the Savoy Doucet Cajun Band might be thought of as merely an offshoot for Doucet).

There is also the **Savoy Smith Cajun Band** (with state fiddle champion **Ken Smith**), and a bevy of solo projects by all three principals.

The essence of the band lies in its devotion to old-time Cajun music; don't listen expecting progressive forays into the next century of the form. Their repertoire is largely based on restored and all-but-forgotten material from the masters, and the original songs they write are sculpted to fit with the past.

"It's through Marc that the band started," Ann Savoy told me. "It's a given in our part of Louisiana that you play traditional music in your home. But Marc had toured with D. L. Menard and the Balfa Brothers and knew the value of playing Cajun music outside Louisiana. Because visitors come in and don't know the difference between Cajun and zydeco and they think everything is going to sound like BeauSoleil. Sometimes it confuses and disappoints them when we don't; more often, they're fascinated. BeauSoleil has drawn people to the music, and when they get here it's like seeing the variety and beauty of the tradition."

While Doucet has a nice day job with BeauSoleil, Marc Savoy spends his days as one of the most renowned instrument makers in the world, and

Ann, a Cajun by marriage, has jumped with unbridled enthusiasm into the job of folklorist. Still the band has time to tour, record, and maintain a high group profile in their own corner of Acadiana (Saturday morning jams at Marc's Savoy Music Center near Eunice are legendary).

Of their recorded output, *Live! At the Dance* and *Sam's Big Rooster* are suggested acquisitions. Ann Savoy lists other Cajun and Creole music that should be heard to understand the form: "Arhoolie's complete works of Amédé Ardoin; Iry LeJeune (the Gold Band and Ace Collections; Ace is really cool—from the original 78s with no bass); Dennis McGee, the Shanachie set; some Lawrence Walker; *The Balfa Brothers Play Traditional Cajun Music.* And Rounder just released the Lomax collection of early Cajun recordings."

Ann Savoy likes to talk about "Food! My favorite subject! For Cajun, in Eunice, there's Joanie's Cajun Connection or Mathilda's Country Kitchen. But I'm afraid it's not possible to be a vegetarian in this area. Though Ruby's in Eunice is a nice mom-and-pop place that has vegetables."

From the reporter's notebook:

(Rhodes-on-Pawtuxet Ballroom, Rhode Island, Mardi Gras party, February 1999)—A misty, foggy night and we've traveled from New London to approximate Fat Tuesday. Nice bill: Savoy-Doucet Cajun Band, BeauSoleil, Chris Ardoin & Double Clutchin' . . . I'm pressed up front by the stage, and someone smells like ham. This is the first time I've seen this band; they're hypnotically great. Marc Savoy is seated on a stool, wiping his face repeatedly with a towel. Is he well? He seems to be having a good time, but his grin pops up only occasionally; he seems rapt with attention.

On fiddle is Michael Doucet, wearing a Hawaiian shirt and apparently content to lay back, rock-out wise. Ann Savoy, who married into the Cajun culture and is damned serious about it—she's brought me a copy of her book—is a wonderfully warm stage presence. The only problem I can see with this stuff is that, for all its innate danceability, I would literally prefer to be on the Savoys' front porch, with a bowl of gumbo and a beer, listening on a spring night. It's a decidedly intimate music.

Another segue from past to future is fiddler **Hadley J. Castille,** a white-water-quick player with a militant sense of Cajun tradition—his most popular song is "200 Lines: I Must Not Speak French," which he wrote after being disciplined for doing just that. (The tune won Castille a Cajun French Music Association Heritage award in 1992.)

He grew up near Opelousas, learned to play from his father, Francois, and Uncle Cyprien; he listened heavily to the recordings of Harry Choates and Leo Soileau, melding their influences with Bob Wills and other such western swing folk. From that group he forged his own style; he's also an emotive vocalist and songwriter who enjoys composing with his son, Blake, and playing around with his Sharecroppers Cajun Band. Castille's work has also graced the Clint Eastwood film *A Perfect World*.

The recommended CD is *200 Lines: I Must Not Speak French*, though all his albums are good and *Cajun Swamp Fiddler* is a cut above.

Of the Even Younger nouveau Cajun acts, **Steve Riley** (1969–) **& the Mamou Playboys** are road warriors who have exponentially growing and international fan bases. Riley, born in the town of Mamou, is an accordion-ist with a rock-star sensibility and a vibrant band that focuses on all nu-ances and implications of Cajun music, including (until the last few years) exclusively French-language tunes. Founded in 1988 by Riley and the as-tounding fiddler and songwriter **David Greely** as a devoutly traditional outfit, and inspired by both men's respective tutelages with and affection for Dewey Balfa, the Mamou Playboys have over the years evolved into one of the most visionary outfits in the field.

Riley grew up deeply appreciative of Cajun music—he played triangle as a kid at house parties with such august jammers as Dennis McGee and (second cousin) Marc Savoy, and he never really wanted to do anything else. "Yeah, I was interested in the Beatles when I was young," he told me, "and I did play bass guitar in a high school rock band. But I kept wanting to play Cajun music during rehearsal breaks."

Musicians' ages spanned three generations in the earliest incarnation of the Mamou Playboys; it wasn't until after a rough but exciting, self-titled first CD—produced by Zachary Richard—and some growing pains that the band has arrived where Greely and Riley are truly happy. They've toured intensely, and their enthusiasm, fine songwriting, and onstage sense of Big Fun have paid off in a huge way.

"There are probably more zydeco bands on the road than Cajun bands," Riley told me. "I think BeauSoleil and Balfa Toujours and us are the three main Cajun bands traveling extensively. But the circuits are such that we're always playing with or running into C. J. Chenier and Geno De-lafose, and it's all getting more and more popular—which is healthy for the music of southwest Louisiana."

Over the course of six CDs—most of them for Rounder and including the Grammy-nominated *Trace of Time*, *La Toussaint*, *Friday at Last*, and 1998's terrific *Bayou Ruler*—Riley & the Mamou Playboys's sound has ex-panded to include traces of rock, country, and swamp pop. "I think every-thing that we love is sneaking its way into our songwriting and playing," he told me. "*Ruler* was definitely a change for us; we were writing material in English, I was hanging out with producer [and guitar hero] C. C. Adcock, who had a huge influence on us. So at any time you might hear us do old-time twin fiddle tunes or some rocked-out swamp pop."

The latest and most stable lineup of the band includes longtime drummer **Kevin Dugas,** bassist **Blaine Gaspard,** and guitarist **Roddie**

Romero, a fine player who replaces another fine player, **Jimmy Domengeaux,** who died in 1999.

In addition to their work in the Mamou Playboys, Riley and Greely have been active in the Little Band o' Gold, a supergroup roots–swamp pop amalgam with a highly regarded CD out in 2000.

The five albums of Louisiana music everyone should own? According to Steve Riley: "A Balfa Brothers album, *any* Clifton Chenier—they're all great—a Fats Domino collection . . . You need some swamp pop guys so, hell, get some Warren Storm. And a Dennis McGee one with Amédé Ardoin and Sady Courville."

Venturing even further afield than Riley and company, **Wayne Toups** of **Zydecajun** (1958–) is an onstage madman who wields his accordion like a flame thrower: He flings sheets of notes over the crowd as he personally orchestrates a mob-rule approach to good times at every one of the band's shows.

Born in Lafayette and raised by a French-speaking rice farmer in Crowley, Louisiana, Toups was versatile on accordion by the time he was thirteen, obsessed as he was by such giants as Iry Lejeune. Instinctively, Toups enjoyed the traditional aspects of Cajun music and the funkier sides of zydeco; when he formed his band (guitarists **Ray Ellender** and **Rhett Glindmeyer,** bassist **Timmy Broussard,** drummer **Timmy Dugas,** and keyboardist **Phillip Knowlton**), the name was an obvious choice.

But he was also heavily influenced by southern rock and classic soul music, and thought a swirling sampling of the recipe might attract folks of his own generation who might not otherwise be open-minded about the indigenous music of southwest Louisiana. And if the band's stylistic versatility puts off the traditionalists, it has opened the doors for Toups to play with a variety of artists in other genres—particularly country stars Sammy Kershaw, George Jones, Mark Wills, and Garth Brooks.

Zydecajun has released ten firebrand CDs—including *More Than Just a Little, Blast from the Bayou, Back to the Bayou,* and *Little Wooden Box* (Wayne's euphemism for his accordion)—one of which, *Fish Out of Water,* was on Mercury Records. The band's touring roadmap is astonishing in its range: everywhere from South America to Southeast Asia.

Filé is another cool band, and not just because they had the good sense to call themselves "Filé" instead of "Ground Sassafras." Founded in Lafayette by Cajun accordionist Ward Lormand and Creole fiddler and multi-instrumentalist D'Jarma Garnier, the group started out in a fairly strict traditional sense, aligning themselves closely with older Creole fiddle wizard Canray Fontenot. With his passing, though, Filé tossed a few more colors on their palette.

That they have a piano player—pretty much unheard of in Cajun music—and that he's David Egan, an R&B–happy vet of country artist Jo-El Sonnier's band, pushes the group in a decided honky-tonk direction.

All three of the principals write material, and an Appalachian-tinged rhythm section (drummer Peter Stevens and bassist Kevin Shearin) gives the whole recipe a bit of hillbilly spice.

Their latest releases include *Hang On to Your Chapeau; Filé: Cajun Dance Band; La Vie Marron: The Runaway Life; Two Left Feet;* and their first, *Live at Mulate's.*

The **Jambalaya Cajun Band** is certainly worth mentioning as another standout. It was formed in the late seventies by fiddler **Terry Huval** (1956–). Born in Port Arthur, Texas, Huvel grew up in Breaux Bridge, Louisiana, with his drummer brother, Tony. The Jambalaya Cajun Band is a musical sampling of All Things Acadian. Playing a heavy regional festival and club schedule, as well as recording for Louisiana's prestigious Swallow label (most notably *C'est Fun!* and *Laisse les Jeunes Jouer!* as well as the new *Lessons Learned*), the band is a virtuosic instrumental unit with solid vocals that is more than a little interesting compositionally.

Tasso, which some folks realize is a Louisiana term for a dried, jerky-type of ham, is a nouveau-trad trio with superb abilities that features fiddler **Mitchell Reed,** accordionist and vocalist **Phillip Allemond,** and guitarist, vocalist, and composer **Randy Vidrine.** Their second CD, *Viens à Ma Maison*, was produced by Michael Doucet.

Despite tourists' assumptions to the contrary, New Orleans isn't exactly bustling with Cajun and zydeco music. But Marksville's **Bruce Daigrepont** (1958–), a fine singer, accordionist, and guitarist, set up shop in the Crescent City years ago and, with his **Cajun Band,** purveys a fine and authentic brand of Cajun music; his Sunday-night house gigs at Tipitina's are as prestigious as they are fun.

Raised in New Orleans, Daigrepont was exposed to Cajun music on trips back to the country to visit relatives. After attending the Festivals Acadiens in 1979, he was seized by an accordion frenzy and set about becoming a virtuoso. Within a year, he was heading up the Bourre Cajun Band, whose regular gigs at New Orleans's Maple Leaf Bar (a spot that is perhaps more associated with R&B pianists James Booker and Jon Cleary) helped start a healthy Cajun music scene in the wicked city.

A proud archivist with several hundred traditional songs in his repertoire, Daigrepont has little interest in re-creating the old songs in the studio. As solid a writer as he is a singer and performer, Daigrepont eventually formed the Cajun Band and signed with Rounder. *Stir Up the Roux, Paradis,* and *Petit Cadeau* are all recommended CDs of solid original material. He and his band have toured Europe and the United States extensively, in addition to his regular work in New Orleans.

Younger even than Billy Gilman, who is rocketing up the country charts as the hottest thing since Leann Rimes, **Hunter Hayes** (1991–)—a Cajun-born accordion prodigy who could pass for Gilman's kid brother—

has been barbecuing Louisiana audiences recently with his extraordinary talent. Hayes has performed at the "Le Cajun" awards show for the Cajun French Music Association in Lafayette.

Belton Richard (1939–) might be thought of as a slightly older, considerably less intense Zachary Richard. An accordionist who looks like Elvis and who dabbled extensively in rock before focusing on his Cajun roots, Richard was born near Rayne, Louisiana. He learned the instrument at the hands of his father, was playing professionally in his early teens, and at eighteen started his own rock 'n' roll band, The French Rockets.

Richard soon became enamored of his heritage, formed a group called the **Musical Aces** and merged the rockier tendencies with his French-language ancestry by working a heavy swamp-pop angle in the context of Cajun structures. He's enjoyed a series of big-selling releases (particularly the singles "The Cajun Streak" and "Une Autre Soir d'Ennia") for the Swallow label and became a tremendously popular artist in Louisiana and East Texas throughout the sixties and seventies; when the biz began to wear him out, he stepped back from his live performance schedule. Richard continued to record, though, until 1987, when he took an extended respite. After a solid 1993 release called *Modern Sounds of Cajun Music*, the 1995 Festivals Acadiens was dedicated to him. He's since come out of retirement at a more relaxed pace and released the 1996 CD *I'm Back!*

Earlier recommended albums include *The Essential Belton Richard Cajun Music Collection* and *Good 'n' Cajun*.

Sheryl Cormier (1945–) is a fine accordionist born in Grand Coteau-Sunset and billed (with some justification) as the "Queen of Cajun Music"—though Ann Savoy and Christine Balfa could certainly demand a recount on that vote. A traditionalist whose band, **Cajun Sounds,** is a tight and supportive outfit, Cormier grew up sitting in with her dad's band, Andrew Guileau and the Sunset Playboys. Mom was the drummer, so Cormier had plenty of support as a woman entering a "man's world." Cormier took a break when she decided to get married and raise a family, but the call of music was too strong and she's been hitting the festival circuit heavily for years. Her husband, singer and manager Russell Cormier, and her son, Russell Jr., are both in her band.

A sizzling player, Cormier can best be heard on the *Queen of Cajun Music* CD.

And speaking of the Female Department, **The Magnolia Sisters** are a pretty terrific quintet—even if some of them aren't authentic, bloodline Cajuns. A sort of female supergroup made up of **Ann Savoy, Christine Balfa, Jane Vidrine, Tina Pilione,** and **Lisa Trahan Reed,** the women are all multi-instrumentalists and fine singers who now live in Louisiana. They play in other Cajun bands, too. Their debut CD was called *Prends Courage,* after which they were picked up by Rounder, and *Chers Amis,* the sophomore effort, was even better. The trad Cajun stuff is wonderfully arranged and performed, and their ventures into folk music are warm and reverent.

Another group of fiercely proud young traditionalists is **Al Berard and the Basin Brothers;** they grew up in the Atchafalaya River Basin, a fine area to absorb the true sounds of Cajun music. Vocalist, fiddler, and multi-instrumentalist Berard learned to appreciate his ancestry and his music when he was on tour with Hadley Castille.

After forming the Basin Brothers, the group signed with Flying Fish/Rounder and has released three albums: *Let's Get Cajun* (nominated for a Grammy), *Stayin' Cajun,* and *Danse la Louisiane (In Louisiana).*

At this time of immense pride in the Cajun culture, it seems that everyone in southwest Louisiana has a Cajun band, and the new generation is heavily represented. If these chapters have indicated anything at all, it's that music is handed down from generation to generation. There are dozens of fine Cajun bands out there: **Mamon, La Bande Feufollet, Paul Daigle, Karlo Broussard & Standard Time, Lee Benoit and the Bayou Stompers, Moise and Alida Viator, Damon Troy and Louisiana Beat, Scotty Pousson and the Pointe aux Loups Playboys,** and **Kevin Naquin and the Ossun Playboys**. (If ever I do form a Cajun band, I'll know enough to call it the Playboys of something.)

Three

---•◆•---

ZYDECO

*I*n our hotel room, conveniently located near the French Quarter and, for Dixieland Steve's purposes, the Harrah's Casino at the foot of Canal Street, I am playing zydeco tunes on my portable CD player. I've brought along just a sampling: Chris Ardoin & Double Clutchin', Beau Jocque & the Zydeco Hi-Rollers, an early Clifton Chenier with the Zodico Ramblers, and Geno Delafose and French Rockin' Boogie.

I'm here with my former college roommate, Steve Pace, whom I have begun to call Dixieland Steve since, in the spirit of the Mardi Gras we've come to experience, he continually mimes playing a trombone. He opens a postbreakfast Dixie beer and stares at the boom box as though he can *see* the music, like germs under a microscope. "Goddamn, Koster," he protests with easy good humor, "We come to Mardi Gras and here you are listening to this *accordion* shit." He gives the word "accordion" such an odious inflection that I have to laugh.

"It's zydeco, amigo," I tell him.

"Okay," Dixieland Steve says agreeably. "I can tell that. But where do these people come from? It all sounds alike."

To the uninitiated, most zydeco music (briefly discussed in connection with the blues in "The Baton Rouge Scene," Part 3, Chapter 1) *is* repetitive. It's usually sung in French and, as it's derivative of the Creole and Cajun musical forms, most often features two- and three-chord waltzes and dance numbers. Because early accordions were available only in the keys of A and F, and the primordial single-row diatonic accordions limited the notes you could play, many of the songs in the repertoire are restrictive.

At the same time, like any other musical form, the more you listen to it, the more the nuances and subtleties begin to emerge. It has not always been this way, but accordions now come in many different styles and keynote systems, which bolstered the zydeco evolution, and the music has mutated over the years as it incorporated influences from blues to funk to hip-hop and even country. A few things remain constant: You're *going to* hear an accordion and a *frottoir* (or "rubboard," a sheet-metal vest sorta like a giant cheese shredder that hangs against one's chest and is played percussively, usually with a spoon). Also, zydeco is *going to* be danceable.

In an effort to impart to Dixieland Steve that zydeco is diverse, I pop in Double Clutchin', cueing up "Lake Charles Connection," which I will state right now is the greatest zydeco song of all time. By most standards, true, it's not typical zydeco. Following in the innovative tradition of Clifton Chenier, then Buckwheat Zydeco, Boozoo Chavis, Beau Jocque, Chris Ardoin, and fellow youngsters Keith Frank, Lil' Brian and the Zydeco Travelers have taken zydeco to a new level, heavily infused with funk and even elements of hip-hop and alt-rock. It's called nouveau zydeco. Most of it is in English and most of it rocks.

Dixieland Steve is impressed by the sheer groove and energy of the tune, and his face is etched with the same musical euphoria I saw during our college cruises, when the eight-track in his Monte Carlo would blast out the Gentle Giant album with "Two Weeks in Spain" on it.

"*This* I can handle," he says. "These guys rock. It's like Fishbone if they ate crawfish."

Zydeco, simply, is a mixture of several dances and a musical style. The sound is what happened when black Creoles took the rootsy acoustic music of their ancestors and the land-sharing Cajuns and mashed it together with modern electric blues, soul, and R&B. Accordion dominates—as I have said, there is no zydeco without accordion. The music is so danceable because by definition that's why it evolved—and the older material was often three-chord uptempo pieces or slower waltz songs that the youngsters expanded to incorporate the blues of Clifton Chenier, R&B, elements of hip-hop, modern funk, rock, and even country.

Eventually, players brought in various combinations of electric guitars, horns and saxophones, and bass and drums along with the accordion and *frottoir*; but note that the Cajuns' fiddle and triangle were *not* part of the equation.

"Zydeco is the only American music supported by the people indigenous to the region in which it was created," Sean Ardoin, who heads up a band called ZydeKool, told me a few years ago. Sean is Chris Ardoin's brother, Lawrence "Black" Ardoin's son, and Alphonse "Bois Sec" Ardoin's grandson, so he is as much a student of the music as he is a legacy and an innovator. "Blues started down here in the South and it's supported by the rest of the country and the world, but not really here [in Acadiana]. But zydeco is absolutely supported here and was for a long time. It's just that, now, we're exporting it to the rest of the world."

Like Cajun and Creole music, zydeco is predominantly a French-language form—or it was. A lot of the young tigers, the nouveau zydecoists, have gone English. That has brought a new, younger audience to the lucrative dance circuit that extends from Lafayette to Houston. The region is white-hot with zydeco clubs; both older traditional bands and the *nouveau* zydeco kids work heavily.

Though there are schisms between young and old bands, and new and traditional interpretations, one of the most significant differences is in touring tendencies: those acts content to work only the circuit compared to those breaking out and taking zydeco to the world. It is possible (and profitable) for zydeco bands never to leave southwest Louisiana or east Texas; clubs such as Slim's Y-Ki-Ki in Opelousas, Richard's in Lawtell, and El Sido's and Hamilton's Place in Lafayette are all within a one-beer ride of one another in the heart of Acadiana. They are gold mines where Keith Frank will sell out on any night. Four-night weekends are nonstop parties in southwest Louisiana, and between horse races, gumbo cook-offs, trail rides, rodeos, and the preponderance of nightclubs, it's almost impossible to *not* hear great zydeco.

The music is gaining a worldwide reputation, too. First, Louisiana-born Queen Ida moved with her family to California as a child and became a zydeco power on the West Coast several years ago. Buckwheat Zydeco, though, was probably the first true pioneer to take zydeco global. For those artists who want to hit the road, every year sees more and more opportunities at Cajun and zydeco and roots festivals not just throughout the United States but all over the world. That practitioners of both Cajun and zydeco are touring together, recording together, and sharing stages together indicates not only a welcome solidarity but a healthy attitude for the music of southwest Louisiana.

"In general, the south Louisiana Creole culture is very insular," Rounder Records's producer Scott Billington, who has worked with a rich variety of zydeco and Cajun artists, told me. "I have such admiration for Buckwheat Zydeco, not just as a musician but also as a worker. He knew he could expand the borders of zydeco. He would play a show on the East Coast in front of ten people and it didn't faze him. 'Next time we'll have a hundred,' he'd say. And it has taken off."

Buckwheat Zydeco is modest but emphatic about his role in the explosion. "Definitely," he told me, "zydeco music is important to Creole people and the culture, but I've thought that traveling all these years to bring the music to an international crowd, and educating people, is important for Creoles, too."

Geno Delafose, arguably the best of the young accordionists, who works predominantly in French and plays a largely traditional style of zydeco, is a road dog who enjoys touring beyond the boundaries of Louisiana and Texas, but sees advantages for those who stay behind. "Keith Frank is the hot local band now," Delafose told me, "and he doesn't take it on the road too much. He's making money. The thing is, Keith's dad [zydeco legend Preston Frank] and his band didn't travel. But my dad [another zydeco hero, John Delafose] and his band did. Zydeco is very much a family thing, so you can see how one generation influences the other. From my perspective, the crowds have grown a lot, and we get a chance to show the different levels of zydeco."

As noted earlier, Creole and Cajun musicians have worked together since the days of Amédé Ardoin and Dennis McGee. In both camps, experimentation beyond tradition has blurred the two styles considerably, though it's safe to say that zydeco artists are definitely more adventurous and involved in blues and funk and the Cajuns are more conservative and focused on rural and country music. In general, it's not surprising to see Cajun musicians Steve Riley or BeauSoleil's Michael Doucet guesting on zydeco albums, or zydeco players Geno Delafose and Chris Ardoin sitting in on Cajun records. The same formula applies to gigs, although backwoods racism still rears its pathetic head on occasion.

A few years ago, Geno Delafose, his mother, and a friend went to a Cajun nightclub to dance because Balfa Toujours—friends and touring partners of Geno's—were performing that night and Delafose was scheduled to get up and jam with them. But when Delafose and company arrived at the nightclub, he was pulled aside and told that it wasn't a good idea to dance in a white nightclub.

"I was dumbfounded and didn't know what to say," Delafose told me. "But when I got onstage and played music with Christine [Balfa], everything was fine. On the one hand, it's encouraging that the music helps people get along. On the other hand, I just assume that if I go into a pure Cajun club . . . well, a black guy's gonna get some looks."

Chris Ardoin knows what Delafose is talking about. "I've never run into something like that personally," he said to me, "but that sort of thing is alive. You go into some of the smaller country towns . . . "

As usual, it's the musicians who seem to get along in a way that transcends the bigotry. As Cajun accordionist Steve Riley told me, "The Cajuns and Creoles have been hanging out together for years, and for the most part, intelligent folks understand each other and borrow from each other and get along."

If we accept, then, that the musicians understand and appreciate the differences in the music and culture even as they celebrate the similarities, it's time to examine the form a bit. To appreciate zydeco, you have to understand the importance of the accordion, which can have single, double, or triple keys, or have the range of a piano.

The piano accordion came into prominence with **Clifton Chenier** (1925–1987). He's the Jimi Hendrix of accordion, the Bob Marley of southwest Louisiana—and, unfortunately, like both of them, he's dead. In his time, though, Chenier, a.k.a. The King of Zydeco, was a tremendous player and innovator. Taking the simple but infectious Saturday night Creole dance music they called "la-la," adding piquant dashes of Chuck Berry rhythm and Jimmy Reed blues—along with the modern guitar, drums, and horns instrumentation that made those forms possible—Chenier transformed a simple, almost precious batch of indigenous folk songs into some roof-raising party anthems.

When Chenier protégé Buckwheat Zydeco (né Stanley Dural Jr.) described his first gig with The King, the natural excitement in his voice kicked up a notch: "I wasn't sure what to expect, and then I got up on stage and we played four hours without an intermission." He laughs. "I'd never seen anything like it before. I got up on that stage and I stayed two years."

Chenier was born into a sharecropping family in Opelousas. He transformed a love of blues and the French-language songs of his culture into a natural curiosity about music. Clifton grew up working in sugarcane fields and learning the piano accordion—an instrument given to him by Isiae Blasa and unusual in its range for Creole and Cajun music at the time. Fascinated by the technique of accordionist Amédé Ardoin, Chenier, along with his washboard-playing brother Cleveland, were soon playing weekend dances at their Uncle Morris's nightclub after spending their weeks driving oil trucks for nearby refineries in Lake Charles, Louisiana, and Port Arthur, Texas.

Almost instantly, Chenier's approach to the repertoire was mischievously creative. He was heavily into bluesmen Muddy Waters and Lightnin' Hopkins, and was also absorbing the New Orleans R&B of Fats Domino that permeated radio airwaves. Tossing it all into the French language music he grew up with was pretty revolutionary.

In 1954, Chenier was discovered playing on the side of the road by J. R. Fulbright, an ex–circus worker who had turned independent record-producer. Fulbright was looking for a blues harpist. At Lake Charles radio station KAOK, Chenier made his first recordings, released by Elko Records, and within a year he'd been picked up by Specialty Records out of Los Angeles. Even in that short time, the growing influence of blues and R&B was obvious on songs such as "Boppin' the Rock" and a hit called "Ai 'Tit Fille (Hey Little Girl)."

With his band the Zodico Ramblers, Chenier was soon based in Houston, soaking up that town's R&B grooves and touring full time as he carved a loyal following for his energized approach to the old ways. In 1964, he moved to the folk-loving Arhoolie label after being introduced to label honcho Chris Strachwitz by his cousin (Lightnin' Hopkins's wife). A year later, he recorded an old traditional song called "Zydeco Sont Pas Salé"—loosely translated as "the snap beans aren't salty." Updating the rhythm of the piece, Chenier recorded what has been called the Anthem of Zydeco and gave the new style of the music its name.

Chenier worked the Gulf Coast and festival circuit hard, gradually expanding the line-up of his band, now known as the Red Hot Louisiana Band, to include electric guitarist Paul Senegal and saxophonist "Blind"

John Hart. Ever the natural performer, Chenier started wearing a cape and crown onstage, supplemented by a luminous gold tooth and a rhinestone-spangled accordion. Almost by instinct he began to infuse the perform-ances with elements of big-band jazz. Among the guitarists who played in the Red Hot Louisiana Band were Lonnie Brooks and Lonesome Sun-down. Youngsters Johnny Winter, Steve Miller, and Elvin Bishop were all Chenier's friends and influenced by him.

He continued to record extensively—1976's *Bogalusa Boogie* and *Zy-deco Legend* are high points. It should be remembered that Chenier wrote most of his own material. He also toured overseas, and essentially took zy-deco to the world on sheer talent and determination. It's true that, depend-ing on the crowd or geographical region he was playing, Chenier tailored his song list according to language demands, but his infectious partying cries and unique patois were probably more accessible than he imagined. In any case, he eventually appeared in the 1973 film *Hot Pepper*, won a Grammy, and even played for President Ronald Reagan in the White House.

Chenier suffered from diabetes, which affected his output during the last ten years of his life. As he told Ann Savoy in her book *Cajun Music—A Reflection of a Culture*, "I brought French music further than anyone down here. And everywhere I went with it, they received it, you know. And I've been places with French music, I don't think people here is ever gonna get there."

As Steve Riley, the young Cajun accordionist, told me: "Clifton was and always will be the King of Zydeco. There was nothing contrived about him. He grew up poor and living the blues—and he was an incredible blues musician. You listen to him sing and play and it comes through in the mu-sic. It's who he was and the notes he played and sang were extensions of his soul. Plus: there's not too many people who looked that cool, either."

If you accept the premise that, in the world of zydeco, there is Clifton Chenier and then everyone else, it's fair to say that on that second-level or-bit around Clifton's sun, in no particular order, you'd find Buckwheat Zy-deco, Beau Jocque, Rockin' Dopsie, and, the longest-runnin' of the bunch, Boozoo Chavis.

After Chenier's passing, a new king, Rockin' Dopsie, was crowned. And following Dopsie's death seven years later, in 1993, yet another crowning installed Chavis as the third king of zydeco. As for who deter-mined these things, well, it all goes back to the origins of Chenier's tag as the King of Zydeco.

It is pretty clear that there was no Acadiana-wide referendum, and plenty of people assume that Chenier came up with the whole persona himself. But Chenier claimed in an interview with writer and musician Ben Sandmel, excerpted in Michael Tisserand's *The Kingdom of Zydeco*, that the royalty thing was official—insomuch as it came from his winning a crown as part of the first prize in an accordion contest in Europe. In nightclubs across

Louisiana and East Texas, plenty of artists have called themselves zydeco kings or princes or queens or princesses, but the subject was never questioned until Chenier died.

Maybe it all started when Chenier protégé **Buckwheat Zydeco** (1947–) defected from the Red Hot Louisiana Band in 1978. Zydeco's career ascended even as Chenier's was in decline, and in 1980 Buckwheat was crowned Texas King of Zydeco in a ceremony in Houston, a fishy event because it was organized by no one of particular importance, though it *did* generate publicity. Today Buckwheat says he went through the whole thing reluctantly.

At the time, though, flames were further fueled when Buckwheat's first Rounder Records release was titled *Turning Point*, which many interpreted as a passing of the torch—particularly as the album cover showed Buckwheat in full cape-and-crown regalia. A royal battle between the two took place in October 1982 when they shared a bill at the first Texas–Louisiana Blues and Zydeco Festival in Houston. The reports are that Chenier, stung that the situation had taken place, kicked no small amount of ass, both in his playing and in what he said to the crowd. He also stopped wearing the cape and crown after that gig; he seemed to say that he didn't need the finery, that the royalty was within.

At that point, probably chastened because the thing had happened at all, Buckwheat, too, stopped with the Halloween costume stuff, and one supposes that Chenier lived out the rest of his life as the unspoken and undisputed king. It's said that his crown was buried with him.

As for Buckwheat, his career has developed sufficiently that, as probably the most successful zydeco recording artist ever, he doesn't need the ego boost of self-proclaimed royalty. He was born one of twelve kids in Lafayette, and showed a marked propensity for R&B piano before he was six. At nine, he was a pro in Lynn August's band. Although accordion and traditional Creole music were prevalent in his family bloodline, Buckwheat—so called because his childhood braids reminded folks of the "Little Rascals" character—worked the Gulf Coast throughout his teens with a variety of blues and soul players, including Barbara Lynn and Clarence "Gatemouth" Brown.

In 1971, he started his own band, **Buckwheat and the Hitchhikers**, and got a taste of working as a leader. Five years later, when Chenier asked Buckwheat to join his band as an organist, the youngster was blown away by the opportunity and began to develop an appreciation for the rootsy zydeco style. After an apprenticeship and a switch to piano accordion, Buckwheat peeled off and formed his own **Ils Sont Partis Band**. Mixing showmanship with a yeoman's work ethic and an open mind about exploring new frontiers, Europe among them, Buckwheat began to win fans all over the world.

"The music is definitely important to the Creole people," Buckwheat told me, "but the [reason for] traveling all these years has been to break the music internationally and to educate people as to what zydeco is all about. Where I come from in Louisiana is almost like New York City. We have *all* nationalities, not just the Creoles and Cajuns."

His visionary sound—blending relentless party tunes with contemporary touches of rock, synthesizers, and trumpets—was evidenced on a series of records, including *Take It Easy Baby*, for the Blues Unlimited label. The band moved over to Rounder for *Turning Point* and its successor, *Waitin' for My Ya Ya*, which earned a Grammy nomination. It wasn't long before Buckwheat signed a major label deal with Island Records—an unimaginable coup for a Creole–zydeco artist.

The label debut, *On a Night Like This*, copped another Grammy nomination. Hailed the biggest zydeco act ever, the band was highlighted in the popular film *The Big Easy* and became jammed at parties with Eric Clapton and Steve Winwood.

Since then, Buckwheat Zydeco has stayed busy. He recorded for several major labels before forming, a few years back with manager Ted Fox, a new self-owned label, Tomorrow Recordings, which has issued *The Buckwheat Zydeco Story: A 20-Year Party*. The label is committed to the discovery and support of younger artists, among them Houston's Lil' Brian & the Zydeco Travelers.

Buckwheat listens to a variety of music. His advice: "You buy some Cajun and you buy some zydeco. There's plenty of great artists out there, so I'd suggest you go in the stores and you put those things on your head and listen to the music and decide what you want. I like everything and I learn from everything." He also appreciates how food reflects tradition: "Well, you start at Pat's Restaurant in Henderson and just keep going. Go to Prejean's in Lafayette and then on to Pat Claiborne's on North University. You're not gonna go hungry."

Rockin' Dopsie (pronounced Doop-see) (1932–1993) was born Alton Rubin in Carencro, Louisiana, and, despite the crown thing, was never the virtuoso or individual stylist that Chenier was. But Dopsie rocked the house when he played, and his music was wildly popular.

He grew up spending more time working in the fields than in school; in any case, he learned about accordion from his father, who played the instrument at house parties in the area. With a disciplined practice ethic and a keen ear turned toward blues as well as Creole music, which allowed him to cop tunes from the radio, Dopsie quickly scored gigs in local clubs. He acquired the "Dopsie" moniker from a touring Chicago dancer, got married, and spent several brutal years working construction by day and playing music at night.

Eventually, he became an electrical contractor; but by that point, the music was starting to work for him. Zydeco was in its infancy at the time, and Dopsie instinctively knew how to fill a dance floor. When Chenier befriended him, he began to work the new exuberant style into his act. It was a hard road but, after years of gigging with his band (called the Cajun Twisters, the Zydeco Twisters, and eventually just the Twisters), he began to trickle recordings into the marketplace. In 1973, he signed with a Swedish label and recorded a succession of fine albums that broke his reputation—and furthered that of zydeco—to an international audience; at this time, his name in the United States was barely known beyond the borders of Louisiana.

In 1985, Dopsie was part of a zydeco coterie (along with Terrance Simien and Buckwheat Zydeco) selected to take part in Paul Simon's Grammy-winning *Graceland* project. Then by 1992, Dopsie released his major-label debut for Atlantic, *Louisiana Music*, and worked sessions for such diverse artists as Cyndi Lauper and Bob Dylan. A few years later, though the King of Zydeco matter had died down somewhat in Louisiana and Dopsie was reaching new acclaim elsewhere, he re-ignited the issue when he publicly decreed Boozoo Chavis as his "prince," who by rite of passage would take over the kingdom upon Dopsie's death (a scenario that happened all too quickly).

For all the ill feelings that arose over the "King" biz, it's maybe best to remember that Dopsie and Chenier were friends who together carried the torch of zydeco. To appreciate their music, listen to *Louisiana Music; Big Bad Zydeco;* and Simon's *Graceland*, if for no other reason than to hear their duet on "That Was Your Mother."

The new king, **Boozoo Chavis** (1930–2001), was responsible for the first hit recording in the annals of zydeco, a tune called "Paper in My Shoe." He was born Wilson Anthony Chavis in Lake Charles, where his dad was a tenant farmer and his mom ran a dance club and sold barbecue at rural horse races. Boozoo, a childhood nickname that perhaps captures in some sense his capricious spirit, grew up playing accordion and listening to primordial zydeco and cowboy singer Gene Autry. By his teens, he was pulling in needed cash playing house-party gigs in his hometown.

A farmer and horseman, Chavis took a spirited but low-tech approach to his music and button-row accordion; he relied on traditionalism even as he demonstrated a penchant for goofy songs rendered in a throaty rasp. In youth, some of his early jamming companions were Clifton and Cleveland Chenier. Only by happy chance did Chavis enter the recording studio—a year before Clifton recorded "Zydeco Sont Pas Salé"—to lay down a tune called "Paper in My Shoe," a testimonial to the crafty ways the impoverished keep their feet warm when too poor to buy socks.

The song was a hit and it's still a staple in dancehalls throughout Louisiana and East Texas. Unfortunately, Chavis was less than pleased with the accounting figures on the single. He claimed it sold perhaps a million copies, but he was credited with sales of only 150,000. Being a man of principle, Chavis simply decided he didn't want to work in such a business.

He spent the next few decades training horses. If he played accordion at all, it was probably for his own entertainment on the back porch. It was only in the 1980s, when Chavis heard about an impostor touring as Boozoo Chavis, that he decided to return to the stage. His raw energy and full-blown enthusiasm, and a blastin' album called *Down Home on Dog Hill*, immediately caught the fancy of a new and larger generation of zydeco fans.

Even though he always said all he needed was an accordion to rock the house, Chavis and his band brought the stomping *in vivo* rhythm to trad zydeco that plenty of the younger artists have incorporated into their own versions of the music. In Chris Ardoin's words, "Boozoo put the double-kick bass drum in the music. It jumped it up."

He began to write, record, and tour with a vengeance, and over time a series of albums—all solid and some spectacular—named *Zydeco Trail Ride; Boozoo, That's Who!; Hey Do Right;* and *Live! At the Habibi Temple, The Lake Charles Atomic Bomb, Louisiana*—established his name and style as immortal within the form. He was also a fine ambassador who was supportive of younger artists and engaged in headline-grabbing faux battles with contemporaries such as Beau Jocque.

As for his escalation to "kingness," Chavis was anointed in April 1994 in a civic ceremony in Lafayette that reflected the artist's dignity. (Tisserand's *Kingdom of Zydeco* has an excellent account of the coronation.) When the crown was passed to Chavis, he pretty much tucked it away. Though he put a commemorative silver tiara on the front of his de rigeur cowboy hat, he discreetly let the royalty thing fade into the shadows—where, perhaps, it should be.

Chavis's catalog was covered with joyous reverence by younger zydecists, even as he propelled his own music forward. In 1999, his *Who Stole My Monkey* was invigorating and feisty and even threw a bit of R-rated lyricism into the mix. He seemed to view his music as a way to keep the party fueled.

Rounder's Scott Billington, who has worked with several seminal zydeco and Cajun artists, told me, "Boozoo is very primitive compared to someone like Buckwheat Zydeco, but when he came back onto the scene, he brought young people to the dance halls." In 2001, Chavis died after collapsing onstage.

As Chavis's foe in the grandiose mock battles of the last decade, Andrus Espre—known the world over as **Beau Jocque** (1957–1999)—was a terrific and bigger-than-life foil. Despite a Job-like early life in which a back injury paralyzed him from the waist down, Jocque brought a wild, zealous enthusiasm and scholar's approach to zydeco.

Espre was born in Kinder, Louisiana. His dad was a traditional accordionist, which was sufficient to cause the rebellious young Andrus to shun the instrument. He loved music, though, and played tuba in garage R&B bands. After high school and a stint in the military, Espre became a licensed electrician until 1987, when a fall exploded a disc in his back and he was told he would never walk again. For mental therapy during convalescence, he picked up his father's accordion and began to play. He discovered an instinctive talent for the squeeze-box, dug the danceability of zydeco, but admittedly found the traditional style of his dad's generation a bit snore-inducing. Feeding from his own preference for rock, funk, and reggae, Espre began to experiment with structures.

About a year after his accident, he miraculously began to walk again and, curious about the possibility of zydeco as a career, he and his wife, Michelle, began a studied analysis of the business—what worked and what didn't—and began to turn his quest into an energized science. He played in public for the first time in 1991 and shortly after formed the Zydeco Hi-Rollers. With a devotion to party music that rivaled his idol's, Boozoo Chavis, Espre had a fresh, experimental style, a bellowing, raspy voice, and the massive frame of an NFL linebacker. Indeed, the newly christened Beau Jocque was an indelible figure onstage.

The band was equal to his pyrotechnic energy, and the Hi-Rollers rapidly became one of the hottest units in Louisiana zydeco. They recorded a self-titled album for a local label, then signed with Rounder and released *Beau Jocque Boogie*, a high-water mark in modern zydeco that featured the original tune "Give Him Cornbread"—the song that has become, one might say, the "Stairway to Heaven" of zydeco.

As his career rocketed and the tours went farther from home, the succession of albums sold extremely well for the genre—among the recommended CDs are *Check It Out, Lock It In, Crank It Up!* and *Gonna Take You Downtown*—and suddenly Jocque was no longer the upstart newcomer. Boozoo Chavis and Beau Jocque together provided a one-two punch in the evolution of zydeco. "Boozoo started the double-kick drum," Sean Ardoin told me. "Then Beau Jocque came along and funked it all up." Jocque and Chavis started showing up at one another's gigs, taunting and engaging in the sort of staged rivalry and chicanery that more than one critic has accurately compared to that of professional wrestling.

Keith Frank, maybe the biggest of the younger generation, wasn't happy at all with Jocque. He and Jocque had serious disputes involving back-and-forth accusations of song theft. Before any ill-will could be resolved, unfortunately, Jocque died of a heart attack following a gig at Mid-City Lanes Rock 'n' Bowl in New Orleans. Scott Billington, who produced five CDs for Jocque, commented, "He was absolutely driven. He was reckless with life but in many ways he was like a cat with nine lives. He overcame a lot, and when he invented the character he called Beau, he made a whole new persona and was just so determined to succeed. When I first saw him play, he was so driven, so full of abandonment it was scary, but in that good way like with Howlin' Wolf."

"I put support beams underneath the dance floor for Beau Jocque," John Blancher, owner of the Mid-City Lanes, told the *New Orleans Times-Picayune*. "People danced harder when he played."

The old guard of a relatively new form, Rockin' Sidney, Queen Ida, Terrance Simien, John Delafose, and Lawrence "Black" Ardoin have all contributed to the evolution of zydeco.

Born in Lebeau, Louisiana, Sidney "**Rockin' Sidney**" (1938–1998) Simien is a zydeco immortal for the outta-left-field success of his 1985 song, "My Toot Toot"—zydeco's first international hit single. Though his grandfathers were Creole musicians, he grew up digging R&B and swamp pop, learned guitar, organ, and harmonica, and, after apprenticing as a keyboardist in lounges, recorded dozens of rhythm 'n' blues tunes for the regional labels Goldband, Fame, and Jin.

But it wasn't until Sidney learned accordion in the late seventies and switched to playing his own intuitively unique brand of zydeco, a recipe that included everything from country and rock to pop and soul, that he began to carve a true identity. Maison de Soul released his debut zydeco album, *Give Me a Good Time Woman*. There followed a series of self-released cassettes until 1985, when a record called *My Zydeco Shoes Got the Zydeco Blues* was released. A cut on the record was "My Toot Toot," which started getting punched on Louisiana jukeboxes until a groundswell of attention pushed the cut first nationally and then global. The song sold in rock, pop, and country markets and earned Rockin' Sidney a Grammy award.

The smash turned Sidney into a perpetual club draw and, if he never again enjoyed similar success before his death, several CDs on his own Bally Hoo label did consistently well. Some complain that his insistence, earlier in his zydeco career, on playing all the instruments on each album—and employing a cheesy drum machine—gave the material a sameness. Eventually, he used backing bands in the studio. Suggested listening: *Talk of the Town, Boogie Blues 'n' Zydeco*, and an import called *Live With the Blues*.

As one of the few women zydeco stars, **Queen Ida** (1929–) has indeed made a mark in zydeco, though she went west to do so. A longtime resident of California, Ida Lewis Guillory was born in Lake Charles to a musical family of farming stock. After World War II, the family moved to the San Francisco Bay Area, and mother Elvina returned from one of her frequent trips home to Louisiana with a triple-row accordion. Her brother Al Lewis became proficient on it and began to play professionally, and Ida would sneak it out when he wasn't around.

Ida was driving a school bus and contemplating life after forty when, after being coerced into sitting in with her brother's band during a school Halloween benefit, she instantly became a regional force. A writer from the *San*

Francisco Chronicle was there that night and started the "Queen Ida" tag; she was eventually crowned in an official ceremony in San Francisco.

In the meantime, Ida played briefly with an outfit called The Playboys before officially joining her brother's band, Al Lewis and the Barbary Coast Bon Ton Band, where she quickly became the focus of attention. When a successful appearance at the Monterey Jazz & Blues Festival increased her popularity, she began to tour. With early production and songwriting help from Al, who changed his name to Al Rapone, and with the infusion of her son Myrick "Freeze" Guillory, Queen Ida has become the premier zydeco presence on the West Coast. Hers is a style that incorporates calypso influences and *conjunto* masters, among them Flaco Jimenez.

Ida has released probably a dozen albums over the years for the GNP/Crescendo label—1982's *Queen Ida & the Bon Ton Zydeco Band On Tour* won a Grammy—and has been nominated for three other Grammys. She was the first zydeco artist to have toured Japan, appeared in Francis Ford Coppola's *Rumble Fish*, and continues to stay active. Though Al left the Bay Area fold and returned to Louisiana several years ago, Ida's latest CD, *Back on the Bayou*, which came out in 1999, is a fine reunion effort.

With a voice that *Rolling Stone* described as a melding of Sam Cooke and Jimmy Cliff, **Terrance Simien** (1965–) is quickly bridging the gap between the old masters and the young lions of zydeco.

He's also the most likely zydeco artist to load up the CD changer in the tour bus with everything from Amédé Ardoin and John Delafose to Bob Dylan and Phish. Born in Mallet, Louisiana, Simien, a handsome guy with hippie aesthetics, grew up fascinated with music. He loved gospel and hymns and spent Saturday afternoons listening to zydeco programs on the radio. A bricklayer by trade, Simien learned single- and triple-row accordion and on weekends tried to conquer local roadhouses. But with his amped natural energy and instinctual attempt to blow traditional zydeco into a new era, his work met with deaf ears and he figured out he'd have to hit the road to win a crowd.

The strategy worked. Not only did Simien—and his band the **Mallet Playboys**—help broaden the music's appeal beyond its limited geographical borders, he began to draw younger fans to zydeco. The Mallet Playboys is maybe the best band in zydeco. With the wild-man *frottoir* wizard Earl Sally competing with Simien in the Irresistible Stage Presence department, and with a rock-happy twin guitar attack, these guys are over the top.

In 1984, Simien seized the attention of Paul Simon and was recruited for that singer's *Graceland* project. Simien was also featured in the film *The Big Easy*—and suddenly he was an internationally recognized presence. From there, his zydeco career exploded. Simien and the Mallet Playboys kicked their efforts into an even higher gear, often playing up to 250 gigs a year, to the delight of fans called "beadheads" (originating from Simien's habit of launching Mardi Gras beads from the stage). Still, it took until 1990 to release their inaugural album, *Zydeco on the Bayou*, as good a debut as one could hope for. Though it is anchored in the traditional—two songs in French—it also uses the past as a trampoline to the future.

Over the last decade, Simien and the Mallet Playboys have just worked harder. CDs *There's Room for Us All* and *Positively Beadhead* and the EP *Jam the Jazzfest* are incendiary efforts that cross Simien's soaring voice and great songwriting with a touch of reggae and funk, a purely rock approach to performance.

The new generation of zydeco is anchored in three separately unique but equally dynamic young titans: Keith Frank, Geno Delafose, and Chris Ardoin. Not surprisingly, each are from zydeco-playing families.

Delafose is more traditional, frequently performing in French and not straying from the older formula, even with his original songs. Frank and Ardoin, though, are at the forefront of *nouveau* zydeco, music that's highly cross-pollinated with all sorts of contemporary aural influences.

"There are a lot of young zydeco bands trying to follow what we're doing and what Keith Frank's doing," **Chris Ardoin** (1981–) told me. "[The scene had been] very conservative. [But] we use a lot more guitar patterns, vocal harmonies, different rhythms. . . . Some of the older folks say what we're doing isn't zydeco. And I say, 'Yeah, it is.' It's time to change and what we do *is* zydeco. We'll play traditional stuff sometimes because we play to a lot of people and sometimes they wanna hear that stuff. But we have a lot of younger fans who didn't care about zydeco until lately, and they wanna hear where we're taking it."

Ardoin is the youngest of a Lake Charles clan that goes all the way back to Great Uncle Amédé, the first great Creole accordionist, and Grandfather Alphonse "Bois Sec," another monster player still kicking ass well past Medicare (both are discussed in an earlier chapter). While still a high school sports star, Chris's instinctual approach to accordion blasted him to prominence on the circuit along with his band **Double Clutchin'**.

Chris gravitated to music and first appeared onstage at the age of four, playing accordion at a gumbo cook-off. At nine, he performed at Carnegie Hall, playing *frottoir* with father Lawrence "Black" Ardoin, Bois Sec, and several generations of family musicians. Soon after, Chris and older brother Sean were playing full-time in their father's band, Lagniappe, but eventually Chris's headstrong insistence on bending and molding traditional zydeco with a variety of fresh, funky ways caused Dad to see the writing on the wall, and he set the kids free.

And so Double Clutchin' was born. Titled after the bass drum pattern that fuels the groove in the nouveau zydeco, the band quickly made inroads with its unique style. Though they'd play the old songs from the universal zydeco canon if requested, Double Clutchin' was more interested in writing their own music or interpreting R&B and rock tunes. With Chris's Hendrix-like runs and (even at thirteen) booming baritone voice, and Sean's pumped-up drums and high-pitched vocals, they quickly sawed a niche in the rejuvenated zydeco scene. They signed with the local Maison de Soul label for two sit-up-and-take-notice CDs, *That's Da Lick* and *Lick It Up!* which resulted in an international deal with Rounder.

Gon' Be Jus' Fine came out in 1997 and remains arguably the best album yet made by the tenderfoot zydeco generation. The bright thread of tradition runs through the quilt of the work, anchoring the set along with Derek Dee Greenwood's vitamin-strength bass—but once that's established, all bets are off. Chris and Sean each have individual songwriting strengths that, when pieced together in their co-written tracks, emerge as a wondrous new whole. The previously mentioned "Lake Charles Connection" leads off the record like the gate explosion at the start of a horse race, a tantalizing indication of what's to come: four-part harmonies, irresistible dance tempos, and bouncy tunes such as "When I'm Dead and Gone," "Cowboy," and "We Are the Boys." With a nod to the past—Amédé's "Ardoin Two Step"—thrown in as a gesture of respect, the package is pretty terrific. The follow-up, *Turn the Page*, is another high-energy record with amazing arrangements of other artists' material—Jackie Wilson's "(Your Love Keeps Lifting Me) Higher and Higher" and Musical Youth's "Pass the Dutchie," cleverly tacked onto an original song called "Stay in or Stay Out."

Soon the brothers began to head steadfastly in different directions. Eventually, Sean split off to form his own band, ZydeKool. As for the question of whether the lack of Sean's powerful onstage personality and soaring vocals would affect Double Clutchin''s sound, well, sure, it did. Too, mainstays Tammy Ledet (*frottoir*) and Greenwood are gone.

The remodeled edition of Double Clutchin' includes cousin Dexter Ardoin filling the drum chair, Nat Fontenot on guitar, Curly Chapman on bass and *frottoir*, and backing vocalist Charles Elam III. Though he doesn't sing, Dexter pumps the titular beat effortlessly, and, as on the 2000 Rounder CD, *Best Kept Secrets*—fueled by a wonderful arrangement of "Papa Was a Rolling Stone"—the strong vocals stay intact with Elam and various members stepping up to fill Sean's spots.

As for Chris, his accordion skills just get better and his strides in songwriting and singing are ever more assured. He's a high school grad now, and, when faced with football scholarship offers or the certainty of zydeco stardom, he made the choice for music.

"Chris is shy, like me," Geno Delafose said by phone one afternoon shortly before I met him at a roots festival in Rhode Island. "Part of the early credit for Double Clutchin' goes to Sean, because he's a people person and he flat-out entertains people. But Chris has stepped up; he's a great accordion player and, though he grew up in the old school, he's pushing it in new directions."

While we're on the subject, **Sean Ardoin 'n' ZydeKool,** which in-cludes ex–Double Clutchin' bassist Greenwood, doesn't yet have the pres-tigious deal with a label such as Rounder. But Sean has refueled his own accordion skills, and their self-titled debut CD, released in 1999, is a strong effort that relies on Sean's free-spirited vocal extravaganzas and perhaps a heavier pure funk base than Double Clutchin'. Behind the kit or out front on accordion, Sean is a dynamic entertainer.

The music of the Ardoin Brothers might indeed be different, but they're more similar to each other than they are to their playing in their fa-ther's band. Still active on his own, **Lawrence "Black" Ardoin** (1946–), son of Bois Sec Ardoin, was born in Duralde, Louisiana. A drummer, accordion-ist, and bandleader of considerable skill, he joined siblings **Morris** and **Gus-tave** with his father in the **Ardoin Brothers Band,** a superb, tight dance outfit that worked steadily and profitably until slowed by the death of Gustave in an auto accident. Shortly after, Bois Sec retired from duty, and Black shifted from drums to accordion and took over the reins of the band.

When the Ardoin Brothers Band never really regained momentum, Black conceived a new unit called **Lawrence "Black" Ardoin and the French Zydeco Band**, which added elements of swamp pop and Cajun to the zydeco roots. They released an eponymous effort in 1984, which was re-released in 1999 under the title *Tradition Creole*. With its French-language tunes and sparkling interplay between accordion and fiddle, it's a sweet record. Of late, Black's newest project is **Lagniappe**—which occasionally employs Chris's skills—and their first CD is out, *Hot and Spicy Zydeco*.

About Black, Sean Ardoin told me, "The unsung hero in the Ardoin line is my father. For fifteen years, my dad was the man in southwest Louisiana and Texas with the Ardoin Brothers Band, and he kept it rolling when the members began to fall off. That's where I got my pride." Inas-much as Black manages Chris, and Chris guested on Sean's debut CD, it appears that all is happy in the House of Ardoin. It's comforting to know there will probably always be an Ardoin wielding an accordion in divine Louisianan fashion.

Without question the kingpin of young zydeco is **Keith Frank** (1972–) **and the Soileau Zydeco Band,** which collectively might be thought of as the Bruce Springsteen & E-Street Band of the genre. Noted for great tunes and a barnstorming ability to rock the house for marathon five-hour dances, Frank is a wonderful talent. One of the best things he does is graft a hip-hop influence onto a variety of contextually bizarre older tunes, from Peppermint Harris's classic "I Got Loaded" and a medley of fifties popsters ("Blue Moon," "Stay") to reggae and even Katrina & the Waves's inanely catchy "Walkin' on Sunshine."

All Soileau Zydeco Band performances are rife with witty pop culture references; one of his best tunes is "Going to McDonald's," which is pretty self-explanatory—chiefly in the form of quick musical quotes from popular television theme songs. The interesting thing about Frank is that, for all his ability to absorb new grooves and rely on hip-hoppery in his style, he writes material that's structurally similar to rock 'n' roll. Though his voice isn't as technically skilled as either Sean or Chris Ardoin's, his sound evokes a sheer party flavor that's unequaled in modern zydeco.

A graduate of McNeese State University with a degree in electronics, Frank was born in Soileau, Louisiana. As with many of the other zydeco scions, young Frank learned a variety of instruments as a novice, played drums full time with his father's family band—the Preston Frank Swallow Band—tooled guitar in a friend's band and, in the early nineties, took charge of his own career when he formed the Soileau Playboys (which now includes sister Jennifer Frank on vocals and six-string bass, drummer and vocalist brother Brad Frank, guitarist and vocalist George Lee, and James "Chocolate" Ned on *frottoir* and vocals).

"I guess I first picked up my father's accordion when I was six," Frank told the *Lake Charles American Press* in 1998. "I had to put it down though because I'd get a whipping. Every few years I'd go back to the accordion but I'd always put it down because I couldn't get the sound I wanted out of it."

The band immediately made an impression on the so-called crawfish circuit, releasing a local cassette before coming out with a CD called *Get on Boy!* in 1993, which Frank released with partners Fred Charlie (producer) and Scott Ardoin (sound engineer). The material was perhaps derivative of Beau Jocque's modern stylistic fusions. The issue of song theft was complicated because many of their songs *did* sound remarkably alike, and, zydeco, a fairly rudimentary style to begin with, borrows heavily from itself. That CD sparked a massive and bitter feud between the two artists that ended only with Jocque's untimely death. The pair issued barbed comments at one another from the bandstand and, in Frank's case, the recording studio. His *What's His Name?*, the fastest selling CD in the history of the Maison de Soul label, contained a blatant sonic attack on Jocque in the song "One Shot."

It's unfair to judge Frank's estimably great career by that unfortunate rift—as indeed his popularity and superb canon of recorded work indicates. Churning out a catalog at the rate of about a CD a year, highlights include *Only the Strong Survive, Live at Slim's Y-Ki-Ki*, and *Ready or Not.*

For sheer fun, there's no better Frank tune than "If Your Mama Don't Mind," off *Ready or Not.* Frank runs through a list of his paramour's relatives whose permission he might need to take her out on a boozy good time—as in, "If your uncle don't mind / let's go out and drink some moonshine." Frank's assured vocals jump into an overstylized falsetto that, in conjunction with a simple but fetching accordion riff and sister Jennifer's bass line, create the ultimate Saturday-night dance tune.

Keith—and Brad and Jennifer—come from a bloodline linked with music. Dad, of course, was the titular head of the **Preston Frank** (1947–)

Swallow Band, a traditional group formed in 1977 with Uncle Carlton in the fold. Preston was partially responsible for "Why Do You Want to Make Me Cry?" which he co-wrote with drummer Leo Thomas, a certifiable staple in the great zydeco canon.

Preston was born in Oberlin, Louisiana, and grew up playing accordion even as he worked at a plywood plant. After the Swallow Band began to earn a regional reputation playing around Eunice and Mamou, they released albums for the local Lanor label, including 1991's *Let's Dance.* More recently, under the appellation the **Family Zydeco Band,** they've picked up their performance schedule.

Musically, **Geno Delafose** (1972–) looks backward more often than forward, but his popularity and skill are equal to that of Chris Ardoin and Keith Frank. Born in Eunice, Louisiana, Delafose is yet another zydeco legacy.

"I can remember as a little boy wanting to play the accordion," Delafose told me. "My father played me Amédé Ardoin records. He said if I could play like that I'd never have any problems working anywhere. Well, nobody can play like that, but at least I'm working."

It makes me sound like a broken record to say it again, but Geno, like most of today's zydeco stars, grew up playing first *frottoir* and then drums in his father's band, John Delafose and the Eunice Playboys. As he mastered accordion, he began trading vocal licks with his dad, then took the reins of the band. Eventually, the group segued into his present unit, **French Rockin' Boogie** (of late, **Joseph "Cookie" Chavis** on guitar, **John "Popp" Esprite** on bass, and vocals, *frottoir* artist **Steve Nash,** and drummer **Germaine Jack**).

A master of every nuance of zydeco, as well as single- and triple-row and piano accordions, Delafose is as enticing a singer as he is a player, with immense charm and gentle personality. "Geno is such a real performer and writer," Cajun accordionist Steve Riley told me. "He grew up playing the traditional French tunes with his father. He still does it to this day, but he's doing his own stuff, too—and he's one of the only ones doing it. I love to see that. It's who Geno *is*."

He and French Rockin' Boogie signed with Rounder Records in 1993 and a year later came out with *French Rockin' Boogie,* a record so special it didn't take the listener back in time to early zydeco so much as pull that era into the nineties. Two years later, they released *That's What I'm Talkin' About!,* another neat mix of great old-time dance tunes and fresh originals.

In 1998, Delafose and French Rockin' Boogie upped the ante with the *La Chanson Perdue* album. With his own tunes like "The Lost Song" and "I'll Never See Her Again," Delafose elevated himself from a virtuosic interpreter and promising writer into a creator of new classics. His warm, warbling voice is perfect for the French delivery, and his ability to come up with catchy accordion licks and memorable melodies—even for those of us who are impeded by language inadequacy—is impressive.

Rounder's Scott Billington, who produced all three of Geno's CDs, told me, "In the best ways, Geno has picked up the torch from his father and is carrying on in true Delafose style. On his last album, [Cajun guitarist] Christine Balfa came in and did some stuff with us. She's from another great family musical tradition. There is an element about these artists that's a conscious mining of history, and that's in its own way progressive."

As for Geno, he regards what he's doing as perfectly natural. "For a while," he told me, "when you said 'zydeco' in southwest Louisiana, it was strictly for people thirty and over. Now it's for people aged two to a hundred. Some of them want a funkier beat and different sounds thrown in; some want the old stuff. I like 'em all—and I like to think we're adding to a tradition."

What would Delafose suggest as an introduction to the traditional music? "Clifton Chenier, of course. Balfa Toujours is a great Cajun band. If you wanna know the nouveau Cajun, anything by Steve Riley. For nouveau zydeco, possibly Keith Frank and Chris Ardoin and the Double Clutchin' stuff. And maybe if you want to hear how the traditional stuff sounds today, our last album, *La Chanson Perdue*, is pretty good, I think."

It'd be cool if Geno's dad, **John Delafose** (1939–1994), born in Duralde, Louisiana, were still alive to see what his son is doing with the music the old man loved. He was also a fine practitioner of the form. He and his band, **The Eunice Playboys,** served as a segue between old-time Creole music and post-Chenier zydeco.

Delafose learned single-row accordion when he was eighteen, after building and mastering his own fiddles and guitars as a kid. A farmer by trade, he also played harmonica and pursued music only as a hobby, though he played often for weekend zydeco bands by the early seventies. In the middle of the decade, he decided to form the Eunice Playboys with his sons, John "T. T." Delafose on *frottoir* and Tony Delafose on drums and later bass, and Charles and Slim Prudhomme on guitar and bass, respectively. Blending a manic onstage energy with conservative dance zydeco, moving in the direction of country rather than blues when it came time to experiment, the Eunice Playboys became one of the most sought-after bands on the Gulf Coast circuit.

Over the years, several other cousins, uncles, and offspring worked in the band—Geno of course paid some serious apprenticeship dues—and a high point occurred in 1992 when John and the group were featured in the film *Passion Fish*. The group released several albums—*Heartaches and Hot Steps; Joe Pete Got Two Women;* and *Zydeco Excitement* are all recommended—and were important in many ways. Delafose was a fine writer and inspiration; Beau Jocque, Chubby Carrier, Terrance Simien, and even Boozoo Chavis were fans.

John had heart problems but, though a heart attack forced his retirement at one point, he recovered enough to play a few more dates and, perhaps more important, to see Geno achieve early success as a solo artist. By all accounts a gentle man who taught his musicians and children to respect others, the music, and the culture, Delafose was as fine a person as he was a musician.

"My dad was a really, really nice fellow," Geno told me. "And he was a really funny guy. I think it was hard for him to act like a dad because, being around him in the band so much, it was more like being with a brother. He'd try to say something stern or tell us what to do, and he couldn't do it. He'd always turn it into a joke."

Given the accessible stew of influences that marks nouveau zydeco, and the music's unprecedented popularity, it has suddenly ceased to be a "family responsibility" passed from one generation to the next. While the bloodline approach is clearly working, more and more youngsters who have no ancestral ties to zydeco are getting into it.

Whether umbilically connected or not, here are some of the other zydeco artists you should be aware of.

Nathan & the Zydeco Cha-Chas are anchored in the lively piano accordion runs, often clever tuneage, and distinctive singing voice of **Nathan Williams** (1963–), who was born in St. Martinville, Louisiana. His father died when he was seven and he left home in the ninth grade to work in Lafayette with his older brother Sidney, who gave him an accordion because he knew Nathan was a huge fan of Clifton Chenier.

Sidney Williams, it should be pointed out, is the titular Sidney who owns primo zydeco club El Sid-o's, and he nurtured Nathan's enthusiasm for accordion, letting the kid hang around the club and watch such folks as Buckwheat Zydeco perform. In fact, Buckwheat provided lessons and encouragement. Eventually, when Buckwheat went on tour, young Nathan and his newly formed band started playing without a fee in El Sid-o's, slowly developing a following.

When he released a single, "Everybody Called Me Crazy," on his brother's El Sid-o's label—formed to help Nathan out—the tune became a regional favorite. It caught the ears of Scott Billington; Rounder signed the young band, whose instinctive ability to segue slices of R&B into their zydeco made for dance-hall success.

The first album, *Zydeco Live!*, was recorded at Sid's club, and featured a guest boost from Boozoo Chavis. A series of CDs followed, including *Steady Rock, Your Mama Don't Know, Follow Me Chicken*, and another live piece, *I'm a Zydeco Hog!* There's also a record with Cajun fiddler Michael Doucet, *Creole Crossroad*. Throughout, Williams and his band focus on fun, demonstrate an adept appreciation of form, and have a terrific instinct for what works; for example, a fine, French-language adaptation of Stevie Wonder's "Isn't She Lovely" ("Elle Est Jolie") that showed up on *Follow Me Chicken*.

The latest Cha-Chas release, *Let's Go*, features mainstay Cha-Chas guitarist Dennis Paul Williams, Allen "Cat Roy" Broussard on alto and tenor saxophones, Mark Anthony Williams on *frottoir*, Wayne Burns on bass and Gerard St. Julien Jr. on drums.

With Queen Ida happily ensconced on the West Coast, few women accordionists are infiltrating the ranks of Louisiana zydeco—despite her success and reputation. But **Rosie Ledet** (1972–), known as the Zydeco Sweetheart, who took over her husband's band after sneaking self-taught lessons on his ax while he was working during the day, is a true star. With sultry good looks, fine chops, and a slightly suggestive approach to song craft, Ledet should probably be an inspiration to women curious about the possibilities of leading or playing in a zydeco band.

Ledet was born in Church Point, Louisiana, spoke French growing up, and was taught English by her parents only to make schoolwork easier. Always a music fan, she was into a wide range of artists, from Koko Taylor and Tina Turner to Boozoo Chavis and Terrance Simien. She met her future husband, bandmate and producer, Morris Ledet, when he sat in with Boozoo Chavis at a dance; six months later they married.

Morris's own band, the Zydeco Playboys, was working weekends when Rosie admitted that she'd been playing Morris's accordion; she quickly went from sitting in with the group to fronting it, and Morris shifted to bass guitar. Rosie's way with the accordion was as impressive as her original songs—most of which, whether teasing or scolding, reflect the woman's point of view in the admittedly one-sided zydeco world.

Ledet has by now released several CDs, each one better than the last. Of the catalog, the initial *Sweet Brown Sugar* stands up there with later releases, *I'm a Woman* and *It's a Groove Thing!*

Zydeco Force, a young Opelousas band that formed in 1988, started out as a Clifton-esque melding of traditional zydeco and blues but, over time, has evolved the millennial funk sound of the nouveaux. Anchored by the superb skills of accordionist Jeffery Broussard and songwriter, vocalist, and multi-instrumentalist Robby "Mann" Robinson, the Z-Force, as they're known to fans, are perhaps best noted for the mid-nineties dance phenomenon that sprang forth from their song "The Zydeco Push."

The band split up for a while, overshadowed as they were by the sudden growth of younger bands, but are back together. Among their albums (all for the Maison de Soul label) are *The Sun's Going Down*, *The Zydeco Push*, *It's La-La Time*, and the buoyant reunion, *We're Back!*

Fascinated by the accordion since he was a youngster, **Corey Arceneaux** parlayed his uncle's being a security guard at El Sid-o's nightclub in Lafayette (so he could witness zydeco royalty Nathan & the Zydeco Cha-Chas) with a devoted work ethic that led him to master the diatonic and piano accordions.

Corey first played in his Uncle Fernest Arceneaux's band, Fernest & the Thunders, before forming his unit, **The Zydeco Hot Peppers,** in the early nineties. He's since worked the nouveau highway with the nod toward the traditional despite a furiously infectious performing style that seems more contemporary. They've released two CDs, *Hit and Run* and *Tell Me Why.*

As the youngest of yet another high-powered zydeco family, the Carriers, **Roy "Chubby" Carrier** (1967–) is a fiery performer who used his traditionalist background to explore a variety of rock- and soul-based extensions—including cool versions of the Who's "Squeezebox" and War's "The Cisco Kid." His dad, **Roy Carrier Sr.,** is a traditional accordionist who taught his son the instrument. By twelve, Chubby was playing drums for his father's band, and a few years later took over the accordion when gigs interfered with his dad's job.

After high school, Chubby toured for three years, playing *frottoir* with Terrance Simien's Mallet Playboys, then returned home to form The Bayou Swamp Band with brothers, *frottoir*-meisters Troy "Dikki Du" Carrier and Kevin Carrier. A self-released album, *Go Zydeco Go*, sold well regionally and paved the way for subsequent efforts on small but national labels— *Dance All Night, Boogie Woogie Zydeco, Too Hot to Handle*, and the brilliantly titled *Who Stole the Hot Sauce?*

Still another scion is **David "Rockin' Dopsie Jr." Rubin,** an energized singer, songwriter, and *frottoir* wizard who'd played with his father's Zydeco Twisters and inherited the group after Sr. passed away in 1993. Brother **Anthony Rubin** (accordion and vocals) and **Alton Rubin Jr.** (drums) are also in the band, which has admirably carried on Dopsie's style even as they seek to push it into the new century.

Unlike many of their kind, Dopsie Jr. & the Twisters travel fairly extensively and even play a regular gig at the Maple Leaf Bar in New Orleans. With a healthy appetite for rock, funk, and roadhouse fun, Dopsie Jr. and company interpret everyone from Hank Williams to Jessie Hill—and make it work. Among their library are *Zydeco Man, Feet Don't Fail Me Now*, and *Everybody Scream.*

Still active from the old-timer's coterie is **Willis Prudhomme** (1931–) **and Zydeco Express**. Prudhomme, born in Kinder, Louisiana, is a fine accordion player. Two things are particularly interesting about him: He didn't learn the instrument until he was in his forties, and his mentor was Cajun musician Nathan Abshire. There's an obvious rural feel to Prudhomme's sound that probably has more to do with Abshire than Prudhomme's day job as a life-long farmer. This pastoral touch is immediately noticeable not just in the Cajun flair and periodic waltzy output but also in his down-home original dance material, which includes (typically French-language) songs such as "Chickenhead Zydeco" and "Standin' in the Door Naked as a

Worm." Prudhomme has released several cassettes and CDs in the last fifteen years, including *Fais Do Do, Zydeco Express*, and *Crawfish Got Soul*.

Another artist who came to accordion in middle age is **Lynn August** (1948–), a blind musician who played professionally for years as a keyboardist and drummer in various outfits, including Buckwheat Zydeco's band, before learning accordion when he was forty and starting a solo career. A splendid singer whose involvement in church choirs is evident in the gospel touches he brings to his zydeco, August was born in Lafayette. He led a big band in his voyages, and made a point of studying Alan Lomax's field recordings of the seminal *juré* voicings. A wonderful and openly curious player, August's *Sauce Piquante* album, which features a guest spot from New Orleans blues guitarist Snooks Eaglin, is a sparkling effort. Also recommended are *Creole Cruiser* and *Creole People*.

It seems that at times there's a zydeco musician in every house, farm, and apartment in southwest Louisiana—and as an indicator of the form's exploding popularity, that's a good thing. Among other names that are worthy of consideration are **Jo Jo Reed, the Creole Zydeco Farmers, Sam Brothers, Joe Walker, Jude Taylor, the Zydeco Blazer, T-Lou,** and **Major Handy.**

V

LOUISIANA ROCK

One

THE
INDIGENOUS SOUND

*I*t's a late afternoon sound check at the House of Blues in New Orleans's French Quarter, the Friday before Fat Tuesday, and in typical fashion, Mardi Gras has hit town with the raw power of a Force 5 hurricane. Hometown band Cowboy Mouth, in recognition of the occasion and for this second and final of back-to-back sold-out carnival shows, has just finished running through material such as "Mardi Gras Mambo," as well as obscure songs from their vast and varied catalog—stuff with true Louisiana flavor they want to trot out in celebratory fashion.

As the band exits the stage and mingles with friends and well-wishers, the house sound system comes up and cranks out Mardi Gras tunes and old-style rock and R&B, and at one point Jerry Lee Lewis, Louisiana's first rock star, comes over the speakers. It's a symbolic moment, representing the old and the new in Louisiana rock 'n' roll.

It occurs to me that homegrown rock in Louisiana has been overlooked; I mention this to Cowboy Mouth's lead guitarist, John Thomas Griffith, who is lingering in front of the stage, water bottle in hand. "Rock is definitely the bastard child of Louisiana music," Griffith agrees.

As part of an earlier and moderately successful New Orleans punk–new wave act called Red Rockers, Griffith had to relocate to the West Coast to get attention. It's a feeling a lot of Louisiana rockers know. The late, popular band the subdudes moved to Colorado to seek attention, and, as their guitarist and vocalist Tommy Malone told me, "The rock scene in New Orleans was and is a struggle. You continue to fight the reality of what the culture dictates. This is the birthplace of jazz and it's *strong*. In southwest Louisiana, it's Cajun and zydeco—and it's *strong*. I'm neither of those; none of us were. That's wonderful stuff—nice to go out and hear.

But people think it must be wonderful to be a musician and be around the New Orleans music scene. I hate to say it, but it's made it difficult where I'm coming from."

Now, as he looks around the empty House of Blues, Griffith gestures towards the sounds of revelers outside. "The attitude [in New Orleans] seems to be, 'You can get rock 'n' roll anywhere, so let's promote the indigenous stuff." He grins. "Of course, at Mardi Gras, even rock is cool."

Drummer Fred LeBlanc, holding a basket of catfish nuggets, wanders up and absorbs the flavor of the conversation.

"Mardi Gras, man," LeBlanc says with a reverent tone. "If you think about it, Mardi Gras *is* pretty much a rock 'n' roll holiday. Though it's much more, too, of course. It's everything New Orleans, but it's rock 'n' roll, too." He offers me a nugget, then continues. "Cowboy Mouth is a Mardi Gras band—which is to say, we play *Louisiana* rock 'n' roll. We're part of a tradition of music that extends from gospel and jazz and zydeco all the way to rock 'n' roll—and every night onstage, no matter where we are, I emphasize that we play *Louisiana* rock 'n' roll." He gestures overhead at a speaker, still cranking Jerry Lee. "Take it back to Jerry Lee Lewis, man. He mighta had Memphis influences, but he *made* it Louisiana."

It's something to think about as I head out to let the band get ready for their show—what makes rock 'n' roll Big Easy–style? What is it about Cowboy Mouth, the subdudes, the Radiators, Randy Newman, the Blue-runners, Dale Hawkins, and Tony Joe White that to hear them is to *know* they're from Louisiana? As I leave, "Whole Lotta Shakin' Goin' On" fades out and yet another version of "Mardi Gras Mambo" comes up. In the two hours since I arrived at the airport, I've already heard about fifteen versions of "Mardi Gras Mambo," and by the time I leave I will be convinced the only arrangement I *haven't* heard will be the Gregorian chant version—which doesn't mean it doesn't exist.

I've just flown in from New England for Carnival, my first one, and now that I've checked in with my pals in the Mouth, I head back to the hotel to meet Dixieland Steve. *Mardi Gras* literally means "Fat Tuesday," the apex of Carnival and the day before Ash Wednesday, and it marks the end of the forty days of wanton debauchery that begins at the Krewe of Reveler's Ball. Fat Tuesday is the last hurrah before those holy days between Ash Wednesday and Easter.

Mardi Gras is as old as the city of New Orleans, and has grown and evolved in parallel ways with the community itself. To be sure, it represents different things to different people, but the images of parades, floats, maskers, street parties, and round-the-clock revelry are accurate. From there, the celebration takes on other aspects, whether you're from a suburban neighborhood or a gentrified family; whether you're a blood-line member of one of the elite krewes, a member of a Mardi Gras Indian Tribe, or a frat boy from Kansas looking for a place to party 'til spring break.

Music permeates Mardi Gras—and though it is historically jazz, parade music, and R&B, even upstart rockers now have a claim to the holiday if for no other reason than they've bullied their way into the proceedings in fine fashion.

I find Dixieland Steve and we head out to absorb the aura. Though it is only late afternoon, the streets outside are already clogged with revelers, most of whom don't live here. The French Quarter represents one aspect of Carnival: the side many would recognize from viewing the Delta rushparty sequence in *Animal House*, the side that causes most New Orleanians to cringe when the footage airs on CNN. Indeed, after experiencing five protracted days of lunacy, I will describe the French Quarter during Mardi Gras as the Battle of Gettysburg sponsored by Anheuser-Busch. To set foot on Bourbon Street at Canal Street and then attempt to negotiate a path all the way to, oh, Lafitte's Blacksmith Shop on St. Peter, at the edge of the lower and more residential part of the Quarter, is an exercise in gummy mayhem.

"I don't know whether I'm kicking beer bottles or dead bodies," Dixieland Steve says at one point as we negotiate the sardine can that is Bourbon Street.

In many ways, Mardi Gras in New Orleans parallels the relationship of Louisiana rock 'n' roll to the state in general. Its practitioners come from all over the state and contribute legitimately to the event, but they are sneered at by the locals. No matter, for all the attention given to other forms of music in the state, Louisiana does have an impressively rich rock 'n' roll tradition because the segue from R&B to rock 'n' roll was fairly easy.

New Orleans writer Jeff Hannusch, whose book *I Hear You Knockin': The Sound of New Orleans Rhythm and Blues*, is one of the finest ever written about music, says that part of what put early rock 'n' roll in a different category from rhythm & blues was race. Rock was nothing more than R&B sung by a white guy rather than a black one (see "The Foundations and the Piano Giants," Part 2, Chapter 1). Louisiana, thanks to its stewpot approach to diversity was an ideal spot for the music to mix, too. "You have to remember that New Orleans is the birthplace of blue-eyed soul," he says. "It is literally the first place where white singers worked with black bands."

The phenomenon happened largely because, as certain restrictions began to loosen after World War II, two best friends and visionaries, Cosimo Matassa, a white record producer, and Dave Bartholomew, a black musician, arranger, bandleader, and songwriter, joined together and *made* it happen. Working out of Matassa's French Quarter recording studio, using both black and white artists in varying and intermingling cooperatives, the pair created the New Orleans R&B scene that would give birth to rock 'n' roll (Bartholomew and Matassa are profiled in "The Foundations and the Piano Giants," Part 2, Chapter 1).

Hannusch further suggests that white radio stations did their part to spread the new style by playing R&B records. It worked to attract black listeners, but it also wound up turning white listeners on to the black music. "So you had middle-class white kids wanting to be Fats Domino or Lee Allen," Hannusch says.

As discussed in the chapter on rhythm & blues, the white R&B that evolved became known as rock 'n' roll. And while there *were* subtle differences—Jerry Lee Lewis, for example, brought major rockabilly and Memphis influences to the table—the two forms were similar. Eventually, it became a matter of almost arbitrary labeling. Was Lewis a rockabilly artist? Was Chuck Berry a rocker? What about Little Richard?

Whatever Lewis was, he rocked his ass off. I've often wondered what it must have been like to see Jerry Lee in his prime. Performance photos show a handsome if darkly creepy young man with the gaze of a serial killer, his leg cocked at an obtuse angle from the piano, and wild, wavy red-blonde hair rocketing outward in defiance of gravity as he hammered the keys with rabid zeal. To listen to his early classics—"Great Balls of Fire" and "Whole Lotta Shakin' Goin' On"—is to remember the glorious and primitive possibilities of rock. They remain pagan triumphs of barely distilled energy and they created a frenzy in intoxicating ways.

Roaring out of the woods of Ferriday, Louisiana, where he was born, **Jerry Lee Lewis** (1935–) would become everything Buddy Holly and Roy Orbison weren't: a kind of Anti-Elvis with Attitude to the third power who had a lot more to do with Little Richard than he did with "Love Me Tender." Lewis's parents were poor, but his father, Elmo, dug swing and Al Jolson, and the youngster became fascinated with Jimmie Rodgers, Gene Autry, and Robert Johnson's Faustian "Hellhound on My Trail." Jerry Lee's mother, Mamie, remembers that as a kid her son sang tunes of his own invention that blended all sorts of available musical styles.

His immediate and extended family indulged in a curious mix of religion (hardcore Pentecostal) and profession (bootlegging) that offered peculiar juxtapositions of experience. These things had predictable outcomes for Jerry Lee and his two closest cousins, Jimmy Swaggart and Mickey Gilley, both of whom would become famous, respectively, as a tainted evangelist and a country singer.

All three learned piano, but from the first time he sat down at one, at his Aunt Stella's house when he was eight, Jerry Lee was the best, and it wasn't long until his father managed to come up with a rickety old Starck upright for Jerry Lee to practice on. The kid would sneak out at night with Swaggart, and the two would head to Haney's Big House, a black juke joint, where they'd absorb the sounds of various chitlin' circuit blues and boogie-woogie artists such as B. B. King and Champion Jack Dupree.

Those must have been influential outings, stylistically, for by the time he was fourteen the barely pubescent Killer had made his musical debut and demonstrated a vigorous and unique style. On the sales lot of a new Ford dealership, Lewis sat in with a local country band and blew the crowd away with a simmering version of "Drinkin' Wine Spo-Dee-O-Dee," a tune that would pop up numerous times during his career.

As an adolescent, Lewis was torn in a struggle between the very real call of the church and the very real call of his loins. He enrolled in a fundamentalist Bible school in Waxahachie, Texas, a well-intentioned maneuver that blew up in spectacular fashion when the curriculum succeeded in arousing the more Bacchanalian instincts within the young man. He was kicked out within three months.

He made perfunctory attempts at day jobs, and took a series of roadhouse gigs where he learned a tune by a former nightclub employer named Roy Hall called "Whole Lotta Shakin' Goin' On"; he also developed an appreciation for amphetamines. There were also a couple of "warm-up" marriages that failed to work out, chiefly thanks to Lewis's inability to stay out of live-music bars. By the time he headed to Memphis and Sam Phillips's Sun Studios in 1956, the young man was on a mission. He'd added an affection for rockabilly music to his recipe, and Sun, of course, was where young Elvis Presley, another kid fascinated by rockabilly, had become a star.

In rapid fashion, "Whole Lotta Shakin' Goin' On" and "Great Balls of Fire" established Lewis as a star alongside Elvis and Carl Perkins. He crashed over America like a tsunami and celebrated his cash and fame by marrying Myra Gale Brown, the teenage daughter of his bass-player uncle.

But while the little-publicized marriage roused negligible controversy in the United States, a snippy British press reacted more strongly when he brazenly sported Myra Gale during a tour of Britain. Though he claimed she was fifteen (presumably thinking it was better than, say, fourteen), it made no difference, and an uproar of disapproval caused the tour to be aborted after only a few dates.

The Killer headed back to the United States, where investigative reporters discovered that Myra Gale was actually *thirteen*—and America recoiled as well. Lewis thrust his stubborn chin at the world, continued to tour relentlessly, and released dozens of singles, few of which scored respectable success. In 1963, he left Sun and signed with Smash/Mercury, and for the next five years he wore it out on the road and in the studio to no avail.

Eventually, Lewis made the conscious switch to country music, a shrewd decision; but it's good to remember that Lewis's rock years shone as intensely as a blowtorch. Confirm it by listening to "Little Queenie," "Roll Over Beethoven," "Johnny B. Goode," and tunes by other writers: "Chantilly Lace," "What'd I Say," and "Rockin' My Life Away." Country music didn't know what it was in for.

Pianist Jon Cleary, the Crescent City piano professor, says this about Lewis: "My uncle was completely nutty over Jerry Lee and I can say that, as a player, Lewis is another underrated giant. I don't know if he's a lazy pianist; he's pretty rudimentary a lot of times but every once in a while he'll pull something out that's just incredible. . . . The glissandos and the hammering at the top. Listen to the end of the solo on 'Cold, Cold Heart.' That's what piano playing is about."

Collectors might want to search for original singles or even vinyl albums, but the uninitiated can find plenty of greatest hits packages. *Jerry Lee Lewis: The Essential Sun Collection* is a solid two-disc set.

Another great piano guy whose work is clearly sautéed in hot sauce is **Randy Newman** (1943–), and defining him as a rock musician may be doing him a great disservice. But there's nothing wrong with good rock 'n' roll, and in any case it is correct to say that Newman has dabbled generously in the genre while carving a pop music reputation that might be better compared to earlier songwriters such as Cole Porter, Stephen Foster, Kurt Weill, and the Gershwin siblings; or contemporaries Warren Zevon, Harry Nilsson, and Lyle Lovett, and even satirists Spike Jones and Frank Zappa.

Although he was born in Los Angeles, Newman has big-time New Orleans roots inasmuch as he and his mother—a native of the city—summered there through much of his impressionable youth while his dad bounced around as a career military man. Those summers would indelibly imprint his future piano style with a rollicking gait that falls somewhere between Louis Gottschalk, Champion Jack Dupree, and Professor Longhair. In a 1988 interview with journalist Timothy White, Newman said, "[New Orleans is] my favorite place in the country. I think . . . the people are sorta sweet, the music is sweet . . . I love the music, it sounds so good to me."

Two of Randy's uncles, Alfred and Lionel Newman, were successful film composers, and even Randy's dad, Irving, wrote a tune that ended up as a B-side on a Bing Crosby single. So when Newman realized early that his dream of being a baseball player wouldn't happen, he succumbed to the music. He had taken piano lessons since he was seven, and by his early teens had studied harmony and theory. When pushed by lifelong friend (and future record producer) Lenny Waronker to try to write tunes for a living, Newman had a small gig with a Hollywood music publisher called Metric Music within a year.

He wrote for a variety of artists, including Cilla Black, P. J. Proby, Manfred Mann, Judy Collins, Gene McDaniels, the Fleetwoods, Jackie DeShannon, the O'Jays, Harpers Bizarre, and even the Everly Brothers, Ricky Nelson, Eric Burdon, and Ella Fitzgerald. During that period he also got his feet wet in the lucrative world of writing scores for television: *Lost in Space, Peyton Place*, and *Judd for the Defense*. (He is now famous for his film scores, among them *Ragtime, The Natural*, and *James and the Giant Peach*.)

Randy Newman (1968) and *Twelve Songs* (1970) were his first two solo discs; they contained some brilliant material, including the remarkable "I Think It's Going to Rain Today," "Bet No One Ever Hurt This Bad," "Let's Burn Down the Cornfield," "Cowboy," and the original version of "Mama Told Me Not to Come," a song Three Dog Night would rocket to #1 within a few years.

Newman had a helluva lot to offer: a skewered worldview, innovative chord patterns, and, though his singing voice hasn't been described by many as "angelic," it has a charm to it, particularly in the context of his own material. It's almost a musical sneer, delivered in such a lazy southern drawl that it sneaks up on you.

Newman hit a stride with the next three records: *Sail Away* (1972), *Good Old Boys* (1974), and *Little Criminals* (1977). They all contained moments of such brilliance and attitude that it seemed almost as though Newman didn't want to be a success; for this reason, it was probably cruel that he scored hits for all the wrong reasons. The boobs he was lampooning on such songs as "Rednecks" and "Short People" didn't get it, so of course the songs were as successful as they were controversial. His 1974 album *Good Old Boys* was a statement-in-song about the stellar aspects of Dixie culture.

Indeed, the album holds up brilliantly. "Rednecks," "Marie," and "Kingfish"—Newman's version of Governor Huey Long's "Every Man a King" (that's right, Long wrote and recorded a song)—are often mentioned in connection with the album. But what could be better than "Louisiana 1927," a highly visual vignette about President Calvin Coolidge's visit to Louisiana to assess damage from a flood? With its haunting refrain, "Louisiana, Louisiana, / they're trying to wash us away," it's three minutes of lyrical and melodic genius.

Newman's career hardly peaked with *Good Old Boys*. A succession of well-crafted and thoughtfully constructed records (among them *Land of Dreams*, *Bad Love*, and the must-own collection *Guilty: 30 Years of Randy Newman)*, soundtracks *Ragtime* and *The Natural*, and his peculiarly great take on *Faust*, have issued forth at Newman's oft-languid pace.

Though he doesn't tour much, he has been getting out of late, and in any case shows no sign of drying up creatively.

Three rockers who followed in the Killer's wake are even today instantly identifiable as Louisiana artists.

Bobby Charles (1938–) is an important figure whose name should be etched in the admittedly feeble memories of rock fans everywhere. Though most noted for penning R&B and swamp-pop tunes, we already know that the line of demarcation between those styles and rock is gray at best. Throughout his career, Charles's songs have been covered by such diverse performers as Kris Kristofferson, Fats Domino, Bo Diddley, Joe Cocker, Ray Charles, and Tom Jones.

Because Charles also recorded with members of The Band, chiefly bassist Rick Danko (with whom he also co-wrote material), and because he released decidedly rocky albums, among them *Bobby Charles* and *Wish You Were Here Right Now*, he qualifies as a force in the genre.

Born R. C. Guidry in Abbeville, Louisiana, the soon-to-be-known-as Bobby Charles grew up with his ears hungry for Cajun, country, jazz, and rhythm & blues music—everyone from Louis Armstrong to Fats Domino to Hank Williams—and by his teenage years he was writing and recording his own material. He was one of the first white artists to work with black musicians in Louisiana, backed in numerous sessions by Paul Gayten's all-star band (which included Lee Allen, Red Tyler, and Charles Williams), a pairing that added substantially to Charles's hipness factor.

Not that he wasn't responsible for writing cool tunes. The first of his songs to garner widespread appeal, written when he was fifteen, was called "Later, Alligator," which owed a substantial debt to Guitar Slim. (It would later land on the charts for Bill Haley & the Comets under the title "See You Later, Alligator.") It's true that, on the recommendation of a local record store owner, Charles sang the tune over the phone to Chicago record label impresario Leonard Chess—yeah, *that* Chess—who assumed that Charles was a savvy black kid.

Though Charles turned out to be white, Chess arranged for the youngster to enter Cosimo Matassa's studio in New Orleans, where Charles insisted on using his own band, the Cardinals, rather than Fats Domino's group, which had been booked for the session. "Later, Alligator" became a regional hit until it broke nationally with the Haley version.

Other memorable titles would follow: "Walking to New Orleans," "On Bended Knee," "Why Can't You," "Bye Bye Baby," "One-Eyed Jack," "Take It Easy, Greasy," "But I Do," and "Before I Grow Too Old." An interesting foot-note: Charles neither plays an instrument nor reads or writes music. He comes up with a lyrical concept, jots it down, and memorizes a melody un-til he can sing it into a recorder or to a musician. His voice seems plain, yet he has a way with a melody, particularly on ballad material. In the early seventies, he signed with Bearsville Records, a small "artists' label" owned by Albert Grossman, the influential manager who steered the careers of Bob Dylan, The Band, and Janis Joplin. Because the resulting, self-titled al-bum (1972, reissued on Island in 1996) didn't fare well in the marketplace despite nice reviews, Charles essentially retired for the remainder of the decade.

He resurfaced in the early eighties with his own Rice 'n' Gravy label, though luck hasn't exactly been on his side in that venture. For a variety of reasons, albums such as *L'il Cajun* (1984), which includes cameos by Willie Nelson and Neil Young, and *I Wanna Be the One* (1992) have never been distributed. In '86, Chess re-released a best-of collection called *Chess Masters* and in 1995 the Stony Plain label released a batch of tunes from the Rice 'n' Gravy sessions called *Wish You Were Here Right Now*. Other re-leases that made their way to the marketplace include *Clean Water* and *Se-crets of the Heart*.

Jimmy Clanton (1940–) is one of those guys who falls into the rock category because he is white and his good looks won him a starring role in the Alan Freed teen idol film *Go Johnny Go*—even though he was a true R&B talent. Born in Baton Rouge, Clanton discovered Fats Domino and

Little Richard before he could qualify for a driver's license—and when it turned out he could sing his ass off *and* write songs, he was on his way.

A few early bands—the Dixie Cats and the Rockets—earned Clanton a recording date in New Orleans at Cosimo Matassa's studio, and the producer scored record deals for both Clanton and his pal Dick Holler. Clanton scored a hit with "Just a Dream."

A guest shot on *American Bandstand* followed, and with it came a succession of hits over the next several years (including "Letter to an Angel," "Go Jimmy Go," and "My Own True Love." A truly nice guy who seemed mildly comfortable in his role as a poppy balladeer, Clanton spent two years in the army, a situation that eventually allowed him to return to his more rockin' roots. He had a few more hits, the biggest being "Venus in Blue Jeans" (1962), but the oncoming British invasion ultimately left Clanton an oldies show staple. He also spent time as a disc jockey.

Dale Hawkins (1938–), born in Goldmine, Louisiana, was another white guy who recorded the early Louisiana sound for Chess Records. In 1957, he left a permanent imprint on rock history when he co-wrote a hit called "Suzie Q," defining his sound as what might be called "bayou bluesabilly." The song established him as a primary influence on future rockers and would-be Louisianans such as John Fogerty.

Hawkins churned out a series of replications in the years following "Suzie Q," though with dwindling success. He worked as a producer for a while, and then, astoundingly, in 1999, outta nowhere, he came out with a fine CD called *Wildcat Tamer* that showed a Ronnie Dawson–like resiliency and an enviable ability to turn back time. It's a great, roaring, highway cruise of a record—well worth owning.

Travelling down the chronological road, it probably seems at times to **Tony Joe White** (1943–) that he's never done anything but write and record a song called "Polk Salad Annie." And that tune *was* a big hit in 1969 for the Oak Grove, Louisiana, musician. But he's done more than that. A completely unique country–rock–swamp artist, he grew up in Texas and broke as a songwriter in Nashville, but he retains a lyrical quality redolent of his home state.

He penned "Rainy Night in Georgia" (how much better does it get than that?) and had tunes covered by Elvis Presley, Hank Williams Jr., Dusty Springfield, Tina Turner, and Rory Gallagher, who did a version of White's "As the Crow Flies." *Closer to the Truth* and *One Hot July* are recent (if hard to find) albums, and White remains an underappreciated treasure.

Moving into the modern era, rock acts imbued with the organic sounds of their home state have had more critical success. Cowboy Mouth, the subdudes, the Radiators, and Mulebone have managed to capture elements of Louisiana's unique lifestyle, geography, culture, and music into their own rock 'n' roll, and might well be defined as cult bands—but in the best possible sense of the word.

"If we never made another record," **Cowboy Mouth** bassist **Rob Savoy** told me, "I'm convinced we could tour regularly as long as we wanted—and make a great living. That's the nature of Cowboy Mouth—we take Louisiana to the world, and kids are hungry for it."

Their major-label debut *Are You with Me?* sold about 300,000 copies and had a hit in "Jenny Says." But whatever momentum they'd generated had pretty much leveled out after a series of corporate buffooneries that would have split up a lesser band.

But based on *every* Cowboy Mouth show I've seen, whether it's in front of 50,000 at JazzFest or eight frozen people on a twenty-below night in the dead of a Vermont winter, Cowboy Mouth refuses to quit until they've won over everyone.

Though there are (and have been) more successful rock acts in the state's history—for example, the New Orleans trio Zebra whose debut album enjoyed the biggest-selling first week in Atlantic Records's history, or the Baton Rouge–spawned, alt-poppers Better Than Ezra, who crashed platinum status more than once, and of course Britney Spears—the members of the Mouth are irrepressible. It's an attitude—a spirit of celebration and reverence and good will—imbued in their music and stage show that rings genuine. Virtually anyone who has seen the band play knows the joys of being alive.

Mouth frontman **Fred LeBlanc** is one of the more instantly recognizable figures in contemporary Louisiana music. A short, muscular guy with a heavy brow and piercingly intelligent eyes, there is a bit of the drill instructor's countenance to LeBlanc's features and Chautauqua tent–styled emcee skills, but he is simply one of the greatest rock bandleaders ever, and he's unwilling to let the crowd have anything other than a great time. Fellow New Orleans percussionist Cyril Neville agrees. "The thing I like about Fred," he told me, "is that he's a showman. At the end, it's about entertainment. And coming from New Orleans, where we have the greatest drummers in the world, you watch Fred and he knows how to dispense the city's history, how to make people laugh and dance and think. That's what it's about, whether you're playing rock or jazz or funk or whatever."

Cowboy Mouth was formed in 1991 by Fred LeBlanc and **Paul Sanchez** after each had spent productive time in the seminal New Orleans acts Dash Rip Rock and The Backbeats. Sanchez, with a strong affection for melodic folk music, and LeBlanc, whose Dashic reputation for wildly appealing Keith Moon–styled folly obscured a solid affection for pop songs, recognized in one another a unique musical chemistry.

When Sanchez faced disillusionment after trying to work in the film business, and a post-Dash solo deal fell through for LeBlanc, the two reunited and quickly assembled Griffith, who'd experienced moderate fame at the dawn of the MTV era in the punk band Red Rockers, and bassist Steve Walters (ex-Normals). They called themselves Cowboy Mouth after a character in a Sam Shepard play who wants to be "a rock 'n' roll Jesus with a cowboy mouth."

From the word go, the Mouth had a quantifiable magic: The four personalities were sufficiently different that there was no danger of coming off as a stereotypical rock band. Too, Griff, LeBlanc, and Sanchez were all strong writers whose disparate styles—each expressing, coincidentally, respective snippets of their Louisiana upbringings—came together splendidly when the songs were run through the Mouth blender.

As such things must, Cowboy Mouth hit the Dixie frat and beer-bar circuit heavily, admittedly using LeBlanc's Dash reputation to get the news out. A hearty and loyal following developed almost overnight and, armed with a backlog of tunes from previous bands as well as new material, the quartet released *Word of Mouth* independently in 1992.

Though the record has strong moments, particularly "Maggie Don't Two-Step," "Rose on Fire," and "Jenny Says" (the latter would become the most recorded song in rock history, at least by the same band), it's also true that the pieces were still falling into place. Griffith's country-rock tunes had an Eagles quality, and Sanchez's Cajun- and Irish-flavored drinking songs were rousing in the St. Patty's Day choruses. LeBlanc's "Jenny Says," by now an anthem, is one of a canon of tunes he wrote that were inspired by the titular Jenny, a former longtime girlfriend.

Word of Mouth was a promising debut, but nonetheless came off rather like a cake that'd been pulled out of the oven twenty minutes early; doesn't mean it wasn't edible, just not as good as you knew it would have been with a little time and practice.

Capitalizing on their reputation as a hot in-concert attraction, Cowboy Mouth came out a year later with *Mouthing Off (Live + More)*, recorded for the most part at a gig in Rennes, France, and seasoned with a few studio tracks. Though heavy with cover tunes, the Mouth's ability to arrange other writers' material was compelling.

By the time *It Means Escape* came out in 1994, Cowboy Mouth's original material was developing a significantly identifiable band sound. At that point, Walters left the band and Savoy, late of Lafayette's wonderful Cajun-rock outfit the Bluerunners, answered the call.

After a tour with Hootie & the Blowfish, at that point the biggest band in the world, Cowboy Mouth came home and headlined House of Blues during the National Association of Music Marketers; the hometown crowd went berserk, attending executives from MCA made the jump, and the band signed a deal shortly after.

In 1996, they released their major-label debut, *Are You with Me?*—an album stunning in its ability to wrap the flavor of New Orleans in a rock 'n' roll package. Yet again, "Jenny Says" was included, and this time it became a radio hit. Buoyed by the support of a seamless package of tunes, and there isn't one bad song on the CD. *Are You with Me?* became a hit even though the corporate folk who signed the band were fired shortly after the Mouth came onboard and the record was left floundering without promotional support.

The follow-up, *Mercyland*, was released in 1998 and was a fine record. Their next record, *Hurricane Party*, never hit the streets. The disintegrating relationship with the label proved too much; the Mouth decided that having no deal was better than hanging with MCA. They cleared up legal problems and obtained the rights to their earlier indie albums, formed Cowboy Mouth Records and re-released those CDs, then came out with an in-concert document called *All You Need Is Live* in early 2000.

In the meantime, new management negotiated a deal with Blackbird, a subsidiary of Atlantic and, though the *Hurricane Party* CD was probably lost in the Bermuda Triangle of MCA minutiae, the band forged ahead with an even fresher product, *Easy*, which came out in June 2000 and features "Everybody Loves Jill."

Cowboy Mouth will doubtless continue for however long the spirit is alive—and the members all have side projects to keep them from getting stale.

Sanchez continues to nurture his impressive solo folk career; to date, he has released the CDs *Jet Black and Jealous*, *Wasted Lives and Bluegrass*, *Loose Parts*, *Sonoma Valley*, and *Sold Out . . . At Carrollton Station*. LeBlanc has released three solo CDs of his own homemade recordings, *Dammit . . .* , *Playing the Game of My Life*, and *Double Dammit*, all of which demonstrate a poppier side to his songwriting than typically associated with his Mouth tunes.

John Thomas Griffith, who grew up in Texas and is now ensconced in that state's *Buddy Magazine* Texas Tornadoes music hall of fame, released a pre-Mouth solo album, *Son of an Engineer,* and has been working on film scores and ambient keyboard pop.

Griffith and Sanchez have performed together as the Lonesome Travelers, a country-leaning acoustic band that has recently been fleshed out with Savoy and Cowboy Mouth roadie–bonus musician Eddie Ecker.

"A lot of rock bands have a beginning and an end point," Griffith says, "because they're playing fad music—whatever's hot at the moment. Which is okay; that's the way rock goes, in cycles of what's hip. But you can be in Cowboy Mouth and take comfort because it can last forever. We draw so much from the rich styles here, and it seems to work."

The subdudes essentially spawned in the mid-eighties from high school bands of brothers Tommy, Dave, and John Malone in Edgard, Louisiana. After graduation, the siblings migrated to New Orleans and began playing in a shifting variety of groups on and off Bourbon Street. John would eventually end up in the physics lab at the University of Virginia, but Dave and Tommy were hooked on tunes. In the mid-seventies, David fell in with a coterie of musicians who would become the Radiators, and Tommy met a bassist named Johnny Ray "J. R." Allen, and later a keyboardist named John Magnie, with whom he worked in bands Little Queenie and the Percolators.

Tommy's scene was anchored in rock music, though flavored with the country influences indigenous to a rural Louisiana upbringing and, of course, the omnipresent N'Awlins sound seeping into their subconscious like humidity. With Magnie and Allen, Malone formed a country-flavored band called the Continental Drifters. Eventually, with Malone's high school buddy Steve Ademee on drums, they did an impromptu gig at Tipitina's. They impetuously called themselves the subdudes in an effort to describe their low-volume (subdued) approach, but the name stuck and the night went off with a magical buzz of greatness.

The crowd and the band sensed it, and the burgeoning quartet—Malone (voice and guitar), Allen (bass), Magnie (accordion and keys), and Amedee (percussion)—decided to pursue the experiment cautiously. As they rehearsed one day at Malone's house in Algiers Point, working on harmonies, Malone handed Amedee an old tambourine and a wooden spoon to keep time, and so the essential elements of the 'dudes sound fell into place.

All four musicians wrote material, together and separately. With glorious three-part harmonies that sounded like Hall & Oates in a hot tub full of gumbo, their pop lyrics and unique approach to instrumentation created a buzz wherever they showed up.

One of those places was Colorado. They'd worked a regular Monday night slot at Tip's, honing their sound and building a following, but they were concerned about the inability of New Orleans rock bands to win attention from the record business; so the band decided to relocate to Magnie's home territory. They entered a *Musician* magazine Best Unsigned Band contest and finished second to Lonesome Val. After a showcase, the 'dudes had three offers within a week and signed with Atlantic Records.

A year later, in 1990, they released their self-titled first record. Boasting a well-conceptualized batch of original tunes ("Need Somebody," "Got You on His Mind") and a nice take on the hometown's "Big Chief," the album was pretty wonderful.

They followed it in 1991 with *Lucky*, another outing so strong that it was all but ignored by commercial radio and the American public. Though the 'dudes were drawing fans and selling a respectable amount of records, they couldn't seem to take it to the next level, and the Atlantic deal fell through.

"It was a slow go," Malone remembers. "There were times when we thought it was really going to take off and happen—not that we wanted to be the biggest rock stars in the world, but . . . the momentum never stayed even."

It was three years before *Annunciation* emerged on the Windham Hill subsidiary, High Street. The album reflects amazing range between funk and balladry in its songs. Their music turned up in cool places, as on the popular television drama *HOMICIDE: Life On the Streets* ("All the Time in the World"), but it seemed as though momentum had reached a static level.

In 1996, the subdudes came out with *Primitive Streak*, a record that, despite launching with a song called "All the Time in the World," seemed to have a feel of finality, or possibly desperate resignation.

Unfortunately, the band decided to call it an amicable day. They did a farewell tour and recorded for posterity's sake in a variety of venues along the way; the tour produced in 1998 the exhilarating but bittersweet *Live at Last*. With a thoughtful selection spanning the band's career, and a pristine sound, *Live at Last* served as a "best of" record far beyond mere studio replication. It's not a bad choice for the uninitiated, though there aren't any bad subdudes albums.

"We always had hope," Malone says. "I'm very proud of all those records. It was real and it was unique and had some depth to it." He laughs and jokes, "Maybe there was too *much* talent." The 'dudes reconvene sporadically for such occasions as JazzFest or certain charitable events.

The highest-profile post-subdudes project was the participation of Malone and Allen in **Tiny Town,** a Dixie supergroup named after the John Hiatt–Ry Cooder–Nick Lowe–Jim Keltner one-off outfit called Little Village. In the case of Tiny Town, the lineup was augmented with drummer Kenneth Blevins and guitarist Pat McLaughlin.

Blevins, another well-known New Orleans musician-about-town, has a lengthy and impressive list of session credits. McLaughlin is an Iowa-born, Nashville-based songwriter whose tunes and recording guest slots are so popular that it would be easier to list the artists he hasn't been associated with.

Tiny Town's live chemistry was immediately hot, and the obvious potential was more than realized when they released a self-titled CD in 1998 with a subsidiary of Warner called Pioneer. Because of Malone's distinctive voice, the work bore a significant sonic resemblance to that of the subdudes, though McLaughlin's input added a hardy texture that took the edge out of the swamps and into the winding roads of Tennessee.

Unfortunately, it turned out to be a one-time-only venture. "Finally," Malone sighs, "I just wanted to be the one in charge for a change. We gave it almost three years and toured, even though the label folded just after the release of the record. I decided to go home and work on some songs."

The results of *those* efforts were on display in early September when I went to Tipitina's and saw the debut show of Malone's new quartet—a two-guitar–bass–drums outfit featuring drummer Johnny Vidacovich.

It was astonishing. Throwing down the same gorgeous melodic hooks and harmonies one would expect from Malone, the song structures were almost progressive rock, a sort of twin guitar–cross between the Allman Brothers and Wishbone Ash—if all concerned had been raised on crawfish. Speaking of crawfish, Tommy Malone's favorite place to eat is "Liuzza's over by the fairgrounds; the gumbo is outstanding. For po'boys, good Lord, Weaver's in Lakeview. And if you're getting a little out of New Orleans, you gotta go to Mosca's across the river on Highway 90. It's Italian-Louisianian and Carlos Marcello used to eat there." He also lists five CDs by Louisiana artists every thinking person should own: "Well, *anything* by Louis Armstrong. And certainly something by James Booker. *Positively Bonaroo* by Dr. John. A greatest hits collection by Fats Domino. And since I'm a rock guy, get an album by Bobby Charles."

As for the other two 'dudes, Magnie and Amedee, they stayed in Colorado and worked day gigs in a variety of session and club situations before surfacing in 1999 with a band called Magpie, which also includes Coloradans Tim Cook on bass and guitarist Jay Clear.

Like Tiny Town, Magpie also carries hints of the base ingredients that made the subdudes so unique, though the sound centers around Magnie's rollicking New Orleans piano and a songwriting style that uses the frontier expansiveness of his Rocky Mountain upbringing. With Amedee sitting behind a full drum kit, the sound is decidedly more beefy.

At the end of every summer, **The Radiators** play a private gig for the guy who operates their Web site. He lives in a small Rhode Island village not far from me in Connecticut, and the Rads invited me to drive over on a Sunday afternoon and check it out.

It was unseasonably cool—more like early autumn than summer—and I found myself standing in a generous backyard behind a New England, red barn style–house bordered by woods, gathered with perhaps a hundred other lucky souls, friends of the band and friends of the Web-site guru, to watch the Rads ease through two long, loping sets.

I had to keep pinching myself because the sheer intimacy of the event, the pure *casualness* of the whole thing, was wonderful. More than that, it said so much about the Radiators' worldview and how they, like Cowboy Mouth, will always survive regardless of label associations. Between sets, drinking a beer in the garage–dressing room with guitarist and vocalist Dave Malone, who exudes good cheer with smoldering intensity, it occurs to me that the Radiators are the sort of people you'd summon if you had a flat tire in the middle of the night.

The Radiators recall the Grateful Dead in their laissez-faire approach to live structure. If anything, the band is a loving musical batch of New Orleans components as filtered through a sort of Little Feat–esque prism. Formed in January 1978, when the principals of such historical bands as Dust Woofie, Ritz Hotel, and the Rhapsodizers got together, the Rads have blasted into their third decade together with the same lineup: keyboardist Ed Volker, drummer Frank Bua, guitarists Camile Baudoin and Dave Malone, and bassist Reggie Scanlon.

After a jam session in Volker's garage one afternoon, the disparate segments collectively quit their respective bands the next day and the Rads were born. Heavily taken with the primal funk of civic giants Professor Longhair, the Meters, Champion Jack Dupree, Allen Toussaint, and even Jelly Roll Morton, yet raised in the era when rock was stretching out to experiment with country and jazz, the Radiators instinctively assimilated all those resources with their own compositional skills to create what is lovingly called Fish-Head Music.

The first order of business was to secure venues. The band settled in for a regular Wednesday night date at Luigi's Pizza Parlor on Elysian Fields—payment: pizza and beer. The gig bolstered their burgeoning songwriting skills as well as their reputation until, in a moment born of his inability to hear himself over the guitars (and also because they were playing the song "Texas Chainsaw Massacre"), Bua literally took a chainsaw and performed a bit of surgery on one of Luigi's antique tables. End of gig, pizza, and beer.

No matter. By then the Rads had developed a small but rabid fan base, and the gigs started rolling in at joints such as Jimmy's and the Dream Palace and, inevitably, Tipitina's; an astounding guest list of prominent New Orleans and touring musicians who showed up to watch and sit in began to grow.

The time seemed ripe for a recording, but given the scarcity of signed acts in New Orleans at that time, the Radiators formed their own record company even as those early gigs were bubbling into the recognizable, free-form, and at-length musical circus that keeps them a major live draw to this day.

Croaker Records, as the company is still called, was surely one of the first of the Do-It-Yourself labels later popularized by indie rock bands in the eighties and nineties. The idea furthered the Rads' young but effective "buck the trend" philosophy, and Croaker released the band's first record, a double-live album called *Work Done on Premises*, in 1980.

Though an in-concert document is a bit strange for a debut effort, the concept seemed natural enough in light of the band's improvisational magic and given that folks had taped shows—à la the Dead—almost from the first Rads gig. And, in the spirit of the Dead (and later Phish), the Radiators encouraged the bootlegging. As Scanlon told Scott Jordan of *Offbeat* in 1997, "We figured if people were going to go to all that trouble to haul all that [recording] gear down, let 'em have it."

Later in 1981, a second Croaker album, *Heat Generation*, came out and the Radiators soon started playing Mardi Gras shows. When they finally made it to New York City's Lone Star Café in 1985, the joint was so stuffed with Tulane grads and other Louisiana transplants to the Big Apple that Epic Records signed the Radiators to a major-label contract.

Given that the Grateful Dead and Little Feat were cult bands with enormous record sales, it was an admirable move by the label to ink a band with the same organic roots system and a propensity for playing extemporaneous songs that lasted several minutes each. After all, one could rest assured that Journey could crank out five perfect three-minute slabs of radio-friendly pablum in the time it took for the Rads to work through one easy version of "Jigsaw" or "Nail Your Heart to Mine."

The experiment was moderately successful. The Radiators released three albums for Epic, *Law of the Fish* (1987), *Zigzagging Through Ghostland*

(1989), and *Total Evaporation* (1991). Radio airplay resulted: "Doctor Doctor" off the first album, "Confidential" from *Ghostland*, and "Soul Deep" from the last are the ones I've heard the most. But "Memories of Venus," "Red Dress," "Let the Red Wine Flow," "Party 'Till the Money Runs Out" and "I Want to Go Where the Green Arrow Goes" all comprise a wonderful cauldron of songs that bubbles with raw New Orleans sound.

The minor hits didn't translate to massive record sales, and the group and Epic eventually parted ways, but the Rads had built a fervent legion of Fish-Heads who turned every gig, regardless of locale, into purple-, gold-, and green-tinted Mardi Gras.

And there was always Croaker Records. Not long after the Epic chapter was closed, the band embarked on a zealous tour schedule and a variety of live and studio recordings. In 1992 and again in 1994, Croaker released live albums (*Snafu* and *Bucket of Fish*, both of which contained plenty of new original material as well as innovative covers).

Louisiana is rife with rock bands whose careers were criminally overlooked, but **The Bluerunners** are maybe the most underrated and ignored. Guitarist and vocalist Mark Meaux and vocalist, accordionist, and multi-instrumentalist Steve LeBlanc founded the band as a bunch of brash Lafayette Turks whose affection for the Cajun music of their ancestry was matched by unbridled enthusiasm for the Replacements, Bob Dylan, and Los Lobos. Though the two have had a shifting lineup of surrounding performers (including present Cowboy Mouth bassist Rob Savoy) and gleefully vacillate between French- and English-rendered tunes, driving electric rock, and warm acoustic arrangement, a discernible consistency adheres to the Bluerunners's work.

The self-titled debut CD, shrewdly released by Island Records in 1991, should have broken them out in the fashion of bands such as Big Country (though, come to think of it, *that* band was mostly ignored, too). In 1994, Monkey Hill Records put out the gleeful *Chateau Chuck*, but it also experienced problems with sales. The most recent album, 1998's *To the Country*, out from Rounder, found the Bluerunners's career downshifting. It's one of the best Louisiana albums ever made, and, sadly, the public's indifference leaves the existence of the Bluerunners a big question mark.

Royal Fingerbowl is a rock band very different from any of the above, though they share the others' appreciation for the charms of Louisiana. Formed in 1995 in New Orleans to critical exultation not commonly associated with ultra-hip industry types, this trio came together after various of their bands collided in Faubourg Marigny spots such as the Dragon's Den Mermaid Lounge. Royal Fingerbowl is anchored in guitarist, vocalist, and songwriter Alex McMurray's pastiche of urban influences: a New Jersey upbringing (the Boss, Miles Davis, blue-collar diners ethic) and passion for New Orleans (Walter "Wolfman" Washington, Snooks Eaglin and, well, New Orleans), all sandpapered with a Kurt-Weill-Lives-In-A-Rampart-Street-Flophouse-And-Reads-Charles-Bukowski approach to tunecraft.

With the able and resourceful support of drummer Kevin O'Day (who took lessons from Johnny Vidacovich) and bassist Andrew Wolf, McMurray has the observational skills one would expect if his bowling partners were Randy Newman and Tennessee Williams. His nicotine-raw vocal finesse is the perfect complement to a batch of songs that wouldn't work the same way if he sounded like Freddie Mercury.

McMurray has said that he tries to keep New Orleans from over-saturating his material, but if, somehow, Royal Fingerbowl had formed in, say, Wichita, this would be a different band indeed. In 1997, they released a pretty fine CD for TVT Records called *Happy Birthday, Sabo!* The album, peopled with loons and street folk, was funny with an undercurrent of indefinable sadness. The CD was happily embraced by industry illuminati everywhere and sold as well as such an idiosyncratic act might be expected. Finally, in 2000, they followed up with *Greyhound Afternoons,* on which McMurray sounds occasionally older and more introspective, though the kick-off tune, "Fine-Ass Chemise," more than balances the surprisingly gentle "Echoes in My Mind."

A group worth talking about in this context is a band I saw play an unbelievably boiling show for about fifteen drunk and/or sleepy people late on Lundi (Monday) Gras night at Tipitina's French Quarter. Carnival was at that eye-of-the-hurricane ebb between the weekend madness and the final wild countdown to Fat Tuesday, but **The Iguanas** were happy to be there.

The Iguanas are a magical amalgam of Mex-pop, tropical rock, honky-Tex, and swampy R&B. A unit with the sort of brotherly loyalty folks want bands to have, the Iguanas are made up of Ron Hodges (guitar and vocals), Joe Cabral (sax, guitar, and vocals), Derek Huston (sax), Rene Coman (bass), and Doug Garrison (drums). They got together from the usual matings of the New Orleans music scene and solidified their sound at Café Brasil and Rock 'n' Bowl. Soon after, they caught the ear of Jimmy "Wait, I'm gonna stop writing this novel long enough to open a restaurant and start a record label" Buffet, who signed them to Margaritaville Records. They released three discs: a self-titled album; *Nuevo Boogaloo;* and *Super Ball.* A fourth, *Sugar Town,* came out in 1999 on their own Blowout Records label, and carries on their musical tradition; that is, it celebrates the multiculturalism that only a few towns other than New Orleans (or Austin) would support.

A final, tasty band not to be missed is **Mulebone,** a determinedly New Orleans rock group fronted by trombonist Mark Mullins (who also tours and records with Harry Connick Jr.). Their debut CD, *5 Shakes 7 Spirits,* is a danceable sampling of rock by a rich and collective pedigree that has seen its members play with Louisiana artists from George Porter Jr. to Better than Ezra to the Continental Drifters.

Two

IT ROCKS,
BUT IT'S GENERIC

*I*n the annals of songs about New Orleans and Louisiana—ranging from Doug Kershaw's many-times-covered "Louisiana Man" and the immortal "Do You Know What It Means to Miss New Orleans" to more recent songs by Louisiana LaRoux's "New Orleans Ladies" and Cowboy Mouth's "New Orleans"—the song "WWOZ" is pretty damn great. With its lullaby melody and evocative descriptions of young lovers going to sleep in a Garden District home, hearing the horns of the tugboats on the Mississippi through breeze-kissed open windows, and drifting off to the muted sounds of WWOZ playing over the stereo, the tune is a sterling bit of hometown scene-setting that rivals anything Anne Rice has done, at least about people who haven't been killed.

It's one of my all-time favorites, and it was recorded by Louisiana's alternative rock band, **Better than Ezra.** Yet although one of their biggest hits is called "King of New Orleans," and the lush, humid sounds of their third major-label CD, *How Does Your Garden Grow*, seem to have been consciously arranged to create a New Orleans–style mood—à la the Neville Brothers's *Yellow Moon*—Better than Ezra isn't a band that particularly reflects its Louisiana lineage. For the most part, they could be from anywhere.

"I'm not so much a student of New Orleans or Louisiana musical history," guitarist and songwriter Kevin Griffin (1968–) told me once. "I'm certainly a fan of Fats Domino and the Meters, but I was born in Atlanta and grew up listening to KISS and Elton John rather than Louis Armstrong. But I *do* think that, if you live here, even if you're not a scholar of New Orleans music, you're certainly influenced by it on some level."

Maybe that influence is becoming more apparent the further the band goes, or as Griffin develops as a songwriter. In the early nineties, the Baton

233

Rouge–spawned band, now one of the most successful Louisiana groups ever, sounded like hundreds of other rockers. A textbook alt-pop band glued together by Griffin's strong choruses, Better than Ezra (BTE) found favor despite its clean-cut persona.

Griffin grew up in Monroe, Louisiana, and graduated from Louisiana State University, where he was a member of the Kappa Sigma fraternity. This last piece of information is important only because Better than Ezra *sounds* like a frat band, and because it's interesting to note that Griffin was at a party once and accidentally walked into the bathroom where then-student Shaquille O'Neal was sitting on the commode. Not many folks can say that. "I was at a friend's house who actually played on the LSU basketball team," Griffin told me, "and I opened the door, and there was Shaq, sitting on the toilet, you know? He said, 'Hey man, what's up?' and I said, 'Sorry, Shaq.' That was about it." Griffin thought for a moment. "Well, his knees certainly were high up."

Anyway, it's not all bad to sound like a frat band. To be sure, there's nothing threatening about BTE; one of the reasons the fellas in Ezra make good rock stars is that they're such big fans themselves. Griffin learned music by listening to his favorite records and playing his father's seldom-used classical guitar. He played in bands throughout high school before hooking up with drummer Cary Bonnecaze and lead guitarist Joel Rundell at LSU. They imported Shreveport bassist Tom Drummond and, by 1988, BTE was a presence on the local bar and frat party circuit. Progressively infusing their sets with original material, the band released a cassette called *Surprise* and began to attract label attention. But when Rundell committed suicide, the band was devastated and broke up.

For a few years the members scattered. When Griffin ended up in Los Angeles and a demo tape he'd circulated drew attention from A&R folks, Bonncaze and Drummond flew to the West Coast. The rejuvenated BTE began competing in the grimy but neon-hued town that launched Jim Morrison, Tommy Lee, and Axl Rose. They learned a lot, refined their sound, put together a composite sixteen-track album called *Deluxe* on their own Swell label, then returned to Louisiana to see what would happen.

Deluxe sold 10,000 copies and the band's showcase at the prestigious South-by-Southwest festival in Austin caused a major buzz in label land. Before long the band had a deal with Elektra, which re-released *Deluxe*.

On the strength of "In the Blood," "Good," and "Rosealia," *Deluxe* would eventually go platinum. A follow-up, *friction, baby*, their best album, tried to counter some of the wimp factor by beefing up the guitar tones and the tempos, and sold respectably if not as well as the first. "The King of New Orleans," the leadoff single about homeless kids in the French Quarter, was a hit, as was the infectiously yearning "Desperately Wanting," a bittersweet piece about looking back at youth after fate pushes old friends in different directions. "WWOZ" is also on the record. (Request it the next time you see them.) Those are the best tunes Griffin has written, and they reveal a depth and maturity as well as a graceful lyrical touch that elevated the band above the genre.

In 1996, drummer Bonnecaze fell by the wayside and New Orleans native Travis McNabb stepped in. By all accounts, the segue was smooth. (Onstage, the band is typically complemented by Jim Payne, a close friend who started out as their guitar tech.)

With *How Does Your Garden Grow*, BTE's third CD, recorded in their own New Orleans studio with Malcolm Burns at the production helm, the band made major strides in developing a unique identity. Malcolm, a protégé of Brian Eno's who'd worked in one sonic capacity or another with Peter Gabriel and U2, introduced atmospheric textures to BTE's recording and conceptual process. With Griffin's melodic and lyrical muse expanding exponentially, *How Does Your Garden Grow* became the first Better than Ezra CD that exhibited a personality rather than just a collection of nice tunes.

From the Spanish moss–draped introduction of "Je Ne M'en Souviens Pas" to perfectly constructed pop songs—"One More Murder," "Under You," "At the Stars," and "Everything in 2's"—*Garden*'s playfully dark mix of electronica, soundscapes, and great tuneage was a fine accomplishment. Griffin's increasing awareness of Louisianian musical heritage also played a role.

"If you listen to [*Garden*], there's a lot of second-lining going on," he says. "Travis is heavily influenced by [Meters drummer] Zigaboo Modeliste . . . [and] I've just started getting into James Booker. I've become a huge fan of Henry Butler and Kermit Ruffins and Mulebone and Astral Project.

"And lyrically, I'm starting to draw characters from New Orleans. I'd love to say that I find myself sauntering down an oak-lined street in the Faubourg Marigny, soaking up the atmosphere and writing songs. Maybe I'm so immersed in the city day by day that I don't even realize it's having an effect on me. But as far as overtly going out and walking around the city . . . I *wish* I did but unfortunately I don't."

But he does own some Louisiana music: "The Meters's *Fiyo on the Bayou*; a collection of some kind by Louis Armstrong; *Law of the Fish* by the Radiators; the first album by the Bluerunners is great, and the first album by Dash Rip Rock slayed me. And you should have a representative album by the Balfa Brothers."

Though it's true that their sales figures have declined with each album, it probably came as a surprise to the band when, after spending the summer of 2000 recording, they were dropped by their label. In the meantime, they've self-released a collection of rarities called *Artifakt*.

If BTE is the most successful Louisiana rock band ever, one of the first bands to break out of the state in the post-Beatles era was a Baton Rouge sextet called **Louisiana's LeRoux,** a melodic rock outfit that might be thought of as a swampy Boston (shy of a few billion record sales).

One of their songs, a slick piece of AOR harmony-rock called "New Orleans Ladies" off their 1978 debut album, *Louisiana's LeRoux*, was a big success on FM radio—an anthem in the southeast—and apparently has enjoyed staying power. In the summer of 1999, for example, readers of New Orleans's alternative weekly newspaper, *Gambit*, voted "New Orleans Ladies" the best New Orleans song of the century.

While "Ladies" is admittedly an addictive bit of seventies-style pop, even LeRoux's Leon Medica, who co-wrote the song, admits his tune may not have the history of other possibilities for such an award. "I was honored, of course," he told me. "When someone from *Gambit* called to tell me, my wife answered the phone and I was helping my son with his math homework. I didn't realize it was for me and that she'd set the phone down on the table. So the poor guy had to sit there and listen to me explain math for five minutes and, finally, I looked up and saw the phone. He must've thought I was an idiot.

"Anyway, I appreciated the news, but I thought, well, 'Do You Know What It Means?' and 'When the Saints Go Marching In' are classics and maybe more appropriate."

In any event, Louisiana's LeRoux was essentially formed when Lafayette guitarist, vocalist, and songwriter Jeff Pollard met up with the house session musicians at Bogalusa's Studio in the Country: bassist, vocalist, and producer Medica, keyboardist and vocalist Rod Roddy, drummer and vocalist David Peters, and multi-instrumentalist and vocalist Bobby Campo.

Splitting their time between session work for Clarence "Gatemouth" Brown, Clifton Chenier, and other such artists, the outfit first coalesced when Brown asked Medica to organize a band to back him up on a State Department tour of Africa. Medica was producing Pollard at the time, asked him if he wanted to be part of it, and the new outfit took the dates, opening Gate's shows as The Jeff Pollard Band before turning to the stage to back Brown.

The band was rechristened Louisiana's LeRoux when Capitol Records secured their services in a bidding war in 1977, at which time guitarist Tony Haseldon came onboard. The self-titled album came out the next year. With the help of the single "New Orleans Ladies," which Medica had originally co-written with his pal Hoyt Garrick for Dick Rivers, a French Elvis-type who turned it down, Louisiana's LeRoux began to take off.

Their cause was helped significantly by an amazing work ethic that kept them on the road. They opened for acts such as Journey and headlined clubs on the big shots' nights off—and the band developed an estimable cult following.

Over the next few years, they released two more albums, *Keep the Fire Burning* and *UP*, after which LeRoux switched labels to RCA for 1982's

Last Safe Place. Though the singles "Nobody Said It Was Easy" and "Addicted" attracted attention and rekindled earlier momentum, Pollard, the songwriting mainstay in the group for ten years, renewed his religious convictions and quit rock music for the ministry. At that point, the group was experiencing a resurgence they hadn't anticipated, and Medica had hoped the two hits would convince Pollard to remain. But he was resolute. The loss creatively eviscerated the band. Campo also split and, after much debate, LeRoux carried on with Baton Rouge guitarist Jim Odom, who joined up along with Michigan native Dennis "Ferdie" Frederikson on bass and vocals.

The band recorded one more album, *So Fired Up*, but afterwards, in the words of Medica, "We just sort of dissipated. The energy was gone."

Tommy Malone, guitarist and vocalist for the subdudes and Tiny Town, remembers LeRoux from his high school years. "They were a damned good band. I'd go to Thibodeaux and see them back when they were called the Levee Band. Even then, they were just amazing players and songwriters. I don't know whether there's a curse on Louisiana rock bands, but LeRoux should have been huge."

LeRoux remains a viable if sporadic entity. Medica, a renowned Nashville producer, writer, session player, and talent manager who has worked with Anders Osborne and Wayne Toups, keeps LeRoux bubbling on a back burner of sorts. Haselden, Roddy, Peters, and Odom are still in the band, and also onboard are relative newcomers Nelson Blanchard (keys and vocals), Bob Pourciau (drums, percussion, and vocals), and lead vocalist Randy Knaps.

Razor & Tie Records released a greatest hits compilation called *Bayou Degradable* in 1999, and in the same year the new lineup gathered and recorded a CD of original material that was released on their own imprint in time for Mardi Gras 2000.

Which are the Essential Albums by Louisiana Artists Everyone Should Own? According to Medica, "*New Orleans Home of The Blues Vol. 1 & 2*; Dr. John's *Gumbo*; the Meters's *Rejuvenation; Clifton Chenier and His Red Hot Louisiana Band*; and, I hate to add this one because of my involvement, but *Louisiana's LeRoux*, our first album. It's a good record."

Although LeRoux was the most high-profile of the mid-seventies Louisiana rock acts, several other bands made marks, too. Preceding LeRoux was another Baton Rouge act called **Pot Liquor,** whose George Ratzlaff was the main creative source. A power rock band, they signed with Chess/Janus and released several albums, including *First Taste, Levee Blues*, and *Louisiana Rock 'n' Roll.*

Far more successful was New Orleans's **Zebra,** a three-piece progressive power trio that ventured into areas previously explored by Led Zeppelin and Rush, and who would later be emulated by such acts as Kings X. It was (and is) a highly accomplished and ambitious group that honored virtuosity in rock, which isn't quite the paradox it seems.

Zebra formed in New Orleans in 1975 with native songwriter and guitarist Randy Jackson, native bassist, keyboardist, and vocalist Felix Hanneman, and a transplanted Californian, drummer and vocalist Guy Kelso, yet another shrewd human who came for Mardi Gras (in 1972) and just never left. The trio rapidly gained popularity on the club circuit, coughing up amazing renditions of Zep, Bowie, and various hard rock du jour.

Early on, they began sprinkling Jackson's originals into their sets and, dividing their time between New Orleans and the thriving Long Island, New York, circuit, became quite the bi-coastal draw. A demo tape earned regional radio airplay and Atlantic Records signed the band to a five-album deal.

The self-titled debut, produced by Jack Douglas (of Aerosmith fame), remains a wonderfully arty hard-rock record—and became at the time the fastest selling LP in Atlantic history, moving over 75,000 units the week it was released. Anchored by the ambitious, acousto-electric "Who's Behind the Door," about how residents of our planet must appear to folks from elsewhere, *Zebra* peaked at #29 on the Billboard charts and stayed around for eight months.

It's one thing to write driving hard-rock riffs and another to come up with hooks, but rarely do songs have both, at least not on the level of Zebra's debut. But every tune is good, particularly "Take Your Fingers from My Hair" and the harmony-salted "The La La Song." (While his lyrics frequent the same landscape as those of most pop writers, throughout his career, Jackson would also tackle some interesting topics—like hunting, cocaine abuse, aliens—with a clever wit.)

Jackson, a soft-spoken and friendly guy, nonetheless feels awkward about discussing his material. "I don't think the songs are as much about specific things as they are a series of musical questions," he told me by phone from his Long Island home. "They are . . . ruminations . . . just stuff I wonder about."

The immediate impression, listening to a Zebra record, is that there is no way the three of them could pull the dense arrangements off live—but they do. I saw them in the early 1980s at a Dallas club called Cardi's, known to some as the place where a pre-remorseful David Crosby was busted for firearms possession while entwined with a glowing crack pipe.

Each of the band members sang really well and, with Hanneman nimbly segueing from keyboards to bass, simultaneously tapping Taurus bass pedals, the sound was amazingly rich.

The band's follow-up, *No Telling Lies*, was noticeably weaker despite the inclusion of such fine tunes as "Bears" and Jackson's gorgeous hymn to the recently murdered John Lennon, "Lullaby." Sales of the record were tepid at best, and Jackson says today that the overwhelming and sudden success—and the subsequent demands—of the debut record left

them without enough time either to write or to prepare for the sophomore effort.

"I mean, how old is *that* story?" Jackson laughs. "You hear your whole
career about bands that have several years to write songs for their first
album, then, between touring and publicity, you turn around and it's time
to record the second one—and you've got two weeks to write ten songs."

Zebra's third album, *3.V,* is arguably their finest and most cohesive.
Sadly, though sales topped *No Telling Lies,* the elusive "hit" never materialized and Atlantic dropped the band in spite of the true and consistent
quality of the work.

Zebra kept the faith, and continue to do so. They tour frequently and
maintain a solid fan base in the Deep South and the Long Island areas,
and their extraordinary live shows caused Atlantic to heat up the presses
for a "postscript" *Zebra Live* release in 1989. Recent releases include *In
Black and White—the Best of Zebra* and *Zebra—King Biscuit Flower Hour,*
as well as solo discs by Jackson and Hanneman.

In the modern era, before there was a Cowboy Mouth or a Better than
Ezra, there was **Dash Rip Rock.** Every American town has the equivalent of
Dash Rip Rock: *the* rock band that first drew significant attention, the one
that you *knew* would become stars—but for some reason never quite pulled
it off. These bands are like metaphorical sacrificial lambs that have to go
through the wringer and experience all the bad breaks so that the wave of
acts behind them can profit.

Dash Rip Rock was born in 1983 when Louisiana State University
master's degree candidate Bill Davis met ex-LSUer and local barroom
kook Ned "Hoaky" Hickel Jr. Davis, a guitarist, vocalist, and songwriter in a
band called the Human Rayz, and Hickel, a bassist and vocalist in Scooter
& the Mopeds, had similar onstage philosophies—drunken energy cubed—
and it wasn't long before the two joined forces and formed a band that
would fuse the country punk energy of Jason & the Scorchers with the
Dixie-pop flair of REM.

Though original drummer Clark Marty had introduced Hickel to
Davis, he was gone by the time the band recorded their first record. Behind
the kit instead was Fred LeBlanc, late of New Orleans new wave–punk acts
the Backbeats and the Mistreaters, and whose unique mentality fit with
dovetail precision into Hickel's and Davis's worldviews.

Dash became the bar-band equivalent of a mid-air collision between
two whiskied-up trapeze artists performing to a great soundtrack. It's not
everybody's idea of highbrow entertainment, but it's great fun if you don't
mind getting blood in your popcorn.

Their Navy SEAL–like approach to conquering the southern club circuit was successful, and in 1986 they recorded a rockin' self-titled album
for 688 Records. The trio stayed on the road, slaughtering crowds with
their everything-goes-every-night attitude.

Mammoth Records signed the band and in 1989 they released *Ace of Clubs*, one of the fine albums in Louisiana history for no other reason than it rocked and had good songs. The band's reputation began to seep beyond the Deep South and across the nation. Davis, LeBlanc, and Hickel made the reasonable assumption that they would go to the next level, and when it didn't happen (one major-label A&R guy died in the process of getting the band a deal), LeBlanc experienced an adjustment in lifestyle. He split and eventually formed Cowboy Mouth (see "The Indigenous Sound," Part 5, Chapter 1), which cynics have described as a sort of Dash Rip Rock post–Betty Ford.

In any case, Dash signed up drummer Chris Luckette and plowed ahead. Two more albums for Mammoth came out, *Not of This World* and *Boiled Alive*—both more holding-pattern efforts than steps forward—before the band's relationship with the label rotted through. A pair of indie efforts, *Tiger Town* (Doctor Dream) and *Get You Some of Me* (Sector 2) followed before Luckette opted to return to the sanity of home life. A scrub-faced, post-high-school neophyte named Kyle Melancon, whose approach to rock is energizing in its childlike glee, is the latest Dash drummer.

Suddenly, despite less-than-stellar sales of their last effort, Dash had a single, an afterthought recording of "(Let's Go) Smoke Some Pot," an admittedly hilarious novelty parody of Danny & the Juniors's "Let's Go to the Hop." An indictment of the cannabis-reeking jam-band culture, the song took off in several municipalities and became a hit.

Considering that during their years of insane club popularity, Dash's composite album sales totaled less than 100,000, any hit was surely welcome.

Davis and Melancon penned a fine set of tunes and the trio gathered in 1997 to record *Paydirt*, their best album in years. Produced by none other than old pal LeBlanc, *Paydirt* (PC Records) contained plenty of Dash attitude in addition to a compact set of punchy country-punk rock songs.

By 2000, the toll of years of recording and touring had become too heavy for Hickel and he left the band. Harry Nelson signed on, proving that Davis is probably right: nothing can keep Dash Rip Rock down for long. The refurbished trio continues to sing its way onward, though Davis has shifted his home base to Nashville for business purposes. The intensity of the shows never diminishes, and an in-concert set called *Live From the Bottom of the Hill* was released at Mardi Gras 2000.

A few other homegrown, modern Louisiana rock bands have made noise. While cities like Baton Rouge and Shreveport had their share of metal club bands and even original acts in the late eighties and early nineties, the most successful was a New Orleans group called **Lillian Ax,** headed up by guitarist and songwriter Steve Blaze.

Formed in 1984, Lillian Ax signed with MCA for three albums before moving over to IRS for a fourth. The highlight is *Psychoschizophrenia*, a compelling collection with classico-gothic chord structures, banshee lead guitar, and marketable melodies. Blaze says the band consistently sold from 100,000 to 150,000 copies of each album; solid numbers, to be sure, but he eventually started a darker band called **Near Life Experience.**

As for trying to make it as a metal band in Louisiana, Blaze told me, "We're so tourist friendly here that everyone perceives New Orleans as only having R&B and jazz bands. That's not the way it is; there are a lot of great rock bands here but no club or media support. The newspapers don't really help you out unless it's blues and jazz. You'll see stories about acts that sold five thousand records; Lillian Ax has sold hundreds of thousands of records and no one ever wrote about us."

New Orleans's guitar poppers **Deadeye Dick,** presumably so-titled in honor of the Kurt Vonnegut novel, seemed on the verge of long-term success after scoring a Top 50 hit single, "New Age Girl," off 1994's debut CD, *A Different Story.* The peppy tune was also included on the soundtrack to the film *Dumb and Dumber.* But the group, comprised of guitarist and vocalist King Muse Calem Guillote, bassist Mark Miller, and drummer Billy Landry, couldn't move to the next level.

Singer and saxophonist **Jerry La Croix** (1943–) was born in Alexandria and is known as "The Count." He came to prominence as the ultrapowered wailer in Edgar Winter's band White Trash, and billions of cannabis-happy teens in the seventies roared along with La Croix on that band's epic version of "Tobacco Road." La Croix also worked with Blood, Sweat & Tears and Rare Earth, as well as the Boogie Kings, a legendary, off-again and on-again swamp-pop unit.

Shreveport's **The Bluebirds,** fronted by brothers Buddy and Bruce Flett, emerged from the ashes of the popular cover band The A Train. Cranking out serviceable if not particularly distinguished blues-rock, the band's *Swamp Stomp* and *South from Memphis* sound like a grits-and-gravy Foghat.

In the mid-nineties, Baton Rouge modern rockers **Becky Sharp** released one album for the MCA imprint, Way Cool Records. Treading heavily in the wake of Seattle grunge, but with a twist of honeyed melody, not much happened despite the infectious regional hit "Beach Ball."

Other bands that have made their way around the rock circuit include **The Cold,** a significantly influential punk band in the eighties who ruled the New Orleans scene; and **Little Queenie and the Percolators,** headed up by vocalist Leigh Harris (now a fixture on the city's R&B circuit), which had a sort of revolving door membership policy that featured many of the town's best rock players. **Tom's House** is a New Orleans pop quartet determined to follow firmly in the gold and platinum footsteps of Better than Ezra. These harmonizing hunks established a rabid following virtually overnight, bringing to the table a natty instinct for songwriting and an easy-to-like collective persona.

Some Louisiana rock bands and artists whose work isn't distinguishable as being from Louisiana have realized they couldn't make it in their home state and headed to greener pastures.

Lucinda Williams (1953–) is well on the way to national success. Toward the end of the nineties, she went from ordinary cult status to large cult status. Every critic has anointed her as a singer and songwriter goddess, and with good reason. A native of Lake Charles, Williams took up guitar before she was a teenager. When she was a kid, her family traveled to and lived in various exotic locales, including Santiago, Mexico City, the Deep South, New Orleans, and Austin. She began to learn songs by Bob Dylan, Judy Collins, Van Morrison, and Buffalo Springfield. The influence of her father, a professor of poetry, led her to seek out the writings of Flannery O'Connor and Hank Williams. She went to college and began to play the local folk circuit; she dropped out to pursue music full time in 1971.

As geographically curious as her father, Williams honed her burgeoning craft and lived all over the United States. Her early aspirations for folk stardom were somewhat realized when, following a lead given to her by a New Orleans friend, she signed with Folkways in 1978. She recorded two albums for the label in the eighties, *Ramblin'* (made for $250 in one day, and which contained her interpretations of such staples as "Ramblin on My Mind," "Great Speckled Bird," and "Jambalaya") and *Happy Woman Blues* (containing many promising originals, including the yearning "Lafayette" and "King of Hearts").

Neither attracted much attention, but the work promised a bright and talented artist. The Folkways experiment over, Williams continued traveling, writing, and working a variety of jobs; eventually she settled in Los Angeles, where she played clubs and took voice lessons.

Other lessons came from an ill-fated marriage to Greg Sowders of the Long Ryders. When Williams recycled her experiences in song format, she won a new deal with Rough Trade; in 1988, she released a self-titled album for the label. To casual observers who weren't aware of the work Williams had put in, *Lucinda Williams* must have looked as if it had dropped from heaven.

Indeed, her persona—that wonderful straw cowboy hat bent at acute angles as if she'd raided Elvin Bishop's closet, her hard but pretty face, the drugstore sunglasses, and a monster voice like a trailer-park Chrissie Hynde—had become an intriguing cross between a hell-raising folk poet and a rock-dabbling bar babe. And the music, which had evolved from country-folk to what can best be described as rootsy Americana, reflected all these elements: the aching plea in "I Just Wanted to See You So Bad" virtually bleeds pain; the dreaming waitress in "Sylvia" may never be happy; and "Passionate Kisses" (later recorded in Grammy-winning fashion by Mary Chapin Carpenter) is a remarkable, evocative three-minute portrait of a woman who ain't asking for much.

She packed a horse-kick punch, too, as on "Changed the Locks" (later covered by Tom Petty) and her version of Howlin' Wolf's "I Asked for Water (He Gave Me Gasoline)."

Williams, by this point, was a "musician's musician," which means that such people as Elvis Costello were hanging around and doing guest bits on her record. Unfortunately, Rough Trade went belly-up without providing much support, and it was four years before Williams would release *Sweet Old World* (on the Chameleon label). This long-awaited album, best noted for its synthesis of all her influences, set her up for two things: another massive delay before she'd have another record and a mature and cohesive work called *Car Wheels on a Gravel Road.*

That it took six years to make that CD was to a large extent Williams's fault. Ever the perfectionist, she recorded the piece from scratch twice; but when it was finally issued by Mercury, the CD was critically worshipped by every music writer in this solar system.

At that point, Williams crossed over into mainstream consciousness as a recognizable entertainer. Williams's 2001 disc *Essence* continues her joyful evolution. The album might be thought of as a happy but reflective sonic bridge across the river Maturity—if its muddy flow were comprised of blood, beer, and tears. But she remains quite visible, wandering around JazzFest in 1999, for example—and that only makes her cooler.

A Lake Charles singer named **Bobby Kimball**, born Bobby Toteaux, possesses a voice of almost operatic beauty—and if you listened to rock radio at all in the eighties, you are intimately familiar with it. As the frontman for Toto, Kimball is the man who sang "Rosanna," "Africa," "I Won't Hold You Back," and "Hold the Line," and presumably still has the cluster of Grammys the band won over the course of their run. Kimball left Toto in 1984, but recently rejoined the resurrected band.

Jesse Winchester (1944–), who is without question a highlight in the admittedly limited Louisiana folk-rock scene, is the Shreveport-born expatriate who became a Canadian citizen after fleeing the United States in 1967 in protest of the Vietnam War. He spent his early years in Memphis, graduated from Williams College and, upon receipt of his draft notice, hauled ass to Montreal. In 1970, the Band's Robbie Robertson produced Winchester's first album, a truly great record of superb songs ("Snow," "Black Dog," and "Yankee Lady"—"I lived with decent folks / In the hills of old Vermont / Where what you do all day / Depends on what you want"). If a bit more of a "rock" record than his future catalog would reflect, it's an important work. The follow-up, *Third Down, 110 to Go,* is considered by many to be his best, although others prefer his early stuff in the country-tinted *Let the Rough Side Drag.*

In 1977, when Winchester was pardoned by President Jimmy Carter, he returned to the United States, where he has since quietly pursued a career devoted to solid craft. The Sugar Hill label has put out Winchester's most recent recordings; 1999's *Gentleman of Leisure* is a strong, melodic record. If anything, his voice has more "Louisiana soul" to it than his earlier feisty work.

Winchester's defection from Louisiana shouldn't necessarily be connected with a lack of folk or folk-rock scenes in the state, although they're low-key compared to much of the music. Cowboy Mouth rhythm guitarist, vocalist, and songwriter Paul Sanchez, who has released several splendid folk solo discs, assures me that a vibrant folk scene does exist in New Orleans, often populated by musicians whose higher profile careers are with more popular electric bands. Carrollton Station, a fine music club in that city, is a testament to the existence of such a scene, but it would be incorrect to say major careers have blasted off from the folk launching pad.

From another world than Winchester's—in virtually every possible way—is a New Orleans singer named **Phil Anselmo** (1968–). Although Anselmo still lives in and loves his hometown, he became the lead vocalist of a Texas metal act called **Pantera**, a group of glam-metal wannabes whose new approach to rock was to play faster and louder than anyone had before.

Pantera has puzzled critics and Billboard types for years; while their brand of metal has its place in the sales demographics, that they've debuted on the charts at #1 (1994's *Far Beyond Driven*) and consistently score platinum status with almost every record runs contrary to passing fads. Their best CDs are probably *Vulgar Display of Power* and *Cowboys From Hell*, and a live album released in 2000.

As for Anselmo, he's alive and busy, despite almost dying backstage in Dallas of an overdose of heroin some years ago. By all reports, he seems to have learned his lesson. He's also been part of a metal supergroup, Down, whose 1995 CD, *Nola*, is a satisfyingly "swallow some Comet" experience.

Probably the most famous Louisiana punk–new wave band was New Orleans's **Red Rockers,** who formed in 1979 after meeting at Louisiana State University in Baton Rouge. Comprised of vocalist and lead guitarist John Thomas Griffith (now with Cowboy Mouth), lead guitarist James Singletary, bassist Darren Hill, and two drummers, first Patrick Jones and then Jim Reilly, the Rockers were heavily influenced by the rebellion inherent in the British punk scene.

Frustrated by their inability to be taken seriously in New Orleans, the band relocated to Los Angeles and later San Francisco. They recorded three major label albums for Columbia imprint 415—*Condition Red, Good as Gold*, and *Schizophrenic Circus*—and scored a huge MTV hit with the ultra-catchy song "China." Ultimately, following the muse that would eventually lead him to Cowboy Mouth (see also "The Indigenous Sound," Part 5, Chapter 1), Griffith abdicated and the band broke up.

A generation down the road, a loose-knit confederacy of Ruston, Louisiana, kids with a jones for the symphonic propensities of Brian Wilson and the Beatles and the brain-galaxy explorations of Pink Floyd would whittle quite a niche in the American indie rock scene. Known en masse as the Elephant 6 collective, bands such as **Neutral Milk Hotel, Olivia Tremor Control,** and the **Apples in Stereo**—formed by hometown kiddos Bill Doss (OTC), Jeff Mangum (NMH), and Will Hart and Robert Schneider (AIS)—came into being as a musical Utopian enterprise to combat the boredom of life in small-town Louisiana. (So boring was small-town Louisiana that the migratory E6 tribes have resettled in such burgs as Athens, Georgia, and Denver, Colorado.)

Perhaps the most commercially successful of the lot is the Apples in Stereo—true darlings of indie rock—though the other groups enjoy devoted followings. Enamored of a life style that looks back to prime sixties communal hippiedom, and perfectly happy recording albums on primitive sounding equipment, the Elephant Folk demonstrate an alluring propensity for cranking out product, much of which is great.

As for folks who've migrated *into* Louisiana, and in particular to New Orleans, several rock transients come to mind. Whether New Orleanians *want* them there depends on the star in question. Consider **Trent Reznor** (1965–), for example. The Captain Angst of computer-metal superheroes Nine Inch Nails moved to the city in the early nineties, not long after his enraged *Pretty Hate Machine* CD sold millions of copies.

Reznor was born on a Pennsylvania farm and raised in Cleveland; he mastered a variety of instruments while playing in New Wavey bands. Then he took The Cure's corpse-like pallor, mixed it with American sarcasm, and poured it all into his own cocktail of metal guitar, emotional rage, and industrial electronics.

1994's *The Downward Spiral* took his muse to new heights, essentially circumventing whatever melody had existed on his earlier work—and sold millions anyway. It's clear that the youth of America related to Reznor's self-analysis.

But while his complaining is indeed self-absorbed, and he lashes out at, well, everything, it's hard not to like some of Reznor's tunes; and, too, he takes his dog with him everywhere. Since moving to NOLA, he has set up a recording studio in an old funeral home (what a surprise), dresses in black a lot, and in addition to working with Marilyn Manson, took several years to craft 1999's *Fragile*, which hit #1 and stayed just long enough to prove it could.

It's probably safe to say that Reznor doesn't hang out a great deal playing poker with **Jimmy Buffett** (1946–), another occasional resident of the town. Buffett is the one-man industry built around his own liberally garnished reputation as the beachcombin', Heineken-swillin', yacht-residin', plane-flyin', clam-digger wearin', book-writin', good-timin' songster who incurred the wrath of many French Quarter residents when he brought his circus to town and opened one of his Key West–styled fern bars, Margaritaville, on Decatur Street.

Margaritaville is a comfortable joint and they do some good things. Most important,, they support live original music of an eclectic chemistry (blues great Coco Robicheaux plays there on occasion).

You know the drill on Buffett's music: the Florida-based songwriter hit it big with his calypso-flavored, vaguely amusing approach to beach-themed folk. Every tune was crispy with beach sand and crinkly with the sound of empty aluminum beer cans tossed on a boat deck.

For years, every studio album Buffett made was a hit: *A White Sport Coat and a Pink Crustacean; Living and Dying in ¾ Time; Changes in Latitudes, Changes in Attitudes* (from whence the beast, "Margaritaville," sprang); and *Coconut Telegraph*. Get the idea? After spending mucho time early in his recording career on his boat, Buffet formed his infamous Coral Reefer Band in the mid-seventies and shifted his focus to touring.

He remains one of the highest grossing concert acts in the universe. His next live album should put the total of in-concert CDs at four—and there's no end in sight.

A former head-muse for the mid-eighties Welsh band The Alarm, **Mike Peters** (1959–) ended up in New Orleans after the band splintered and he'd traveled the country on a sort of Steinbeckian exploration.

Sharp released two solo efforts, *Hard Travellin'* (1991) and *Downtown America* (1996), which had more to do with Woody Guthrie and Jimmie Rodgers than Marshall amps and hairspray. Landing in New Orleans, he enjoyed his first few years as an anonymous folk-tinted solo artist, playing for sympathetic expatriates in Kerry's Irish Pub. He still holds court there regularly, heading up a loose aggregate of local musicians who morph into various units on the Kerry's stage. It's a nice little scene.

Alex Chilton (1950–) is an expatriate from Memphis, where he became a legend in first the Boxtops and then Big Star; he maintains a moderately low profile in New Orleans. He's stayed productive with albums like *Like Flies on Sherbet/Live in London* and the all-covers *Set*, which combine his innate charm with a lackadaisical approach to production.

Ex–new waver **Willy DeVille** (1950–), with his carved cheekbones and vaguely vampiric air, is the New York–born guitarist, singer, and songwriter whose band Mink DeVille was popular in the seventies. After he went solo several years ago, DeVille moved to New Orleans. His subsequent CDs do reflect a bit of a Crescent City feel, particularly on *Backstreets of Desire* and *Loup Garou*, though he's such an individual stylist that it can't be said that his work is distinctly Louisianan.

Legions of musicians have called Bourbon Street the musical equivalent of graduate school, but there is particular charm to guitarist **Mason Ruffner** (1953–) and his matriculation.

A Texas native who grew up enamored of Jimi Hendrix and Bob Dylan, Ruffner played lead guitar in Fort Worth's legendary R&B outfit, Robert Ealey's Five Careless Lovers, before settling in New Orleans in 1979. With his stalwart backing band, The Blues Rockers, Ruffner set up camp on Bourbon, where the protracted intensity of his live shows quickly became a city-wide topic of amazement. Soon, visiting rock dignitaries such as Bruce Springsteen, Billy Gibbons, Carlos Santana, and Jimmy Page (who even clambered onto the tiny stage and jammed) were dropping by after concerts to see whether Ruffner was as cool as the rumors indicated.

He was. Ruffner remains a throwback to the rollicking days when rock was less about posturing and a lot more about sweat and a sense of discovery—[whether that might be] the next beer, a beautiful girl, or the addictive powers and horizon-less possibilities of a guitar fretboard.

One tourist who dug Ruffner happened to be an executive for CBS Records who signed Ruffner in 1985. The Rick Derringer–produced debut, *Mason Ruffner*, came out in October that year. But, though his second LP, *Gypsy Blood*, sold over 200,000 copies, and he was highly sought after for session work, he lost his deal, moved to rural Texas, and shifted his work to suit his own pace.

Of late, he's lived in Nashville, and in 1999 came out with the superb and aptly titled *You Can't Win*.

One of the more intriguing bands to develop in New Orleans is the **Continental Drifters,** not only because of its quasi-supergroup status, but because most of its principals moved to New Orleans from other states. They are Peter Holsapple (jangle-guitarist supreme, former member of the dBs, touring member and confidante of REM, and guest artist on a virtual hall-of-fame of rock records); Vicki Peterson (ex-Bangles) and Susan Cowsill (yes, one of the Family Cowsill who recorded "Indian Lake"); bassist Mark Walton (ex–Dream Syndicate and Giant Sand); drummer Russ Broussard (ex-Bluerunners and Terrance Simien); and multi-instrumentalist Robert Maché (ex–Steve Winn band, Lydia Lunch).

They came together after an initial merry-go-round approach to membership and, in 1994, recorded a self-titled CD released on New Orleans's Monkey Hill label and in Germany on Blue Rose. *Rolling Stone* called the Drifters one of the two best unsigned bands in the United States.

But despite these accolades and although the CD had its charms, it quickly faded. The band settled into a typical New Orleans–type torpor, working a variety of day jobs and performing a regular Tuesday night gig at Howlin' Wolf that turned into a residency famous for the band's easy, family-like vibe.

In 1999, the Drifters released their long-awaited second CD, *Vermilion*. Forged from a vaguely folky background, with joint lead vocals from Cowsill and Peterson or Holsapple, *Vermilion* sounds as if the Band, the Indigo Girls, and the Mamas and Papas got together for a game of Twister.

Finally, from Kentwood, Louisiana, there's **Britney Spears** (1981–), who will probably end up being the largest-selling Louisiana artist *ever*. Spears auditioned at the age of eight for a gig on the Disney Channel's new *Mickey Mouse Club* show. Though she was thought too young, the network brujos saw that she had talent and arranged for Spears to study at New York's prestigious Off Broadway Dance Center and the Professional Performing Arts School. When she turned eleven, she was awarded a spot on the *Mouse* show.

After two years as a Mouseketeer and working in commercials and in an off-Broadway show, Spears decided to move back to Louisiana and attend high school. After about a year, she returned to New York City. Eventually, Jive Records signed her to a contract and, in early 1999, released *. . . Baby One More Time*. By her sixteenth birthday, Spears had become the youngest artist in recording history to achieve Diamond status, which is what happens when someone sells ten million copies of an album. The album and its title cut reached #1 simultaneously.

Considering that Pink Floyd's *Dark Side of the Moon* spent 741 weeks on the *Billboard* charts and finally achieved Diamond status, that ought to present an idea of just how astonishing Spears's accomplishment is. The awards and honors just keep rolling in—too many to list here—and, as I write this, her second CD, *Oops! . . . I Did It Again*, and third CD, *Britney*, are carved into the charts like lettering on a tombstone.

Efforts to ask her whether she considers Professor Longhair a musical hero have not been successful.

VI

THE WONDROUS SOUNDS

One

THE MUSIC
OF VOODOO

*N*ew Orleans's Bywater district is located between the Faubourg
Marigny and the Mississippi River. Once known as one of those "you
don't wanna be there alone after dark" areas, the Bywater has in recent years
undergone the upsurge that neighborhoods typically experience when
young, poor, creative, and industrious folk invade a place and, beneath an
unconscious cloud of esprit de corps, settle in and set about cleaning it up.
Indeed, since about 1980, the same kind of thing has happened in the lower
Quarter and the Marigny, and the Bywater's facelift is encouraging. There
are now fine restaurants and nightclubs the denizens can call their own—
Vaughan's has become the regular Thursday night residence for Kermit
Ruffins and the Barbecue Swingers (see "Modern Jazz and the Disparate
Paths of Young Warriors," Part 1, Chapter 2). Of particular interest to us,
though, is the Island of Salvation, the Bywater's authentic voodoo shop.

On a hot September Saturday, Louisiana Black and I wander in with
our friend Tom Crosby so that I can speak with the proprietress, Sallie Ann
Glassman, an authentic and ordained voodoo priestess (Manbo) who happens to be from New Haven, Connecticut, home of Yale University and
very little voodoo. Don't kid yourself, though. Glassman is the real deal—
pick up her book *Vodou Visions*, out from Villard Press, if you want to
know about voodoo. She sits serenely behind a desk in the small shop,
which is fragrant with incense smoke and stuffed with various powders
and apothecary necessities, trinkets, idols, candles, and minutiae helpful to
the practitioner of voodoo.

I'm there to speak with Glassman about the music of the religion. The
original plan was for me to attend a voodoo ceremony and observe, among
other things, the music that is integral to the ritual. Glassman heads up the

ceremonies, and I was invited with her approval by an initiate, reverend Elissa Maistros (a.k.a. Scully Elly), a voodoo hounsi who operates the Voodoo Shop inside Louie's Juke Joint at 1128 Decatur in the French Quarter. (The Juke Joint, by the way, is a superb outlet for Louisiana music of all kinds.) Alas, one of the ritual drummers is ill and the evening gathering has been cancelled. Instead, I talk with the bird-like Glassman, whose blonde hair and Jewish ancestry don't fit the stereotype implied by Marie Laveau. However, stereotypes aren't what I'm after—authenticity is—and the music and drums regularly proffered at Glassman's ceremonies are just what you want to hear.

For all the hype, hunting down real voodoo and its music is not that easy. What I find, though, is that pockets of New Orleans and Louisiana voodoo do exist and are fine historical repositories of actual voodoo and voodoo-inspired music, even if the ritual drums and chants that regularly take place in Haitian voodoo ceremonies are scarce. While the music of such artists as Dr. John, Coco Robicheaux, Bo Dollis, and the Wild Magnolias Mardi Gras Indian Tribe (see "The Mardi Gras Indians and Carnival Tunes," Part 6, Chapter 3), certain cuts by the Neville Brothers, and the albums by the late Shreveport-born bluesman John Campbell are often rife with allusions to voodoo and the spiritual church, none of the work is representative of the music and rhythms one might hear at an authentic voodoo ceremony.

"I go to ritual once a week and music and drumming are very important," says Scully Elly. "We have drummers on three different drums—the papa, mama and baby. There is music for each of the different gods and a different rhythm to help invoke them; their rhythm is played and their song is theirs only."

It's important to understand that voodoo is essentially a religion based on communication with the spirits of ancestors. The most illuminating work on ceremonial voodoo is *Divine Horsemen: The Living Gods of Haiti*, written by Maya Deren, a Russian-Jewish filmmaker who died in 1961 and whose exploration into Haitian voodoo resulted not only in the *Horsemen*—probably the most myth-busting work published on the subject yet—but also Deren's own conversion to voodoo.

Through the influx of slaves from Haiti and Africa, voodoo entered New Orleans and Louisiana. Although the religion was outlawed and its practitioners were "converted" to Catholicism by frightened whites, the faith has persisted here and in rural parts of Louisiana in various strains that include certain rituals and saints from Catholicism. Offshoots include the spiritual churches that dot Orleans Parish and that were once particularly strong in the black community. In Haiti, voodoo is still a prominent faith.

In 1998, Lyrichord Discs released a CD of representative Haitian voodoo music called *Divine Horsemen: The Living Gods of Haiti*. But perhaps the finest collection, *Angels in the Mirror: Vodou Music of Haiti*, came out a year earlier from the Ellipsis Arts label. A beautifully and informatively packaged CD and booklet, *Angels in the Mirror* features thirteen tracks of field recordings of various songs, rhythms, and call-and-response chants applicable to a variety of rituals in a typical voodoo ceremony. The hypnotically rhythmic material relies not just on drums but on a variety of percussion instruments as well as flute—and, of course, singing and chanting.

"Singing is a tool we use to manipulate energy," says Mimerose Beaubrun, founder and lead singer of the Haitian voodoo pop group Boukman Eksperyans, in the liner notes to *Angels in the Mirror.* "It's a way of controlling the energy above, to be able to control the energy in yourself. . . . Singing is where you express your emotions. Singing is praying. It's the way you communicate with other forms of energy, because prayer means putting you in communication."

Though Boukman Eksperyans have released a variety of CDs in the United States, they are considered radical and revolutionary in their native land—"Boukman" is the name of the slave who initiated the island's 1804 independence uprising—and much of their work has been banned in Haiti. Using Creole dialect, voodoo ceremonial rhythms, rock instrumentation, and dance and costume, the band is remarkable and unique.

"In Haiti, everyday life is touched by religion," says Scully Elly, "and frequently that means voodoo. They have a saying that Haiti is 90 percent Catholic and 110 percent voodoo. So if you see someone walking down the road singing, it might be a song to Azaka, the god of the harvest. Even the songs by Boukman Eksperyans that don't sound like they're about voodoo, are. You have to remember that voodoo is everywhere there, and that even the songs of revolution were keyed across the island by voodoo rhythms."

In New Orleans, of course, the rhythms and songs were first heard by white audiences in Congo Square on Sundays when plantation owners allowed the slaves to gather there and celebrate (see "Spontaneous Combustion and the Birth of an Art Form," Part 1, Chapter 1). Ultimately these sounds influenced the development of jazz. The beats cross-pollinated with the military-style brass bands that cropped up late in the nineteenth century, resulting not only in the second-line parade rhythms but in the spirit of freedom inherent in jazz improvisation.

"Everyone is encouraged to sing along [during ritual]," says Scully Elly. "Many 'outsiders' find this hard to do since the songs are sung in Haitian Creole. The more people sing the more powerful the 'prayer' is." She explains that an initiate called an *Ounjenikon* leads the singing and is responsible, along with the drummers, for keeping the tempo and the order of the ritual correct. Typically, during a ceremony, there are at least five songs sung.

Bill Summers, percussionist for Los Hombres Calientes, has been an initiate in the voodoo religion since 1967. Though he didn't grow up in

New Orleans, his grandparents owned property here and Summers moved here some time back. He's not happy with the way America has corrupted the word "voodoo." "The only thing I've ever seen about voodoo in this country was on the Saturday night creature feature," he said. He is adamant about how positive the faith is and the purity of its music. "As a percussionist, I find the rhythms of the ceremonies and these special drums beautiful," he says. "There's a rhythm for everything. I can sing and play to herbs, for example. But not just anyone can play [the drums at the ceremonies]. In order to do so you have to have your drums consecrated and your hands baptized; without that there will be no visit from *Orisi* or *loa*. Without the music, you have no juice."

Mac Rebennack and his Dr. John persona (see "The Foundations and the Piano Giants," Part 2, Chapter 1), as exemplified on the 1967 album *Gris-Gris*, is probably the most successful of the contemporary artists who have used voodoo as inspiration. Who can forget Rebennack's original and heavily theatrical Dr. John character—based of course on the nineteenth-century conjure man and contemporary of Marie Laveau—who in Rebennack's guise came onstage in a hybrid of Mardi Gras Indian finery, various serpentine icons, and surrounded by props?

The idea of the Dr. John character had been percolating within Rebennack for some time. He'd been exposed to New Orleans' spiritual churches and various voodoo characters growing up. But it wasn't until he and his band were out in Los Angeles and ran into Harold Battiste, then heading up the talent on the Sonny and Cher show, that it all came together. Rebennack and his band of renegade New Orleanians recorded *Gris-Gris*—also discussed in the earlier chapter, a wonderfully creepy album that may not be anthropologically or spiritually accurate but sure *sounds* like voodoo—and Battiste wrangled a contract for them with Atlantic.

Even before he became Dr. John, Rebennack had sought approval from the New Orleans spiritual churches to record some of their music. As he recounts in *Under a Hoodoo Moon:* "One of the first of my serious contacts with the reverend mothers [who traditionally head up the New Orleans spiritual churches] happened a bit before I did the *Gris-Gris* album. I ran into Mother Shannon, a well-known reverend mother, and told her I wanted to cut some voodoo songs. She said, 'Oh, no, you can't do that.' Then I said, 'Well, how about if I just used the tune but changed the words?' and she gave me her okay."

He also describes the music of a "typical hoodoo" ceremony at the start of a ritual: "Sometime during the litany, someone would begin to chant and play sacred rhythm on broomsticks nailed with bottle caps, Coke bottles, pots, pans—anything available. A person or two might bring congas and start to build a rhythm. All these voices, congas, bottles, and pans would work together until a mesmerizing chant was laid down to help with the healing. The music was a way of getting into the spirit."

Dr. John went on to become a figurehead and partner in a *gris-gris* apothecary, the Dr. John Temple of Voodoo on St. Philip Street. He ran it as a business, but Dr. John was also thoroughly schooled in the theories and practices of the spiritual church during the shop's run.

Shreveport-born blues guitarist John Campbell, who died at the age of forty-one, was known as "The Hoodoo Man" (see also "Young Pups," Part 3, Chapter 2). Although his last album, *Howlin' Mercy*, bears no musical similarities to the ceremonial rhythms described by Scully Elly or Bill Summers, its blistering electric blues-rock contains plenty of references to voodoo accoutrements. His onstage persona and liner notes were also rife with such spirituality.

But, according to Campbell's close friend Barbara Hoover, host of WWOZ's *Planet Waves* blues show, the "hoodoo man" tag was mostly record-label hype. "He was called the hoodoo man," she says, "but to confine John's spirituality to a phrase like 'voodoo' or 'hoodoo' doesn't cover all of it. For sure, there were elements of that, but John surrounded himself with all things spiritual."

Also a fervent believer is the swampy bluesman Coco Robicheaux (also discussed in "Young Pups," Part 3, Chapter 2), though his music is considerably more optimistic. Each of his albums—*Spiritland*, *Louisiana Medicine Man*, and *Hoodoo Party*—are mightily infused with the anecdotes and allusions to voodoo. These days, Robicheaux, who was initiated years ago into the cult of *elegua*, a Santerian offshoot of voodoo, speaks eloquently of the ceremonies and music of his faith in that distinctive and folksy style. "Mostly, these days, I *am* now the ritual," he says. "I carry it within me. But there are a lot of different ceremonies and songs and rhythms. They're mainly to attract *loas* [the spirits who are gatekeepers to ancestors]. The music is stylized and the rhythms are all African-based."

So whether you listen to the Halloween-style frivolity of Bo Dollis and the Wild Magnolias's *1313 Hoodoo Street* (a collection of voodoo theme music, much like an early Beach Boys album that celebrates cars and surfing) and other voodoo-influenced blues and rock records, or attend an authentic ritual and learn first-hand how the *loas* are summoned through rhythm and song, you will find that the music inspired by voodoo is still wide-reaching in Louisiana.

Two

SWAMP POP

*I*t's perhaps too cruel to describe swamp pop as a tiny sonic helicopter that disappeared into the Bermuda Triangle of Music. For one thing, it hasn't disappeared, at least not entirely. Just this year a group called Lil' Band o' Gold—really a nine-member supergroup of Acadian musicians that includes seminal swamp poppers Warren Storm, Steve Riley, and David Greeley from the Mamou Playboys (see "Early Cajun and Creole Music," Part 4, Chapter 1), and country musician Richard Comeaux from River Road—released a great self-titled CD. It's not exactly swamp pop, but it's the closest thing out in a while.

Indeed, the very diversity of its musicians makes Lil' Band o' Gold a metaphor for the entire genre called *swamp pop*. Swamp pop evolved in the early-to-mid-fifties at a time when young folks in the twenty-two parish section of southwest Louisiana called Acadiana were itching to Americanize the French-speaking culture of their parents and grandparents. The swamp poppers infused traditional forms of Cajun and Creole with large doses of early and electrified rock 'n' roll and R&B, mingling the music of white and black cultures in the process. These emerging artists and songwriters expressed their musicality through the electric possibilities of amplified guitars and drum kits—and without some of the codgerly instrumental baggage implied by fiddle and accordion. Swamp pop musicians were also black *and* white artists who not only interacted with one another in a time and location not known for racial harmony but collaborated with each other and performed publicly together.

As it evolved over its short life span, swamp pop songs, in my interpretation, anyway, were either wonderful slow dances that mixed the "high school crush" anthems of Buddy Holly with the New Orleans R&B balladry of early Aaron Neville or Johnny Adams, or high-energy tunes whose sounds evoked the image of a rockabilly artist skiing down a mountain and colliding with a drunken Hank Williams. The songs rely on piano triplets and usually a battery of saxophone lines competing with electric guitar. As touched on earlier in the book, the ancestral elements of zydeco and Cajun music in swamp pop are always unmistakable; the purveyors of swamp pop couldn't have completely eradicated the genetic ties even if they'd tried.

In his terrific book *Swamp Pop: Cajun and Creole Rhythm and Blues*, Shane K. Bernard (whose father is swamp pop icon Rod Bernard) lists familiar songs in the swamp pop style. Although the artists are not by definition swamp poppists themselves, or even from Louisiana necessarily, just a few of these titles give you an idea of the genre: "Before the Next Teardrop Falls" by Freddie Fender, Phil Phillip's "Sea of Love," and Johnny Preston's "Running Bear."

Though swamp pop only lasted a few years—and by the way, the term *swamp pop* is credited to British journalist John Broven—there were several significant acts in the genre, and more than a few hit songs blasted out of Louisiana under the swamp pop banner.

Cookie & the Cupcakes made a name for itself in the 1950s with the genre's biggest hits. The "Cookie" is **Huey Thierry** (1936–), who was born near Roanoke, Louisiana. Heavily influenced by Fats Domino and Hank Williams—as defining a set of bookends as swamp pop could want—Thierry wanted to sing and joined a band called the Boogie Ramblers, anchored by keyboardist and trumpeter Ernest Jacobs. Thierry's voice revitalized the club band, which was soon rechristened Cookie & the Cupcakes. In 1955, they released a single, "Cindy Lou," on Goldband Records, one of several local labels—Carl, Jin, Hallway, Arbee, and La Louisianne among them—noted for their swamp pop artists. A few years later, they hit the Shot Heard Round the World of swamp pop when they recorded a self-penned ballad called "Mathilda," which went to #47 in *Billboard*.

Other hits included "Betty and Dupree," "Got You On My Mind," and "I'm Twisted," but the band's subsequent singles did less and less well. In the mid-sixties, Thierry left the band and went to Los Angeles, where he was literally missing in action for several years. He eventually resurfaced to lead another version of the Cupcakes in the early nineties, though their viability in any sort of national marketplace is questionable.

King Karl (1931–), born Bernard Jolivette in Grand Coteau, Louisiana, and **Guitar Gable** (1937–), born Gabriel Perrodin Sr. in Bellevue, Louisiana, are two more Creole kingpins of swamp pop, both as writers and performers; unfortunately Gable is perhaps best (or most recently) remembered as being the longtime victim of an imposter who toured extensively using his name.

In any case, Karl, a singer and saxophonist, grew up writing songs while he worked day jobs for a veterinarian. Gable taught himself guitar at the age of twelve, and both were more influenced by blues artists than any zydeco happening at the time. After they met and formed Guitar Gable and the Musical Kings Featuring King Karl, they found a surprising amount of work playing original material, mostly composed by Karl.

A single, "Congo Mombo," produced by Jay Miller and leased to the Excello label, broke big. Two more of Karl's songs, "This Should Go On Forever" and "Irene," both did well, the latter for Karl and Gable and the former for Rod Bernard, a white swampster who collaborated frequently with Karl. The band continued to perform off and on before calling it quits in the late sixties. Both Karl and Gable are now retired and have children busy as Louisiana musicians.

Guitarist and vocalist **Rod Bernard** (1940–) was born in Opelousas, and worked as a teen deejay on various radio stations and in a country band called the Blue Room Gang. After meeting Texas record honcho Huey Meaux, Bernard started recording his own material. He formed a band called the Twisters, who covered Karl's song "This Should Go On Forever," which was not only one of the first swamp pop songs, it also slowly gained momentum and went Top 20. The success led to Bernard's appearance on *American Bandstand* and a short-lived deal with Mercury Records. When that didn't pan out (the label ultimately only released four of the over forty sides Bernard recorded), he formed the Shondells—no, not the Tommy James version—with fellow swampos Warren Storm and Skip Stewart. They enjoyed some regional popularity, but Bernard never equaled the original success of "This Should Go On Forever."

Bernard's pal **Warren Storm** (1937–) was similarly successful. Known—possibly at his own encouragement—as the Godfather of Swamp Pop, he was born Warren Schexnider in Abbeville, Louisiana, and started out when he was twelve playing drums in his father's band. Through high school he played in a variety of country bands, became a top regional session player, and signed a deal as a singer when he was eighteen. His first single, for the Nasco label, was called "The Prisoner's Song," which sold a quarter-million copies.

He followed with several singles for local labels, played with Bernard in the Shondells, and, after swamp pop died out, stayed busy in a variety of musical projects including the band Cypress (with Willie Tee). Since the mid-eighties, he's sporadically released a few albums, including *Heart and Soul* and *Warren Storm Live and in the Studio*.

Johnnie Allan (1938–) was born near Rayne, Louisiana, and has enjoyed a life in music. He worked his way through a variety of Cajun bands in his youth. When rock 'n' roll reared its head, he started the band Krazy Kats, whose debut single, "Lonely Days, Lonely Nights," came out on the

MGM label. He released numerous singles and albums during the swamp pop years, and has gone on to work with artists ranging from Joe Cocker and Van Morrison to Gloria Gaynor and T. Graham Brown. In 1981, Allen produced the first Swamp Pop Music All-Star Show—for all practical purposes, the first reunion of the giants of the form. In 1995, his swamp-poppy arrangement of Chuck Berry's "Promised Land" went gold. A retired schoolteacher and principal, Allen has also written and self-published three books on music and musicians in southern Louisiana.

It's probably safe to assume that **Tommy McLain** (1940–) is the only swamp popper to have released a CD called *Cajun Rod Stewart* (1999, Crazy Cajun Recordings), though one supposes that, should he ever record an album of Louisiana music, Rod Stewart could do it. In any case, McLain, who was born in Jonesville, Louisiana, had a substantial swamp-pop hit with "Sweet Dreams" (#15 in *Billboard*) in the 1960s. An admittedly curious figure with a Herman Melville beard, McLain scored another hit with fellow swampist Clint West on "To Find Another Man," and continues to work regularly. He's played in the Boogie Kings and with his own Mule Train Band.

Gene Terry (1940–) brought a big-band sense to swamp pop, though certainly not by any Benny Goodman definition. He did use a larger-than-average horn section, an addition to the concept that worked in clever ways. Born Terry Gene DeRouen in Lafayette, the singer grew up in Port Arthur, Texas, and with his band, the Down Beats, made swamp-pop magic with a strutting single called "Cindy Lou." Terry recorded numerous singles for the Goldband label, but never equaled the success of "Cindy Lou." Nonetheless, he and the Down Beats remained a live entity to be reckoned with for years.

One of the Down Beats's big rivals, chiefly because of their incendiary live shows, were **The Boogie Kings.** The band was formed as a trio in Eunice, Louisiana, in 1956. Douglas Ardoin, Harris Miller, and Bert Miller were three white kids who played exclusively black music, a move which was, for the time, pretty gutsy. The group would eventually evolve into a raucous swamp-pop outfit whose ranks swelled periodically, peaking at twelve members. Though they were part of the swamp-pop movement and deserve mention here, it was probably after swamp pop faded in the mid-sixties, and trumpeter Ned Theall took over, that they reached the height of their popularity as a rockin' showband.

Still, they never forgot their roots. In the mid-nineties, the Boogie Kings headed up a swamp pop tribute CD that featured guest vocalists from the genre's golden years.

Joseph Barrios was born in Cut Off, Louisiana, and came to music with the help of cousin Vin Bruce. Under the stage name **Joe Barry** (1939–), he achieved notoriety for being what might be described as the

Keith Moon of swamp pop. His memorable material was heavy on heart-felt ballads, yet his offstage habits—file under "massive and eternal party"—perhaps defined him more than his music did. Still, his self-penned "I Got a Feeling" scored a record deal. It also served as a B side to Barry's version of "I'm a Fool to Care," which Huey Meaux leased to Mercury Records, reportedly selling over a million copies worldwide. Subsequent tunes on the Jin and Smash labels, "Teardrops in My Heart" and "You Don't Have to Be a Baby to Cry," did well enough in all demographics that Barry recorded for a time as Roosevelt Jones—the better to appeal to a black audience that might not dig his crossover style if they knew he was a white guy.

By the late sixties, fed up with the business, Barry quit. He returned to record some country singles for Nugget in the seventies, quit his intoxicant-driven lifestyle, turned to religion, and even recorded a gospel album; unfortunately, he encountered a Job-like run of bad luck and ill health that plagued a comeback attempt. For all the ups and downs, Barry's work is truly extraordinary—he was one of the terrific true talents of the swamp-pop genre.

Other swamp-pop artists you should be aware of include: **Lil' Bob & the Lolipops,** forever immortal for their call-to-party anthem "I Got Loaded," still a Mardi Gras fave; **Clint West** (1938–), who played in the Boogie Kings and eventually as the solo artist who released such swamp-pop hits as "Big Blue Diamonds" and "Mr. Jeweler"; **Randy & the Rockets,** a band headed up by Randy Davis and remembered for two songs: the ballad "Genevieve" and "The Cajun Twist"; **T. K. Hulin,** the St. Martinville kid who recorded "I'm Not a Fool Anymore" and one of the greatest tearjerk titles of all time, "As You Pass Me By (Graduation Night)." Also notable are **Rufus Jagneaux,** a latter-day swamp-pop band described by author Shane Bernard as a "Cajun hippie" outfit. Led by Benny Graeff, the band further added to the chemistry of the swamp-pop formula by tossing in the influences of early sixties British rock bands. It is ironic that when certain echoes of swamp pop hit it big in the United States, they were recorded not by indigenous artists but by rockers such as the Rolling Stones and, later, Robert Plant, who had listened favorably to swamp pop. A final note: A pair of Louisiana artists who cranked out great swamp pop were Bobby Charles and Jimmy Clanton. But since each made a larger splash in rock and R&B, they're covered elsewhere in this book (see "The Indigenous Sound," Part 5, Chapter 1).

Three

THE MARDI GRAS INDIANS AND CARNIVAL TUNES

*T*onight Louisiana Black and I are staying in the rear apartment of a home owned by friends in the Lower Garden District. Technically, I guess, it's located in Central City, but "Central City" doesn't have that Anne Rice ring to it. The house is a lovely Greek-columned National Registry place but, with many of the neighborhoods and streets of New Orleans, its location is iffy: You can travel one block and go from historical luxury to war zone.

In this case, we're within vomiting distance of the H&R Bar, the home-turf drinking and rehearsal spot of the Wild Magnolias, one of the more prominent of the Mardi Gras Indian tribes. Although it's September, and traditionally the Indians don't start practicing for Fat Tuesday until October or even Thanksgiving, the Wild Magnolias have a higher public profile than most tribes, thanks to a series of recordings and musical performances they've done that mix the Indian chants with N'Awlins R&B. As such, their rehearsals are more of a year-round proposition.

To the uninitiated, Mardi Gras Indians (also see "Singers and Hitmakers," Part 2, Chapter 2) are a trip. They're basically social clubs, of sorts, based in New Orleans' black community, each comprised of men from one neighborhood, who mask—that is, they make and don glorious and elaborate feather and bead costumes complete with headdresses, then set out on meandering parades through the city, but only three times a year: Mardi Gras Day, St. Joseph's Night (March 19), and, most recently, at JazzFest (late April–early May). They're joined on these marches by brass bands and social aid and pleasure clubs. Thousands of citizens who will never attend a

Mardi Gras ball come out of their houses on Mardi Gras Day, awaiting that first glimpse of the resplendent Indians.

Since we're in the neighborhood for a few days, Louisiana Black and I figure we'll drop by the H&R Bar and say hello; I've read more than one article about journalists who hang out there during the Indian rehearsals. But that idea is punished immediately. We are sitting in his car, the bright red Firebird, dressed in T-shirts and wearing sunglasses with trapezoid-shaped lenses, our elbows jutting out the open windows, and, with our scrubbed faces and short hair, we aren't the typical H&R customer. So, as we're cruising slowly down the pockmarked side street towards the bar—in an area where several black males of varying ages are drinking from tall cans, their brewery logos masked by paper bags, and standing on the corners or sitting on stoops in front of rotting buildings—we aren't really surprised when one of the fellows looks at us, spits disdainfully, and says loudly and with a touch of strident resignation, "Here comes the police again."

They think we're undercover cops! Hell, we probably *do* resemble undercover cops, a realization that makes us laugh; that is, until we reach the bar and find it locked up. This means we'll have to come back—and the only thing worse than being mistaken once for policemen, by people who don't *like* policemen, is to do it again. For some reason, though, the H&R, which has a huge banner proudly proclaiming it as the home of the Wild Magnolias Mardi Gras Indian Tribe, is closed for the duration of our stay, our personal symbol of futility. Each day we get in the Starsky-and-Hutch-mobile and set off down the street to the baleful glare of the locals, any one of whom invariably mutters, "Mothafuckin' po-lice" just loud enough for us to hear. Confirming that the bar is still closed, we head out to friendlier climes in search of the Indians.

Eventually, we learn that each tribe consists of the Big Chief, who gives the orders, leads the chants, and ultimately decides whether to confront another tribe; as many as three Spy Boys, whose job it is to scout for rival organizations; three Flag Boys, who in turn carry banners and signal the warriors as to the Chief's intentions; an assortment of Trail Chiefs; and Wild Men, who make up the rank and file.

When a tribe encounters another tribe, a "confrontation" might take place involving various rituals, not the least of which is based on sartorial finery. The Indians are instantly identifiable by their intricately beaded and feathered costumes—each tribe's leader, the Big Chief, looks astonishing in his peacock-like, larger-than-life headdress—as well as by their respective dances, second-line-flavored percussion, and chants of decades-old carnival and street patois and newly minted improvisations. Some of the more nationally familiar of these calls and phrases include "Mighty Kootifyo" (the traditional call of the Big Chiefs); "Jocomo fee na nay" (which you'd know from the tune "Iko Iko" [see "Singers and Hitmakers," Part 2, Chapter 2]; it is a phrase that dates back to earlier battles between Mardi Gras Indian tribes, and translates roughly as "Get the fuck out of the way"); and "Hey Pocky A-Way" (see also "Rhythm & Blues," Part 2, Chapter 2), a song title theoretically derived from the Indian chant "Too Way Pocka Way," which in turn may be a twist on the Creole French idiom *Toi Pas Kwe,* "You can't believe that."

Maybe the most famous Mardi Gras Indian tribe of all time is the **Wild Tchoupitoulas** (recently risen from the dead), a group at one time headed up by the late George "Big Chief Jolly" Landry (see also "Singers and Hit-makers," Part 2, Chapter 2), a former professional dancer who happened to be an uncle of Art, Aaron, Charles, and Cyril Neville. As the force behind the formation of the Neville Brothers, Chief Jolly gathered the boys—then mostly in the Meters—to provide musical backing for Indian chants, thus getting his now-famous nephews recorded together for the first time. The subsequent album, *The Wild Tchoupitoulas,* originally released in 1976 on Island Records (and also discussed in greater detail in the R&B section), remains extremely important—bringing the Mardi Gras Indians to an international audience.

The Wild Tchoupitoulas wasn't the first co-mingling of the Indians and rhythm & blues, though. A few years earlier, the **Wild Magnolias,** fronted by Big Chief Bo Dollis, hooked up with the Souls, a band formed by R&B musician Wilson "Willie Tee" Turbinton, and recorded the song "Handa Wanda." The genesis of the project came when Quint Davis, honcho of the New Orleans Jazz & Heritage Festival, was standing backstage at the Tulane Jazz Festival while the Souls were setting up. Out front, Indian groups the Wild Magnolias and the Golden Eagles were performing. Behind the curtain, members of the Souls started to jam along quietly—and Davis jumped on the sound.

Turbinton and company went into the studio with the Wild Magnolias to record the Polydor album called *The Wild Magnolias.* A year later, a second album was recorded, this one featuring a Willie T composition called "New Suit," a tribute to the Indian tradition that requires each of the painstakingly created (and expensive) Mardi Gras suits be retired at the end of each year. Since then, the Wild Magnolias have regularly incorporated a band into their ranks, at least for purposes of nightclub performances, and have recorded several more albums: *I'm Back at Carnival Time, World Wide Hoodoo, 1313 Hoodoo Street,* and *Life Is a Carnival* (produced by Cyril Neville and featuring guest performances from Robbie Robertson and Bruce Hornsby). Worth noting is guitarist June Yamagishi, because he's such a bad-ass player. Also included in the band is Big Chief Monk Boudreaux of the **Golden Eagles Tribe**—the same one that shared the stage at the seminal Tulane festival. The Golden Eagles also share the H&R Bar with the Wild Magnolias; the two groups are friendly, though occasionally tension has come between the strutting chiefs. The albums of the

Golden Eagles include *Lightning & Thunder*, which avoids the live-band backing and relies solely on the chants and Indian-generated percussion.

The Wild Magnolias, the Wild Tchoupitoulas, and the Golden Eagles are just three of this unique fraternity. Tribes past and present include, in no particular chronology or order: Red, White & Blue Indians, Golden Arrows, Comanche Hunters, Young Hunters, Seminole Warriors, Bayou Renegades, Ninth Ward Hunters, Mohawk Hunters, Carrollton Hunters, Creole Wild West, White Cloud Hunters, Golden Star Hunters, Black Eagles, Young Cheyennes, Creole Osceolas, Mandingo Warriors, and Guardians of the Flame. The Native American association isn't just a catchy contrivance. New Orleans blacks have always felt a strong affinity for Indians, perhaps because both their cultures were trampled and plundered by marauding white folk. The best description I've ever read of the essence and mission of Mardi Gras Indians is from the pen of John Sinclair, the WWOZ disc jockey, poet, historian, and musician. In 1998, he wrote an article called "Out After Dark with the Wild Indians," which can—and should be—accessed at the *www.wwoz.org* Web site.

> New Orleans tribes are living manifestations of an age-old ritual, preserved and practiced by the descendants of African slaves held captive in America. Their traditions go back to the perambulating societies of West Africa, to their call-and-response chants, and to their secret societies of masked warriors which are common to both African and Native American cultures.
>
> It's a ritual that continues to live in the mean streets of 21st-century New Orleans and in the hearts of the people of the most run down, destitute, stripped-bare-and-left-for-dead underclass neighborhoods of the city. This is where the Wild Indians of Mardi Gras perennially represent the triumph of spirit, creativity, and beauty of song and dance over every obstacle placed in their arduous path.

That's inspired rhetoric, and it's true—though it doesn't get into the early years, when the battles between Indian tribes were often violent and bloody skirmishes that left not only Indians but also observers killed or wounded. George Porter Jr., bassist for the Funky Meters and Runnin' Pardners, told me, "When we were children, it wasn't very safe to be at the Indian parade routes. My parents wouldn't let me go out on St. Joseph's night because there were bodies on the ground. It wasn't so much the Indians or the second liners, though they could get violent, but the people on the streets. Music and alcohol and too much fun . . . It's a lot better today than it was thirty years ago."

Some reports say the Mardi Gras Indians date all the way back to the late eighteenth century, but most certainly the first tribe, the Yellow Pocahontas, formed in New Orleans's Seventh Ward in 1883 and was headed up by Bacate Batiste. The groups are traditionally male and black, though a woman named Barbara Sparks was the Big Queen of the Yellow Jackets. Maurice M. Martinez, a professor at the University of North Carolina who produced and directed *The Black Indians of New Orleans*, a 1976 documentary about the tribes, suggests they evolved in three ways: 1) through genetic and intercultural intermarriage between blacks and Native Americans; 2) because, for years, Mardi Gras Day was the least restrictive opportunity for those groups to express their cultures; and 3) using the masks from the African diaspora, the Indians were presenting images and icons they felt would best appease the whites in power.

Over the years, the rituals and nuances have developed. The brotherhood of the tribes is symbolized by the annual color schemes and the year-long labor of making the costumes, kept secret until their debut on Mardi Gras morning. Typical gewgaws on the hand-sewn outfit are sequins, glass beads, velvet, rhinestones, lace, ribbons, and maribou. The headdresses—or crowns—are elaborately festooned with colored turkey or ostrich feathers that cost as much as $200 a pound.

That the costumes are extraordinarily heavy and hot goes without saying, but until you've watched one of the tribes march through the fairgrounds at JazzFest in the cruel heat of early May, it's hard to imagine the will and dedication required to parade with a tribe.

Other things you might want to know about the Mardi Gras Indians and their music:

1. The late Big Chief Donald Harrison of the Guardians of the Flame was the father of New Orleans modern jazz alto saxophonist Donald Harrison Jr. Father and son decided to collaborate on a project featuring the music of the tribe; the resultant album, *Indian Blue*, was a wonderful creation. "That was the project where I realized that swing music could actually incorporate the music of the Mardi Gras Indians," Harrison Jr. told me. "I mean, I knew it had been done with R&B, but what we laid down, I thought, 'Man, Art Blakey could do this.'"

2. "Brother John," a standout tune for both the Neville Brothers and the Wild Tchoupitoulas, was written by Cyril Neville about John "Scarface" Williams, who not only sang with Huey "Piano" Smith & the Clowns but was a Mardi Gras Indian. The tune is based on Williams's mythic life and death; he was stabbed outside a bar at the corner of Rampart and St. Andrews.

3. A Big Chief is the equivalent of royalty: He's the Big Chief until he dies or abdicates the throne.

As long as we're discussing the Mardi Gras Indians, it's probably not a bad idea to list a few of the other best Carnival songs:

✦ "Wild Injuns" by the Neville Brothers, off the *Yellow Moon* CD. Utterly infectious and more contemporary than most of the R&B chestnuts.

✦ "Mardi Gras Mambo" by the Hawkettes. The most famous version is the original, by Art Neville's first big-time band.

✦ "Go to the Mardi Gras" by Professor Longhair. Everywhere else on earth, beginning piano students learn "Chopsticks." In Louisiana they learn "Go to the Mardi Gras." But you gotta be able to whistle.

✦ "Who Shot the La-La" by Oliver Morgan. A contrary rumor is that Prince La La, the R&B star, composed this tune, but Morgan has so convincingly explained the tune's origins and his creative process that most accept it as his.

✦ "Don't You Just Know It" by Huey "Piano" Smith.

✦ "Carnival Time" by Al Johnson. Influenced by Professor Longhair's "Go to the Mardi Gras," Johnson says he wrote the song because the word "carnival" hadn't been used and it sounded cool.

Postscript: I have seen Bo Dollis and Monk Boudreaux and the Wild Magnolias in the flesh. They were booked at the Funky Butt during Mardi Gras of 2000. They were two hours late, a common problem during peak party times in New Orleans, and especially disappointing for tourists like me, who have mapped out a grid of shows we want to see but who will be out of luck unless the performers start on time. By the time they came on-stage, I was supremely irritated and uncomfortable. Fitting all the Wild Magnolias, their band and krewe into the cramped and already crowded up-stairs staging area was an unacceptable experiment in physical geometry—rather like John Holmes trying to fit into a pair of Kathy Rigby's panties.

So after twenty feedback-drenched minutes, I hauled ass and got a Lucky Dog.

Four

GOSPEL AND
RELIGIOUS MUSIC

*B*aylor University in Waco, Texas, is the largest private Baptist university in the world, and anyone who knows me even slightly isn't at all surprised to discover that I flunked out—particularly when they hear the required curriculum of courses on religion. Of course, these same people are pretty amazed that I went there in the first place—voluntarily, too— but that's another story.

In any case, in light of my historic screw-ups there, and given our history of debauchery together, it seems incongruous that Dr. Larry (my dog's veterinarian and my frequent pal in the pursuit of fun) and I are standing in the *Gospel* Tent at JazzFest in New Orleans. Yet we are, and I anticipate soaking up the very music that I used to rebel against when it was force-fed to me at what William Blake might've called Baylor's "green and pleasant land." But I've happily found that the music wafting from the tent is not the same at all. The wondrous panorama unfolding before us differs from the southern or country gospel I grew up with. This is black gospel and it's a lot more fun than the other.

The Gospel Tent is geographically if not spiritually separated from the main circuit of activity, so you have to leave the broad circumference of stages, food booths, and beer and T-shirt stands and seek it out. The Dynamic Smooth Family of Slidell is onstage in all their groove-fueled glory. It's a full-scale production, and no matter which hymn they're pouring out, it sounds as though God hired James Brown to arrange and choreograph the performance. This is decidedly *not* a Baylor-styled church setting—if we'd had this sort of stuff in Waco, I would have graduated with an advanced degree in divinity. Looking around, I see plenty of church folk peppering the SRO tent, but the fervent believers here are happily sharing the space with a crowd of secular JazzFest fans. So it's typical that a large older woman attired in Sunday finery (despite the muggy heat) and carrying a Bible is sandwiched between Dr. L and a Yankee couple clad in cut-offs and Pittsburgh Steelers jerseys.

"These guys could blow the Neville Brothers off the stage!" Dr. Larry shouts. They *do* rock, and I think about telling Dr. Larry about the New Zion Trio + One, the original triumvirate with whom Aaron Neville started singing gospel. Aaron shows up every year in the gospel tent to sing with them—which accounts for the curious "+ one" title. Onstage is a sky-high soprano, a Jaco Pastorius–styled player on bass, a set of bleachers with a six-piece backing male choir, and a matronly tambourinist wielding the instrument as though it were her own private flying saucer to heaven. In the crowd, all of us, church members or otherwise, are going absolutely nuts, dancing with one another, toasting with beer cans and lemonade, shrieking. The roof-blowing funk of the music hammers home the sheer release of gospel, providing as it did a sort of primal therapy years before Arthur Janov conducted John Lennon and Yoko Ono in his shriek-and-feel-all-better therapy.

"Gospel" is a phrase coined in 1920 by Georgia composer and pianist Thomas Dorsey to describe a new kind of songwriting. He'd just penned his first religious tune, "If You See My Savior," and when he started a company to keep track of the publishing rights for such material he attached the name to the form.

Gospel was stylistically born out of the music sung or chanted by black slaves toiling in the fields of the Confederacy. While it's probably true that some of the material was from Africa and adapted, other songs evolved in the fields and were passed down over time. Further indignities were heaped on the slaves when they were forced to attend Protestant church services conducted by white preachers. By melding the Protestant hymns with spirituals—blues-based songs expressing frustration and pain—and incorporating the African rhythms and emotional field hollers, gospel music came into being. The writer Eileen Southern, in her book *The Music of Black Americans: A History*, suggests: "The slave repertory of the nineteenth century includes many variations on the theme. . . . One spiritual, 'In That Great Getting-Up Morning,' is a song of almost epic proportions" and probably served as a creative and thematic beginning for the gospel repertoire.

Like everything else at that point, gospel music broke down along racial lines; white folks sang what came to be called "country" or "southern" gospel and black people sang "black gospel." It was *all* southern, but black gospel took on decidedly individual characteristics that were first compositionally defined in Thomas Dorsey's song "Precious Lord, Take My Hand": music with big arrangements, usually featuring a big choir and significant audience participation. It might be said that, in the performance of black spirituals or gospel, there are no nonparticipants—only singers and nonsingers. In addition to the swaying and clapping in time, there's a lot of impromptu shouting from the "audience" members, who call out in a sort of response born of the inspiration of the moment and the music. The range of the performances has also expanded from simple piano or keyboard accompaniment for one solo singer or a quartet to full-blown choirs and electric bands, and the level of improvisation and audience participation is high indeed.

As in any style of music, trends in gospel music shift and respond in cycles. There was a period where quartets and four-part harmonies ruled. That's not so true anymore; the Kirk Franklin–esque, full-blown production that reminds one of Prince if he formed the New Jesus Generation seems to be hip today.

Without question, though, the Louisiana gospel identity both past and present was developed in no small part by a New Orleans–born singer named **Mahalia Jackson** (1911–1972). Growing up in poverty, Jackson started singing at the age of four at Plymouth Baptist Church and went on to become the greatest gospel singer of all time. Growing up in a sanctified church, and in an area fairly drenched in blues—Bessie Smith and Ma Rainey were favorites—Jackson moved to Chicago when she was sixteen; there, she was inspired by the eminent Mississippi gospel singer Willie Mae Ford Smith. During her early years in Chicago, she worked as a domestic. She supplemented her income by singing solo at funerals and in churches, then touring for five years with the gospel pioneer (and her mentor) Thomas A. Dorsey, with whom she began a lifelong musical and business association.

In 1934, Jackson recorded her first song, "God Shall Wipe Away All Tears." But it was "Move On Up a Little Higher," released on the Apollo label, that sold an astonishing eight million copies. The song made her a household name in a field clouded with obscurity.

"I loved Mahalia Jackson," Irma Thomas told me. "I grew up listening to that lady. I didn't get to know her, but she was a trailblazer who opened a lot of doors—not just for gospel singers but for black artists in general."

After the success of "Move On Up a Little Higher," Jackson was known nationwide as the Gospel Queen. Much was made about her status as a black artist who rose to fame largely—at first, anyway—through the support of black citizenry. And she ran with it. She could sing beautifully and moved many to tears with the crystalline simplicity of a melody—or she could transform a hymn into a blues-shoutin' work of frenzy. Her voice was undeniably forceful (I don't doubt that she could've shattered a concrete wall had she so desired), but her precise technique and sense of dynamics were profound. Such was her stage persona and personal magnetism that she was able to parlay her supreme spirituality into something enjoyed by the masses; in this way, she did quite a bit of the Lord's work for her people during a cultural revolution.

With her own national radio and television programs, massive real estate holdings, and several private business ownerships, Jackson emerged as an icon who represented true influence and provided ample opportunity for blacks. She was a significant force in the civil rights movement of the fifties and sixties, and it's not unrealistic to say that she was a precursor to Dr. Martin Luther King in drawing public awareness to the unjust racial situation of the times. King requested that she sing directly before his "I have a dream" speech; she also sang at the inaugurations of President Eisenhower and President Kennedy. Jackson's motto was "Don't let the devil steal the beat from the Lord," and it's an appropriately aggressive statement for a woman whose sincere devotion did not preclude an unwillingness to take any shit.

During her career, Jackson recorded about thirty albums, chiefly for Decca and Columbia, and several singles, many of them gold records in an era before there was the platinum designation. Of them, a nice sampling would include *In the Upper Room* and *Gospels, Spirituals & Hymns.* I also recommend her autobiography, called *Movin' On Up.* And if you've never seen the film *Imitation of Life* or the documentary *Jazz on a Summer Day,* do so at once.

Jackson is undeniably the greatest gospel artist ever, but it's true that Louisiana is full of talented spiritual singers, white and black. New Orleans in particular has a huge gospel music base. The music is of a distinct black gospel demographic, not particularly different from the gospel one would find throughout the South in churches from Memphis to Texas. But, as always, that decided and innate New Orleans rhythm creeps into the music and gives it just that extra bit of flavor.

Among Jackson's contemporaries were two other singers. **"Sweet" Emma Barrett** (1897–1983) was another Louisiana artist who established a blues and jazz presence in New Orleans. Her name is synonymous with the French Quarter's famous Preservation Hall jazz room. **Bessie Griffin** (1922–1988) could sing just like Jackson (and frequently amazed people as a child by doing just that). Born in New Orleans, she left the city at a young age to pursue better opportunities in less racially tense environs. Her first brushes with fame came as a member of the Southern Harps and later, the Caravans. Finally, she recorded her first solo effort, Thomas A. Dorsey's "Someday Somewhere" in 1948. In the fifties she signed with the prestigious Specialty gospel label and worked with Professor Alex Bradford, the noted gospel composer.

Griffin hooked up with **The Gospel Pearls,** with whom she was recorded for the fine Epic/Legacy album, *Live at "The Bear" in Chicago.* As on the collection *Even Me,* Griffin's voice is overpoweringly strong and beautiful; she sounds like an angel who could blow Satan's minions out of the sky at a skeet shoot.

Though she came to religious music fairly late in a remarkable life, **Mable John** (1930–), born in Bastrop, Louisiana, and raised in Arkansas and Detroit, was known as a talented blues and R&B singer. She released several records for Stax and Tamla, but her church singing brought her to the attention of Motown honcho Barry Gordy. The first female artist assigned to the label, John started recording blues at the end of the fifties, just as the soul explosion was about to take place—miserable timing, but John continued to cut solid and underappreciated R&B before retiring from secular music and devoting her voice and work to Christianity. Few recordings of her religious work are available, but she was happiest in the gospel context. Based on secular material such as "Your Good Thing Is About to End," it's a solid bet that John could shiver the walls in any church in which she opened her mouth to wail.

Of the male post-Mahalia solo artists, a few have grabbed national attention. **Raymond Anthony Myles** (1957–1998) is probably chief among them, though, tragically, his renown may stem in part from his murder by a carjacker.

Not that he wasn't already famous. Born in New Orleans, Myles grew up in the St. Thomas housing project and, because he was a remarkable singer even as a child, he entertained in area churches as part of a mother-son act called Christine Myles and Son. Following a straight gospel path despite an Al Green–Little Richard voice that would probably have guaranteed him a great career as an R&B star, Myles was aware of the power of the spiritual and the secular. When he was twelve, he sang at the funeral of Mahalia Jackson. He followed with a recording called "Prayer from a Twelve-Year-Old Boy," a paean to peace at the height of the Vietnam War and fresh after the assassinations of Martin Luther King Jr. and Robert Kennedy. The flip side, though, was the precociously sensual "You Made a Man Out of Me, Baby," which caused a significant uproar in the kid's local church schedule.

But Myles didn't slow down or look back. His career as a gospel star blossomed with frightening speed and intensity; by adulthood he'd recorded several albums and toured with Shirley Caesar, Andre Crouch, the Mighty Clouds of Joy, and the Reverend Al Green. With his choir, named RAMS, Myles split his time between recording his own tunes ("Jesus Is the Baddest Man in Town") and creating all manners of rockin' arrangements of traditional material. Onstage, influenced by in-concert powerhouses Ray Charles, Donnie Hathaway, and Aretha Franklin, Myles was an awesome act to follow. It's true that he was planning on recording a CD of message–R&B and secular soul balladry at the time he was killed, but his roots deep within the church were never in doubt. Suggested albums from his repertoire include *Heaven Is the Place* and *A Taste of Heaven*.

If Myles represented a true bright spot for the future of Louisiana gospel, **Bishop Paul S. Morton Sr.** (1950–) is helping to bear Myles's torch.

Born in Ontario, Canada, he followed a call to the ministry in 1967 and eventually became pastor at the Greater St. Stephen Missionary Baptist Church in New Orleans. In addition to expanding the membership of the church from 600 to over 18,000, writing numerous books, and heading up radio and television evangelism, Morton is also a successful gospel recording star. On his own and backed by the church's Mass Choir, Morton has recorded five CDs for the Gospocentric label, including *Crescent City Fire, The Sun Will Shine After a While,* and *Jesus, When Troubles Burden Me Down.* Working a slick, millennial funk sound, Morton sounds a bit like Doobie Brother Michael McDonald, and most of the women I know would tell you this is a wonderful thing.

Several quartet-styled harmony groups are worth noting in the Louisiana gospel canon, and the **New Zion Harmonizers** are one of the best. Formed with some of his teenage pals in 1939 by **Benjamin Maxon,** who was a nephew of and inspired by Alberta French Johnson, lead singer of the famed, golden-age female gospel group the Southern Harps, the Harmonizers learned traditional four-part harmony as an after-school exercise, and have since maintained a reputation as one of the finest quartet harmony groups in the world.

One of the early leaders of the Harmonizers was **Sherman Washington,** whom Maxon met while the two worked at the shipyards together. After early tours opening for the Southern Harps, the Harmonizers earned their own headlining status and, after Maxon quit the group to preach, started to tour internationally. Starting in the mid-fifties, the New Zion Harmonizers began to record for Booker, Avant, and Gotham labels (some of those now-rare offerings can be found on the *Gospel Heritage* collections out of England).

In 1969, the Zion Harmonizers made their first appearance at the New Orleans Jazz & Heritage Festival; Washington was subsequently placed in charge of the new Gospel Tent. They continued to record through the seventies and eighties—for such small but prestigious outfits as Flying Fish—and have in the last two decades released a series of traditional but forward-looking works of close quartet harmony. Maintaining a high profile in the New Orleans church community, the group is still sought after on the festival circuit. I suggest you buy *The Best of New Orleans Gospel,* crank up "Jesus Walked the Mighty Water" or "He That Believes," and languish happily in the full-force of their joy-inducing vocal blend.

The **New Orleans Spiritualettes,** formed by **Mrs. Ruby Ray** after she moved to the city from her native Mississippi, are devoted to the old-school delivery of classic gospel music in the tradition of pure, distilled harmony. They are a sort of house band at St. Thomas Baptist Church in New Orleans, and it's interesting to note that their pastor is the same Reverend Benjamin Maxon who founded the Zion Harmonizers. They have toured the United States and Europe extensively, and the CD *I Believe* is a nice introduction to their music.

Also great fun are the **Soulful Heavenly Stars,** another traditional New Orleans outfit who deserve recognition. Under the leadership of **"Big" Al Johnson,** the group has gradually expanded their tour base from hometown to international, and CDs such as *Who We Are*, with tight arrangements of classics like "Swing Low, Sweet Chariot" and "Down by the Riverside," are fine instructionals of the form.

Other such groups are the **Mighty Chariots** (buy the CD *Remember Me, Oh Lord*), the **Southern Bells** (together in New Orleans for over thirty years), and of course the **New Zion Trio.** To see them at JazzFest is an exercise in the sublime; it'll sober you up if you're drunk and get you high if you're sober. Take it from me and Dr. Larry.

In the context of contemporary Christian music—from Kirk Franklin to Amy Grant it is admittedly a huge business—there are some Louisiana artists doing nice work.

Trin-I-Tee 5:7 is a young trio from New Orleans comprised of singers **Chanelle Hayes, Terri Brown,** and **Angel Taylor.** They've released two CDs for major label Interscope, *Trin-I-Tee 5:7* and *Spiritual Love*, and work a contemporary Christian sound extremely similar to what you'd find if En Vogue and the Ohio Players experimented with hip-hop while at a church service together. One single, "God's Grace," has gone Top 10, and exposure on tour with Kirk Franklin's Nu Nation has helped sales of both CDs vault into the gold-record bracket. Aside from their smooth groove and harmonies, one of the cool things about the group is that they write a lot of their own material.

Also making waves in the contemporary Christian market is **Blessed.** Offering a solid gospel message within a glossy, ultra-contempo shell, Blessed is also from New Orleans. Members are **Cynthia Liggins Thomas** (who sang with the New Orleans Symphony when she was five and also speaks four languages), **Angela Fenniday Stewart, Ronda Stewart Singleton,** and **Joslyn Elliot Blackburn.** The group has released two CDs on the Orchard label, the self-title debut and *Journey for the Heart*.

Just to prove that every notable gospel artist in Louisiana *isn't* from New Orleans, consider **Ruby Terry,** the black gospel singer who has released several fine CDs for the Malaco label. Though she grew up in Mississippi and Oklahoma, she currently works her ministry out of Lake Charles, where her husband is pastor of the Saints Memorial Church of God in Christ. She's been nominated for a Stellar award, and has built a nice following around such recommended CDs as *God Can Do It* and *What a Time*.

The Cox Family, an act out of Cotton Valley, Louisiana, has made headlines in the fields of country, bluegrass, and gospel music, the subsequent amalgam of which sounds as though their siblings were the Everly Brothers. Formed in 1976 by father Willard, son Sidney, and daughters Evelyn and Suzanne, the Cox Family were doing nicely working the county-fair circuit when they caught the ear of bluegrass giant Alison Krauss; she later scored them a deal with Rounder Records, recorded several of Sidney Cox's songs herself, and produced all the clan's albums except for their inaugural release on Wilcox Records.

The group's profile increased exponentially after Counting Crows front man Adam Durvitz invited the band to open several dates on the Crows' mega-huge 1994 tour of the United States. Soon afterwards, they were featured on the surprise smash-hit soundtrack to the Coen Brothers film *O Brother Where Art Thou* and the follow-up *Down From the Mountain*. Though it's fair to say the Cox Family's bluegrass flavorings are probably the overwhelming characteristic of their music, it's also true that country gospel is never far from the core of their work. And though they've been nominated for a Grammy for Best Bluegrass album for their *Beyond the City* CD, they also shared a Grammy for their participation in the collaborative *Amazing Grace—A Country Salute to Gospel* CD. Also recommended listening is *Just When We're Thinking It's Over.*

Finally, there's one more young turk worth mentioning, an impressive male gospel singer from New Orleans, **Jo "Cool" Davis**. Crescent City music fans know Cool not just for his bubbly personality, his George Foreman puppydog persona, and his booming, reach-the-clouds voice, but also because he's the doorman at Tipitina's, the world-renowned live-music club. He subscribed to the theory that gospel music as "entertainment" is every bit as valuable—perhaps more so in its potential to reach the masses—as just "sitting in the church on Sunday" music. Heavily influenced by Sam Cooke's secular tunes as well as religious, Davis grew up singing in the New Covenant Baptist Church on Touro Street. A childhood friend of Raymond Miles's, Davis opened for touring gospel performers such as the Zion Harmonizers, and eventually he went on the road with John Lee and the Rocks of Harmony.

Davis hasn't, to my knowledge, released any records. But to see him host the Sunday Gospel Brunch at the House of Blues, or open for the Neville Brothers at the club where he's the doorman, is a realization of the wondrous and interpretive possibilities of gospel music.

Naturally, in a state as spiritually intense as Louisiana, it's important not to overlook those artists who are perhaps better known in a secular context but have released gospel albums. Off the top of my head, that would include **Irma Thomas** *(Walk Around Heaven—New Orleans Gospel)*, **Aaron Neville** *(Devotion)*, **Hank Williams Jr.** *(Gospel Favorites)*, and several others who loved singing gospel and probably have something on tape somewhere: **Marva Wright, Johnny Adams, Jerry Lee Lewis, Luther Kent,** and **Fred LeBlanc.**

Five

COUNTRY MUSIC

*T*he first time I remember being aware of country and western music in Louisiana was through my father, who owned Koster's Lone Star Trailer Sales. In 1959, he sold a mobile home to Elvis Presley, who was at that time in the military, serving at Fort Hood in Killeen, Texas. I don't remember the sale—I was barely out of diapers at the time—but at a certain point it did register when my father showed me a full-page ad he ran in the *Dallas Times Herald*, something about "When Elvis needs a trailer, he comes to Koster's Lone Star." There was a picture of Presley, of course, dressed as I remember in crisp GI finery and shaking hands with my dad, a handsome man in his own right.

As I grew older, just before the Beatles hit our shores, I realized who Elvis was, and the magnitude of my father's deed began to sink in. I had a transistor radio that I played softly in my bed each night after I was supposed to be asleep, listening to WRR broadcasts of Chicago White Sox games—why a Dallas radio station aired that particular franchise, I've no idea—or KRLD, which carried the then–Houston Colt .45s. When the ballgames ended, the stations returned to regular music programming. One of the two had some form of primordial Top 40 format, I can't remember which. Like many kids, I assumed the songs weren't records but were being performed at the station by the artists, and I distinctly recall hearing Elvis's "Crying in the Chapel" in the darkness of my room, feeling a connection through radio signals across the night sky to the radio station where, it seemed, my dad's pal Elvis was performing.

"Elvis bought a trailer from Righteous Richard," I'd think drowsily, for one of my father's early advertising personas cast him as "Righteous Richard, the Poor Man's Friend." (Not that my dad was a con man or anything, though I must admit his right-hand salesman was a guy called Dr.

Jeffrey Toner, who had a bogus divinity degree from Yale hanging on his office wall. The two of them also had an organ in one corner of the room on which dad would clump out the chords and Dr. Toner would lead prospective customers of religious persuasion in a version of "What a Friend We Have in Jesus" when it seemed important to seek spiritual guidance over the advisability of selecting a new domicile. Invariably, God recommended buying top-of-the-line trailers.)

It was only when I told my folks that I'd heard Elvis singing at the radio station that they explained to me the concept of disc jockeys spinning records. Generally, they said, the artists didn't actually show up in the studio and perform every time I heard a song on the radio, any more than three-inch people were actually acting in our television set.

"Now what you might run across," Righteous Richard said, "is something like *Louisiana Hayride*," a show broadcast out of Shreveport where the singers on any given night *were* performing live on the radio. "All kinds of stars have been on *Louisiana Hayride*."

Had Elvis been on? I wondered.

"Elvis practically invented *Louisiana Hayride*," Dad assured me.

In fact, *Louisiana Hayride*, which originated in 1948 and was broadcast out of Shreveport's Municipal Auditorium on Saturday evenings for the next twelve years, served as a launch pad in the early stages of Presley's career, though it can hardly be said that he "practically invented" the show.

The program originated on the 50,000-watt KWKH station and provided prime weekend entertainment throughout Louisiana, Texas, Arkansas, Mississippi, and Alabama, as well as selected other spots across the South and the West. The format was that of a live variety show, with regular station hosts Horace Logan and Frank Page, guest emcees, and comics peppered amongst live-music segments of blues, gospel, pop, jazz, western swing, and hillbilly performers in addition to its primary draw, country and western.

Hayride, also known as "the Cradle of the Stars," is predominantly associated with country music because it was indeed responsible for boosting the careers of many of that era's biggest country and western stars, including Hank Williams, George Jones, Johnny Cash, Jim Reeves, Kitty Wells, Slim Whitman, Governor Jimmie Davis of Louisiana, Webb Pierce from Monroe, Louisiana, and Shreveport's own Faron Young and Johnny Horton.

A lot of those young performers hopscotched from *Louisiana Hayride* to radio stardom and eventually the Grand Ole Opry in Nashville, the latter of which was by all counts a bastion of musical conservatism following stringent traditional guidelines, in direct contradiction to the free-wheeling *Hayride*. As a matter of entertainment, *Hayride* encouraged younger, hungrier performers, had folks dancing in the aisles, offered door prizes, and even allowed Gene Autry to ride his horse onto the Municipal Auditorium stage.

The show struggled at first, but when an up-and-coming Hank Williams appeared in July 1948 with a rousing version of "Move It On

Over," the tide began to turn. Hank Williams hovered in the Shreveport area for a year or so (Hank Williams Jr. was born in Shreveport about nine months after that inaugural performance), and had his own daily morning program on the station for a while. By the time of Hank's last appearance on *Louisiana Hayride*, during which he encored seven times with his then-number-one hit "Lovesick Blues," he was a superstar. And *Louisiana Hayride* was firmly established as a major force in country music.

Williams wasn't the only artist who established temporary residence in Shreveport to work on the program. Slim Whitman of Tampa, Florida, who yodeled classic pop material, worked for a time as a Shreveport mail carrier while building his reputation as a performer on *Hayride*, and it wasn't unusual for would-be stars to pop up from all over the country, hoping to get a shot on the show. For our purposes, the big news is that *Louisiana Hayride* established the state, for a while, anyway, as a prime player in the burgeoning country music industry. One would think that, given its geographical location Louisiana would be a huge exporter of country and western talent.

But one important aspect has kept Louisiana from becoming a flood-tide of country stars: The rural foundations that are essential to the formation of a country tradition have been channeled into Cajun and zydeco music rather than country. And because those two forms are almost exclusive to Louisiana, many of the musicians who might have been pure country artists had they grown up in similar rural conditions anywhere else were channeled into Cajun or zydeco music instead. Rising country star Andy Griggs, who hails from Monroe in northeast Louisiana, subscribes to this theory: "I've fought really, really hard to not get a Cajun image," he told me. "As soon as the label signed me they were getting ready to promote me as a Cajun. The head of the promo department wanted a picture of me with a washboard and hay bales and crawfish. I was scared to death." Another of the northern Louisiana C&W artists who battled the Cajun perception is one of Griggs's contemporaries, Springhill native Trace Adkins. "It's quite possibly true that a lot of rural musicians in southwest Louisiana, who might've been predisposed to country, went into Cajun music," he said in a phone conversation. "But I grew up in north Louisiana and it's a different state. Northwest Louisiana is culturally a lot like east Texas. Where I grew up, Hank [Williams Jr.], who's from Shreveport, was a huge influence. Plus, I grew up about ten miles from Joe Stampley's hometown. There's a big country presence; in the fifties, at the height of *Louisiana Hayride*, Shreveport was second only to Nashville."

Still, the draw of Cajun or zydeco for otherwise country-inclined musicians is particularly obvious in a family such as the Kershaws, a Cajun clan that features third cousins Doug and Sammy. Doug is a fiddler of astonishing technique who is best known for his rambunctious Paganini-in-Crawfish stage show and the song "Louisiana Man," which has been covered by more artists than there are germs. He also tightropes styles, having dabbled extensively in traditional Cajun music, country, and a uniquely personal mixture of the two. Sammy is more of a mainstream entertainer whose star shines most brightly in Nashville country, albeit in a fashion that displays his obvious affection for southern rockers Lynyrd Skynyrd and Molly Hatchett.

More on the Kershaws a bit later, but the point is that although country music exists in a big way in Louisiana history, it's probably not what it would have been without the huge body of work in Cajun and zydeco music. Still, this music, and in particular the enormous status of *Louisiana Hayride*, shaped the careers of several Louisiana artists.

Randall Hank Williams (1949–) was not influenced at all by the Cajun-zydeco factor—probably because he never had a chance to be. Williams is known to millions of country and rock music fans, as well as to every human who ever watched the intro credits to *Monday Night Football*, as **Hank Williams Jr**. Though he's no longer the biggest country star out of Louisiana—that would be Tim McGraw or Kix Brooks (of Brooks & Dunn) at the moment, and Trace Adkins right behind—Junior was without question a superstar for a long, long time. He's released about seventy albums by this point, and has a über-loyal fan base that will probably buy anything he puts out until the day he dies. And since he's barely fifty, that could be a while.

As mentioned above, Junior was born in Shreveport. He was only three when his father passed away, but by that time the Old Man's nickname for his son, Bocephus, was in place. It may have come from ventriloquist Ron Brasfield, who played the Grand Ole Opry with his dummy named Bocephus. Country music was probably a discernible part of the kid's DNA; raised in Nashville and Alabama, Bocephus was at an early age tutored on guitar and the Biz by Johnny Cash, Jerry Lee Lewis, Brenda Lee, and others who'd been friends with the Old Man.

Under the guidance of his mother, Audrey Shepherd Williams, he began touring as one of those show-biz cuties, performing pre-adolescent tributes to his father. Williams debuted on the Opry when he was eleven, scored his first radio hit with a version of his dad's "Long Gone Lonesome Blues" at fourteen, released his first album, *Sings the Songs of Hank Williams*, a year later on the MGM label and, by the time he was old enough for a driver's license, he had become the youngest songwriter ever to earn a BMI citation (for his Top-5 self-penned hit, "Standing in the Shadows").

Out of school since sixteen, Williams toured heavily, working his daddy's image and material with a band called the Cheatin' Hearts. Like anyone ushered into national fame under such circumstances, Bocephus had his share of problems. He rebelled against forces that would have had him spit out Xerox renditions of his father's material, and by twenty-five he had undergone two divorces and displayed a penchant for drink and dope.

But he started to forge his own identity. Influenced by both the redneck rock movement, which had generated in Austin with Willie Nelson and Waylon Jennings (and southern rockers Lynyrd Skynyrd and the collective Allman Brothers, Marshall Tucker, and Charlie Daniels Bands), Bocephus recorded an album with several of those artists called *Hank Jr. and Friends*. It was a musical revelation celebrating a new and genuine persona that combined all the outlaw elements of country music, rock 'n' roll, and the proud South.

Then, in 1975, he fell five hundred feet down Ajax Mountain in Montana and nearly died. His skull was crushed and his face had to be reconstructed, but he used the recuperative time for soul-searching and to play his guitar. He decided to follow his own creative muse regardless of what the ghouls wanted—and it paid off in a big way.

Throughout the eighties, Williams became a huge success, selling tons of records and becoming a larger-than-life hero to misfits everywhere. His work espouses a peculiar existentialism that's one part Nietzsche, one part marijuana, and one part *Field and Stream*, all simmered in a broth of Jack Daniels; all this can be found on such hits as "All My Rowdy Friends (Have Settled Down)," "Gonna Go Huntin' Tonight," "Whiskey Bent and Hell Bound," "If the South Woulda Won," "A Country Boy Can Survive," and "Good Friends, Good Whiskey, Good Lovin'." "When *Whiskey Bent and Hell Bound* came out, I learned every song on the album," Trace Adkins told me. "What an amazing record. When you think about it, *any* of Junior's are worth owning."

The theme he wrote for *Monday Night Football* earned him four Emmy awards and probably enough royalty checks to buy Saudi Arabia. In the mid-nineties, ABC execs decided to give Hank a rest from the *Monday Night Football* theme and hired regionally appropriate artists to sing variations on the tune instead. The concept backfired in a big way, and Hank was back quickly enough, but one of the really interesting efforts was for a Saints game in New Orleans when the Neville Brothers sang the song.

Williams has been the Country Music Association's Entertainer of the Year three times, has recorded twenty-four gold, ten platinum, and one quadruple platinum albums, and if his reputation as a songwriter can never eclipse his daddy's, folks from Alan Jackson to Kid Rock cover his material proudly. (One of Williams's latest singles is something he recorded with Kid Rock called "Naked Women and Beer.") Most important, Williams has come to terms with himself and with his father's legacy. So it's cool that, in 1990, he won a Grammy for "There's a Tear in My Beer," a duet he recorded with his father through the magic of technology.

If Williams seems eternal, he's still what might be described as a second-generation Louisiana country music star. Plenty of artists came before him.

One was **Webb Pierce** (1926–1991) from West Monroe, Louisiana, whose ninety-six chart hits during the golden era of pure honky-tonk remain an estimable achievement. But it was Pierce's reluctance to abandon honky-tonk during times when public tastes were changing that probably left him, in the long run, with a lower public awareness quotient than many of his contemporaries. It was all in the cards by the time he was sixteen, when he was already hosting his own radio show on a Monroe station.

Pierce was called to the service, and after a three-year stint he moved to Shreveport to re-energize his career while working as a shoe salesman. It wasn't long before he joined *Louisiana Hayride*, and in 1951 he was signed to Decca. A year later, a single called "Wondering" settled onto the charts with glue-like adhesion, and the machine they called Webb Pierce was underway. Several Top 10 singles later, Pierce scored with what would become his signature tune, "There Stands the Glass." He became renowned not only for finding obscure material but also for writing his own great beer-soaked songs. In 1955, Pierce finally moved to Nashville and the Grand Ole Opry, where for the next four years he continued to reel off hits with almost creepy regularity, including the 1959 hit "I Ain't Never," a tune co-written with Mel Tillis that gave Pierce a whole new audience. He also had what might be described as a Large Time, living a gaudily flamboyant life in his custom Nudie suits, neo-pimpmobiles, and guitar-shaped swimming pool. (At its peak the pool was drawing 3,000 visitors a week, a nuisance that so irritated neighbor Ray Stevens that he and fellow annoyees filed suit to stop the influx. Pierce simply built a duplicate pool on Music Row.)

The honky-tonk train derailed in the mid-sixties as a newer, poppier Nashville took charge of the genre. When Pierce declined to adapt, his momentum began to stall. He continued to make records, though, and didn't suffer financial problems: He had invested wisely in music publishing and had purchased numerous radio stations despite the Nashville honchos who had frowned on his entrepreneurial spirit. He thumbed his nose at them all and enjoyed his Liberace-goes-country lifestyle and his place in country-music history: He is credited with being the first non-western act to employ twin fiddles, and also for being the first person to feature a pedal steel on a record (1954's "Slowly"). Only his being overlooked by the Country Music Hall of Fame might have pained him until he succumbed to pancreatic cancer at the age of seventy-four.

Pianist **Floyd Cramer** (1933–1977) helped usher in the Nashville pop sound that was the death sentence for Pierce's honky-tonk era. Cramer was one of the most unique country artists, mostly because he played piano, standard practice in Louisiana but much rarer for a country musician elsewhere. Born in Sampti, Louisiana, he grew up in Arkansas and played a piano his parents bought him while he was still a kid. He credits his mournful, whole-note slides to the influence of Mother Maybelle Carter's technique on the autoharp, and he was accomplished enough to join the *Louisiana Hayride* after leaving high school.

While on the show, he backed Webb Pierce, Jim Reeves, and Elvis Presley, among others, and started recording on his own behalf in 1953. His strength as a session player was tattooed into the collective consciousness of Nashville after he moved there in 1955. He toured with The King and Hank Williams, and had some success recording for RCA Victor. In 1960, his rendition of Hank Locklin's "Please Help Me I'm Falling" was a monster hit, holding down #1 for fourteen weeks. Two subsequent singles, "Last Date" and "On the Rebound," made him a star—a position he maintained for years on the strength of annual *Class of* albums, which contained his arrangements of that year's big hits in pop and country. As the synthesizer age dawned, Cramer adjusted easily, using technology to move into the Easy Listening field.

Because of his widespread session work and willingness to experiment technically and stylistically, there's a lot of schlock out there with Cramer's name on it. If you really want to hear him kicking ass, get RCA's *Essential Series.*

Jimmy C. Newman (1927–) born in Big Mamou, Louisiana, grew up listening to the Cajun music indigenous to the area, as well as western singers such as Gene Autry. He sang in his early days with Chuck Guillory's Rhythm Boys, recorded with little success for Baton Rouge baron J. D. Miller, then moved on Miller's recommendation to Dot Records out of Nashville. In 1953, he had a hit with "Cry, Cry, Darling," which landed him a full-time gig on *Louisiana Hayride.* Over the next several years (and labels), Newman established himself as a mid-level star with "A Fallen Star," "Blue Darlin'," "You're Making a Fool Out of Me," and "Grin and Bear It." Along the way, he graduated from *Hayride* to *Opry* status.

His biggest accomplishments came in the early sixties, when Newman used his popularity to record a bilingual album heavily infused with Cajun material: *Folk Songs of the Bayou Country.* His subsequent recordings pinballed between typical Nashvillean fare and the Louisiana stuff. He continued to be a strong musical proponent for Cajun culture, and always toured with bands of Cajun musicians; he even gave himself his middle initial and decreed that it stood for "Cajun."

Following in the fusion tradition of Newman is **Jo-El Sonnier** (1946–), born to a hardworking family of sharecroppers in Rayne, Louisiana. Sonnier is a Cajun multi-instrumentalist, singer, and songwriter whose efforts to impart the music of Acadiana into mainstream Nashville are creative and admirable if not entirely successful. Sonnier was influenced by monster accordionist Iry LeJeune and, by the time he was thirteen, he had a hit single called "Tes Yeux Bleu." After high school, he moved to Lake Charles and recorded—solo and with the Louisiana Ramblers—for the Goldband label. Not until Sonnier and his wife relocated to California was he inspired by the Bakersfield sound of Buck Owens and Merle Haggard to start singing in English and infusing country music into his material.

Over the next several years, he traveled the nation, recording for diverse labels and playing with everyone from David Lindley to Garth Hudson and Steve Winwood. (He even appeared in movies, including *Mask* and *Wildfire*). More important, Sonnier enjoyed such radio hits as "If Your Heart Should Ever Roll This Way Again," "Rainin' in My Heart," "No More One More Time," and "Tear-Stained Letter" (the latter penned by British folk-rock genius Richard Thompson). Sonnier's mixture of Cajun, country, and rock was as free spirited as it was exhilarating; in 1987, *Performance* magazine named him "New Country Artist of the Year." Sonnier's solo recordings and virtuosity in the studio (he played on sessions for Dolly Parton, Emmylou Harris, and Elvis Costello) were complimented when his material was covered by Johnny Cash, John Anderson, Loretta Lynn, Conway Twitty, and George Strait.

The unexpected death of his wife utterly devastated Sonnier, and though he regrouped, his career had lost momentum. Still, respect for Sonnier in his home state is without parallel, an adulation shared by the important folks in Nashville who recognize his contributions and artistry. To check out Sonnier's finest country stuff, try *The Complete Mercury Sessions*. For more Louisiana seasonings, try Rounder's *Cajun Roots*.

Also heavily influenced by his Cajun ancestry is **Doug Kershaw** (1936–), the Ragin' Cajun fiddler who was born in Tiel Ridge, Louisiana. As mentioned earlier, his "Louisiana Man" is a royalty machine: It's been covered almost nine hundred times, which means that Kershaw probably needs several jukeboxes if he ever wants to sit down and listen to all of the versions back-to-back-to-back. It was even played during the Apollo 12 moon shot.

He was a fiddling prodigy, attracting the shrewd ears of local producer J. D. Miller while Kershaw was only twelve and playing in his cousin's Cajun band. Miller persuaded the French-speaking Kershaw to go English. With his brother Rusty, Doug recorded material that Miller took to Nashville; he came back with recording and publishing contracts.

Known as the Music Makers, the brothers' band joined the *Louisiana Hayride* and then the Grand Ole Opry in rapid succession. After serving their time in the military, Doug and Rusty got out in 1960. One of the first songs they recorded was Doug's "Louisiana Man." The brothers followed up with "Diggy Liggy Lo." Another Kershaw-penned hit, "Cajun Stripper," was next, after which Rusty got out of the business and Doug carried on solo.

For eleven years at Warner Brothers, Doug delivered solid if not spectacular sales and harmony-laced, Cajun-flavored country. He then bounced from one major label to another, always delivering that demon fiddle and high-quality performances. His last charted hit was in 1988, when he teamed with Hank Williams Jr. on "Cajun Baby." His bands—first the Louisiana Men and then Slidin' Jake—were always terrific outfits, employing rock-show energy within the country structures. But over time, Kershaw developed problems with cocaine and alcohol. He finally cleaned up and pulled back on the fevered approach to his career. On any stylistic disparities between his roots music and C&W, he once said, "The difference between Cajun and country is that Cajun was around before country was."

A Texas expatriate who eventually settled in Shreveport and gained everlasting fame for a song he co-wrote called "Honky-Tonk Man," **Johnny Horton** (1925–1960) was a lovable and eccentric ne'er-do-well who took pride in being known as "The Singing Fisherman." An athletic young man whose mother taught him guitar when he was eleven, he received basketball scholarships to several colleges but instead briefly attended seminary with thoughts of becoming a preacher. Somehow, he ended up in Alaska, working as a fisherman and seriously attempting for the first time to write songs.

Later, in California, he won a talent contest, came to the attention of management, and eventually recorded a few unsuccessful sides for Dot and Mercury. He then married Hank Williams's widow, Billie Jean, and relocated to Shreveport, where Billie Jean coaxed him into pursuing his stalled career. When he secured a gig on *Louisiana Hayride*, "Honky-Tonk Man" became the first of a long string of big hits.

Horton's style was all over the map—he moved from rockabilly to honky-tonk—and it wasn't until he took note of the emerging narratives in country-folk music and recorded Jimmie Driftwood's "The Battle of New Orleans" that he became a household name. He followed with similar material; particularly memorable are "Johnny Reb," "Sink the Bismarck," and "North to Alaska." It was around this time that he began to suffer from morbid premonitions of his own premature and violent death. Soon after, following a gig in Austin at the Skyline Club (creepily, the site of Hank Williams's final public gig), Horton was driving back to Shreveport when he and a drunk driver collided head-on and the singing star was killed.

His legacy as a songwriter, country singer, and sweet weirdo are secure; if nothing else, "Honky-Tonk Man" is one of the greatest songs ever. Dwight Yoakam, among others, recorded the tune, and it was the inspiration for the Clint Eastwood film of the same name.

Like Sonnier, **Joe Stampley** (1943–), born in Springhill, Louisiana, bridges the older and newest generation of country music stars. Stampley's family was particularly musical: Both his parents sang, he absorbed a solid gospel foundation from his grandfather, and his dad taught him guitar and piano. After the family moved to Baytown, Texas, Stampley sang for his hero, Hank Williams, at a radio station. The old Hankster was full of encouragement and career advice. After high school, Stampley, by then equally impressed with Jerry Lee Lewis and the Everly Brothers, moved back to Springhill, where he was befriended by a local disc jockey named Merle Kilgore. The two began writing songs together, and Kilgore engineered a few deals for Stampley.

He worked a variety of day jobs while singing and writing songs for a local band called the Uniques before he went solo. By the mid-seventies, he'd scored several Top 5 singles, including "Soul Single," which crossed over to the pop charts. Stampley moved to Epic in the late seventies and continued to be a solid force with self-penned, pop-leaning material. He hit a home run when he started teaming with Moe Bandy for a series of clever honky-tonk duets, "Just Good Ol' Boys" and "Holding the Bag." Stampley's material stayed in the honky-tonk vein, and he continued to enjoy solid popularity through the mid-eighties. Among his top songs were "All These Things" and "Roll On, Big Mama." I recommend *Good Ol' Boy*.

Eddy Raven (1945–) was born Edward Garvin Futch in Lafayette. Yet another baseball-playin' Louisianian, young Futch harbored a childhood dream of playing center field for the Boston Red Sox (smart kid, that one), but turned to music after a broken ankle short-circuited his athletic career. An equal-opportunity musical sponge who grew up playing guitar and singing, he loved Cajun, rock, country, and R&B. The soon-to-be Raven mixed all his influences to become a unique songwriter. He wasn't aware he'd become "Raven" until he saw a pressing of his first single, "Once a Fool," released on the Cosmos label. When it didn't make him rich, he worked at a record store in Lafayette, playing alongside everyone from John Fred and the Playboy Band and Johnny Winter to Professor Longhair and Bobby Charles. The store, La Louisianne, had its own signature label and soon released an album by Raven, *The Cajun Country Sound*, which inspired Jimmy C. Newman to help Raven score a publishing deal in Nashville. His songs started showing up on the country charts, recorded by such artists as Jeannie C. Riley, and Raven toured as the lead vocalist for the Governor Jimmie Davis Band during political campaigns.

At the advice of industry bigwigs, Raven moved to Nashville, continued to write hits for other artists, and eventually started to chart his own mid-level hits ("Dealin' with the Devil" and "Another Texas Song" among them).

It was in the early eighties, though, that Raven finally went to the top with "I Got Mexico." It was followed by a series of Top 10 singles, a run of hits that seemed to abate only with the end of the decade. From that point, Raven's career slowed considerably. But he remains one of the best of the Louisiana country songwriters. A suggested compilation is RCA's *Best of Eddy Raven*, which showcases some of his more Cajun-flavored material.

Of the newer generation of country stars, three stand out.

Kix Brooks (1955–) of Shreveport is one-half of the headlining country group Brooks & Dunn. Kix, born Leon Eric Brooks III, is the son of a pipe fitter and grew up on the block where the widows of Johnny Horton and Hank Williams lived. He loved music early on, and was exposed to the blue-collar sounds of the region; this means that he was absorbing country, rock, blues, and Cajun music.

By the time he was in college, he was a veteran of the regional club circuit: He once played seventy-two consecutive nights on Bourbon Street in New Orleans. In and out of university, he worked day jobs in such diverse climes as Alaska and Maine, honed his songwriting skills at night, and eventually landed in Nashville. Before long, such artists as John Conlee and the Nitty Gritty Dirt Band had scored hits with his material; but though he released a single in 1983, it was six more years before his first solo album, *Kix Brooks*, appeared. The next year, Brooks met and started writing songs with Ronnie Dunn. Their first single, "Brand New Man," went to the top of the charts, as did its encore, "My Next Broken Heart." Since then, they've made few mistakes in their stay at the top in Nashville.

They have an interesting if formulaic onstage partnership: Dunn is the serious guy and Brooks is the madcap. Their material ranges from barroom shtick to tender balladry, and on their albums *Hard Workin' Man, Waitin' on Sundown, Borderline*, and *Tightrope*, the pair uses the strength of their respective personalities to elevate songs that are often just good. Still, their popularity remains steadfast, and it seems they're named Duo of the Year by the Country Music Association every other week.

At the turn of the new millennium, the hottest Louisiana country & western draw is **Tim McGraw** (1967–), whose wife is Faith Hill; whose dad is ex–Philadelphia Phillies and New York Mets relief pitcher Tug McGraw; and whose early hit, "Indian Outlaw," stirred up storms of controversy in various Native American groups for lyrics that allegedly reinforce stereotypes.

McGraw was born in Delhi, Louisiana, near Monroe. He was raised in nearby Start by his mother, divorced from the Tug, and until he went to college he seemed to be following in his dad's jockish footsteps. McGraw went to Northeast Louisiana State on a multiple athletic scholarship, fooled around with rodeo, and considered first the legal profession and then sports medicine before sour grades intruded.

A guitar picked up in a pawnshop on a whim changed his life. Before long, he was working clubs in the southeast, writing his own songs, and learning that his deep, emotive voice worked well on sad material. In 1989, he moved to Nashville. Within two years, he had landed a deal with Curb Records on the strength of a demo tape. His debut CD, *Tim McGraw*, charted three minor hit singles. His sophomore effort was *Not a Moment Too Soon*, which included "Indian Outlaw." But it was the follow-up single, the weepy but gorgeous "Don't Take the Girl," that gave McGraw some much needed credibility, and the album landed three more hits on the charts. McGraw was huge; over 5 million folks bought the record.

The third album, *All I Want*, went multi-platinum, though it was a fairly mundane effort that relied on too much whimsical and vaguely goofy material. The next CD, though, *Everywhere*, was a solid step forward. It also set a country music record when six singles went to #1.

When McGraw hooked up with Faith Hill, whose career is riding on the same rocket that fuels such folks as Shania Twain and the Dixie Chicks, his ascension to stardom was complete. The most recent CD, *A Place in the Sun*, is a continuation of his style. Like Kix Brooks, McGraw does show some of his Louisiana upbringing, mostly in instrumental flourishes. Still, he's a mainstream Nashville mover—over 15 million CDs sold and counting—so don't expect anything too radical.

Another relative youngster who's done well is Springhill, Louisiana's **Trace Adkins** (1962–). Drawing from two Louisiana strongholds, gospel and, sports, as well as from the traditional country and the rock that any kid who grew up in the seventies would have been exposed to, Adkins grew up playing guitar and football—activities that occupied him well at Louisiana Tech. After graduation, he worked for several years on oil rigs; eventually, he decided to give music a shot and used his baritone in the gospel quartet New Commitments.

In the early nineties, he went solo and switched to country music, the thematic core of which he described on his Web site as "Pain and sex. That's life, man." After playing clubs for a few years, he was approached at a gig in Nashville by an exec from Capitol Records and offered a deal. His 1996 debut, *Dreamin' Out Loud*, went Top 20 on the strength of four powerful singles, including "Every Light in the House Is On" and "I Left Something Turned On At Home." Two CDs and a rash of major awards followed. *Big Time* and *More* offer intriguing and well-conceived mixtures of whimsical honky-tonk and more sensitive material. Like Sammy Kershaw, Adkins seems to have an overlooked penchant for balladry. At six-foot-six, and weighing about 250 pounds, Adkins is a large man whose roughneck upbringing is balanced by such an articulate worldview that he's guested several times on Bill Maher's *Politically Incorrect* television program. His innate Louisiana-ness doesn't lie in anything obvious—he's not Cajun and didn't mow Fats Domino's yard or anything—but he did grow up hardscrabble in Louisiana's oilfields. And among the pitfalls that have befallen Adkins on his way to stardom are three marriages; an accidental shot through the heart from his second wife; a hurricane he endured while on an offshore rig; a severed finger, lost in a car accident and surgically reattached; and a 400-gallon oil tank that blew up while he was trying to fix it.

Adkins recommends several must-own CDs by Louisiana artists: "Pick out any Hank Jr. record. Kix Brooks has written some good songs that he and Ronnie [Dunn] have recorded . . . and that first Britney Spears album was pretty big. I've never met her, which is probably a good thing."

In 1999, **Andy Griggs** (1973–) of Monroe, Louisiana, roared out of the Nashville chutes like a beer-charged bronco with his MCA debut, *You Won't Ever Be Lonely*, the title single of which went to #1. The video for

"She's More," featuring his eye-pleasing wife, Stephanie, went to #1. A follow-up single, "I'll Go Crazy," also rocketed to the Top 10, and the album peaked at an impressive #15. Griggs negotiated all this with easy confidence and a high-quality product. More important, he did it without pandering to the Nashville instinct to overly sweeten it all. He's got the pure honky-tonk voice, the Hollywood looks, and the creative inclinations of a youngster who lived through the grunge rock years and came out with the opinion that Dwight Yoakam was really what was cool.

Other seminal and early Louisiana country artists you should know:

Another alumnus of *Louisiana Hayride*, **David Houston** (1938–1993), born in Bossier City, Louisiana, counted among his ancestors Robert E. Lee and Sam Houston, and was in the sixties and early seventies a terrifically successful country performer. Possessed of an almost operatic voice, he started singing lessons as a child, encouraged by his godfather, Gene Austin, a popular singer from the twenties. He also learned guitar and piano, and in his teens he attracted the attention of Johnny Horton's manager, who secured him the *Hayride* gig. After a few slow years, during which he sold insurance, Houston recorded "Mountain of Love," which was released in 1963 and roared to #3. His next several singles also charted, the best being "Almost Persuaded," which earned him two Grammy awards. He went through several labels and continued to churn out nice country pop—two duets with Barbara Mandrell did pretty well—but he never really ascended again. He died of a ruptured brain aneurysm.

Evangeline is a talented female group from New Orleans. Guitarist Kathleen Stieffel, bassist, and washboardist Sharon Leger, keyboardist Beth McKee, and lead guitarist Rhonda Lohmeyer form the core of the group. The harmony-laced outfit is known best for being discovered by Jimmy Buffett and signed to his Margaritaville label. Two early CDs, a self-titled disc and *French Quarter Moon*, demonstrate a fine sense of harmony, an affection for their hometown, and an intriguing way of integrating the Crescent City's charm into contemporary country material.

Al Terry (1922–), another of the coterie of Cajuns who segued into a successful career in mainstream C&W, was born in Kaplan, Louisiana. An accomplished guitarist and clarinetist (!) who liked Django Reinhardt and developed an affection for early honky-tonk and western music, Terry and his brothers formed a band and were playing on a Lafayette radio station by the time he was fifteen. They graduated to other stations in the area and, called Al and the Southerners, released their first single in 1946. A few years later, blues producer J. D. Miller signed the band. They released a single called "Good Deal Lucille" that appealed to the Cajun populace because of its bilingual lyrics. The single went Top 10 and, going solo, Terry joined *Louisiana Hayride*. Though he was asked to record Cajun material, he opted to stay with the country stuff, for better or for worse. In 1957,

Country & Western Jamboree called Terry the "No. 1 New Singer." Behind in the balloting were Elvis Presley and Sonny James.

A singer and songwriter from Centerville, Louisiana, **Peggy Forman** is probably best known for penning "Out of My Head and Back in My Bed," which went to #1 for Loretta Lynn in the late seventies. She also wrote material for Conway Twitty, Bill Anderson, George Strait, and Jean Shepherd. She had some minor chart success on her own with songs like "That's What Your Lovin' Does to Me" and "I Wish You Could Have Turned My Head and Left My Heart Alone."

Let's face it, you're not gonna run into too many country singers who are black, and probably even fewer who are cardiologists, but **Cleve Francis** (1945–) is both. Born in Jennings, Louisiana, Francis as a kid made a guitar out of a cigar box. His mom later bought him a real one, and by med school he was playing summer gigs as a country singer. He recorded three self-released albums, then eventually caught the attention of a patient whose brother was in the R&B group the Heartbeats. A subsequent album for indie Playback featured a video that attracted Liberty Records; since 1991, Francis has released such CDs as *You've Got Me Now*, *Walkin'*, and *Tourist in Paradise*.

Another Shreveport guy, **Claude King** (1933–1983), will be forever associated with the hit song "Wolverton Mountain." He attended college in Montana on a baseball scholarship—has anyone besides me noticed the high percentage of Shreveport country singers who had athletic scholarships?—and returned to appear on *Louisiana Hayride*. A singer whose easygoing songs effortlessly crossed over to pop charts from their country origins, King had dozens of hits over the years; but nothing approached the success of "Wolverton Mountain," the saga of the birds and bees on the titular peak who protected the lovelorn hermit that lived there.

A songwriter named **Red Lane,** born in Bogalusa, Louisiana, mastered Chet Atkins–styled guitar in the service and only started to compose tunes after an idle rumination on what he'd do for a living if something happened to his hands. Although he recorded extensively on his own, and enjoyed some minor success, Lane's tunes were hits for Roger Miller, Waylon Jennings, Conway Twitty, Dottie West, Hank Thompson, Roy Clark, Eddy Arnold, Jac Greene, John Conlee, and Ed Bruce, among others.

John Wesley Ryles (1950–), born in Bastrop, Louisiana, grew up playing guitar and singing in a family band, the Ryles Family Singers. He worked professionally on Dallas's *Big D Jamboree* before he could drive a car. They relocated to Nashville and, in 1968, Ryles released a solo single called "Kay" that scored the youngster a Top 10 crossover hit. Over the next two decades, he had several mid-level successes with a smooth, country-pop sound, but the years were marked with frustration over his inability to move to the superstar level. He scored one Top 5 song, "Lifetime Thing," in the late seventies, but eventually he retired from the pursuit of stardom and is instead a respected session player and jingles singer.

A fine singer whose honky-tonk successes showed a bluesy, gospel-drenched background, **Margie Singleton** (1935–) was born in Coushatta, Louisiana. A guitarist and songwriter of substantial ability, she wrote many of her songs, including her 1957 debut single, "One Step Near to You" b/w "Not What He's Got." A member of the *Louisiana Hayride* for several years, Singleton scored a few more hits, then began a series of duets with George Jones, chief among them the wonderful "Waltz of the Angels." She also wrote some nice material for other artists (including Marty Robbins and Charley Pride), enjoyed some solo success ("My True Confessions"), and sang on the Grand Ole Opry. It was also Singleton, not Jeannie C. Riley, who was the first to record Tom T. Hall's "Harper Valley PTA." After the sixties, her chart days were essentially over. If you can find it, *Crying Time* (United Artists) is a nice representation of her work.

Glenn Sutton (1937–). was born in Hodge, Louisiana. An important country songwriter, his career has spanned almost forty years. He grew up in Henderson, Texas, but in Nashville he penned, among others, "Almost Persuaded," "Your Good Girl's Gonna Go Bad," "Bedtime Story," "The Day That Love Walked In," and the immortal "What Made Milwaukee Famous (Has Made a Loser Out of Me)." Sutton co-wrote several other biggies with Billy Sherrill and even sang some of his own songs

And of course: **Linda Gail Lewis** (1947–). Yes, Jerry Lee's sister. To be charitable, she had a reasonably nice voice, and probably wasn't particularly interested in a show-biz career. But her brother encouraged her, and with his influence she recorded some singles and probably had some fun. Her hits were few though, amazingly, her latest effort is a collaboration with none other than Van Morrison (!)—"You Win Again."

Six

RAP AND
HIP-HOP

*Y*ou might be surprised to find that, even in the tourist-laden environs of the French Quarter, the House of Blues books hip-hop shows, but when it comes to musical power and popularity, New Orleans's rap scene is astoundingly successful—platinum quality successful—and the city has a healthy club scene. Here's how it all started.

After rap and hip-hop established the boundaries and rivalries of East Coast and West Coast styles, it was inevitable that other parts of the country would emerge as serious players. Houston was probably first, rising to national prominence on the strength of the Geto Boys. But Louisiana wasn't far behind, and when it hit, it did so in a big way. First rose the No Limit empire, under the leadership of rapper, entrepreneur, and would-be NBA star Master P, who has become powerful enough to sign hip-hop hero Snoop Dog, which if nothing else constitutes a major coup against the Los Angeles and New York labels. Then came Cash Money Records, headed up by siblings Bryan "Baby" Williams and Ronald "Godfather" Williams.

The state has even created the "bounce" phenomenon: a rap-fueled dance craze seemingly indigenous to New Orleans's projects. It spontaneously evolved in the St. Thomas project in 1989 when a young DJ, Kevin Tucker—a.k.a. **MCT**—improvised a series of street slogans in the fashion of Mardi Gras Indian call-and-response chants, and an immediate crowd gathered. The result was a local scene that spawned dozens of "bounce" songs, all infectiously danceable, rap-pop fusions that glistened with summery possibility. Block parties sprang up with mobs of men, women, and kids choking the courtyards of housing projects, all exuberantly bouncin'— which requires the participant to bend forward, thrust ass proudly, and shimmy in appropriately rhythmic behavior. While it hasn't caught on worldwide, it's been extremely popular in the inner-urban sections of New Orleans for years now.

Without question, the monarch of the scene is **DJ Jubilee,** an infectiously enthusiastic schoolteacher and coach in the New Orleans school district whose bounce anthems routinely cluster in the lower levels of the *Billboard* charts; some music-label folks predict that thanks to his work, the phenomenon will bubble over and break nationally in a big way.

Now, the first thing I wanna say is that I do not presume to "get" rap and hip-hop. I understand where it comes from and why, but that doesn't mean I understand it. As a forty-five-year-old white guy, I would elaborate by saying I don't think that rap is *designed* for me to understand or like, and that, indeed, if I *did* get it and like it, then its practitioners would probably consider themselves failures.

During my college days, though, I was heavily into Gil Scott-Heron, whose work might legitimately be considered a major precursor to rap. His tunes are scathing and often hilarious—a sort of spoken-word jazz-and-poetry that, sadly, many of the hip-hop generation have never heard. "Whitey's on the Moon," "Winter in America," "The Revolution Will Not Be Televised," "B-Movie"—those are terrific and powerful songs. One can directly trace the evolution of the music from Scott-Heron to Public Enemy, whose *Fear of a Black Planet* and *It Takes a Nation* and *Apocalypse Now . . . The Empire Strikes Black* are records I not only understood but dug listening to because the tunes sound good.

But that was all years ago.

My personal issues aside, it can't be denied that hip-hop is now and will continue to be a powerful force in Louisiana music, thanks in large part to Percy Miller, who would become **Master P** (1970–). He grew up in New Orleans's Calliope housing projects and began to divide his time between California and Louisiana after his parents split up and his father relocated to the West Coast. A fine athlete, he received a basketball scholarship to the University of Houston. After inheriting $10,000 from his grandfather, P opened an indie record store called No Limit Records in Richmond, California. When that was successful, it was a logical segue from selling other people's music to his own, and in 1991, P subsequently released a debut single, "Ghetto's Tryin' to Kill Me."

When sales of the follow-up EP, *99 Ways to Die*, doubled, P correctly figured he was onto something. He reached a distribution agreement for his fledgling No Limit label with Priority Records, then formed the group **Tru** with his brothers, Silkk the Shocker and C-Murder. Their self-titled CD sold about a half-million copies in 1995. After P oversaw some nice-selling compilations, especially the *West Coast Bad Boyz* series, he began releasing his own solo CDs, including *99 Ways to Die, Ghetto Dope, Getaway Clean, MP*

Da Last Don, and *Ice Cream Man,* which debuted in 1996 at #3 on the *Bill-board* R&B chart. And, despite being without benefit of radio support, the floodgates opened.

Since the mid-nineties, working out of his hometown, he's consistently signed other local rappers to record deals, along the way proving that it's impossible to overload the underground marketplace with hardcore gangsta rap. The theory is that, coming along at a time when the Music Biz was crawfishing over the violence of gangsta rap, Master P provided a service because the kids *wanted* it. His in-house production team—**Beats by the Pound,** comprising Craig B., KLC, and Mo B. Dick—*does* rock, and has backed virtually all the material that volcanoes forth from the label. As his personal wonderland expanded, P branched into film and video, Internet communications, and even sports agenting.

A former member of the No Limit rap stable is **Mystikal** (1970–), who, as I write this in late autumn 2000, is one of the hottest hip-hop artists in the world. Born Michael Tyler in New Orleans, Mystikal is a Gulf War veteran who grew up in the Baptist church and represents a paradoxical approach to the gangsta style—as if he can't decide whether it's okay to not proselytize for dope and violence. A talented wordsmith with a machine-gun delivery and a clever way with rhymes, he released a self-titled CD in 1995 and drew the attention of Jive Records, for whom he put out *Mind of Mystikal* two years later. No Limit then came calling, for whom he released a third CD, *Unpredictable,* which seemed to represent the more incendiary side of his nature.

After the follow-up, *Ghetto Fabulous,* he split from No Limit and went back to Jive for a 2000 release, *Let's Get Ready.* Sales of that album have moved him to the top of the heap on the strength of the bounce hit "Shake Ya Ass," an infectious piece of Hustler-flavored nonsense.

Mia X is another of the more talented of the No Limit house artists and was the label's first female. She was born in New Orleans, grew up in Queens, and spent a few years in the rap outfit New York Incorporated before returning to her hometown to work in a record store. Master P heard one of her demos, called her up and, acting on an almost freestyle rap she churned out after the violent death of a friend, came out with the single "Bout It Bout It." The song was a big hit and Mia X was on her way. She's released *Good Girl Gone Bad, Unlady Like,* and *Mama Drama,* the latter of which went Top 20. On the occasions when she genuinely emotes—as for lost friends or family—she can be heartbreakingly good.

Both of Master P's brothers, **Silkk the Shocker** (1980–) and **C-Murder** (1982–), have also enjoyed successful careers. For a few years, C-Murder was mostly relegated to a lot of the "mob rules" compilations the label is famous for. But he's had two solo CDs, *Life and Death* and *Trapped in Crime.* The latter features songs such as "Urban Jungle" that demonstrate what might be construed as weariness of the lifestyle.

Silkk got his start in a unit called the Down South Hustlers, but was quickly swept into the No Limit fold. He's made three solo albums, *The Shocker, Charge It 2 Da Game,* and *Made Man.* "Ghetto Rain" is a standout track.

Fiend is one of the more unique members of the No Limit roster, known for his "I just chewed some gravel" delivery. *There's One in Every Family* is the Fiend CD to listen to.

The best No Limit album comes from one of the more recent signees, a guy called **Mr. Marcelo from the Ghetto,** named in (misspelled) honor of Carlos Marcello's New Orleans crime family. The CD in question is his debut, *Brick Livin'.* On the title cut, Marcelo puts forth the finest explanation I've heard of why I, as Whitey, can't possibly hope to understand the logic and meaning behind gangsta rap.

Also found on the No Limits catalog are **Young Bleed,** interesting if only because one of his CDs is called *My Balls and My Word;* **Prime Suspects,** whose *Guilty Until Proven Innocent* sorta says it all; **Big Ed,** whose Navy-Seal-in-the-Projects approach on discs such as *The Assassin* and *Special Forces* puts him in the company of label-mates **Mac** and **Soulja Slim,** both of whom continue the paramilitary motif on such CDs as *Shell-Shocked* (Mac) and *Give It 2 'Em Raw* (Slim). **Kane & Abel** are expatriate New York rappers and authors (of the novel *Eyes of a Killer/Behind Enemy Lines*) who were turned on to the No Limit folks by Mia X. **Skull Duggery** emerged from the ranks of a New Orleans dance and rap crew called the Nature Boys and graduated to No Limit, imprints of which have released *These Wicked Streets* and *Third Ward Stepper* (the latter features the chilling "Big Easy" with its horror soundtrack piano line); and **Lil Soldiers,** nine- and seven-year-old-brothers, signed to the label in time for a 1999 release called *Boot Camp.*

By comparison, Cash Money Records is the upstart label in town, though it is no less successful than No Limit. **Brian "Baby" Williams** and **Ronald "Godfather" Williams** started Cash Money in 1991 and, with the help of house producer Mannie Fresh and a couple of stars such as Juvenile and B.G., the company has carved a substantial slice of the nationwide pie. Where No Limit has ridden the gangsta horse as if it were Secretariat, the Williams brothers have incorporated the bounce phenomenon into their signature sound. With Fresh's ever-evolving formula—live backing instrumentation *à la* the Roots, an element of gangsta-ism to keep it cutting edge, and a distinct, almost lazy southern beat and flavor—Cash Money manages to compete with No Limit without striding too heavily on the elder label's turf.

Like that of No Limit, the roster at Cash Money is incestuous (if not nearly so large); its artists perform on one another's CDs and record together as various groups, for example, the Hot Boys are made up of Lil Wayne, Turk, Juvenile, and B.G., all of whom have solo albums out. But unlike Master P, the Williams brothers weren't artists themselves, just the honchos behind the label. (Though in 1998 Bryan did hook up with Manny Fresh and released *How U Luv That? Volume I,* followed later that year with a *Volume 2* and in 2000 with *I Got That Work.*)

The first artist to break for Cash Money was **B.G.**—short for Baby Gangsta (real name Christopher Dorsey). The name is more or less appropriate because he signed with the label when he was only eleven, and also because he's already done time on a weapons charge and fought the Demon Heroin. Still, he found time to release an amazing seven CDs before he turned twenty. The Williamses originally signed him as part of a duo called the Baby Gangstas (the other was Lil Wayne, but the pair split up early on), along with several other area artists, including UNLV and Kilo G. But rough times in the early years resulted in a housecleaning from which only B.G. emerged.

In 1995, he came out with *True Story,* the CD that perhaps saved the label. Unifying B.G.'s characteristic, molasses-slow rhymes with Manny Fresh's imaginative tracks, the record caught on in a big way in the South. Even without benefit of a national distribution deal, B.G.'s next few CDs—*It's All On You, Volumes I* and *II*—were so successful that they, along with the emergence of Juvenile as a promising artist and the inaugural effort by the Hot Boys (1997's *Git It How U Live*), were instrumental in scoring Cash Money a huge deal with Universal Records. B.G. recorded two more CDs, *Chopper City in the Ghetto* and *Checkmate,* both of which have sold solidly. But he was bypassed by **Juvenile** as the label's big attraction.

A more melodic rapper with a distinctly slurring southern drawl, Juvenile—born Terius Gray—grew up in New Orleans's Magnolia projects and scored his deal with Cash Money by literally pestering the Williams brothers every day until they rewarded him with a contract. He'd drawn a lot of attention in the city for his contributions to DJ Jimi's "Bounce for the Juvenile." An immediate kinship with Manny Fresh resulted in a Cash Money debut, *Solja Rags;* the CD sold over 200,000 copies. The encore effort, *400 Degreez,* scored a hit with the single "HA."

A second single, "Back That Azz Up," with an almost reggae feel and utterly infectious beat, was a huge hit and tattooed Bounce throughout the atlas. (Snooks Eaglin is clearly a fan too; see page 140.) The CD went double platinum and the Williams brothers came up with the idea of forming the Hot Boys, whose initial *Guerrilla Warfare* not only furthered the reputations of Juvenile and B.G. but lent instant credibility to Lil Wayne and Young Turk. Juvenile has followed with even more solo success—CDs such as *G-Code* and *Playaz of da Game*—and he's now one of the biggest hip-hop artists going, despite being arrested on an assault charge in the summer of 2000 when a bathtub incident with some strippers went awry. (You were expecting, what, a jaywalking summons?)

Lil Wayne has also experienced success—both with the Hot Boys and on his own. *The Block Is Hot* is Lil Wayne's 1999 debut. He's probably seventeen by now, and it's disconcerting to hear his adenoidal, cartoony voice pipe up with all manner of ghetto gangsta-isms, but Manny Fresh is again a star—putting solid tracks behind the words—and Wayne pulls off some nice R&B–flavored stuff on "Fuck the World" and "Up to Me."

The influence of Cash Money and No Limit have made a lot of people hungry for success; in any case, the global lifestyle and affluence represented by hip-hop would have made thousands of Louisiana youngsters aspire to the business. So it's no surprise that successes have occurred outside those two New Orleans entities.

A Baton Rouge rapper called **Beelow** signed with Universal Records and has released two CDs, 1999's *Ballin' 4 Billions* and *Ballaholic*, which came out a year later. There's not much more to say about him, other than his tune "Big Bodies" is *very* educational.

Sisters Tonya and Tremethia Jupiter, known as **The Ghetto Twiinz** and raised in New Orleans's Ninth Ward, used influences as varied as Salt 'n' Pepa and Scarface to get started in hip-hop. Another influence was a short-lived career in dealing dope, though they rethought their collective path while in jail. They released a CD called *Surrounded By Criminals* on the city's fledgling Big Boy Records, then signed with Virgin Records for *In That Water* (1997) and *No Pain No Gain* (1998). Their reality-based rap hasn't caught on in a big way, and probably won't, though it would be a mistake to sell short any of the city's hip-hop artists at this juncture in the culture's explosion.

Seven

CLASSICAL AND WORLD MUSIC

𝒯he first time I visited New Orleans, my dad put us up in a nice hotel at the corner of Bourbon and Toulouse. At the time it was called, I believe, the Downtowner. It's pretty famous, I suppose, for its licorice-twist second- and third-floor balconies, prime people-watching areas at any time of year and—no big surprise—really spectacular Nudist Posts during peak tourist events.

The hotel has changed hands a few times in the last thirty years, and in any case it's now called the Ramada Plaza Inn on Bourbon Street. Sure, it's a chain, but so is the Holiday Inn Chateau Lemoyne on Rue Dauphine, which is where I married my lovely wife—and neither of 'em are exactly Red Roof Inns, buddy. Besides, the Inn on Bourbon Street has been other things besides the Downtowner. It was once the New Orleans Opera House, which is one way of saying that, though Ernie K-Doe may be slightly more flamboyant than *Madame Butterfly*, classical music has always had its place in Louisiana.

To prove it, I walked down the street from our newspaper office here in New London, Connecticut, and had a short but insightful interview with Xiao-Lu Li, the conductor of the Acadiana Symphony Orchestra in Lafayette, Louisiana. Why is Maestro Li hanging out in a New England seacoast town? Well, sometimes things just work out for you. Li recently took on the additional job of conducting the Eastern Connecticut Symphony; this means he's here about half the year, during which time he and I can lament together the lack of anything remotely approaching gumbo in our little Robert Frostian section of the world.

Li, a friendly, folksy man with a sharp wit and a far more accessible attitude toward nonclassical music than most critics I've ever met—he speaks compellingly about Cajun and zydeco, for example—says many illuminating things during our conversation, although one in particular sticks out.

"I still find," he told me, "that Louisiana is a place where world-class musicians come from and where world-class music is performed. But it isn't always easy. The New Orleans Symphony has gone bankrupt twice. Symphony and opera are very expensive art forms, and right now it isn't just New Orleans that's having difficulties. Baton Rouge and Shreveport have trouble, too."

Li points out, though, that Louisiana is hardly unique in the country when one is describing classical music organizations that have to hustle to stay afloat—regardless of available talent.

And despite the struggles, the **Baton Rouge Symphony** (under music director and conductor Timothy Muffit) presented a strong 2000 season featuring a performance by the recent winner of the Van Cliburn competition (more about Cliburn below since Van is a Lou'sanna boy); the **Shreveport Symphony** (Dennis Simons, music director and conductor) celebrated its fiftieth season in 2000; the **New Orleans Civic Symphony** (under the direction of Dr. Joseph Hebert) is holding its own in a town that enjoys serious musical options on any night of the week; and Li's **Acadiana Symphony Orchestra** is healthy, servicing eight parishes in the heart of Cajun country. All present seasons of significant quality.

There are also the **Shreveport Opera** and the **Shreveport Metropolitan Ballet,** the **Baton Rouge Concert Band** and **Baton Rouge Ballet Theater,** the **Jefferson Symphony Orchestra,** the **Louisiana Philharmonic Orchestra,** the **Lake Charles Symphony,** and the **Lake Charles Civic Ballet,** several ballet companies in New Orleans and Baton Rouge, and many brass quartets, children's choirs, and string quartets, chorales, and choruses.

So if the classical contingency doesn't get as much attention as, say, the Marsalis family, it doesn't mean it ain't happening.

"It's hard to have classical music in the Louisiana environment when so much of the marketing money goes to R&B and jazz," Li told me. "I sat on the Louisiana Music Commission and 90 percent of the money goes to jazz. *But,* there is exciting, encouraging stuff going on. About five years ago, we started a Young Person's Conservatory in Lafayette. When I met Ellis Marsalis, he told me, 'Maestro, I commend you on what you're doing.'" Li also pointed out that "Tulane has a fine music department, and LSU is a top ten music school. There is a history in Louisiana. It's just that nobody talks about it much."

Indeed, in the vibrant early years when the city first earned its reputation as a European collision-on-the-bayou, there was a festive opera tradition and no shortage of classically trained musicians and composers. Whether Louisiana's classical musicians are identifiable as spawn of the state, well, by the very nature of classical music, which is rigid and repertory in performance, there's little room for the bassoonist from Lake

Charles, for example, to blast into a zydeco-flavored riff in the middle of Glazunov's "Russian Funeral March."

One of the country's most famous pianists hails from Louisiana. **Van Cliburn** (1934–) was born in Shreveport, the diametric other end of the state from New Orleans' cosmopolitan demographics. His mother studied with Arthur Friedheim and, when young Van showed a prodigal aptitude for the piano at a tender age, she trained him extensively until he entered Juilliard at seventeen.

The family had moved to Fort Worth, Texas, where Cliburn won the Texas State Prize when he was thirteen, and the next year he copped the National Music Festival Award. At twenty-four, Cliburn melted the Cold War freeze when he went to Moscow and won the First International Tchaikovsky Competition—after which he was treated to a ticker-tape parade in New York.

For two decades and beyond, Cliburn was the toast of the world—and that's not an exaggeration. He played with the top symphony orchestras and was a de rigueur invitee at all sorts of governmental, black-tie society occasions on any continent where pianos are tuned. As titular overseer for the globally renowned Van Cliburn International Piano Competition (first held in 1962), Cliburn effectively cemented his name to generations of the finest young piano talent in the world. In 1978, tired of the travel, Cliburn retired and devoted his time to philanthropic causes.

A decade later, Cliburn came out of the shadows to perform first for President Ronald Reagan and, shortly after, in Moscow at the invitation of Premier Mikhail Gorbachev. Since then, his live performance schedule has intensified. He still works the Tchaikovsky—it's sort of his "Stairway to Heaven"—and commemorated the start of the one-hundredth anniversary season at Carnegie Hall with a concert.

Cliburn has established scholarships at several colleges and conservatories—including Louisiana State University—and if you're going to own any of his numerous fine recordings, check out the moderately recent *Van Cliburn: A Romantic Collection*, an eight–CD set released by BMG Classics. And: there is decidedly no "Louisiana" in Cliburn's style.

Other Louisiana pianists of renown, all from New Orleans, would include **Edward Knight Jr.** (1795–1833), **Henry Albert Long** (1854–1930), and **Sydney** and **Lucien Lambert**.

Now, if Cliburn is the state's best known classical performer, surely New Orleans's **Louis Moreaux Gottschalk** (1829–1869) is Louisiana's finest classical composer. And Gottschalk's work did heavily reflect his New Orleans upbringing. Gottschalk was a fine pianist, too, and toured extensively, performing his stirring mix of Creole, French, and African–Caribbean music.

He was born on the border of the French Quarter, at the corner of Royal and Esplanade. He was a Creole who grew up in a city heavy with Creole influences; biographers have written that, as a kid, he would stand on the balcony of the family's next home—on Rampart—and listen to the Sunday slave gatherings across the street in Congo Square (see "Spontaneous Combustion and the Birth of an Art Form," Part 1, Chapter 1).

A piano prodigy who early on mastered the French operas that permeated New Orleans at the time—before the opera house burned down, anyway—he scored plenty of early gigs playing in the Garden District homes of the local rich. When he was thirteen, he left to study in Paris, where his New Orleans influences paradoxically worked well within the rigid structures of his classical studies.

A handsome guy in a Proustian way, Gottschalk was a performer who was immensely popular with young women, a sort of Deep South cross between Paganini and Paul McCartney. Though he returned to the United States on several of his nonstop concert tours, Gottschalk traveled extensively in South America and the Caribbean. He was particularly enamored of his Creole heritage and ancestral roots in St. Dominique, and eventually settled there, never returning to New Orleans save for rare and brief visits. He regularly staged performances in Rio de Janiero and Havana, and some think his early passing was caused, at least in part, by his exhaustive work schedule.

Though scholars today discount a lot of his work as fanciful and wide-ranging at best and mediocre at worst, Gottschalk was a composer of some importance. Chief among his works are probably "Souvenirs D'Andalousie, Caprice de Concert," "Night in the Tropics," and "Mort, Opus 60." His compositions were typically shorter than one might associate with "classical music," and his spicy rhythms were certainly forward-thinking if not revolutionary. It should be noted that Gottschalk's brother, **L. Gaston Gottschalk,** was a singer, teacher, and composer who performed with Saint Saëns in Paris and later taught at Chicago Musical College.

Edmund Dédé (1829–1903) was also a composer of some note who was born in New Orleans and died in Paris, France. A black violinist and clarinetist of considerable skill, Dédé was also a conductor; he wrote "Le Sement de l'Arabe," "Vaillant Belle Rose Quadrille," and "Le Palmier Overture." The Naxos label has recently released some of Dédé's works.

Eugene Prosper Prevost (1809–1872) was born in Paris but died in New Orleans. A conductor and composer, he studied at the Paris Conservatory and won first and second prizes in composition. He came to New Orleans in 1837 and was conductor of the French Opera Company there for almost thirty years.

Other composers of note from Louisiana include **Basile Barés** (a black, post–Civil War composer); **Emile Johns** (a native Frenchman who moved to New Orleans, taught music, and published a collection of original pieces called *Album Louisianais*); **Samuel Snaer** (1833–?), born in New

Orleans, a black pianist and composer who performed regularly in concerts and musical theater in the city and who wrote dance suites and a mass; **Claude Almand** (1915–), born in Winnsboro, Louisiana, whose work includes "The Waste Land"; **James Gutheim Heller** (1892–1971), born in New Orleans and composed "Four Sketches for Orchestra"; and **Mitchell Parish** (1900–1993), a famous lyricist born in Shreveport. Two of his more famous songs: "Star Dust" (music by Hoagy Carmichael, of course), and "Deep Purple" (with Billy de Rose).

There was even an abundance of Louisiana singers and musicians who didn't play piano—and patrons—who made an impact on the world of classical music.

Contemporary soprano **Elizabeth Futral** is a household name—if you are an opera lover, that is—and maybe even if you aren't. She is a North Carolina native who grew up across Lake Ponchartrain from New Orleans. Though a classically trained pianist and flutist, Futral focused early on singing. She eventually earned a master's degree in voice from the fine opera program at the University of Indiana, then spent two years training with the Chicago Lyric Opera before turning professional. She's sung all over the world with the finest companies and symphony orchestras, and is most noted for her roles as Cleopatra in Handel's *Julius Caesar,* Gilda in Verdi's *Rigoletto,* and Susanna in Mozart's *The Marriage of Figaro*—as well as for being the first to musically interpret the part of Stella in the San Francisco Opera's version of *A Streetcar Named Desire* (available on CD and DVD).

New Orleans's **Nathan Franko** (1861–1930) was a violinist and conductor who toured the world when he was eight and later performed as a member of the Metropolitan Opera Company in New York City; **Leo Kofler** (1837–1908) was an Austrian who died in New Orleans and was the choirmaster and organist of St. Paul's Chapel in New York City in 1887; **Joseph White** (1838–1890), born in New Orleans, was a black violinist who studied at the Paris Conservatory and successfully toured the United States before writing *Violin Concerto;* soprano **Amy Fay** (1844–1928) was born in Bayou Goula, Louisiana, studied in Weimar with Franz Liszt, and debuted at the Mendelssohn Glee Club in New York City.

Mezzo-soprano **Shirley Verrett** is a black opera star who was born in New Orleans in 1933 and can be heard on the album *Anna Bolena* (which also features Beverly Sills); musical theater singer **Linda Hopkins** (1925–), born in New Orleans, played the lead in *Inner City* at the Ethel Barrymore Theatre in New York City in 1972; **John Davis** (1773–1839), who was born in Paris, France, moved to New Orleans in 1809 and, after opening a theater there, formed an opera company that presented over eighty operas by thirty-two composers; **Louis Tabary** (1773–1831), who was born in France and became a resident of New Orleans in 1804, was director of a theater on

St. Peter Street and later St. Philip Street, produced dozens of operas, and later opened the Orleans Street Theatre, which was destroyed by fire.

My wife is an unapologetic fan and supporter of National Public Radio. Since they don't broadcast Red Sox or Saints games, I never turn it on. But I *do* ride in her car a lot, which means I hear NPR frequently. And though I swear they keep running the same news story over and over—a tense, subdued report from a guy with a clipped British accent who starts off by saying, "Violence erupted on the West Bank today . . . "—she is far better informed about life on our planet than I am.

When NPR plays music, it's one of two kinds: either classical or what I might describe as world music. I can enjoy both; indeed, we have extensive classical and world music collections, even though, until I turned twenty years old, I didn't own an album that didn't have a derivative of the word "boogie" in the title.

All this means that I sonically associate classical music and world music. Along with jazz, they represent the "brainy" end of the music section. But Louisiana, as you now know, has a substantial jazz history worthy of its own section; for this reason, I'm going to group classical and world music together. In a large and cosmopolitan sense, the state's music is pretty damned wholly ethnic. I mean, what are Cajun and zydeco but ethnic music? It could be argued that blues and jazz are ethnic, too—in origin, anyway. But let's go beyond that into the context of "world" music that one might find in a CD in, say, Lincoln, Nebraska.

In other words, is reggae or Irish music going on in Louisiana? The answer would be yes, certainly. As in any big city with a thriving music scene, New Orleans has plenty of world music going on.

For example, Cyril Neville, the band's youngest sibling, has a healthy interest in reggae. Not only does he encourage plenty of reggae acts in the city, his own **Uptown All-Stars** are billed as the world's only second-line reggae band. The only time I ever saw them, though, they came on about 3:00 A.M. after my pal Carl Daniel and I had already sent the *esposas* back to the hotel in cabs and were too drunk to get much out of it—other than grooving happily for ninety minutes. Because we *thought* we remembered digging them, we both bought copies of *Fire This Time*, which is probably hard to find but worth the effort.

The rest of the city's reggae scene is healthy. There used to be annual reggae fests in New Orleans, and bands such as **Irie Vibrations, Cool Riddums & Sista Teedy,** and **Exodus** are just three of the area's standout bands.

The Latin scene, not surprisingly, is hot, too. Not only are jazzers **Los Hombres Calientes** incredible proponents of Cuban influences, singer **John Boutte** recently sang lead with ¡Cubanismo! on their fiery *Mardi Gras Mambo: ¡Cubanismo! In New Orleans* CD. **Mas Mamones, the**

Freddy Omar Latin Band, and **Acoustic Swiftness** are also fine representatives of the Latin sound vibrating in the city. There are African seasonings, too, particularly with the long-lived **Kumbuka Drum & Dance Collective.**

Maybe the most famous of the ethnic bands in the city is the **New Orleans Klezmer All-Stars.** Superb proponents of that fine Jewish folk music—rendered with a Crescent City twist—the All-Stars have released two hoppin' CDs, *Big Kibosh* and *Fresh Out of the Past.*

A sturdy Irish scene is also alive in New Orleans, where acts such as **Danny O'Flaherty** and the **Poor Clares** hold court regularly. Admittedly, the big labels are not gnashing their teeth at one another to sign a lot of the ethnic acts—and that's the nature of the increasing commercialization of the record business—New Orleans certainly upholds its reputation, musically, as being a cosmopolitan city.

ACKNOWLEDGMENTS

For Eileen (The Great God Pan is *alive*—thanks to you. Love ya, babe).

And in gratitude to my mom—the Thelm Unit.

The traveling companions: Dr. Larry "Dr. L" Williams, Steve "Dixieland Steve" Pace, Brett "Louisiana Black" Blackwell, Dan "The Weird Guy" Pearson, John "Howlin' Goat" Mosier (and *in absentian* spirit: Elizabeth Mosier), Carl "King Andouille" Daniel and his *esposa* Gail, Deanna Williams, Beverly Malouf, Dan Malone and Katherine Jones, and Tim and Madalyn Choate.

Of course: Mic "The Doctah" Koster; Ernie "Minor Chords and Screenplays" Myers and Sarah Harpst; Ol' Jeem Dalton; Bob and Joyce Jenkins; Harry and Lynette Dukeman; Steve and Janet Powell; Andy and Monica Timmons; Keith and Mikey Rust; The Entire Dallas Supper Club Contingency; Bob and Sara Jenkins; Dan Waters; Mark Weaver; Dr. Tandy "Man, Who Did That to Your Knee?" Freeman; Bob Compton and Cheryl Chapman (forever united in Mexican food); Dr. Linda Vogel; Dr. Jim Proulx; Dodie's Seafood; muffulettas for David Hale Smith and Seth Robertson and Courtney Dreslin at DHS Literary; and for my editors at Da Capo: Andrea Schulz and Jane Hobson Snyder as well as Fred Francis, Jennifer Blakebrough-Raeburn, and Alex Camlin; criminally overlooked the first time around: Loyal Gould and Basil Rafferty of the Baylor University Journalism Department; Chris Todora and Jason Christley; the Great God Pan loves the Dixie and Abita breweries, as well as the Bank St. Roadhouse and Dutch Tavern.

Special appreciation for Kristina Dorsey, Milton Moore, Lance Johnson, and all at the *Day* in New London. Ditto: Judy and Albie Glassenberg.

Would that we could all run again: Puppy Brown and Moosie.

Never underestimate: Jan Ramsey and Joseph Irrera, and the staff at *Offbeat*, the magazine that says it all; Louie Maistros and Scully Elly and the Juke Joint; Ian "One-Man Marriott" McNulty; Johnny Palazzotto and the Baton Rouge Blues Festival; the good folks at Raful Neal's Lounge; William Ranson Hogan Jazz Archives at Tulane University; the Preservation Research Center of New Orleans; Roger Hahn, David A. Jones, and Scott Jordan; The Olivier House Hotel, New Orleans—and in particular Pat Mitchell, she of the wonderful voice, superb personal library, and a host of phone numbers, anecdotes, and a Hall of Fame roster of stunning N'Awlins musical pals.

To Fred LeBlanc: love ya, bruh.

Hugs for John Thomas Griffith, Rob Savoy, Paul Sanchez, and the Cowboy Mouth family.

Help beyond the call: Steve Burton and Rounder Records, Mark Samuels and Basin Street Records, Tom Cording and Randy Haecker at Sony Media, Rhino Records, Alligator Records, and Mardi Gras Records.

New Orleans Police Officers: Iain Watt, Jeff Jacob, and Michael McLeery of the 8th District—without their fine work this book wouldn't exist.

Welcome: Katie, Emily, and Natalie Jenkins, Jack Mosier, and Flynn Choate.

I can't believe you'd pay attention to the likes of me dept: Luann Rice, Doug Clegg, Chris Schildt, Ace Atkins—and special thanks to James Lee Burke, whose gracious generosity and friendship remains humbling.

Stunningly talented photographers: Skip Weisenburger, Dana Jensen, Tim Martin, Jacquie Glassenberg, Bob Patterson, Tony Walstra, Al Pjura, Eileen Koster, Ian McNulty, Larry Williams, Mike Remus, and Jackie D'Antonio.

Apologies to those I've missed; it was unintentional and you know you deserve it. The mistakes are mine.

In memoriam: Aunt Dolly, Mike Hyrka, Satchmo (a hundred years and counting).

And of course R. L., still doin' that tailgate ramble in the vast beyond.

BIBLIOGRAPHY AND SOURCES

INTERVIEWS

Trace Adkins. Musician.

Chris Ardoin. Musician (Double Clutchin').

Sean Ardoin. Musician (Double Clutchin', ZydeKool).

Marcia Ball. Musician.

Tab Benoit. Musician.

Scott Billington. Producer and record-label executive (Rounder).

John Birge. Manager (Cowboy Mouth).

Stevie Blaze. Musician (Near Life Experience).

Clarence "Gatemouth" Brown. Musician.

James Lee Burke. Author.

Sam Butera. Musician (Louis Prima).

Henry Butler. Muscian.

Jon Cleary. Musician (Absolute Monster Gentlemen, Bonnie Raitt).

Bill Davis. Musician (Dash Rip Rock).

Gregory Davis. Musician (Dirty Dozen).

Geno Delafose. Musician (French Rockin' Boogie).

Bo Diddley. Musician.

Michael Doucet. Musician (BeauSoleil).

Scully Elly. Voudoun.

Sallie Ann Glassman. Voudoun.

Kevin Griffin. Musician (Better than Ezra).

John Thomas Griffith. Musician (Cowboy Mouth, Red Rockers).

Andy Griggs. Musician.

Roger Hahn. Journalist.

Jeff Hannusch. Journalist and author.

Donald Harrison Jr. Musician.

Barbara Hoover. Disc jockey (WWOZ, New Orleans).

Joseph Irrera. Journalist and editor.

Randy Jackson. Musician (Zebra).

Fred LeBlanc. Musician (Cowboy Mouth).

Tommy Malone. Musician (subdudes, Tiny Town).

Ellis Marsalis. Musician and educator.

Wynton Marsalis. Musician and author.

Cosimo Matassa. Producer.

Bunny Matthews. Journalist and artist.

Irvin Mayfield. Musician.

Ian McNulty. Journalist.

Leon Medica. Musician (LeRoux), producer, artist, and manager.

Pat Mitchell. Musician.

Keb' Mo'. Musician.

Charles Neville. Musician (Neville Brothers).

Cyril Neville. Musician (Neville Brothers).

Bill Nowlin. Record company executive (Rounder).

Anders Osborne. Musician.

Johnny Palazzotto. Promoter.

George Porter Jr. Musician (The Meters, Funky Meters, Runnin' Pardners).

Jan Ramsey. Publisher and journalist.

Zachary Richard. Musician.

Steve Riley. Musician (Mamou Playboys, Lil' Band O' Gold).

Coco Robicheaux. Musician.

Paul Sanchez. Musician (Cowboy Mouth).

Ann Savoy. Musician (Savoy-Doucet Cajun Band) and author.

Rob Savoy. Musician (Cowboy Mouth, Bluerunners).

Reggie Scanlon. Musician (The Radiators, Professor Longhair, James Booker).

Kenny Wayne Shepherd. Musician.

Bill Summers. Musician (Los Hombres Calientes).

Michael Tisserand. Journalist, author, and editor.

Mark Walton. Musician (Continental Drifters).

Walter "Wolfman" Washington. Musician.

George Winston. Musician.

Buckwheat Zydeco. Musician.

BOOKS

Armstrong, Louis. *Satchmo—My Life in New Orleans.* 1954. New York: Da Capo Press, 1986.

———. *Swing That Music.* New York: Da Capo Press, 1993.

Barker, Danny, and Jack Buerkle. *Bourbon Street Black—The New Orleans Black Jazzmen.* New York: Oxford University Press, 1973.

Bechet, Sidney. *Treat It Gentle—An Autobiography.* 1960. New York: Da Capo Press, 2002.

Bergreen, Lawrence. *Louis Armstrong—An Extravagant Life.* New York: Broadway Books, 1997.

Bernard, Shane K. *Swamp Pop—Cajun and Creole Rhythm and Blues.* Jackson, Miss.: University of Mississippi Press, 1996.

Berry, Jason, Jonathan Foose, and Tad Jones. *Up from the Cradle of Jazz—New Orleans Music Since World War II.* New York: Da Capo Press, 1992.

Broven, John. *Walking to New Orleans—The Story of New Orleans Rhythm & Blues.* Bexhill-on-Sea, Sussex, England: Blues Unlimited, 1979.

Bufwack, Mary A., and Robert K. Oermann. *Finding Her Voice—The Illustrated History of Women in Country Music.* New York: Henry Holt & Company, 1993.

Carr, Roy. *A Century of Jazz.* New York: Da Capo Press, 1997.

Chilton, John. *Sidney Bechet—The Wizard of Jazz.* New York: Da Capo Press, 1996.

Claghorn, Charles Eugene. *Biographical Dictionary of American Music.* West Nyack, N.Y.: Parker Publishing Company, 1974.

Davis, Ronald L. *A History of Music in American Life—Volume II.* Huntington, N.Y.: Robert Krieger Publishing Company, 1980.

Erlewine, Michael, Chris Woodstra, and Vladimir Bogdanov, eds. *All Music Guide.* San Francisco: Miller-Freeman Books, 1994.

Erlewine, Michael, Vladimir Bogdanov, Chris Woodstra, and Cub Koda, eds. *All Music Guide to the Blues.* San Francisco: Miller-Freeman Books, 1996.

Feather, Leonard. *The Encyclopedia of Jazz.* New York: Da Capo Press, 1960.

Feather, Leonard, and Ira Gitler. *The Biographical Encyclopedia of Jazz.* New York: Oxford University Press, 1999.

Flint, Joe, and Judy Nelson. *The Insiders Country Music Handbook.* Salt Lake City, Ut.: Gibbs-Smith Publisher, 1993.

Friedlander, Lee. *The Jazz People of New Orleans.* New York: Pantheon Books, 1992.

George, Nelson. *Hip Hop America.* New York: Viking, 1998.

Giddins, Gary. *Satchmo.* New York: Da Capo Press, 1998.

Govenar, Alan. *Meeting the Blues.* New York: Da Capo Press, 1995.

Glassman, Sallie Ann. *Vodou Visions.* New York: Villard Books, 2000.

Graff, Gar, Josh Freedom du Lac, and Jim McFarlin. *R&B—The Essential Album Guide.* Detroit: Visible Ink Press, 1998.

Gregory, Hugh. *Soul Music A–Z.* London: A Blanford Book, 1991.

Herzhaft, Gérard. *Encyclopedia of the Blues.* Fayetteville, Ark.: University of Arkansas Press, 1992.

Hannusch, Jeff. *I Hear You Knockin'—The Sound of New Orleans Rhythm and Blues.* Ville Platte, La.: Swallow Publications, 1985.

Harris, Sheldon. *Blues Who's Who.* New York: Da Capo Press, 1981.

Haskins, James (with Kathleen Benson). *Scott Joplin—The Man Who Made Ragtime.* New York: A Scarborough Book, 1980.

Jorgensen, Ernst. *Elvis Presley—A Life in Music, the Complete Recording Sessions.* New York: St. Martin's Press, 1998.

Keepnews, Orrin, and Bill Grauer Jr. *A Pictorial History of Jazz*. New York: Bonanza Books, 1981.

Knowles, Richard H. *Fallen Heroes—A History of New Orleans Brass Bands*. New Orleans: Jazzology Press, 1996.

Koster, Rick. *Texas Music*. New York: St. Martin's Press, 1998.

Kronenberger, Louis, ed. *Atlantic Brief Lives—A Biographical Companion to the Arts*. New York: Little, Brown & Company, 1965.

Larson, Susan. *The Booklover's Guide to New Orleans*. Baton Rouge: Louisiana State University Press, 1999.

Lichtenstein, Grace, and Laura Danker. *Musical Gumbo—The Music of New Orleans*. New York: W. W. Norton and Company, 1993.

Marquis, Donald M. *In Search of Buddy Bolden—First Man of Jazz*. Baton Rouge: Louisiana State University Press, 1978.

Marsalis, Wynton, and Carl Vigeland. *Jazz in the Bittersweet Blues of Life*. New York: Da Capo Press, 2001.

McCloud, Barry, et al. *Definitive Country*. New York: A Perigee Book, 1995.

Mitcham, Howard. *Creole Gumbo and All That Jazz*. Gretna, La.: Pelican Publishing Company, 1999.

Neville, Art, Aaron Neville, Charles Neville, and Cyril Neville (with David Ritz). *The Brothers*. New York: Da Capo Press, 2001.

Nyhan, Pat, Brian Rollins, and David Babb. *Let the Good Times Roll! A Guide to Cajun & Zydeco Music*. Portland, Me.: Upbeat Books, 1997.

Oakley, Giles. *The Devil's Music—A History of the Blues*. New York: Da Capo Press: 1996.

Ondaatje, Michael. *Coming Through Slaughter*. New York: Vintage International, 1976.

Rebennack, Mac (with Jack Rummel). *Dr. John—Under a Hoodoo Moon*. New York: St. Martin's Press, 1994.

Richards, Tad, and Melvin B. Shestack. *The New Country Music Encyclopedia*. New York: Fireside, 1993.

Robbins, Ira, ed. *The Trouser Press Guide to 90's Rock*. New York: Fireside, 1997.

Romanowski, Patricia, and Warren George, eds. *The New Rolling Stone Encyclopedia of Rock & Roll*. New York: Fireside, 1995.

Savoy, Ann Allen. *Cajun Music—A Reflection of a People, Volume I*. Eunice, La.: Bluebird Press, 1984.

Scherman, Tony. *Backbeat—Earl Palmer's Story*. New York: Da Capo Press, 2000.

Schwerin, Jules. *Got to Tell It—Mahalia Jackson, Queen of Gospel*. New York: Oxford University Press, 1992.

Stambler, Irwin. *Encyclopedia of Pop, Rock & Soul*. New York: St. Martin's Press, 1974.

Tisserand, Michael. *The Kingdom of Zydeco*. New York: Arcade Publishing, 1998.

Tosches, Nick. *Hellfire—The Jerry Lee Lewis Story*. New York: Dell, 1982.

Trynka, Paul. *Portrait of the Blues—America's Blues Musicians in Their Own Words*. New York: Da Capo Press, 1996.

Ward, Geoffrey C., and Ken Burns. *Jazz—A History of American Music*. New York: Alfred A. Knopf, 2000.

Wexler, Jerry, and David Ritz. *Rhythm & the Blues—A Life in American Music*. New York: St. Martin's Press, 1993.

Wynn, Ron, Michael Erlewine, and Vladimir Bogdanov, eds. *All Music Guide to Jazz*. San Francisco: Miller-Freeman Books, 1994.

ARTICLES

Aiges, Scott. "Gospel Show Adds Shade of Meaning to Soul Queen's Life." *Lagniappe*, 6 May 1994.

_____. "Kermit Ruffins—Satchmo's Smiling Soul." *Down Beat*, July 2000.

Armstrong, Louis. "Ulcerateldly Yours . . . " *Down Beat*, July 2000.

Azcona, Alaine. "They Play. You Dance. That's It. The World According to Re-Birth." *Offbeat*, May 1999.

Billington, Scott. "Call It Soul—An Appreciation of Johnny Adams." *Gambit*, 22 September 1998.

Birnbaum, Larry. "Lonnie Brooks—Back on Track." *Wavelength*, May 1983.

Blumenthal, Bob. "Mayfield Adds Island Flair to New Orleans." *Boston Globe*, 14 July 2000.

_____. "The Century of Armstrong." *Boston Globe*, 2 July 2000.

Blumenthal, Ralph. "A Skid Row Turned Soho in Downtown New Orleans." *New York Times*, 4 September 2000.

_____. "Digging for Satchmo's Roots in the City That Spawned Him." *New York Times*, 15 August 2000.

Bruns, Rebecca. "What It Means to Miss New Orleans." *Travel & Leisure*, January 1994.

Burke, Miguel. "Boyz At War." *Vibe*, 26 August 1999.

Canty, Kevin. "Arhoolie Records—The Label That Searched At the Source for Southern Music." *Oxford American*, July/August 2000.

Caramanica, Jon. "Big Pimpin'." *Boston Phoenix*, 3 April 2000.

Carron, Linda. "Tab Benoit Plays the Blues from the Heart." *Greenville News*, 12 September 1996.

Citron, Pepe. "Amid the Jazz." *New Orleans States-Item*, 24 October 1974.

Coleman, Rick. "The Fatman Sings." *Offbeat*, August 1997.

Collins, Rich. "King of New Orleans? The Son of a Blues Legend Signs with the Majors." *Gambit Weekly*, 24 June 1997.

_____. "Tough Enough—Paul Sanchez Isn't Afraid to Be Sensitive." *Gambit Weekly*, 5 August 1997.

Crouch, Stanley. "Papa Dip: Crescent City Conquistador and Sacrificial Hero." *Village Voice*, 27 August 1985.

_____. "Wherever He Went, Joy Was Sure to Follow." *New York Times*, 12 March 2000.

Cuthbert, David. "Dunces' Hunt." *New Orleans Times-Picayune*, 26 January 1997.

Dahl, Bill. "Boozoo Chavis Defends His Right to Mantle of Zydeco King." *Chicago Tribune*, 26 August 1994.

De Barros, Paul. "Harry Connick Jr.—A Chart a Day." *Down Beat*, October 1999.

Dominici, Michael. "Mardi Gras Music." *Where Y'at*, March 2000.

D'Souza, Jerry. "Nicholas Payton." Jazzhouse.org., 1997.

Dunn, Jancee. "Great Britney." *Rolling Stone*, 19 July 1999.

Farber, Jim. "Hot Boys Getting Hotter." *New York Daily News*, 18 August 1999.

Farley, Christopher John. "Tennessee Two-Step." *Time*, 28 June 1999.

Fine, Eric. "Kenny Neal—Now Is the Time." *Blues Revue*, June 2001.

_____. Review: "Kenny Neal—Warmdaddy's, Philadelphia, June 22–23." *Blues Revue*, October 2000.

Fishead, Zeke. "Champion Jack." *Wavelength*, May 1983.

Fontenot, Robert, Jr. "Al Belletto: The Prodigal Son Returns (again)." *Offbeat*, August 2000.

Forte, Dan. "David Doucet—Where No Cajun Has Gone Before." *Guitar Player*, July 1995.

Fowler, Robin. "New Orleans." *Southwest Airlines Spirit*, March 2000.

Fuchs, Cynthia. "Happy Rapper: Interview with Hip-Hop Artist Juvenile." PopMatters.com, 1991.

Gardner, Elysa. "Britney, One More Time." *USA Today*, 16 May 2000.

Giddins, Gary. "The Armstrong Era Begins." *Village Voice*, 27 August 1985.

Gladstone, Valerie. "They Come to the Dance Floor Bearing a Gift: Jazz." *New York Times*, 14 May 2000.

Glennon, Sean. "Still Dirty After All These Years." *Springfield Advocate*, 13 February 1997.

Gozzo, Anthony. "Michael Doucet and BeauSoleil." *Rhythm Music Magazine* 3, no. 8 (1994).

Green, Tony. "Papa's Got a Brand-New Bag." *Vibe*, November 2000.

Hahn, Roger. "A Centennial of His Own—Dr. Michael White." *Offbeat*, November 2000.

_____. "And the Beat Goes On—The Legacy and Future of AFO Records." *Offbeat*, October 1998.

_____. "High Priest of Funk: Eddie Bo." *Offbeat*, November 1998.

Hall, Cindy S. "Best Bets for Stardom—Dash Rip Rock." *USA Today*, 21 March 1997.

Hannusch, Jeff, and Rick Coleman. "The Smiley Lewis Story." *Offbeat*, November 1993.

_____. "Earl King Backtalk." *Offbeat*, February 2000.

Harbrecht, Gene. "McGraw Delivers." *Orange County Register*, 21 May 1999.

Himes, Geoffrey. "Filé Sharpens Cajun Appeal." *Washington Post*, 1 November 1996.

_____. "Zydeco: The Kids Are All Right." *Columbia Flier*, 5 June 1997.

Hokkanen, Niles. "Cajun Spirit." *Acoustic Guitar*, November/December 1991.

Hurst, Jack. "The Roots of Newcomer Andy Griggs' Passionate Music." *Chicago Tribune,* 28 May 1999.

Ivey, Ed. "Telling It Like It Is." *Onstage,* June 2001.

Jenkins, Sacha. "Soldier of Fortune." *Vibe,* May 2000.

Jensen, Lynne. "Christine Balfa—Musical Daughter of Legendary Fiddler Dewey Balfa Still Dreams of Her Daddy." *New Orleans Times-Picayune,* 22 April 1994.

Johnson, Allen, Jr. "Grave Concerns." *Gambit Weekly,* 17 March 1998.

Jones, David H. "Fest Focus: The Zion Harmonizers." *Offbeat,* May 1997.

Jones, James T. IV. "Branford Marsalis' Hot Brand of Jazz." *USA Today,* 12 October 1989.

Jordan, Mark. "Iguanas—Sweet Sound of Success." *Memphis Flyer,* 29 March 1999.

Jordan, Scott. "A Country Boy in New Orleans." *Offbeat,* May 1996.

———. "Aaron & Clyde." *Offbeat,* November 1998.

———. "Allen Toussaint Decks the (Rock and Roll) Hall of Fame." *Offbeat,* December 1997.

———. "Blues on Wheels." *Offbeat,* November 1995.

———. "One Step Back 2 Steps Forward." *Offbeat,* November 1995.

———. "The Radiators—Rock Solid for 20 Years." *Offbeat,* August 1997.

———. "Talking to New Orleans." *Offbeat,* February 1998.

Joyce, Mike. "Chavis's Music Hard to Resist." *Washington Post,* September 9, 1994.

Judge, Joseph. "New Orleans and Her River." *National Geographic,* February 1971.

Kart, Larry. "All That Jazz: Will America's Very Own 'Art' Music Run Out of Steam?" *Lagniappe,* 1 March 1985.

Kinzer, Stephen. "The Man Who Made Jazz Hot." *New York Times,* 28 November 2000.

Koster, Rick. "Backtalk: Fred LeBlanc." *Offbeat,* February 2000.

———. "BeauSoleil Greets Carnival Season." *New London (Conn.) Day,* 8 February 2001.

———. "BTE Show Pleases New Haven Rock Fans." *New London (Conn.) Day,* 18 March 1999.

———. "Better than Ezra: How Does Your Garden Grow?" *Offbeat,* November 1998.

———. "Blast from the Bayou Boasts Savory Roux." *New London (Conn.) Day,* 6 June 1998.

———. "Bourbon Street Tour Samples Louisiana Musical Smorgasbord." *New London (Conn.) Day,* 24 February 2000.

———. "Brothers Wonderfully Schizo." *New London (Conn.) Day,* 5 July 2000.

———. "Cajun Music Fest Features Younger Generation." *New London (Conn.) Day,* 2 September 1999.

———. "Casinos Embracing Cajun, Zydeco Sounds." *New London (Conn.) Day,* 14 May 1998.

———. "Chris Ardoin: A Zydeco Family Affair." *Offbeat,* April 1999.

———. "Cowboy Mouth—The Oral History." *Offbeat,* March 2000.

———. "Dash Defines Bar Band Possibilities." *New London (Conn.) Day,* 12 December 1998.

———. "Doing Family Time on Planet Earth—The Neville Brothers Love Globally and Act Locally." *Dallas Observer,* 22 September 1996.

———. "Dr. John—Right Place, Right Time." *New London (Conn.) Day,* 24 January 1998.

———. "Elder Statesman Brown Does It All." *New London (Conn.) Day,* 2 November 1999.

———. "Extrapolating Rhythm and Blues—Cajun Monarch Marcia Ball Spreads Her Wings." *Dallas Observer,* 14 August 1997.

———. "Fest Profile: Davell Crawford." *Offbeat,* May 1999.

———. "Funky Meters Bring Bayou Groove Into Frigid Climes." *New London (Conn.) Day,* 18 January 2000.

———. "Gospel Discs Sway Even the Skeptical." *New London (Conn.) Day,* 17 February 1998.

———. "Harrison Brings Jazz Past and Future to Norwich Fest." *New London (Conn.) Day,* 14 April 1999.

———. "Jazz Fest's Homegrown Highlights." *New London (Conn.) Day,* 7 May 1999.

———. "Keb's Star Shines in Musical Galaxy." *New London (Conn.) Day,* 20 November 1999.

_____. "Lip Service—Cowboy Mouth's Manic Responsibility." *Dallas Observer,* 17 April 1997.

_____. "Louisiana Acts Sizzle on House of Blues Tour." *New London (Conn.) Day,* 6 November 1999.

_____. "Lyle Lovett—The Song's the Thing." *Offbeat,* May 2000.

_____. "Mouths to Feed—New Orleans Band Has Many Outlets, One Goal." *Dallas Observer,* 3 July 1997.

_____. "Nevilles Confound Theater Crowd." *New London (Conn.) Day,* 10 November 1997.

_____. "Pops Shimmered Like a Star." *New London (Conn.) Day,* 17 July 2000.

_____. "Preservation Hall Jazz Band Strikes Just the Right Notes." *New London (Conn.) Day,* 31 March 2000.

_____. "Spry and Dry—Gatemouth Brown on Seven-Plus Decades." *Dallas Observer,* 28 March 1997.

_____. "Summer Goes South with B. B., Nevilles." *New London (Conn.) Day,* 20 August 1998.

_____. "The Doctor Is In—Dr. John Making Another House Call At Mohegan Sun." *New London (Conn.) Day,* 22 January 1998.

_____. "Vodou Gains Foothold Despite Hollywood." *New London (Conn.) Day,* 3 August 2000.

_____. "Wynton's Performance Dazzles—Without Horn." *New London (Conn.) Day,* 27 May 2001.

_____. Review: "Zachary Richard—Silver Jubilee: The Best of Zachary Richard." *Offbeat,* March 2000.

_____. "Zydeco Roots Sprout Anew." *New London (Conn.) Day,* 19 February 1999.

Kowal, Rob. "Galactic No Prophylactic." *Where Y'at,* March 2000.

Lane, Julie Kamysz. "Disgrace Notes." *Gambit Weekly,* 25 July 2000.

Levin, Charles. "Dirty Minds—New Orleans' Dirty Dozen Have Transcended the 'Brass Band' Label." *Santa Cruz County (Calif.) Sentinel,* 21 June 1996.

Lewis, John. "Keith Frank—Zydeco At Its Most Irreverent." *Oxford American,* July/August 2000.

Lien, James. "A Brief History of New Orleans Rock." *Offbeat,* March 1998.

_____. "The Iguanas Get Serious." *Offbeat,* April 1998.

_____. "Royal Fingerbowl Going Places." *Offbeat,* March 1997.

Litwin, Sharon. "The Family Marsalis." *New Orleans Times-Picayune,* 4 July 1982.

Louwagie, Pam. "Carnival 'King' Is Famous for Floats." *New Orleans Times-Picayune,* 26 January 1997.

Lovejoy, Sandy. "A Rambling Conversation with Tim McGraw." *Knix Magazine,* May 1999.

Mansfield, Brian. "New Traditions—Geno Delafose." *New Country,* October 1996.

Marks, Sonny. "At Sixteen, He's Used to Seeing Himself on Cds." *Lake Charles (La.) American Press,* 18 July 1997.

Matthews, Bunny. "Barefootin' with Robert Parker." *Wavelength,* May 1983.

_____. "Student Learns from a Jazz Master." *New Orleans Times-Picayune/The States Item,* 17 September 1982.

McCall, Michael. "Life Under the Big Top." *Country Music,* June/July 2001.

_____. "Staring Down Their Future." *Country Music,* August/September 2001.

McDermott, Tom. "New Orleans Piano Giants Past and Present." www.ikoiko.com/tm9704a.html.

McKenna, Dave. "The Singer's Home Run." *Washington Post,* 15 May 1999.

McVey, Richard II. "Tim McGraw Finds His Place in the Sun." *Music City News,* May 1999.

Mead, Walter Russell. "Dancing the Bamboula in Old New Orleans." *GQ,* February 1993.

Menagh, Melanie. "Sexy Wynton Marsalis." *USA Today,* 1–3 December 1989.

Milkowski, Bill. "Astral Project." *JazzTimes,* December 1999.

Miller, Samantha. "Mr. Invincible." *People,* 2 June 1997.

Moreau, Kevin. "House Party." *Gambit Weekly,* 19 August 1997.

Mouton, Todd. "Sonny Landreth—Inside the Slide." *Offbeat,* November 2000.

Newcomer, Wendy. "Andy Griggs' Path to Fame Isn't So Lonely." *Country Weekly,* 16 March 1999.

Oksenhorn, Stewart. "The Dirty Dozen Will Blow You Away." *Aspen (Colo.) Times,* 21 March 1997.

Oliver, Ken. "Better than Ezra: Better Than You Think." *Charleston Free Time*, 9 April 1997.

Pareles, Jon. "Britney Grows Up, Very Carefully." *New York Times*, 14 May 2000.

Parrish, Michael. Review: The subdudes' *Primitive Streak. Dirty Linen*, June/July 1996.

Paxton, Joshua. "Booker: A Pianist's Perspective." *Offbeat*, May 1999.

Piazza, Tom. "Night-Tripping with the Good Doctor." *New York Times*, 22 May 1994.

Pierce, Kim. "Making Gumbo Fit for Commander's." *Dallas Morning News*, 4 February 1998.

Point, Michael. "3 Powerhouses 'Sing It' at La Zona Rosa." *Austin American-Statesman*, 29 September 1997.

Pond, Neil. "Dreaming Out Loud." *Country Music*, June/July 1999.

Price, Deborah Evans. "Griggs Draws on His Musical Heroes for Debut Set on RCA." *Billboard Magazine*, 20 February 1999.

Price, Mark. "Unconventional Wisdom Prevails." *Charlotte (N.C.) Observer*, 18 February 2000.

Ratliff, Ben. "Marsalis's Stylishly Solid Septet, Feeling Right at Home." *New York Times*, 6 January 2000.

_____. "The Solo Retreats from the Spotlight in Jazz." *New York Times*, 28 May 2000.

Reich, Howard. "Jazz Improvisation Gets Its Due with Marsalis' Pulitzer Prize." *Chicago Tribune*, 13 April 1997.

René, Sheila. "Interview: Willy De Ville." Rocknet.com, July 1996.

Reynolds, Simon. "Family Values in the Rap Business." *New York Times*, 12 March 2000.

Rippey, Kathleen A. "Backtalk with Marva Wright." *Offbeat*, November 1995.

_____. "Louisiana Home Grown." *Offbeat*, January 1993.

Salvail, Andre. "Beau Jocque Cranks It Up!" *Offbeat*, April 1999.

Salam, Kalamu ya. "No Jazz, No Wynton." *Wavelength*, May 1985.

Sandmel, Ben. "The State of Music in Louisiana." *Sky Magazine*, March 2000.

Sanneh, Kelefa. "The Big Easy—The Cash Money Label Cashes." *Boston Phoenix*, 23 September 1999.

Simon, Clea. "A Thorough Zydeco History, Meaty, Piquant, and Rich." *Boston Globe*, 8 August 1997.

Sinclair, John. "Backtalk with Ernie K-Doe." *Offbeat*, February 1996.

_____. "Give Me My Flowers Now—the Johnny Adams Interview." *Offbeat*, October 1993.

_____. "Masters of Louisiana Music—Lonnie Johnson." *Offbeat*, June 2001.

_____. "One for All—An Oral History of Harold Battiste." *Offbeat*, May 1994.

_____. "St. Joseph's Night in New Orleans—Out After Dark with the Mardi Gras Indians." WWOZ interview, February 1998.

Spano, Susan. "The Big Easy Doesn't Require a Big Budget." *New York Times*, 1 January 1995.

Spera, Keith. "After Whirlwind Tour, Home Looks Good to Cleary." *New Orleans Times-Picayune*, 22 January 1999.

_____. "Father & Son." *Offbeat*, October 1993.

_____. "Still Smokin'." *Offbeat*, March 1996.

Strauss, Neil. "A Trendsetter on Rap's Fringe." *New York Times*, 28 May 2000.

_____. "Better Songs Through Censorship." *New York Times*, 12 March 2000.

_____. "Mother-In-Law of All Visits." *New York Times*, 17 May 2000.

Swenson, John. "On the Wrong Road with . . . the Radiators." *Offbeat*, May 2001.

Tabak, Jonathan. "Astral Project at 20." *Offbeat*, June 1999.

_____. "A Family Affair—New Orleans Trumpeters Have the Music in Their Genes." *Down Beat*, July 2000.

_____. "Back Talk with Terence Blanchard." *Offbeat*, July 1996.

_____. "Nicholas Payton—Payton's Passion." *Down Beat*, July 2000.

_____. "The Treme Brass Band: You Know Where It's Comin' From." *Offbeat*, January 1996.

Tribble, Scott L. "All a Scene in Ezra's Dream." Internet interview with Better than Ezra, 1998.

Twomey, Jack. "Terence Blanchard Online Chat." JandR.com, March 21, 2000.

Various authors. "Carnival Tales—A Multitude of Local Minstrels Spin Tales of Mardi Gras of Yore." *Offbeat*, February 1996.

Various authors. "In the Drink." *Gambit Weekly*, 3 March 1998.

Wald, Elijah. "Louisiana in Lincoln." *Boston Globe*, 7 August 1998.

Walton, Anthony. "Randy Newman—His Album About the South Remains a Classic." *Oxford American*, July/August 2000.

Walton, David. "Armstrong Played Out His Life in Sweet Harmonies." *Dallas Morning News*, 27 July 1997.

Wirt, John. "Davell Crawford a Veteran at 20." *Baton Rouge Daily Advocate*, 26 April 1996.

_____. "Celtic Label Adding Filé to Its Gumbo." *Baton Rouge Daily Advocate*, 20 September 1996.

Wolfe, Charles. "Gov. Jimmie Davis—The Original Power Player." *Oxford American*, July/August 2000.

Woodward, Richard B. "Nevilles." *Interview*, August, 1990.

Wyckoff, Geraldine. "At Play in the Tent of the Lord—The Story of Jazz Fest's Gospel Tent." *Offbeat*, May 1994.

_____. "Zydeco's Two Camps." *Gambit Weekly*, 26 August 1997.

ARTISTS' WEB SITES

www.astralproject.com
www.betterthanezra.com
www.brooks-dunn.com
www.christhomasking.com
www.cowboymouth.com
www.dougkershaw.com
www.eddiebo.com
www.galacticfunk.com
www.getmusic.com/peeps/mystikal.cm
www.hconnickjr.com
www.henrybutler.com
www.henrygray.com
www.k-doe.com
www.lonniebrooks.com
www.nevilles.com
www.radiators.org
www.rebirthbrassband.com
www.sammykershaw.com
www.sonnylandreth.com
www.spiritland.com (Coco Robicheaux)
www.tabbenoit.com
www.terenceblanchard.com

www.tommyridgley.com
www.tonyjoewhite.net

GENERAL INFORMATION WEB SITES

www.allaboutjazz.com
www.alligator.com
www.allmusic.com
www.amazon.com
www.barnesandnoble.com
www.basinstreetrecords.com
www.bluesaccess.com
www.borders.com
www.cajunfrenchmusic.org
www.cashmoney-records.com
www.cdnow.com
http://commerce.usunwired.net/blues/ (Louisiana Blues Hall of Fame)
www.downbeat.com
www.festivals.com
www.gambit-no.com
www.lafayettetravel.com
www.louisianamusic.org
www.louisianamusicfactory.com
www.mammoth.com
www.mardigrasrecords.com
www.mtv.com
www.neworleansmagazine.com
www.neworleansonline.com
www.nola.com
www.nolimit.com
www.nynorecords.com
www.offbeat.com
www.orleansrecords.com
www.ragtimers.org
www.redhotjazz.com
www.rockhall.com
www.rounder.com
www.satchmo.com
www.sonymusic.com
www.spyboy.org
www.tabasco.com
www.thejukejoint.com
www.tipitinas.com
www.usatoday.com
www.whatbayou.com
www.wwoz.org

INDEX